GRANTA BOOKS

THE BEST OF GRANTA TRAVEL

The Best of Granta Travel

GRANTA BOOKS
LONDON
in association with
PENGUIN BOOKS

GRANTA BOOKS
2/3 Hanover Yard, Noel Road, Islington, London N1 8BE

Published in association with the Penguin Group
Penguin Books Ltd, 27 Wrights Lane, London W8 5TZ, England
Viking Penguin, a division of Penguin Books USA Inc.,
375 Hudson Street, New York 10014, USA
Penguin Books Australia Ltd, Ringwood, Victoria, Australia
Penguin Books Canada Ltd, 2801 John Street, Markham,
Ontario, Canada L3R 1B4
Penguin Books (NZ) Ltd, 182-190 Wairau Road,
Auckland 10, New Zealand

Penguin Books Ltd, Registered Offices: Harmondsworth, Middlesex,
England

First published in Great Britain by Granta Books, 1991

1 3 5 7 9 10 8 6 4 2

Printed in England by Butler & Tanner Ltd, Frome and London

ISBN 0-14-014204-5

CONTENTS

GABRIEL GARCÍA MÁRQUEZ
WATCHING THE RAIN IN GALICIA

My old friend, the painter, poet and novelist, Héctor Rojas Herazo—whom I hadn't seen for a long time—must have felt a tremor of compassion when he saw me in Madrid in a crush of photographers and journalists, for he came up to me and whispered: 'Remember that from time to time you should be nice to yourself.' In fact, it had been months—perhaps years—since I had given myself a well-deserved present. So I decided to give myself what was, in reality, one of my dreams: a visit to Galicia.

No one who enjoys eating can think of Galicia without first thinking of the pleasures of its cuisine. 'Homesickness starts with food,' said Che Guevara, pining perhaps for the vast roasts of his native Argentina while they, men alone in the night in Sierra Maestra, spoke of war. For me, too, homesickness for Galicia had started with food even before I had been there. The fact is that my grandmother, in the big house at Aracataca, where I got to know my first ghosts, had the delightful role of baker and she carried on even when she was already old and nearly blind, until the river flooded, ruined the oven and no one in the house felt like rebuilding it. But my grandmother's vocation was so strong that when she could no longer make bread, she made hams. Delicious hams, though we children did not like them—children never like the novelties of adults—even though the flavour of that first taste has remained recorded for ever on the memory of my palate. I never found it again in any of the many and various hams I ate later in any of my good or my bad years until, by chance, I tasted—forty years later, in Barcelona—an innocent slice of shoulder of pork. All the joy, all the uncertainties, and all the solitude of childhood suddenly came back to me with that, the unmistakable flavour of the hams my grandmother made.

From that experience grew my interest in tracing the ancestry of this flavour, and, in looking for it, I found my own among the frenetic greens of May, the sea and the fertile rains and eternal winds of the Galician countryside. Only then did I understand where my grandmother had got that credulity which allowed her to live in a supernatural world in which everything was possible and where rational explanations were totally lacking in validity. And I understood from where her passion for preparing food for hypothetical visitors came and her habit of singing all day. 'You have to make a meat and a fish dish because you never know what people will want when they come to lunch,' she would say, when she heard the train whistle. She died very old and blind and with her sense of reality completely unhinged, to the point where she would talk about her oldest memories as if they were happening at that moment, and she held conversations with the dead she had known alive in her remote youth. I was telling a Galician friend about this last week in Santiago de Compostela and he said: 'Then your grandmother must have been Galician, no doubt about it, because she was crazy.' In fact all the Galicians I know, and those whom I met without having time to get to know them, seem to have been born under the sign of Pisces.

I don't know where the shame of being a tourist comes from. I've heard many friends in full touristic swing say that they don't want to mix with tourists, not realizing that even though they don't mix with them, they are just as much tourists as the others. When I visit a place and haven't enough time to get to know it more than superficially, I unashamedly assume my role as tourist. I like to join those lightning tours in which the guides explain everything you see out of the window—'On your right and left, ladies and gentlemen . . . '—one of the reasons being that then I know once and for all everything I needn't bother to see when I go out later to explore the place on my own. Anyway, Santiago de Compostela doesn't leave time for such details: the city imposes itself immediately, complete and timeless, as if one had been born there. I had always believed, and continue to believe, really, that there is no more beautiful square in the world than the one in Siena. The only place that made me doubt its authority as the most beautiful square is the one in Santiago de Compostela. Its poise and its youthful air prohibit you from even thinking about its venerable age; instead, it looks as if it had been built the day before by someone who had lost their sense of time. Perhaps this impression does not come from the square itself but from its being—like every corner of the city—steeped to its soul in everyday life. It is a lively city, swept

3

along by a crowd of happy, boisterous students who don't give it a chance to grow old. On the walls that remain intact, plant life makes its way through the cracks in an implacable struggle to outlive oblivion, and at every step, as if it were the most natural thing in the world, one is confronted by the miracle of stones in full bloom.

It rained for three days, not inclemently, but with unseasonable spells of radiant sun. Nevertheless, my Galician friends did not seem to see these golden intervals and apologized for the rain all the time. Perhaps not even they were aware that Galicia without rain would have been a disappointment, because theirs is a mythical country—far more than the Galicians themselves realize—and in mythical lands the sun never comes out. 'If you'd come last week you'd have had lovely weather,' they told us, shamefaced. 'It's very unusual weather for the time of year,' they insisted, forgetting about Valle-Inclán, Rosalia de Castro and every Galician poet who ever lived, in whose books it rains from the beginning of creation, and through which an interminable wind blows, perhaps the very same that sows the lunatic seed which makes so many Galicians delightfully different.

It rained in the city, it rained in the vivid fields, it rained in the lacustrine paradise of the Arosa and the Vigo estuaries; and, over the bridge, it rained in the undaunted and almost unreal Plaza de Cambados; and it even rained on the island of La Toja, where there's a hotel from another world and time, which seems to be waiting for the rain to stop, the wind to cease and the sun to shine in order to start living. We walked through this rain as if through a state of grace, eating shellfish galore, the only live shellfish left in this devastated world; eating fish which, on the plate, still looked like fish; and salads that continued to grow on the table. And we knew that all this was by virtue of the rain which never stops falling.

It's now many years since, in a Barcelona restaurant, I heard the writer, Álvaro Cunqueiros, talk about Galician food and his descriptions were so dazzling that I took them for the ravings of a Galician. As far back as I can remember I've heard Galician emigrants talk of Galicia and I always thought their memories were coloured by nostalgic illusions. Today I recall my seventy-two hours in Galicia and I wonder if they were all true or if I myself have begun to fall victim to the same delirium as my grandmother. Among Galicians—as we all know—you never can tell.

Translated from the Spanish by Margaret Costa

TODD MCEWEN
THEY TELL ME YOU ARE BIG

The technological parade of welcome: I was already dead with fatigue. Thank you for flying with us today, here is your ticket, change planes in Chicago, you'll have to change planes in Chicago, change in Chicago. They said it so often I began to get the idea I should change planes in Chicago. *Change planes*: the phrase began to lose any reference to travel; it acquired a dread phenomenological taint. But I did not change those sorts of planes in Chicago. Rather, in Chicago I *changed size*. For when I deplaned (more tech-talk) I walked into Big People Land.

I was obliged to go a short distance through a glass tube, the story of a life, from one gate to another. I then had an hour, a whole, giant hour to myself. In Big People Land. And there they were. They were all about me: large surely-moving salesmen and mammoth middle managers, corn-fed beef-fed farm-bred monuments to metabolism. Flying from dairy states to beef capitals to commodities centres. From Fon-du-Lac to Dubuque, their huge briefcases *stuffed with meat*. Clinching beefy deals with muscular handshakes. Their faces were florid Mt Rushmores with aviator spectacles and sideburns uniformly metallic; their eyes, bovine, the size of Dutch plates, reflected their Low Country ancestries. Their hands were steam-shovels, their shoes big as our tiny neurotic New York family car. I'm not talking fat, although flesh is essential in Chicago. I'm talking big-boned, as the apologists say. I, a tiny under-nourished New York worrier, had been injected into the enlarged heart of America.

Airports like abattoirs are white. All this moving meat, these great bodies laughing, phoning, making valuable contacts, astonished me. I was overwhelmed by the size of everything and everybody, their *huge bigness!* I had to sit down. But where? Everything I sat in dwarfed, *engulfed* me. I was a baby opossum, writhing in a tablespoon in a Golden Nature Guide. I felt fear, tininess and hunger. I decided the only way to become as big as the Big People was to begin eating.

In the infinite coffee shop, my eyes struggled to take in the polyptych menu and its thousand offerings. Eggs with legs, friendly forks and spoons marched across it. GOOD MORNING! *Barnyard Suggestions* . . . What! I thought. Wanna meet this chicken in the hayloft in half an hour, fella? But these were not that kind of barnyard suggestion. Here in Big People Land, land-o-lotsa wholesomeness, they were suggesting I eat the following: **(1)** 3 strips of bacon, 2 pancakes, 2 eggs (any style), 2 sausages, juice, toast and coffee; **(2)** 6 strips of bacon, 5 pancakes, 4 eggs (any style), 3 sausages, juice, toast and coffee; or **(3)** 12 strips of bacon, 9 pancakes, 7 eggs (any style), $1^{1}/_{2}$ gallons of juice, 3 lbs of toast and a 'Bottomless Pit' (which I took to be a typographical error for 'Pot') of coffee. Thus emptying any barnyard I could imagine of all life. Again I was lost. I felt I was visiting Karnak. I pleaded for half an order of toast, eight pieces.

Outside the window, far away, Chicago was dawning. Obsidian towers, an art deco pipe-organ sprouting from the gold prairie, Lake Michigan still dark beyond. A brachycephalic woman was seated opposite me, biting big things. Her teeth were the size of horse teeth. She said we could see into the next state. She was eating such big things and so quickly a wind was blowing at our table. I turned from this and peered out through the clear air, into the next state. In the far distance I saw great shapes which I knew weren't mountains but my giant Midwestern relatives I am too small ever to visit.

Now I was filled with huge toast. I crawled, miniscule, back through the tubes to the gate. I bought a newspaper and my money looked puny and foreign in the vendor's big paw. In the chairs of Big People Land, my feet never touched the floor. I began to open the *Sun-Times*. But. It was big. Here it wasn't even Sunday and I was suddenly engaged in a desperate battle with what seemed to be a colossal duvet, a *mural* made of incredibly stiff paper. It unfolded and unfolded. It was a whale passing by, it covered me and all my possessions. It surged over the pillar ashtray and began to creep like fog over the gentleman next to me. Help I said. Scuse me, watch your paper there he said. *His tongue was the size of my dog.*

I was exhausted. I could do nothing but wait for my plane to be announced. I watched the Big People. What is it like to move about the world, to travel, free of the fears of the tiny: the fear of being crushed by all the big things Big People make and use? Not just newspapers and barnyard suggestions and airplanes but their Big Companies and their Eternal Truths and the endless statistics of baseball. The airport was hugely hot with Big-People warmth. Warmth from the roaring heaters of their big roaring cars, from the blazing camp-fires of their substantial vacations. And I thought perhaps a few of these Big People were glowing not only from tremendous breakfasts and the excitement and reward of business but from their still-warm still-tousled beds of large love.

Jonathan Raban
Sea-Room

Whenever I find myself growing grim about the mouth;
whenever it is damp, drizzly November in my soul;
whenever I find myself involuntarily pausing before coffin
warehouses, and bringing up the rear of every funeral I
meet; and especially whenever my hypos get such an upper
hand of me, that it requires a strong moral principle to
prevent me from deliberately stepping into the street, and
methodically knocking people's hats off—then, I account
it high time to get to sea as soon as I can. This is my
substitute for pistol and ball. With a philosophical flourish
Cato throws himself upon his sword; I quietly take to the
ship.

Herman Melville, *Moby Dick*

It was the classic last resort. I wanted to run away to sea.

It started as a nervous itch, like an attack of eczema. All
spring and summer I scratched at it, and the more I scratched
the more the affliction spread. There was no getting rid of the thing.
Lodged in my head was an image, in suspiciously heightened colour,
of a very small ship at sea.

It was more ark than boat. It contained the entire life of one man,
and it floated serenely offshore: half in, half out of the world. The face
of its solitary navigator was as dark as demerara. He wasn't flying a
flag. His boat was a private empire, a sovereign state in miniature, a
tight little, right little liberal regime. He was a world away from where
I stood. Lucky man. He'd slung his hook, and upped and gone.
Afloat, abroad, following his compass-needle as it trembled in its dish
of paraffin, he was a figure of pure liberty. He had the world just
where he wanted it. When he looked back at the land from which he'd
sailed, it was arranged for him in brilliant perspective, its outlines
clean, like the cut-out scenery of a toy theatre.

I was plagued by this character. Each time I gave him notice to
quit my private territorial waters, he sailed mockingly past. Smoke
from his pipe rose in a fine column of question-marks over my
horizon. His laughter was loud and derisive. He wouldn't go away.

12

I was landlocked and fidgety. I paced the deck of an urban flat and dreamed of sea-room, with the uncomfortable feeling that I'd picked up a dream which didn't belong to me, as if I'd tuned in my mental radio to the wrong station.

Lots of people would claim the dream as their own. The idea of taking ship and heading off into the blue is, after all, a central part of the mythology of being English. Elias Canetti writes that the 'famous individualism' of the Englishman stems directly from his habit of thinking of himself as a lone mariner; a perception endorsed by whole libraries of bad Victorian novels.

In the books, the English are always running away to sea. The ocean is the natural refuge of every bankrupt, every young man crossed in love, every compromised second son. The Peregrines and Septimuses of the world behave like lemmings: their authors seem powerless to stop them from racing for the nearest quayside at the first sign of trouble.

They do it with such stylish finality too. The bag is secretly packed in the small hours, the farewell letter left like a suicide note beside the ormolu clock on the hall table. Goodbye, family! Goodbye, friends! Goodbye, England!

They close the front door behind them as gently as if they were dismantling a bomb. They tiptoe across the drive, careful not to wake the dogs, their faces grave at the audacity of what they've done. They pass the misty church, the doctor's house behind its cliff of pines, the bulky shadows of Home Farm. By sunrise, they're on the open road, their past already out of sight.

When next heard of, they are up on deck with a full gale blowing out of the Sou'west. The ship is falling away from under their feet in a mountainous swell. They cling to the shrouds, their hands bloody from hauling on ropes and scrubbing decks with holystone. They are changed men.

The sea voyage is more than an adventure; it is a rite of passage, as decisive as a wedding. It marks the end of the old self and the birth of the new. It is a great purifying ordeal. Storms and saltwater cleanse the ne'er-do-well and turn him into a hero. In the last chapter he will get the girl, the vicar's blessing and the family fortune.

I knew that I was pushing my luck, and running against the clock.

Peregrine and Septimus aren't usually men of forty with dental problems and mortgages to pay. I wasn't a scapegrace young tough. I wasn't made for the outdoors. My experience of the sea was confined to paddling in it with the bottoms of my trousers rolled up, collecting coloured pebbles, and lolling on the edge of the ocean in a stripey deckchair until the peeling skin on my nose made me head back to the more manageable world of the hotel bar.

My kinship with the runaways was of a different kind. What I envied in them was the writing of their letters of farewell.

Dear Father,

By the time you read this, I shall be...

Magic words. I was excited by their gunpowdery whiff of action and decision. Both were in pretty short supply where I was sitting. Moping at my worktable, I decided to change a comma to a semi-colon. Framed in the window under a bleary sky, the huge grey tub of the Kensal Green gasometer sank lugubriously downwards as West London cooked its Sunday lunch.

...far away on the high seas. Please tell Mother...

Well, I had fallen out with the family, too. I couldn't put a date on the quarrel: there'd been no firelit showdown in the library, no sign of the riding whip, not even any duns at the front door. It had been a long unloving wrangle, full of edgy silences, niggling resentments and strained efforts at politeness. One day I woke to realize that there was nowhere I felt less at home than home.

Perhaps it was simply that I'd turned into an old fogey a bit earlier in life than most people. At any rate, my own country suddenly seemed foreign—with all the power that a foreign land has to make the lonely visitor sweat with fury at his inability to understand the obvious. *Je ne comprends pas! Min fadlak! Non parlo Italiano! Sprechen Sie English—please!*

I'd started to forget things, as the senile do. Wanting a small brown loaf, I strolled down to the bakery on the corner. I should have remembered. It didn't sell bread any more. It sold battery-powered vibrators, blow-up rubber dolls and videotapes of naked men and women doing ingenious things to each other's bodies. The African Asian who now rented this flesh shop was noisily barricading his windows with sheets of corrugated iron.

He seemed calm enough; a man competently at home on his own patch. He expected a race riot at the weekend.

'The police come and tell us to do it. Saturday, we have trouble here. Too many Rastas—' he waved, in a vague easterly direction, at the dark continent of Portobello, and placidly banged in another nail.

He made me feel like a tourist; and like a tourist I goggled obediently at the local colour of this odd world at my doorstep. Four doors down from the bakery there'd been an ailing chemist's full of stoppered bottles and painted drawers with Latin names. Someone had pulled it out of the block like a rotten wisdom tooth and left a winking cave of galactic war machines. All day long they chattered, bleeped and yodelled, as the local kids zapped hell out of the Aliens. The kids themselves looked pretty alien to me: angry boys, bald as turnips, in army boots and grandfathers' braces; dozy punks with erect quiffs of rainbow hair, like a troupe of Apaches.

Our only patch of civic green space had been taken over by joggers in tracksuits. They wore yellow latex earmuffs clamped round their skulls with coronas of silver wire. They were filling their heads with something: Vivaldi? The Sex Pistols? No. Both would be equally old hat. They quartered the oily turf, blank faced, as exclusive and remote as astronauts.

The streets themselves looked as they'd always done; imperially snug and solid. On a sunny morning, you could easily believe that nothing essential had changed among these avenues of plane trees and tall, white stucco mansions. Even now, there were nannies to be seen—solemn Filipino women, who pushed their pramloads as if they were guarding a reliquary of holy bones in a religious procession. Vans from Harrods still stopped at brass-plated tradesmen's entrances. From a high open window there still came the sound of a child practising scales on the family piano. *Doh, reh, me, fa, ploink. Fa, fa, soh, lah, tee, ploink, doh.*

But there were misplaced notes on the streets, too. At every hour there were too many men about—men of my own age with the truant look of schoolboys out bird-nesting. They huddled outside the betting shops. Alone, they studied the handful of cards in the window of the government Job Centre. The vacancies were for Girl Fridays, linotype operators, book-keepers—nothing for them.

Nor for me, it seemed. I felt supernumerary here. Letting myself in to the whitewashed, partitioned box where I lived, I was met by the wifely grumble of the heating system. It wasn't much of a welcome, and I returned it with a stare of husbandly rancour at the litter of unread books, unwashed dishes and unwritten pages that told me I was home.

I wasn't proud of the way I lived, lodged here contingently like a piece of grit in a crevice. There was something shameful in being so lightly attached to the surrounding world. I wasn't married. I was childless. I didn't even have a proper job.

When I had to give the name of my employer on official forms, I wrote: 'SELF'. This Self, though, was a strange and temperamental boss. He would make me redundant for weeks on end. He sent me on sick leave and sabbaticals, summoned me back for a few days' worth of overtime, then handed me my papers again.

'What am I supposed to do now?'

'Get on your bike,' said Self, not bothering to look up from the crossword in *The Times*.

I'd grown tired of my dealings with Self. He struck me as a textbook example of what was wrong with British industry. He was bad management personified: lazy, indifferent, smugly wedded to his old-fashioned vices. Self loved the two-bottle business lunch. He collected invitations to drinks at six-to-eight. His telephone bills were huge. He poisoned the air with tobacco smoke. It was a miracle that under Self's directorship the company hadn't yet gone bust.

I told him about the Right to Work.

'We'd better lunch on that,' said Self.

By the brandy stage, Self and I were reconciled. We merged back into each other.

I was fogbound and drifting. One morning I breathed on the windowpane and played noughts and crosses against myself. I waited for the telephone to peal. It didn't. In the afternoon I went to the public library and looked up my name in the catalogue to check that I existed. At night I listened to the breaking surf of traffic in the streets, and the city seemed as cold and strange as Murmansk.

An hour of so before the house began to shudder to the can-nonball passage of the underground trains, before the early-morning rattle of milk bottles on steps, I was woken by the bell of the convent down the road. It was ringing for Prime and sounded thin and squeaky like a wheezing lung. The sun never rises on North Kensington with any marked enthusiasm, and the light that had begun to smear the walls of the room looked dingy and secondhand. I didn't much care for the appearance of this new day, and took flight into a deep sea-dream.

In novels, when the black sheep of the family takes ship, his running away is really a means of coming home. His voyage restores him to his relations and to society. I had the same end in view. I wanted to go home; and the most direct, most exhilarating route back there lay by sea. Afloat with charts and compass, I'd find my bearings again. I saw myself inching along the coast, navigating my way around my own country and my own past, taking sights and soundings until I had the place's measure. It was to be an escape, an apprenticeship and a homecoming.

It was a consoling fantasy. I sustained it by going off at weekends and looking at real boats. As a minor consequence of the recession, every harbour in England was crowded with boats for sale: hulks under tarpaulins, rich men's toy motor cruisers, abandoned racing yachts, converted lifeboats and ships' tenders. Their prices were drifting steadily downwards, like the pound; and their brokers had the air of distressed gentlefolk eking out the last of the family capital. They made a feeble play of busyness and spotted me at once as another optimist trying to rid himself of his unaffordable boat. *No dice*, their eyes said, as they shuffled the paper on their desks.

'I'm looking for a boat to sail round Britain in,' I said, trying the words out on the air to see if they had the ring of true idiocy.

'Ah. *Are* you now—' The broker's face was rearranging itself fast, but it looked as if he'd forgotten the expression of avuncular confidence that he was now trying to achieve. All his features stopped in mid-shift: they registered simple disbelief.

He showed me a wreck with a sprung plank. 'She's just the job, old boy. It's what she was built for.'

A sheet of flapping polythene had been pinned down over the foredeck to stop leaks. The glass was missing from a wheelhouse window. It was easy to see oneself going down to the bottom in a boat like that. It had the strong aura of emergency flares, Mayday calls and strings of big bubbles.

'Know what she was up for when she first came in? Ten grand. And that was over four years ago—think what inflation must have done to that by now.' The broker consulted the sky piously, as if the heavens were in the charge of a white-bearded wrathful old economist. 'At two-five, old boy...two-five...she's a steal.'

Lowering myself down slippery dockside ladders to inspect these unloved and unlovable craft, I felt safe enough. The voyage stayed securely in the realm of daydream. I liked the pretence involved in my seaside shopping expeditions, and from each broker I learned a new trick or two. I copied the way they dug their thumbnails into baulks of timber and the knowledgeable sniff with which they tasted the trapped air of the saloon. I picked up enough snippets of shoptalk to be able to speak menacingly of rubbing-strakes and keel-bolts; and soon the daydream itself began to be fleshed out in glibly realistic detail.

As I came to put names to all its parts, the boat in my head grew more substantial and particular by the day. Built to sail out of the confused seas of Ladbroke Grove and Notting Hill, it had to be tubby and trawler-like. It would be broad in the beam, high in the bow, and framed in oak. It would ride out dirty weather with the buoyancy of a puffin; inside, it would be as snug as a low-ceilinged tudor cottage. It was perfectly designed to go on imaginary voyages and make dream-landfalls.

Then I bought a sextant, and the whole business suddenly stopped being a fantasy.

The sextant was old. I found it stacked up with a collection of gramophones and ladies' workboxes in a junkshop. Its brass frame was mottled green-and-black, the silvering on its mirrors had started to blister and peel off. It came in a wooden casket full of accessory telescopes and lenses bedded down in compartments of soft baize.

It had been made for J.H.C. Minter RN, whose name was engraved in scrolled letters on the arc by J.H. Steward, 457 West Strand, London. A certificate vouching for its accuracy had been issued by the National Physical Observatory, Richmond, in July 1907. Its pedigree made it irresistible. I had no very sure idea as to how a sextant actually worked, but this tarnished instrument looked like a prize and an omen.

For the first few days of ownership, I contented myself with rubbing away at it with Brasso until a few of its more exposed parts gleamed misty gold out of the surrounding verdigris. I loosened its hinged horizon- and sun-glasses with sewing-machine oil. I brushed the dust out of the baize and polished the oak case. Midshipman Minter's (*was* he a midshipman?) sextant was restored to a pretty and intricate ornament for a drawing-room.

Next I went to a shop in the Minories and came away with a chart of the Thames estuary, a pair of compasses, a protractor, a nautical almanac and a book on celestial navigation. At last I was in business again with a real vocation to follow. For months I had stumbled along at my old journeywork of writing reviews of other people's books and giving voice to strong opinions that I didn't altogether feel. Now I was returned to being a freshman student, with the art of finding one's own way round the globe as my major subject. I holed up with the sextant and the book on navigation, ready to stay awake all night if that was what was needed to master the basic principles of the discipline.

I read on page one:

We navigate by means of the Sun, the Moon, the planets and the stars. Forget the Earth spinning round the Sun with the motionless stars infinite distances away, and imagine that the Earth is the centre of the universe and that all the heavenly bodies circle slowly round us, the stars keeping their relative positions while the Sun, Moon and planets change their positions in relation to each other and to the stars. This pre-Copernican outlook comes easily as we watch the heavenly bodies rise and set, and is a help in practical navigation.

Obediently I saw the earth as the still centre of things, with the sun and the stars as its satellites. I was happy to forget Copernicus: my own private cosmology had always been closet-Ptolemaic. This geo-centric, ego-centric view of the world was infinitely preferable to the icy abstractions and gigantic mileages of the physicists. Of course the sun revolved around the earth, rising in the east and setting in the west; of course we were the focus of creation, the pivot around which the universe turns. To have one's gut-instincts so squarely confirmed by a book with a title like *Celestial Navigation* was more than I could possibly have bargained for. I became an instant convert. I saw Sirius and Arcturus tracking slowly round us like protective outriders; I watched Polaris wobbling, a little insecurely, high over the North Pole.

For the essence of celestial navigation turned out, as I read, to consist in a sort of universal egoism. The heavenly bodies had been pinned up in the sky to provide an enormous web of convenient lines and triangles. Wherever he was, the navigator was always the crux of the arrangement, measuring the solar system to discover himself on his ship, bang at the heart of the matter.

Here is how you find out where you are. You are standing somewhere on the curved surface of a globe in space. Imagine a line extending from the dead-centre of the Earth, through your body, and going on up into the distant sky. The spot where it joins the heavens over your head is your zenith, and it is as uniquely personal to you as your thumbprint.

Now: your latitude is the angle formed at the Earth's centre between the equator and your zenith-line. You are a precise number of degrees and minutes north or south of the equator. Check it out in an atlas. The latitude of my North Kensington flat is 51°31′ North.

The sun, remember, revolves around the earth. Imagine now that it is noon on one of those rare days—at the time of the spring or autumn equinox—when the sun is exactly over the equator. Get your sextant ready.

Focus the telescope, twiddle the knobs and set the mirrors to work. Excellent. You have now measured the angle formed between your horizon and the sun over the equator. If you happen to be standing in my flat, I can tell you that the figure you have just read off from your sextant is 38°29′.

And what use, pray, is that? inquires Poor Yorick.

It is a great deal of use. Take it away from 90° and what do you get?

51°31′. Our latitude.

Precisely.

I don't understand why.

Think. Your zenith-line cuts your horizon at right-angles. If the sun is over the equator, then the angle formed on the earth's surface between the sun and your zenith-line is the same as the angle formed at the earth's centre between your zenith-line and the equator.

I never did understand spherical geometry.

Nor did I, but the calculation works, and you can play exactly the same game with the Pole Star as you can with the sun. Find the angle between it and your horizon, and you can quickly work out your latitude in degrees north or south.

51°31′ North is not a position: it is a line several thousand miles long encircling the Earth. To find North Kensington on that line, you must time the sun with a chronometer and so discover your longitude.

Longitude—your personal angle east or west of the zero meridian—is measured from Greenwich. 'Noon' is not a time on the clock: it is the instant when the sun is highest overhead above your particular meridian. In North Kensington, which is West of Greenwich, noon comes later than it does to the Royal Observatory, for the sun goes round the earth from east to west at a reliable speed of fifteen degrees of longitude in an hour, or 360° in a day.

Pick up the sextant again and clock the angles of the sun around noon. It rises...rises...rises, and now it starts to dip. What was the exact moment when it peaked? Just forty-eight seconds after noon by Greenwich Mean Time? Please don't argue. Let's agree that it was forty-eight and not a second more or less.

Forty-eight seconds, at a minute of longitude for every four seconds of time, is twelve minutes of longitude. You are precisely twelve minutes West of Greenwich, or 0°12′ W.

So there is home: 51°31′ N, 0°12′ W. St Quintin Avenue, London W10, England, the World, the Celestial Sphere. How easily is the lost sheep found, at least at noon on the vernal equinox, with the aid of Midshipman Minter's sextant. No matter how twisty the lane, or how many back alleys must be broached to reach him, the navigator dwells in the intersection between two angles. His position is absolute and verified in heaven. It all makes a great deal more sense than house numbers and postal codes.

That is the theory. But nautical astronomy is founded on a nice conceit, a useful lie about the way the universe works. It's muddied by the unruly behaviour of the sun and stars as they whizz round us on the celestial sphere. The sun, unfortunately, is a vagrant and unpunctual bird. Only twice in the year is it actually over the equator at noon. Between March and September it strays North, lying at a slightly different angle every day; between September and March it goes south. Solar noon never quite corresponds with noon by Greenwich Mean Time. It can be late or early, according to the clock, by as much as twenty minutes.

It would have been pleasant to go abroad, Crusoe-fashion, with just a sextant and a good clock. In practice, apparently, both were useless without a book of tables called an *Ephemeris*—tables that are meant to keep one posted on what all the heavenly bodies are up to at any particular moment.

I t was time to take my first noon sight. I unfolded the sextant from its wrapping of dusters, feeling that I was handling an instrument of natural magic. From the *Ephemeris*, I'd found that today, because the sun was now down south over Africa, nineteen degrees beyond the equator, it was running three minutes late.

I stood at the kitchen window and squinted through the telescope at the jam of cars and trucks moving slowly past on the elevated motorway like targets in a shooting-gallery, and made my first significant and disconcerting discovery: London has no horizon.

This was serious. Without a horizon, you don't know where you are. Unless you can measure the angle between yourself, the sun and the plane surface of the earth, you might as well be underground. London presented an impenetrable face of concrete, clotted stuccowork, bare trees, billboards, glass, steel, tarmac and no horizon anywhere. No wonder it was famous for getting lost in.

I had to guess at where the city's notional horizon might be, and found a window-ful of typists four floors up in a nearby office block. I focused the eyepiece on the girls and gently lowered the reflected image of the sun to join them in their typing pool. It was three minutes past noon. The girls had a peaky, distracted, time-for-lunch look; the sun, clarified through blue smoked glass, was rubicund and warty. The girls worked on, oblivious to the presence of this uninvited guest, as I twiddled the micrometer-screw with my thumb and laid the sun neatly between the filing cabinet and the Pirelli calendar.

With the swivelling magnifier on the arm of the sextant I read the sun's altitude on the inlaid-silver scale, took away the nineteen-degree declination of the sun, subtracted the total from ninety, and found my latitude—45°30′ N.

Had I only been in Milan or Portland, Oregon, it would have been spot-on. As it was, it did at least put a precise figure on the complaint from which I'd been suffering for the last few months: I was just six degrees and one minute out of kilter with where I was supposed to be.

The details were wonky but the exercise opened a shutter on a tantalizing chink of air and space. It seemed to me that the navigator with his sextant had a unique and privileged view of the world and his place in it. He stood happily outside its social and political arrangements, conducting himself in strict relation to the tides, the moon, the sun and stars. He was an exemplary symbol of solitude and independence. His access to a body of arcane and priestly knowledge made him a Magus in a world where Magi were in deplorably short supply; and I was bitten by pangs of romantic envy every time I thought of him. The fact that he was probably also soaked to the skin, parking his breakfast over the rail, with his circulation failing in fingers and toes, didn't then strike me as being either likely or relevant. This was North Kensington, after all, where the sea-beyond-the-city was always unruffled, bright and cobalt-blue.

I tacked up a quotation from *Purchas His Pilgrims* over my desk:
> The services of the Sea, they are innumerable: it yields...to studious and religious minds a Map of Knowledge, Mystery of Temperance, Exercise of Continence, Schoole of Prayer, Meditation, Devotion and Sobrietie.... It hath on it Tempests and Calmes to chastise the Sinnes, to exercise the faith of Sea-men; manifold affections in it self, to affect and stupefie the subtilest Philosopher.... The Sea yeelds Action to the bodie, Meditation to the Minde, the World to the World, all parts thereof to each part, by this Art of Arts, Navigation.

In the seventeeth century the navigator really had been the hero of the moment: John Donne, for instance, could define passionate love in terms of the movement of a pair of navigator's compasses on a chart, and Purchas's seductive litany had in it all the intellectual excitement of seagoing in the English Renaissance. There was something worthwhile to aim at. It would, I thought, be wonderful to be able to salvage just a small fraction of that sense of the philosophical bounty of the sea.

Leaning out of the window to shoot the sun, the sextant clamped to my eye, I attracted the attention of a good many upturned faces in the street below. Even in North Kensington it's rare to see such an unabashed voyeur in action in the middle of the day, and I came in for a fine selection of sniggers, jeers and whistles. The passers-by were quite correct in their assessment of my case: I was a peeping-Tom. I felt aroused and elated by what I was watching through the telescope—the teasing prospect of another life, a new way of being in the world, coming slowly into sharp-focus.

As soon as I saw it, I recognized the boat as the same craft that I'd been designing in my head for weeks. The tide had left it stranded on a gleaming mudbank up a Cornish estuary. It stood alone, in ungainly silhouette; a cross between Noah's abandoned ark and the official residence of the old woman who lived in a shoe.

The local boatyard had given me the keys and a warrant to view. I slithered across the mud in city clothes, past knots of bait-diggers forking worms into buckets. There wasn't much romance in the discovery of the boat. Each new footstep released another bubble of bad-egg air. The trees on the foreshore, speckled a dirty white with china clay dust from the docks across the river, looked as if they had dandruff. The surface of the mud itself was webbed and veined with tiny rivulets of black oil.

The boat had been lying here untenanted for three years. It was trussed with ropes and chains on which had grown eccentric vegetable beards of dried weed and slime. Its masts and rigging were gone, its blue paintwork bleached and cracked. My shadow scared a sunbathing family of fiddler-crabs in the muddy pool that the boat had dug for itself as it grounded with the tide. They shuffled away across the pool-floor and hid in the dark under the bilges.

No one would have said the thing was beautiful. What it had was a quality of friendly bulk, as solid and reassuring as an old coat. I liked its name: *Gosfield Maid* sounded like a description of some frumpish, dog-breeding country aunt. I've always had a superstitious belief in anagrams. Rearranged, the letters came out as *Die, dismal fog.* Not bad, under the circumstances.

I found a boarding ladder under a dusty tree, climbed nine feet up on to the deck and became a temporary captain lording it over a small and smelly ocean of mud. I inspected my ship with ignorant approval. The deck was littered with pieces of substantial ironmongery that I didn't know the names of or uses for, but I trusted the look of their weathered brass and cast steel. Up front, two anchors lashed down in wooden cradles were big enough to hold a freighter. There was nothing toylike or sportive about this boat: it was the real thing—a working Scottish trawler refurbished for foul-weather cruising.

The wheelhouse stuck up at the back like a sentry box. It was snug and sunny inside, a good eyrie to study the world from. Leaning on the brassbound wheel, I followed the sweeping upward curve of the deck as it rose ahead to the bows. From here, the boat looked suddenly as graceful and efficient as a porpoise. It had been built to take steep seas bang on the nose, and its whole character was governed by its massive front end. Given pugnacious bows like that, you could go slamming into the waves and ride the tallest breakers, with the rest of the boat tagging quietly along behind.

The compass above the wheel was sturdy and shiplike, too. It showed our heading as West-North-West, on course across the wooded hills for Devon, Somerset and Wiltshire. I rocked the bowl in its hinged frame and watched the card settle back into position as the lodestone homed in on the pole; a small satisfying piece of magic...one more bit of the marvellous jigsaw of ideas and inventions by which captains find their way around the world.

Four steps down from the wheelhouse the boat turned into a warren of little panelled rooms: a kitchen just about big enough to boil an egg in, a lavatory in a cupboard, an oak-beamed parlour, a triangular attic bedroom in the bows. The scale of the place was elfin, but its mahogany walls and hanging oil-lamps suggested a rather grand Victorian bachelor elf. Its atmosphere was at once cosy and spartan, like an old-fashioned men's club.

I opened a porthole to freshen the pickled air in the saloon. It was possible now to make out a fine seam down on the far edge of the flats where shining mud was joined to shining water as the tide inched upriver from the sea. I sprawled on the settee, lit a pipe, and generally wallowed in my captaincy. This wasn't just a boat that was on offer; it was a whole estate. Whoever bought it would have a house to live in, a verandah to sit out on, a fine teak deck to pace, acres of water to survey, and a suit of sails and a diesel engine to keep him on the move through life. Who could ask for more of Home?

JAMES FENTON
ROAD TO CAMBODIA

Norman Lewis describes how in 1949 China, which had been open to the West for barely fifty years, closed down again 'for a change of scene': 'If you had wanted to go to China it was too late. You would have to content yourself with reading books about it, and that was as much of the old, unregenerate China as you would know. At this moment the scene shifters were busy and they might be a long time over their job. When the curtain went up again it would be upon something as unrecognizable to an old China hand as to Marco Polo.'

Lewis asked himself which country would be the next to suffer in this way, and he decided that it was high time to visit Indochina. *A Dragon Apparent* was the result which, like *The Quiet American*, is highly revered by the English and American correspondents who worked in the area.* After Dien Bien Phu, however, nobody was able to repeat Lewis's journey throughout the peninsula, unless, like the late Wilfred Burchett, they did so as guests of the Communists: North Vietnam was invented, and closed down. But the remainder of the area stayed open to the traveller for a decade and a half, until 1970. By that time the North Vietnamese had taken over the Cambodian countryside, Laos had become gradually impossible to explore, and South Vietnam was simply too dangerous.

Things improved, from the traveller's point of view, after the Paris Peace Agreement in 1973. Theoretically, western journalists were able to visit any of the 'liberated areas' of the south, and some of us profited from the opportunity. After the fall of Saigon in 1975, there was about a week in which travel was suddenly even easier, because nobody had yet been told to stop us from having a look around. Then we were confined to the capital and starved of news. The curtain descended well and truly over the whole peninsula for what turned out to be the most thorough, and drastic, change of scene.

I had wanted to write some kind of sequel to Norman Lewis's *A Dragon Apparent*, but although much of my book was finished, I could never bring myself to complete the account of the last months of the Phnom Penh regime. As I tried to write about it, I found that nothing but horror could be gained from the experience in Cambodia, and it was impossible to think back to what, for me, had been happier times. There is something hedonistic about travel writing, something egocentric. The masters of the art (Lewis, Greene, Naipaul) may rise above this vice, but, for my own part, it was impossible to complete a travel book about such a catastrophe.

I abandoned the book, but, before doing so, I wrote the piece that follows. It describes a smuggling town to which I believe I was the only Western visitor, and it looks at the Cambodian areas of South Vietnam.

There may also be some contemporary relevance. The Mekong Delta had once belonged to Cambodia, but the Cambodian Empire was in danger of disappearing altogether when, in the nineteenth century, the French established their protectorate in Indochina. In subsequent years, it was not the French, however, but the Thais and the Vietnamese who were always considered *the* historical threat to Cambodia's existence. It was in the face of this threat that Khmer Rouge nationalism developed, but it was the Khmers Rouges themselves, ironically, who ended up destroying their own country and who made it vulnerable to Vietnamese hegemonism. In the Mekong Delta (Kampuchea Krom), the towns are now Vietnamese, but the countryside retains pockets of Cambodian life. But I am afraid that in Cambodia itself the same process will be repeated: Cambodia will be incorporated into a land-hungry empire. Those who oppose this are obliged to answer an impossible question: Are you really prepared to reinstate the Khmers Rouges? Are you really prepared to subject the country to another war?

Towards the end of 1974 I made two trips to the Mekong Delta, where I narrowly avoided meeting the Khmers Rouges (to my great relief) and the Vietcong (to my regret). I enlisted the help of a Vietnamese student as interpreter, and we set off by bus from Saigon to Cantho. At the terminal just outside Saigon, there were vast crowds of screaming touts, who rushed at you and tried to seize your baggage. Little girls were most insistent that you would need sunglasses for the journey. Every form of food and refreshment was pressed into your hand.

The first leg of the journey was by mini-bus, non-stop to Cantho. We fell in with a couple of Vietnamese who were on their way to Ha

Tien, the sea-port by the Cambodian border. You must go to Ha Tien, they said, because of the market. Everything is so cheap: cloth, drink, cigarettes, you could buy whatever you wanted at a fraction of the price in Saigon.

It was impossible to go with our two Vietnamese friends at first, because we were researching into the Cambodian communities of the delta. However, after a couple of days in Ba Xuyen province, where for some reason all the Cambodians appeared to be getting married (it was, I suppose, the Khmer equivalent of Whitsun), we decided to return to Cantho and rejoin them on their journey. As it happened, our friends were nowhere to be found, so we set off on our own to Ha Tien on one of the large, ancient, bone-shaking buses which served the route. The trick with these buses was not to sit at the back, because it would be full of chickens, ducks and catfish, and not to sit in the middle, because there was no room for your legs, and not to sit at the front, because it was absolutely terrifying. For the first part of the journey we sat at the back, and every time the bus hit a bump—that is to say every five minutes—I would hit the roof. Later I sat at the front, and watched a series of near misses. There were two boys on the bus employed to collect the fares and, as we made our rapid progress on the clearer stretches, to hang from the doors screaming at anyone near the road to get out of the way.

Two things held us up. First, there was a series of refreshment stops as vendors climbed aboard and screamed 'Boiled crab!' or 'Shrimp pancake!' in your ear, or proffered chunks of sugar cane. Some of these stops had been arranged with the driver. Others had been ingeniously devised—a sort of commercial ambush. One woman had placed her baby in the path of the bus as if to say: 'Either you buy my rather indifferent madeira cake or you kill my baby. The choice is yours.' The second reason for hold-ups was the activity of the Vietcong frogmen, who had blown up several bridges along the way. This also added to the expense of the trip, since although Thieu's army had plenty of equipment to meet such emergencies, they considered that they should be paid for their efforts. At one point, as we waited for the bus to be precariously loaded on to the pontoon ferry, I went and talked to the small group of soldiers beside the destroyed bridge. They pointed to a clump of bushes about a hundred and fifty yards away and said that the Vietcong were there. I wasn't sure whether they were telling the truth. It seemed ridiculous that the situation could be tolerated. But it was typical of the delta in those times; typical indeed of large areas of Vietnam at that time. The *amour propre* of the Saigon government, and the tolerance of the Vietcong, kept roads open through areas that did not belong to Saigon in any way.

By this time it was getting towards evening, and a woman on the bus advised us that it would be better to sit away from the front seats since it was quite likely that we would be stopped either by Vietcong or by bandits. I remembered the golden rule of travel in Indochina: never be on the roads after dusk. Still, there was nothing to be done, and I was not at all worried about the prospect of meeting the Vietcong. As it became dark, barricades were put up on the roads at either end of every village. We would stop; the two boys would rush to the barricades, parley with the guards and wave us through. The excitement and the hurry mounted. We met more and more Vietnamese Cambodians. One leapt on to the bus and met his mother-in-law. He slapped her so hard on the back that she shrieked. Then he started talking to her with such speed and amusement, holding his head first on one side, then on the other, like some kind of garrulous bird, that he had soon put her into a good mood. The happiness of these two was infectious. My interpreter, who had never travelled in this area, was completely beguiled. He told me that he had never, never seen such a happy group of people in Vietnam before as on this bus.

But at the last village before Ha Tien another bridge had been blown up, and this time it was impossible to get through before dawn. We descended from the bus and went to the village café, where the arrival of a white face at such a time of night caused a great stir. The village was poor and there was nothing much to eat, but in a short while the local police and military chiefs had arrived, and we began talking and drinking together. It was a sad conversation, and much of it consisted of questions posed to me: What did I think of Thieu? What would the Americans do if there was another offensive? Could Saigon last? I tried to answer these questions, in the way I always tried, with tact and about two-thirds honesty. People imagine that the officers of the Thieu regime were corrupt and vicious to a man. In my experience, many of them were no better and no worse than anybody

31

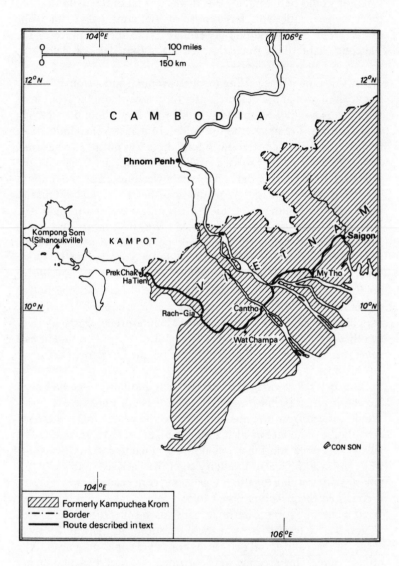

else in the world. But, of course, I only knew them when their fortunes were on the wane, and they had every reason to be reflective about the merits of their own side. In this conversation, there was only one point at which my interpreter refused to translate what I was saying; this was when I pointed out that Con Son island was one of the most notorious prisons in the world, and one of the chief reasons why the Thieu regime was disliked by so many foreigners.

By about midnight, the other travellers had found a place to sleep, either in the huts of the village or under the coach itself. We were invited to stay the next day in order to go fishing: there was a rare and highly-prized species of crab to be found nearby. We accepted the invitation, and were given camp beds and mosquito nets in the military compound. There was a gun nearby, an artillery piece, which fired off at regular intervals into the night, and the guards would occasionally fire shots into the river, to ward off any frogmen. I slept well enough, and woke in an area of most unusual beauty. A dramatic limestone crag lay on the other side of the river, which gave into a calm sea dotted with steep white islands and rocks. We said goodbye to the bus, and climbed into a fibre-glass military dinghy to go fishing.

Of course, said our friends as we prepared to set out, we could use grenades, but it's so wasteful of stock, don't you think? We agreed solemnly, but I noticed we had no tackle with us. There were only two blocks of *plastique* (explosive), one hand-grenade and a landing-net. We sped out among the beautiful islands, passing one on which a white cross stood, marking the cave where the Emperor Gia Long had spent his exile.

Once at the fishing-grounds, we stuck fuses into the *plastique*, lit them with cigarette ends, threw the *plastique* into the water, and retired to a safe distance. With the first explosion, the sea gave a slight heave and brought up a total of one fish. The second, however, succeeded in stunning about sixty sprats and one or two larger items. We decided not to use the grenade, rather to my relief, since I was mortally afraid of it. We never found the highly-prized species of crab.

---

*Published in 1951 and recently reissued by Eland Books.

On our return, we found that the village was being visited by two senior police officers, who were very keen to discuss the problems of Vietnam. When I told them I worked for the *Washington Post*, they were somewhat disenchanted.

'*Washington Post*,' they said, 'the paper that finished President Nixon.'

So I told them that I also worked for the *New Statesman*, which as far as I knew never finished anybody.

'When the Americans were here,' they said, indicating the twisted spans of the bridge, 'this bridge would have been rebuilt in one day. Now...' They shrugged. They said that it was impossible to continue the battle against the Vietcong without more supplies.

I questioned this, pointing out that the soldiers had been firing all the previous night against an apparently non-existent enemy, so they could hardly be that short of ammunition.

They said it was very difficult to combat the Vietcong, because they used such crude methods.

'Crude?' I asked.

'Yes, crude.' The word was spoken with a dreadful scowl.

'What do you mean, crude?'

One of the officers explained. It was these frogmen. They didn't use proper equipment. They just put a clip on their nose, tied round their head a bit of rubber hose to breathe through, attached stones to their feet, and walked along the bottom of the river. They had found from intelligence sources that that was how they had blown up all these bridges. It was impossible to see them coming. It was all very crude.

I had to agree with the officer. It did sound pretty crude. But why didn't they do the same thing in return? Why didn't the Saigon troops go walking around on the bottom of the rivers attacking Vietcong positions?

The officer looked at me with utter contempt. 'That would be quite impossible,' he said flatly.

By this time, another bus had arrived and had been ferried across the river, so we continued on our way, along a palm-fringed coast, towards Ha Tien and the Cambodian border. We could see the Elephant Mountains and the region of Kampot.

Ha Tien itself was an old town, built in the Chinese-French-Portuguese commercial style, with charming, decorated, crumbling stucco houses, and the filthiest market I had seen so far in Vietnam. Was this what we had come for? After a revolting lunch, during which my spirits sank, we asked about the big market. It turned out that we needed a honda cart to take us there. The market was not in Ha Tien. It was in a village called Prek Chak ('Poke Village'), and Prek Chak was in Cambodia.

I must have been a little thick that day: it was already about two-thirty, and not the best of times to be crossing borders. However, we set out along the road, passing rows of Cambodian refugee settlements on the way. About a hundred yards before the border post on the main road we turned left into a small village and came to a pagoda complex, where our driver left us. There was a constant stream of people passing to and fro, their bicycles laden with goods. We walked through the village and, without our asking, people showed us to the unofficial crossing-point. There was a double fence of barbed wire, newly erected, and a Vietnamese soldier stood beside it.

No, he said, it was impossible to go through. Look at the barbed wire.

Yes, I said, it has been cut; all you have to do is roll it back.

No, he said, it was only cut because the Vietcong had cut it the night before. It wasn't really supposed to be cut.

This was obviously a lie, but there were so many people around that I didn't like to try bribing the men in public. Finally I produced my military travel documents, and with ill grace the man let us through.

We walked across a field towards a collection of straw huts. There was nothing remarkable about them from a distance, but when we came closer we realized the place was very odd indeed. The huts, which were clustered around a shallow muddy creek, were crammed full of merchandise of every kind. There were cartons of cigarettes from Singapore, bales of cloth from Thailand, crates of whisky, sacks of cement; there were boxes of Chinese razor-blades and bottles of Chinese wine. Everything was in bulk. The place was a hypermarket of contraband.

James Fenton

As we entered the village, people looked up—not in the normal astonished way to which I had grown used in some of the remoter parts of Cambodia, but in a manner which indicated absolute blank incomprehension. They laughed—the Cambodians among them, not the Chinese—but they laughed in a different way. They seemed embarrassed. They seemed as if they had just been caught out doing something improper. And well they might seem embarrassed. For they were all gambling. Absolutely everybody was gambling. It was like—I suddenly thought—coming into some allegorical town, say in *Pilgrim's Progress*. In the muddy alleys between the huts, the children were gambling with rubber bands, squatting on their haunches and shrieking as they lost or won. In the smaller huts they were gambling with cards, dice, shells. On the other side of the creek, there were larger huts containing full-scale casinos where the really serious stuff was going on. This was run by the Chinese. Numbers or characters were drawn out of a box, and held up to shouts and groans. A vast litter of Vietnamese and Cambodian notes was raked across the tables.

Sitting in one of the many cafés, I got into conversation with some Cambodians who explained part of the history of Prek Chak. It had begun earlier in the year when the Khmers Rouges had attacked Kampot and had destroyed its usefulness as a centre for smuggling. The Cambodian navy had co-operated with the Chinese, and the South Vietnamese had not objected. So the village had grown at an enormous rate, and was still growing. As I walked round, I began to attract a crowd of children, who followed cheering and imitating my every gesture. I wanted to see if, in addition to the Saigon soldiers and police who were walking around, there were any Cambodian military. Yes there were, said somebody, down by the sea. We set off to look for them.

At this point, the children suddenly melted away. I was glad at first, but then I suddenly noticed that nobody was talking to us any longer. We became uneasy, and again we asked the way. This time a Vietnamese woman came up to us and hurriedly explained that if we didn't get out at once we would be killed. It was four o'clock, she said, and at this time the Khmers Rouges came into town. Any foreigners would be killed—one stranger had been killed the day before on the very spot where we were standing. She herself, as a newcomer, had

36

been in terrible trouble. We must get out at once. But how? The route by which we had come in had now been shut up for the night. If we went out along the main road, via the official customs post, we would be arrested. There was one other way.

The woman led us through the village, and as she did so, people stared at us in a new way. Suddenly I realized why they had been quite so surprised when we arrived there in the first place. As the woman explained, Prek Chak belonged to Phnom Penh and Saigon by day. By night it belonged to the Khmers Rouges. Every evening they came in, sometimes trading things, but very often simply stealing them. The Vietcong and NVA [North Vietnamese Army] came in as well, from time to time, but they always paid for their purchases. Prek Chak by day was a paradise for draft dodgers, smugglers and gamblers. By night it was quite a different kettle of fish.

As we made our way through the fields, we met a line of people coming back from Ha Tien to their homes in Prek Chak. As they passed us, they told my interpreter: 'Don't be afraid. Just walk very quickly.' But soon we saw that the route by which they were coming involved at least another mile before the border. Then, we were told, there was a creek, but the ferryman at the creek did not have any authorization, and the previous night his boat had been shot at by the Khmers Rouges. Just at this time, as well.

There was nothing for it but to go back to the official border post and argue our way through the guards. By now I was really frightened, more frightened than I had ever been before. The prospect of arrest by the South Vietnamese seemed nothing compared with the prospect of meeting the Khmers Rouges. We hurried back to the border post, and were obligingly arrested. While this was happening, the South Vietnamese began for some reason to fire shells over our heads into Cambodia, and in Prek Chak the sound of automatic rifle fire began.

The trouble with being arrested was that nobody knew what to do with us. We protested that it had all been a terrible mistake—we had assumed that Prek Chak was in Vietnam, and anyway there were thousands of others crossing the border all the

37

time. The soldiers were sympathetic, but by now they had reported our case, so it was too late to let us go. In Ha Tien we were passed from office to office. Statements were taken, and then the men who took the statements were roundly abused by their seniors for not taking more detailed statements. More detailed statements were taken. The police chief was not around. I was exhausted and irritated and by the end of three hours began to get annoyed. The police station was apparently open to the whole public, and a small crowd of children had gathered to watch the fun.

I turned to my interpreter: 'Will you please tell the officer,' I said in wounded tones, 'that in England it is customary to offer people chairs.'

From the depths of the ancient French building, a chair was brought.

We were approaching the final, most dangerous point, the status of my interpreter. 'Why doesn't he have a press card?' they asked.

I lied through my clenched teeth: 'Because in Saigon, press cards are *never, never* issued to interpreters.'

'Then how do we know he *is* your interpreter?'

'Look,' I said, 'if you want proof, I'll write you out a letter of introduction for him.' I was getting somewhat hysterical. An impressive anger began to sweep through my frame. 'In fact,' I said, 'I'll *type* you a letter for him, and sign it, *with my own signature,* in the name of the *Washington Post!*'

'All right,' they said—much to my surprise.

'Well, where's the typewriter?!!'

They led me into the building. The children milled round.

I sat down in the manner of a man who was about to blow the lid off the Pentagon. 'I'LL NEED SOME PAPER AS WELL, YOU KNOW!'

They hurried off and found a piece of paper. By now the interest was tremendous.

I put the paper in the machine. I did it beautifully. I've since seen Robert Redford do this bit on film, but he was pathetic in comparison. I really gave that paper hell. My fingers poised over the keys. I looked down. It was a Vietnamese typewriter, of course, and all the keys were in the wrong position. Pathetically, I began to look for the *W*. There didn't seem to be a *W*. The children started to snigger. It was perfectly obvious that I didn't know how to type. 'Will you please get these children out of here?' I said, furiously. Then, key by key, I composed the worst-typed letter of introduction ever.

And yet, for some reason, we were let off, and we went and indulged in a celebratory supper. When we got back to our hotel, the manager told us in lugubrious tones that the chief of police had called, and would be back in the morning. We went upstairs with heavy hearts. In the room next to ours, a Chinese merchant had laid out his purchases from Prek Chak, and had erected a small altar, with candles, joss-sticks and offerings of fruit. He was praying, he said, for three things: finance, property and protection from the Khmers Rouges. Soon, there was a knock at the door. It was the police chief, with a couple of his friends. He was profusely apologetic. He had been away all day, otherwise we would never have had all that trouble. His junior officers had not known what to do. How could he make amends? Would we come to breakfast with him the next day? He would take us for the finest Chinese soup in town. At 6.30? Good. The trouble was, he said, that we had been taken through by the military. The military did not know what they were doing. It was very dangerous for a foreigner in Prek Chak. We could have been killed. He was responsible for us. If anything had happened to us, he would personally have been very upset. He considered us, you know, he considered us to be his own sons....

After soup the next morning, the police chief put us on the bus for Saigon, instructing the driver not to charge us for the trip. After we left Ha Tien we persuaded the driver, although with some difficulty, to let us pay half fare. As we went towards Saigon, I noted from time to time that bundles of notes were produced and handed over at the military check-points. This was the protection money on which the racketeers of the Mekong Delta made their fortunes. What I did not realize until some weeks later, when it was independently confirmed, was that Prek Chak's main function was gun-running. Corrupt officials in Kompong Som, together with the Khmer Navy, brought American weapons and ammunition to be sold there to the Khmers Rouges. Later still, I was talking about Prek Chak to a soldier in Kompong Som, and he told me that the place had just been attacked by the Khmers Rouges and burned to the ground. Many of the inhabitants had been killed, the others had fled to South Vietnam where they were continuing their trade. Clearly, the place had outlived its usefulness, and had fallen under the righteous wrath of the insurgents. It certainly had stood for everything they despised.

I said to the solder: 'They were selling arms to the enemy, weren't they?' The soldier looked alarmed. I lowered my voice: 'It was well-known. The FANK [Forces Armées Nationales Khmers] officers were selling their own weapons to the Khmers Rouges.'

'Yes,' said the soldier ruefully, 'they *were* selling arms to the enemy. It is true. But they were only *small* arms.'

While in Ba Xuyen province on this trip, I had found a Cambodian monastery where we had been received very well, and which I wanted to investigate more carefully. The trouble (and the attraction) was that it was in a contested area—the Vietcong-controlled villages were only a couple of miles away. I thought that if I stayed there I might be able to cross over to a PRG [Provisional Revolutionary Government] zone, but it was obviously unfair to try to do so in the company of my interpreter.

A few days later, I therefore set out by myself, on the same sort of minibus, in the direction of Cantho. The driver was fairly careful, but the traffic was heavy. At one point a young girl stepped out from behind a car, and was hit by the bus. We drew to an abrupt halt, and the child was thrown several yards down the road. Then a large proportion of the luggage on the roof-rack slipped off and fell into the road in front of us. The child lay twitching in the road, and the driver, in terrible distress, got out, hailed a honda cart, and took the girl off to hospital. At once, all the passengers on the bus dispersed. Somebody took me gently by the arm, and indicated a large, red, ancient American car, into which we piled. We left the minibus where it had stopped, in the middle of the road.

The miserable aspect of Cantho, with its drug addicts and cripples, has been well described before (for instance, by Richard West in *Victory in Vietnam*). I shall mention just one thing I saw that night. It was a group of legless heroin addicts, sitting in wheelchairs and drinking together on the waterfront. When the time came to pay the bill, an argument broke out among them. Soon the argument developed into a fight—and a vicious fight it was. The purpose of the fight was to pull each other out of the wheelchair. I did not stay to see the result.

The next morning I was dropped from the local bus not far from Wat Champa. As I approached the monastery, walking through the fields, I greeted one of the peasants in Cambodian. At once, he called out to another peasant on the other side of the field, saying that I spoke Khmer. And then I heard the message passed on further, to the adjoining paddies. A sudden surge of happiness came over me, to be walking alone in the countryside, and to be walking into what was, after all, a tiny pocket of Cambodia. The morning was sunny, the occasion propitious. I had never really seen Cambodian village life functioning before, at least not since my trip through Battambang province the year before.

The monastery was set in a spacious grove of tall, umbrageous trees, and the main temple was a work of fantastic imagination. At each corner stood concrete statues of animals, brilliantly painted. The other buildings were more modest, some of them made of wood. The abbot was pleased to see me, and asked after my interpreter. Over a cup of tea, I explained that my purpose was to study a little more of the customs of the monks and to learn a little of the Cambodian language. If possible, I should like to spend a few days at the monastery.

'Aren't you afraid of the Vietcong?' they said.

'No,' I replied, 'the Vietcong always behaved well towards foreigners; I was only afraid of the Khmers Rouges.'

The monks explained that the Vietcong were visiting the village every night to collect taxes, but that they never came into the monastery. The abbot would give me some lessons in Khmer if I gave him some lessons in English. Everything seemed fine.

The monks lived what they were perfectly prepared to admit was a very lazy life. They joined the monastery as young men, at their family's request, and they would leave it when it became necessary for them to work at home. Of course, in wartime the temptation to stay on in the monastery was great. They ate two meals a day, breakfast and lunch. After that they survived on tea and cigarettes, although for senior monks there might be special treats. I once found the abbot chewing sugar-cane, which he said counted as drinking, since one always spat out the fibrous interior. One evening we ate a dish called 'fried milk', which consisted of 'Longevity Brand' condensed milk, mixed with coconut and reduced by heat until it reached the consistency of treacle toffee. The monks' day was spent in lessons—Pali and English—trips to the local villages to beg for alms, attendance at religious ceremonies, and the rest of the time sitting by the monastery pool, feeding the two enormous pet turtles—the monks' stomachs rumbling as evening came on.

The buildings were full of surprises. In one, surrounded by winking lights, the last abbot was lying in his coffin. He had died a year before, and it would be another two years before he was cremated. The present abbot's house was stuffed with souvenirs and junk. It looked like the bedroom of some sentimental bit-part actress. There were photographs, ornaments and knick-knacks, and in a loft above our heads there were piles of embroidered cushions and umbrellas stacked away. But this was nothing to the house occupied by the oldest monk in the establishment, to which we were invited one evening in order to watch the television.

This was a great occasion. There was the strangest altar I have ever seen. On the top level, there was a row of assorted Buddhas—as one might expect. Below these, and partly obscuring them, were a television set and three bottles of pop, flanked by two model Christmas trees with fairy lights, and an illuminated Star of Bethlehem. On the next level there was a row of ancient biscuit barrels and a wholesale tin of Maxwell House instant coffee. At the base there was a coffee table cluttered with china frogs, candlesticks, fluffy animals, alarm clocks and glasses full of old cutlery, all covered with dust.

The old monk also showed me his cupboards, which were full of souvenirs from the seaside, old swords and daggers, and yet more alarm clocks. He had a passion for clocks. He took out one and placed it, with great ceremony, in my hands; it was a travelling alarm, with a cunning, slatted shutter that could be pulled across the clock face.

'Are you—um—giving this to me?' I asked, embarrassed.

'No!' he said quickly, and snatched it away.

Instead, I was given something to eat. By now, the room had filled up with children and adults from the village, the generator had been turned on, the fairy lights and the Star of Bethlehem were blinking away, and I was the centre of attention for about fifty people. As it was evening, the monks were, of course, not eating, so I was going to be the only one.

I looked into the bowl that they put in my hands. It contained crushed rice, coconut and about three hundred ants, swarming all over it. There was nothing to be done. I spooned up the ants, and wolfed them down with appropriate expressions—Mmmm! Lovely! Delicious! But I didn't finish them all. I was absolutely terrified that if I did, they would produce another dish. Finally, when I had done what I considered justice to the bowl, I set it down, and the children eagerly consumed the rest.

But still—no television. The cover had been left on it, and nobody seemed interested in plugging it in. I had noticed vaguely, while eating the ants, that people had been coming in and going out, after whispered consultations with the abbot. Now there were distinctly embarrassed looks. I couldn't understand it, until a little later the abbot explained. The problem was that the Vietcong objected to the monks giving television shows, and had threatened that if they persisted the Vietcong would come into the monastery itself and take away the sets. As it happened, the Vietcong had arrived earlier than usual that night, and were now in the village. They knew perfectly well what was going on, and had sent a message that there was to be no television.

The abbot was desperately worried about losing his televisions. He spoke about them often. He had two, but the one with the twenty-five-inch screen, of which he was particularly fond, was kept in the central pagoda itself, along with the cine-projector, which was also a favourite possession. The abbot used to take siestas there in the afternoon, watching the television and wondering whether he dared turn it on. One night, when the coast seemed clear, a group of young monks did turn it on for me. We watched the local Cantho channel, which was pretty grim: a long programme of excruciating Vietnamese pop music, sung by hideous stars. I quite saw what the Vietcong objected to. However, we lounged at the foot of the great statue of the Buddha and smoked Capstans through the evening.

I went with the abbot and the oldest monk to a funeral ceremony for an old man who had died in a village not far away. We walked along the narrow paths between the houses and the fields, and every time we met someone coming in the opposite direction the oldest monk hit him over the head with his umbrella. I was not sure whether this was custom or mere eccentricity. When people called out from the fields, the abbot told them that I was from Phnom Penh—I was an upland Khmer. This caused great mirth since the upland Khmers (Khmer Loeu) were considered savages, wild tribesmen.

When we arrived in the village, the monks went into the house of the dead man, and soon settled down to a large meal that had been prepared for them. I sat outside with the villagers drinking *soum-soum*, the local rice spirit. We talked about the Vietnamese, whom they despised. There was nothing political about this. They just hated their guts. After all, the Cambodians of the delta, the Khmer Krom, still considered the whole rich area to be theirs. Saigon itself was nothing more than an old Cambodian village called Prey Nokor. The very watches of the villagers and the clocks of the monastery, were set to Phnom Penh time. (Saigon time was an invention of Diem: the North Vietnamese, the Vietcong and the Cambodians were all synchronized.) And although this area paid taxes both to Saigon and to the Vietcong, although the yellow and red Saigon flag was painted on their gates, the allegiance was to Cambodia.

But to a Cambodia with a difference. True, there had been very little interbreeding with the Vietnamese. The people retained their dark skins, which they disliked, their square chins and strong features. If you looked at their ears and lips in profile, the resemblance to the sculptures of the Angkor period was striking. And yet proximity to the Vietnamese, subjugation indeed, had forced them to accommodate to Vietnamese customs to a certain extent. Their dress was similar to the Vietnamese and they were all monogamous—'unfortunately', as one old man put it. Politically and socially they were misfits. A tradition of right-wing nationalist politics had survived there, but only in a degenerate form. I met nobody who had a good word to say for Sihanouk—whereas in Phnom Penh it was hard to find anybody who did not look back on his rule with nostalgia. The hero of the Khmer Krom was Son Ngoc Thanh, but he, after a period with the Lon Nol government, had returned to Saigon, where he was reputed to be too old and sick for any political activity.

Son Ngoc Thanh's memory was still kept very much alive by the Khmers Rouges, who referred to him regularly in their broadcasts as a member of the 'traitorous clique'. He was specially hated by Sihanouk, whose book, *My War with the CIA*, laid special blame on him for the overthrow of the royal government. The Khmer Krom had been trained by the CIA in Mike Force (*Mike*, the letter *M*, stands for 'mercenary'). In the summer of 1970, when the Lon Nol regime was struggling for survival, Mike Force troops were sent to Phnom Penh in large numbers. However, the reception they got from the Cambodians there was lukewarm at best. They were thought to be more Vietnamese than Khmer. Their superior attitude, their military sophistication and their ruthlessness were resented. They were used as cannon-fodder in a series of disastrous campaigns. Eventually, they were almost wiped out. You could still find a few of them in Phnom Penh. They were the gung-ho officers with the perfect command of GI slang. But the experience of fighting for the mother country had not been a success. They had found out, although they would not admit this, that they were not Cambodians after all. And if they were not Cambodians, and not Vietnamese, what the hell were they?

In these villages, the Khmer Krom had adapted themselves to their situation as best they could. Several of the peasants travelled to work in the PRG-controlled areas during the day. For those who lived under the nominal control of the Saigon regime, the PRG taxes were higher than for those in the liberated zones, and in addition they had to pay taxes to Saigon. I asked a large number of them whether there were many Cambodian troops among the Vietcong. Apparently the percentage was not high; this seemed to reflect the alienation of the Khmer Krom from Vietnamese politics. The only respected authority in the region was that of the monks.

To become a monk, to shave your head and eyebrows, to give up women and drink and all forms of games might not be everybody's idea of a good life. But it was a way of saying that you were a Cambodian, a way of avoiding the draft and remaining safe, for the moment at least. Beyond the monastery gates, the pleasant grove, the turtles and the pond, the chances of dying were high. There was gunfire daily as the peasants crossed the lines to and from work, and that afternoon the gunfire was nearer and louder than before. I asked the abbot what was happening. He explained that one of the territorial soldiers was about to be cremated. I went out to the crematorium ground, and watched the ceremony.

The women sat apart, wailing together in a manner which, as it gathered force, turned into what sounded like a ritual chant. The men lit the pyre with bits of old rubber tyres, which gave off a foul black smoke. As the fire began, they hacked at the coffin with axes, in order to make sure that the flames got through to the body. It was a sad and shabby occasion. The men were mostly drunk on *soum-soum*, which they passed around. A young soldier, I think he was about sixteen, was supposed to fire a salute. But he managed to jam his rifle. So the old men took the gun from him and fired the magazines off themselves. Every time they fired, there was an answering volley which came, I think, from the house where the dead soldier had lived. I reflected that the old men had fought for the French, their sons had fought for the Americans, and their grandsons were fighting for the Vietnamese.

By now the coffin was beginning to disintegrate. I wanted to stay and see the whole process to the bitter end. But one of the monks came up to me, pointed at the pyre and screwed up his nose. He told me not to wait around any longer.

Why not? I asked.

Bad dreams, he said, and besides, they were waiting in the monastery for me to give an English lesson.

I walked with him to one of the classrooms, where a group of eager, eyebrowless faces sat patiently. The teacher put a copy of *Understanding English* into my hands, and I began to read out loud. It was a book designed for the type of summer language school that exists on the south coast of England. The main characters in the stories were European students, each with his or her engaging little characteristics. It was full of bad puns and coy little jokes, and as I read the stories out, in a clear, slow, solemn voice, I could hear my own voice ringing round the classroom. No doubt I could be heard as far as the cremation ground, and they would think that the monks were furthering their religious education. By the end of the chapter, I realized that nobody—neither the teacher nor the pupils—had been able to follow a single word.

Every evening I would put on a loincloth and go to the wash-house where my ablutions were an object of great interest and mirth. One thing puzzled the monks. Why did I never relieve my bowels? Was I ill? Was I different in some curious respect? Since I had never had a moment of privacy from the time of my arrival, it was clear that something was wrong. On the third day, therefore, I announced that the time had come. Consternation!

'No have Kiss Me,' said a monk.

This remark might have been disconcerting, had I not been aware that 'Kiss Me' was a brand of toilet-paper. I don't know whether the monks had ever heard the song *Kiss Me Quick*, but one could imagine that they would have well appreciated its urgent rhythms. I took my little can of water down the path, which led past a pleasant stream luxuriant with lotus blossom, beside which the secluded closets stood. A great wave of sympathy and pleasure spread through the monastery.

I used to eat not with the monks—that was forbidden—but with the various lay personnel of the establishment. One evening, as I was sitting with the abbot and a few of the monks, the cook brought in his baby daughter to show me. The child was paralysed from the waist down, and he did not have enough money to get her proper medical attention. In the quietest, most modest way, he asked if I would give him some money, which I was glad to do, since—apart from anything else—I was enjoying the hospitality of the monastery. I gave him as much as I could spare. The man thanked me and left. I overheard the abbot ask the monks how much I had given. It was something like twenty dollars. 'A lot,' said the abbot, rather as if I had overstepped the mark. A few moments later, the cook came back, this time with his wife and the child. They knelt at my feet and placed the baby in my arms. Then they said that they would like to give me the child, since they would never be able to look after it properly. This may sound as if they were deficient in love for the baby, but in fact it was quite the opposite, and I hated having to refuse them.

On the last night, I had bought a gift of coffee for the monks and we sat up till the early hours, talking about politics, laughing and joking. I was very pleased with the way the trip had gone, and even though my Cambodian was only rudimentary and there were few English or French speakers, I had learned a lot in the way that I preferred—not using a notebook more than was absolutely necessary, and allowing events to take their own course. I had missed out on the PRG, but you couldn't have everything, and by now my presence in the area was so well known that it would be impossible to slip across the lines without incurring the wrath of the Saigon authorities. Besides, I doubted very much if it was wise to go from this dotty little pocket of reaction across to the liberated areas.

There was one monk who was much shrewder than the rest. Suddenly he said: 'Of course, we know why you have been staying with us all this time.'

I thought he was going to mention the Vietcong, and indeed he did: 'You're from the CIA, aren't you?'

I laughed. 'If I were from the CIA, I would be afraid to stay here. Besides, I'm not American.'

'That's what you say. But how do we know? This is an interesting area for you. You want to get information about the Vietcong.'

'I'm a journalist,' I said, 'and I hate the CIA.'

'But of course you'd *say* you hated the CIA.'

He was quite serious, and what he said destroyed, at a stroke, all the pleasure of the last days. Of course that's what they'd think. Why else would a foreigner come and spend such a long time with them? What was worst of all was—they didn't *mind*. They seemed almost to be used to it. I was an American spy doing my job; they were Cambodian monks, doing theirs. That was the world as they understood it, and it wasn't until I had thrown what amounted almost to a tantrum that they took the allegation back, and we patched up our friendship.

Redmond O'Hanlon
Into the Heart of Borneo

The situation in Sarawak as seen by Haddon in 1888 is still much the same today. He found a series of racial strata moving downwards in society and backwards in time as he moved inwards on the island.

C.D. Darlington
The Evolution of Man and Society, 1969

As a former academic and a natural history book reviewer, I was astonished to discover, on being threatened with a two-month exile to the primary jungles of Borneo, just how fast a man can read.

Powerful as your scholarly instincts may be, there is no matching the strength of that irrational desire to find a means of keeping your head upon your shoulders; of retaining your frontal appendage in its accustomed place; of barring 1,700 different species of parasitic worm from your bloodstream and Wagler's pit viper from just about anywhere; of removing small, black, wild-boar ticks from your crotch with minimum discomfort (you do it with sellotape); of declining to wear a globulating necklace of leeches all day long; of sidestepping amoebic and bacillary dysentery, yellow and blackwater and dengue fever, malaria, cholera, typhoid, rabies, hepatitis, tuberculosis and the crocodile (thumbs in its eyes, if you have time, they say).

A rubber suit, with a pair of steel-waders, was the most obvious form of protection, I thought. But then the temperature runs to one hundred and twenty degrees in the shade, and the humidity is ninety-eight per cent. Hose and McDougall's great two-volume masterpiece *The Pagan Tribes of Borneo* (published in 1912), Alfred Russel Wallace's *The Malay Archipelago: the Land of the Orang-Utan and the Bird of Paradise* (1869), Odoardo Beccari's *Wanderings in the Great Forests of Borneo* (1904), Hose's *The Field-book of a Jungle-Wallah* (1929) and Robert Shelford's *A Naturalist in Borneo* (1916) offered no immediate solution. And then meek, dead, outwardly unimpressive, be-suited and bowler-hatted Uncle Eggy came to my rescue. Uncle Eggy was in the war against the Japanese in Borneo, and a member of the Special Operations Executive—the SOE. So armed with my newly-remembered ancestor, I decided—before venturing into Borneo untutored—to seek help from the SOE's intellectual descendants, the SAS.

The training area of 22nd SAS near Hereford is the best place on earth from which to begin a journey up-river into the heart of the jungle. The nearest I had ever come to a tropical rainforest, after all, was in the Bodleian Library, via the pages of the great nineteenth-century traveller-naturalists, Humboldt, Darwin, Wallace, Bates, Thomas Belt—and, in practice, a childhood spent rabbiting in the Wiltshire woods. My companion, James Fenton, however, whose idea the venture was, enigmatic, balding, an ex-correspondent of the war in Vietnam and Cambodia, a jungle in himself, was a wise old man in these matters.

Still, as the gates swung open from a remote control point in the guardroom and our camouflaged Landrover climbed the small track across the fields, even James was unnerved by the view. Booby-trapped lorries and burned-out vehicles littered the landscape; displaced lines of turf disclosed wires running in all directions; from Neolithic-seeming fortressed earthworks, there came the muffled hammering of silenced small-arms fire; impossibly burly hippies in Levi jeans and trendy sweaters piled out of a truck and disappeared into the grass; mock-up streets and shuttered embassies went past, and then, as we drove round a fold in the hill, an airliner appeared, sitting neatly in a field of wheat.

We drew up by a fearsome assault-course and made our way into the local SAS jungle. Apart from the high-wire perimeter fence, the frequency with which Landrovers drove past beyond it, the number of helicopters overhead and the speed with which persons unknown were discharging revolvers from a place whose exact position it was impossible to ascertain, it might have been a wood in England.

'What a pity,' said Malcolm, our SAS instructor and guide, 'that you can't come to Brunei with us for a week. We could really sort you out and set you up over there.'

'What a pity,' I agreed, moistening with sweat at the very thought.

'Now,' said Malcolm, taking a small green package out of the newly-designed Bergen back-pack, 'it's all very simple. You find two trees eight feet apart where there's no evidence of any silt on the ground—the rivers can rise eighteen feet overnight and you don't want to drown in a wet dream, do you? Check the tree trunks for termites. Termites mean dead branches and dead branches, sooner or later, mean dead men. We lost a lot of men like that, in storms at

51

night. Tie these cords round the trees, put these metal stiffeners across each end like this, and there's your hammock. Now—here's your mossie net, and you just tie it over your hammock and peg it out by these strings to the surrounding bushes until it forms a good tight box like that—and you really want to watch it, because malaria pills only give you thirty per cent protection. Here's your top cover and that's it. There's your genuine basha.'

A long green tube had materialized above the brambles in front of us, seemingly in a minute or two.

'Stop around three or four in the afternoon,' said Malcolm, 'give yourself plenty of time. Light one of these blocks that makes no smoke and boil up a cup of tea. And just sit by your tree until dark if the enemy are about.'

B ack at the quartermaster's stores we signed for our new kit. One silver and one prismatic compass (black and tight and heavy as a little bomb in its canvas belt-case); two *parangs*— thick knives eighteen inches long which had chopped and slashed their way through the Indonesian confrontation from 1962 to 1966; torches, belts, pouches, powders, insect repellents, parachute cord, water bottles, water purifying tablets, stoves, fuel blocks, mess tins, the complete basha equipment and rations enough (Menu C) for three patrols moving in groups of four for three weeks.

We were in the company of a soft-spoken major. A veteran of Special Forces campaigns in Occupied Europe in the Second World War, of the war in Malaya, of Jebel Akhdar, Aden, Borneo and Dhofar, he was huge. It was vastly reassuring to think that so much muscle could actually squeeze itself into a jungle and come out again undiminished. And his office, hung with battle honours, SAS shields emblazoned with the regiment's motto, *Qui ose gagne*; with a mass of wall charts documenting the progress of his latest candidates; with cartoons of all the wrong ways to resist interrogation; and libraried with strictly practical works of natural history—on edible fungi, on traps and tracking and poaching, on different recipes for the cooking of rats and instructions on the peeling of cockroaches—was an impressive place.

'You'll find the high spot of your day,' said the major, 'is cleaning your teeth. The only bit of you you can keep clean. Don't shave in the jungle, because the slightest nick turns septic at once. And don't take more than one change of clothes, because you must keep your Bergen weight well down below sixty pounds. And don't expect your Iban trackers to carry it for you, either, because they have enough to do transporting their own food. So keep one set of dry kit in a sealed bag in your pack. Get into that each night after you've eaten. Powder yourself all over, too, with zinc talc—don't feel sissy about it—you'll halve the rashes and the rot and the skin fungus. Then sleep. Then get up at 5.30 and into your wet kit. It's uncomfortable at first, but don't weaken—ever; if you do, there'll be two sets of wet kit in no time, you'll lose sleep and lose strength and then there'll be a disaster. But take as many dry socks as you can. Stuff them into all the crannies in your pack. And, in the morning, soak the pairs you are going to wear in autan insect repellent, to keep the leeches out of your boots. Stick it on your arms and round your waist and neck and in your hair, too, while you're about it, but not on your forehead because the sweat carries it into your eyes and it stings. Cover yourself at night, too, against the mosquitoes. Take them seriously, because malaria is a terrible thing and it's easy to get, pills or no.

'Get some jungle boots, good thick trousers and strong shirts. You won't want to nancy about in shorts once the first leech has had a go at you, believe me. Acclimatize slowly. The tropics takes people in different ways. Fit young men here just collapse in Brunei. You'll think it's the end of the world. You can't breathe. You can't move. And then after two weeks you'll be used to it. And once in the jungle proper you'll never want to come out.

'It's a beautiful country and the Iban are a fine people. I was on the River Baram myself, but to go up the Rajang and the Baleh will be better for your purposes. That's a good plan. The Baleh is very seldom visited, if at all, up-river, and the Tiban mountains should be very wild indeed. They look small on a map, those mountains, but they're tough going. One steep hill after another. And you have to be good with a compass. Any questions? No. Good. Well done, lads, Goodbye and good luck.'

James and I drove out past the guardroom and the police post, in a stunned silence, the back of the car bristling with serious dark-green and camouflage-brown equipment; and we fell into the King's Arms. But we were on our way. It was too late to stay at home.

It was midday. Waving goodbye to the thirty or forty children and the thirty or forty dogs which had gathered on the bank, we climbed into our dugout canoe and set off up-river towards the interior, where none of our newly-hired Iban trackers—neither Dana, or Leon, or Inghai (our youngest and our bow look-out)—had ever been. For us, the unknown had begun the moment we arrived in Borneo, at the delta of the great River Rajang; for them, the unknown began now.

After about ten miles hill-*padi* fields gave way to well-established forest. And then the primeval jungle began. The river seemed to close in on us. The two-hundred-foot-high trees crowded down the slopes of the hills almost to the water's edge—an apparently endless chaos of different species of tree, every kind of green; parasitic growths sprouted everywhere; ferns fanned out from every angle in the branches; and creepers, as thick as legs, gripped each other.

The river itself began to turn and twist, too. The banks behind us appeared to merge together into one vast and impenetrable thicket, shutting us in from behind, just as the trees ahead stepped aside a meagre pace or two to let the river swirl down ahead. The outboard motor, manned by Leon and set on a special wooden frame at the stern of the canoe, pushed us past foaming little tributaries, islets, shingle banks strewn with huge rounded boulders, half-hidden coves scooped round by whirlpools. We really were, too, voyaging up-river—at first I thought it an optical illusion, but no, the canoe was actually climbing up a volume of water great enough to sustain an almost constant angle of descent, even between the jagged steps of the rapids.

Spits of land had formed wherever smaller streams joined the main flow, and here driftwood was piled, stacks of hardwood planed smooth by the rush of floodwater, flung together, bleached grey by the sun. We stopped by one such pile to hide a drum of petrol, in case we returned. A monitor lizard, reared up on its front legs, watched us for a moment with its dinosauric eyes and then scuttled away between the broken branches. A Brahminy Kite, flying low enough for us to hear the rush of air through the primary feathers of its wings, circled overhead, its flecked-brown belly white in the sun; watching us, too, before it soared away, mewing its shrill call like a buzzard.

Further up, the rapids began to become more numerous and more turbulent. At each one, as Leon drove the canoe for the central cascade of the current at full power while Dana and Inghai, their back muscles bunched, poled the bow to the left or the right of each oncoming rock, heavy waves of water would crash over us. James, sitting opposite me on the duck-boards in the centre of the canoe, facing upstream, our equipment lashed down under tarpaulins to front and rear of us, was reading his way through Pat Rogers's new edition of the complete poems of Swift. A straw boater on his bald head, his white shirt buttoned at the neck and at the wrists, his trousers no less and no more disgraceful than the ones he wore in Oxford (being the same pair), he would be, I thought, a formidable figure for the jungle to conquer. But he would need, no less certainly, a little discreet assistance against the vagaries of nature.

'Some of this juvenilia is pretty feeble,' James would mutter, displeased.

'Quite so. But–er–James?'

'Yes?'

'Rapid 583/2, Green-Heave Strength six-out-of-ten, is approaching.'

With a second or two to spare, James would shut his book, mark his place in it with a twig, slip it neatly under an edge of the tarpaulin, place his left buttock upon it, shut his eyes, get drenched, open his eyes, squeeze the water from his beard with his right hand, retrieve his book and carry on reading.

Every five hundred yards or so, a lesser Fish-eagle would regard us with its yellow eye, unmoving at first, its grey feet clamped to a favourite branch overhanging the edge of the river, flying off only as we drew almost level, flapping gently just ahead of the canoe to the limit of its territory, and then doubling back. It was odd to be journeying like this, preceded by eagles.

James, his huge head laid back on the hump of our kit under the tarpaulin, had begun one of his five-minute snoozes. The vein on his right temple was distended with blood, a sure sign that his cerebellum was awash with extra dissolved oxygen, and that some piece of programming, vital to the production of a future poem, was in progress.

'James!'

An eye opened. 'What is it?'

'Just this—if you *do* see a log floating *up-river,* let me know.'

'Crocodiles?'

'Well, not the estuarine one that really goes for you. Not up here. But authors Tweedie and Harrisson think we might see the freshwater Gharial. The fifteen-foot one with the five-foot snout and all those teeth.'

'Really, Redmond,' said James, raising himself up on an elbow and looking about, 'you're absurd. You live in the nineteenth century. Everything's changed, although you don't appear to notice. Nowadays you will have no difficulty whatever in recognizing a crocodile. Everyone knows—they come with an outboard motor at the back and a Kenwood mixer at the front.'

I sat back in the boat. When the temperature is one hundred and ten degrees and the humidity ninety-eight per cent, when you're soaking wet and rotting a bit in the crutch, then even weak jokes like that, in the worst possible taste, seem extraordinarily funny.

At four o'clock in the afternoon we entered a wider stretch of river where a tributary joined the main stream and a low ridge of shingle had formed down the centre of the water course. Dana decided to make camp.

'Good fishing. Very good,' said Leon, looking at the swirling white water, the fallen trees and the eddies by the far bank.

We pulled the canoe well out of the water and tied its bow-rope high up the trunk of a tree, in case of floods in the night, and then stretched out on the sand for a rest. Butterflies began to gather. Hundreds of butterflies, flying at different heights and speeds, floating, flapping awkwardly in small bursts, gliding, fluttering like bats, winnowing, some flying fast and direct like wrens in trouble—they made their way towards us and settled on our boots and trousers, clustered on our shirts, sucked the sweat from our arms. There were Whites, Yellows and Blues; Swallow-tails, black, banded or spotted with blue-green; and, just outside the clustering circle of small butterflies, the magnificent species which Alfred Russel Wallace named after James Brooke, *Troides brookiana,* the Rajah Brooke's Birdwing.

Sucking our clothes and skin with their thread-like probosces at one end, the butterflies exuded a white goo over us from their anal vents at the other. Getting up, brushing them off as gently as possible, I walked away from my companions the mandatory few yards and took a pee myself. While my patch of urine was still steaming slightly on the muddy sand, the males of Rajah Brooke's Birdwing (the females, being fully employed laying eggs in the jungle trees) flew over and crowded down on it, elbowing each other with the joints on their legs, pushing and shoving to get at the liquid, the brilliant green feather-shaped marks on their black wings trembling slightly as they fed. I began, prematurely, to feel a part of things.

In fact, having run to the canoe to fetch the shock-proof, water-proof, more-or-less-everything-proof heavy-duty Fuji cameras, I began to feel, as I crawled on my stomach towards the pullulating insects, very much more than a passing pride in the obvious quality of my own offering. It was while photographing this butterfly (with a fixed wide-angle lens which I knew would produce a hopeless picture), a butterfly which later proved to be very common all the way up the Baleh to its source, that I felt the excitement that Alfred Russel Wallace himself describes, on capturing its close cousin *Ornithoptera croesus*: 'The beauty and brilliancy of this insect are indescribable, and none but a naturalist can understand the intense excitement I experienced when I at length captured it.... My heart began to beat violently, the blood rushed to my head, and I felt much more like fainting than I have done when in apprehension of immediate death. I had a headache the rest of the day, so great was the excitement produced by what will appear to most people a very inadequate cause.'

I, too, had a headache for the rest of the day, but then perhaps it was the sun, or the mere thought of our fishing equipment. For after a burning swig all round from the arak rice-brandy five-gallon converted petrol-can, Dana, Leon and Inghai, drawing their *parangs* from their carved wooden scabbards, set off to cut down the saplings for our pole-beds; and I decided it was time that James and I taught them how to fish to maximum effect, like Englishmen. But first a little practice would be necessary.

Withdrawing quietly behind a massive jumble of boulders, well out of sight, I unpacked our precious cargo. Two new extendable rods, the toughest in town. A hundred yards of heavy line. A heavy bag of assorted lead weights. A termite's nest of swivels. A thornbush of hooks. Fifty different spinners, their spoons flashing in the sun, all shapes and all sizes for every kind of fish in every sort of inland water.

'The trouble is,' said James, flicking a rod-handle and watching the sections telescope out into the blue beyond, 'my elder brother was the fisherman. That was his thing, you see, he filled that role. So I had to pretend it was a bore; and I never learned.'

'What? You never fished?'

'No. Never. What about you?'

'Well, *my* elder brother went fishing.'

'So you can't either?'

'Not exactly. Not with a rod. I mean I used to go mackerel-fishing with a line. All over the place.'

'Mackerel-fishing! Now you tell me!' said James, looking really quite agitated and frightening a bright orange damsel-fly off his hat. 'Still,' he said, calming down, 'if *they* could do it, it can't be that diffy, can it?'

'Of course not—you just stick the spinner and swivels and weights on that end and swing it through the air.'

It was horribly annoying. The heat was unbearable. The fiddling was insupportable. The gut got tangled; the hooks stuck in our fingers; the knot diagram would have given Baden-Powell a blood clot in the brain. We did it all and forgot the nasty little weights. But eventually we were ready to kill fish.

'The SAS say it's simpler to stick in a hand-grenade.'

'They're right,' said James.

'But the major said all you had to do was hang your dick in the river and pull it out with fish on it.'

'Why don't you stick your dick in the river?' said James.

Standing firm and straight, James cast the spinner into the river. It landed in the water straight down at the end of the rod. Clunk. James pulled. The line snapped. We went through the whole nasty rigmarole again, with fresh swivels, weights and spinner.

'Try again. Throw it a little further.'

James reached right back and then swung the rod forwards and sideways as if he were axing a tree.

At that very moment, it seemed, the Borneo Banded Hornet, *Vesta tropica,* sank its sting into my right buttock.

'Jesus!' I said.

It was huge and jointed, this hornet, flashing red and silver in the sun.

'You are hooked up,' said James, matter-of-factly, 'you have a spinner in your arse.'

There was a weird, gurgling, jungle-sound behind us. Dana, Leon and Inghai were leaning against the boulders. The Iban, when they decide that something is really funny, and know that they are going to laugh for a long time, lie down first.

Dana, Leon and Inghai lay down.

'You should try it with harpoon!' shrieked Leon, helpless.

With great ceremony we presented our rods to Dana and Leon and a compensatory extra helping of weights and spinners to little Inghai. And with equal aplomb, the Iban took the useless gifts into care, wrapped them in cloth, and placed them in the bottom of the canoe.

Dana, meanwhile, was building a little house. Six-foot tall, two-feet square, with a conventional triangular roof and a small platform half-way up; its use was not apparent. For the spirits? For heads that might saunter by?

'For fish,' said Leon, 'for smoking fish. Now we show you how to fish like the Iban.'

Taking their wooden harpoons from the canoe, Leon and Inghai dived into the river; and disappeared completely, like a pair of Great Crested Grebe. A full forty seconds later they bobbed up again, right over on the far bank. Leon stood up and held an enormous fish above his head, harpooned through the flank. Inghai, as befitted his size, held up a tiddler. Much yelling in Iban took place. Dana, evidently stung into action, took a large weighted net out of the canoe, a *jala*, and made his way upstream to the shingle bank. Swinging it back and forth in both hands, swaying slightly, he cast it out; a slowly spinning circle of white mesh settled on the water, and sank. Jumping in, scrabbling about to collect the bottom ends of the net, Dana finally scooped it all up again, together with three catfish. They looked at us lugubriously, immensely long whiskers, their feelers, drooping down from either side of their mouths. Dana detached them with the greatest care, avoiding their dorsal and pectoral spines which, presumably, were poisonous, and tossed them up the shingle.

Leon and Inghai returned with six fish, all of the same species, *Sebarau,* handsome, streamlined, and, unlike the smooth and mucus-covered catfish, armoured with large silver scales and adorned with a bold black bar down either side.

Inghai collected driftwood and made two fires, one on the beach and the other at the base of the smoking-house. Leon gutted the fish, cut them into sections, placed some in a salting tin, some on the smoking-rack, and some in a water-filled cooking pot. Two ancient cauldrons, slung from a high wooden frame, bubbled over the fire: one full of fish pieces and one full of sticky rice. Dana returned for supper, having set a larger net part-across the current, supported by ropes to an overhanging branch and by white polystyrene floats.

Dusk came suddenly and, equally suddenly, Eared Nightjars appeared, hawking insects, stooping and turning in their haphazard, bat-like way, but always along the tops of the trees above the river banks, seeming half-transparent and weightless in their ghostly agility.

After about ten minutes, they vanished. Which was just as well, because it had dawned on me that the fish and the rice in my mess tin would need all the attention I could give it. The *Sebarau* was tasteless, which did not matter, and full of bones, which did. It was like a hair-brush caked in lard. James had made the same discovery.

'Redmond, don't worry,' he whispered, 'if you need a tracheotomy I have a biro-tube in my baggage.'

It was time to go to bed. We washed our mess tins in the river, kicked out the fire on the beach, and stoked up the smoking-house fire with more wet logs. Slinging my soaking clothes from a tree with parachute cord, I rubbed myself down with a wet towel and, naked, opened my Bergen pack to pull out my set of dry kit for the night. Every nook and cranny in the bag was alive with inch-long ants. Deciding that anything so huge must be the Elephant Ant, and not the Fire ant, which packs a sting like a wasp, I brushed the first wave off my Y-fronts. Glancing up, I was astonished to see my wet clothes swarming with ants, too; a procession of dark ants poured down one side of the rope and up the other; and, all over my wet trousers, hundreds of different moths were feeding. I rummaged quickly in the outside Bergen pocket for my army torch. As my fingers closed on it, everyone else's little fingers seemed to close on my arm. I drew it out fast and switched on: Elephant Ants, this time with massive pincers, were suspended from hand to elbow. The soldiers had arrived. I flicked them off, gratified to hear yelps from James's basha as I did so. It was good to know they also went for poets.

Slipping under the mosquito net, I fastened myself into the dark-green camouflage SAS tube. It seemed luxuriously comfortable. You had to sleep straight out like a rifle; but the ants, swarming along the poles, rearing up on their back legs to look for an entry, and the mosquitoes, whining and singing outside the various tunes of their species in black shifting clouds, could not get in.

'*Eeeeee—ai—yack yack yack yack yack!*' Something screamed in my ear, with brain-shredding force. And then everyone joined in.

'*Eeeeee—ai—yack yack yack yack yack te yooo!*' answered every other giant male cicada, maniacally vibrating the timbals, drumskin membranes, in their cavity amplifiers, the megaphones built into their bodies.

'Shut up!' I shouted.

'*Wah Wah Wah Wah Wah!*' said four thousand frogs.

'Stop it at once!' yelled James.

'*Clatter clitter clatter*' went our mess tins over the shingle, being nosed clean by tree shrews.

The Iban laughed. The river grew louder in the darkness. Something hooted. Something screamed in earnest further off. Something shuffled and snuffled around the discarded rice and fish bits flung in a bush from our plates. A porcupine? A civet? A ground squirrel? The long-tailed giant rat? Why not a Clouded Leopard? Or, the only really dangerous mammal in Borneo, the long-clawed, short-tempered Sun Bear?

I switched off the torch and tried to sleep. But it was no good. The decibel-level was way over the limit allowed in discotheques. And, besides, the fire-flies kept flicking their own torches on and off; and some kind of phosphorescent fungus glowed in the dark like a 40-watt bulb.

I switched on again, clipped the right-angled torch on to my shirt, and settled down for a peaceful bed-time read with Hose and McDougall. Discussing the wars of the Kayan, Hose tells us that

    If the defending party should come upon the enemy

struggling against a rapid—and especially if the enemy is in difficulties through the upsetting of some of their boats—they may fall upon them in the open bed of the river. Then ensues the comparatively rare event, a stand-up fight in the open. This resolves itself in the main into hand-to-hand duels between pairs of combatants, as in the heroic age. The short javelins and spears are first hurled, and skilfully parried with spear and shield. When a man has expended his stock of javelins and has hurled his spear, he closes in with his *parang*. His enemy seeks to receive the blow of the *parang* on his shield in such a way that the point, entering the wood, may be held fast by it. If one succeeds in catching his enemy's *parang* in his shield, he throws down the shield and dashes upon his now weaponless foe, who takes to his heels, throwing away his shield and relying merely on his swiftness of foot. When one of a pair of combatants is struck down, the other springs upon him and, seizing the long hair of the scalp and yelling in triumph, severs the neck with one or two blows of the *parang*.

It was definitely time to sleep.

At dawn the jungle was half-obscured in a heavy morning mist; and through the cloudy layers of rising moisture came the whooping call, the owl-like, clear, ringing hoot of the female Borneo Gibbon.

Replacing the dry socks, pants, trousers and shirt inside two plastic bags inside the damp Bergen pack, tying them tightly to keep out the ants, I shook the wet clothes. A double-barrelled charge of insects propelled itself from inside my trouser-legs. I groomed my pants free of visible bugs, covered myself in SAS anti-fungus powder until my erogenous zone looked like meat chunks rolled in flour, ready for the heat, and forced my way into clammy battle-dress for the day. It was a nasty five o'clock start; but in half-an-hour the mist would be gone, the sun merciless, and the river-water soaking one anyway.

After a breakfast of fish and rice, we re-packed the dugout and set off up-river. The gibbons, having proclaimed the boundaries of their territories, ceased calling. The world changed colour from a dark watery blue to mauve to sepia to pink and then the sun rose, extraordinarily fast.

Inghai put on his peaked cap to shield his eyes from the sun as he sat on the bow and scanned the turbulent water ahead for rocks and logs; Dana, in chiefly style, wore his round hat, as large and intricately patterned as a gaming-table; and Leon, proudly switching his outboard to full power, wore a mutant hybrid of pork-pie and Homburg. James adjusted his boater, stretched out his legs on his half of the duck-boards, and addressed himself to Swift.

Something large and flappy was crossing the river in front of us. Was it a bird disguised as a leaf-skeleton? Was it a day-flying bat disguised as a hair-net? Or was a lattice of tropical worms in transit across my retina? Very slowly, unconcerned, the something made its floating and dipping, floating and dipping, indecisive flight right over the boat: it was an odd idea indeed, *Hestia idea,* a butterfly with grey and white wings like transparent gauze, highly poisonous, and safe. In one of the richest of tropical rain forests, in a natural zone which actually contains more kinds of butterflies and moths than all other habitats of the world put together, it was ridiculously pleasing to have identified just one more species, even if, as I eventually had to admit to James, it was the most immediately obvious of them all.

James, momentarily, re-directed his critical gaze from Swift's sometimes defective scansion, and fixed it upon the surrounding jungle. With A–1 vision in both eyes which are set so far apart that he does, in this one respect, resemble a hammer-head shark, he announced, in a statement which later became formulaic and—for the Iban (and, well, just a little, for me)—the incantation of a shaman of immeasurable age and wisdom summoning the spirits of the forest to dance before him for a span: 'Redmond, I am about to see something *marvellous.'*

The canoe swung into the next bend and there, majestically perched upon a dead branch across an inlet, was a Crested Serpent Eagle.

'How's that?' said James.

The eagle was thick-set, black and brown and grey, his stomach lightly freckled, his head plumed flat. James was sitting up, boatered, bearded-black, his shirt dazzling white. James looked at the eagle. The eagle looked at James. The eagle, deciding that it was too early in the morning to hallucinate, flapped off into the jungle, puzzled.

Gradually, the rapids became more frequent, more difficult to scale. Leon would align the boat carefully in the deep pools beneath each one, open up to full throttle on a straight run, shut off the engine, cock the propeller well up out of the water as we hit the first curve of white foam, grab his pole as Inghai and Dana snatched up theirs, and then all three would punt the canoe up, in wild rhythm with each other.

They were lean, fit, strong with a lifetime of unremitting exercise, their muscles flexing and bunching, etched out as clearly as Jan van Calcar's illustrations to *De humani corporis fabrica*.

The solid tree-trunk keel of the hollowed-out canoe began to thud against the boulders beneath the cascades of water. It thudded lightly at first, and then with alarming violence as the day wore on. We had to jump out beneath each rapid, take the long bow-rope, walk up the stones strewn down beside the fall, wade into the deep current above and pull—guiding the bow up. The water pushed irregularly at our waist and knees, sometimes embracing us like a succubus might (after a year in prison), sometimes trying a flowing rugby-tackle, sometimes holding our ankles in a hydro-elastic gin-trap, but never in a way that could be described as friendly. With nothing but locked spines and clamped cartilages we leaned back against the great flow of water on its way to the South China Sea.

Just in time, by a deep pool, in a harbour formed by two massive fallen hardwoods, Dana ruled that it was noon and we were hungry. The boat was tied up, we collapsed, and Leon went fishing.

Spreading our wet clothes out on the burningly-hot boulders, James and I took a swim and a wash.

Dana, intrigued by Medicated Vosene, shampooed his glossy black hair and then rinsed it by swimming very fast across the pool underwater, a moving *V* of ripples on the surface marking his passage through the spins and eddies. He waded ashore, and even his dark-blue tattooes glistened in the sun. Dana was covered in circles and rosettes, whorls and lines (soot from a cooking pot, mixed with sweetened water, and punched into the skin with a bamboo stick and small hammer). On his throat (the most painful of all to suffer, and the most likely to produce septicaemia) a large tattoo testified to his immediate courage; on his thighs an intricate pattern of stylized Rhinoceros; and on the top joints of his fingers a series of dots and cross-hatchings suggested that he had taken heads in battle—probably from the bodies of invading Indonesian soldiers killed by the SAS, with whom he had sometimes served as a tracker, in the 1962–66 confrontation. Dignified, intelligent, full of natural authority, at forty an old man in the eyes of his tribe, Dana was the law-giver and judge of conduct, the arbiter of when to plant and when to harvest the *padi,* and, perhaps most important of all, the Chief Augurer to his people, the interpreter of the messengers of the gods: the birds.

He regarded us with protective amusement. We were like the white men he had met in the war, Leon had informed us in hushed tones; when we first met Dana, we had stayed in his long-house and behaved like guests he could trust, not offending against custom, well-mannered. James and I, in turn, decided that *Tuai Rumah* Dana, Lord of the House, a Beowulf, or, more accurately, a warrior-king out of Homer, was a great improvement on all our previous Headmasters, Deans and Wardens.

Leon surfaced by the far bank of the river, half-obscured by the roots of a giant tree which twisted into the water, but obviously excited, ferociously excited. He was yelling wildly to Dana and Inghai, '*Labi-labi*!', holding his harpoon cord with both hands, shouting in Iban; and, to us, 'Fish! Round fish! Big round fish!'

Dana and Inghai leaped into the dugout and swam fast across the current. It seemed a lot of fuss about a fish, however big and round.

Dana cut two lengths of our parachute cord, one for himself and one for Inghai and, tying the boat to a branch, plunged in. Something thrashed and splashed, churning up the water between the three of them. Lowering the cord, knotted into a noose, Dana pulled it tight, secured it to the stern of the dugout; and then all three paddled back, towing something. The boat beached; they hauled on the parachute cord. Gradually, a shiny olive dome broke surface, almost round, and about three feet across. Two pairs of webbed, thick claws were thrusting against the water, front and back. Pulling it ashore in reverse, the Iban cut two holes at the rear of its carapace and threaded a lead of rattan through each slit. It was a large Mud Turtle, *Trionyx cartilagineus,* one of whose specific characteristics, described by a so-called closet-naturalist in the nineteenth-century British Museum from trophies in the collection, had been, as Wallace liked to point out, these very same restraining holes at the back of the shell.

Left alone for a moment, the turtle's head began to emerge from a close-fitting sleeve, from folds of telescopic muscle. It had a flexible snout for a nose, a leathery green trunk; and a sad, watery eye. Dana's *parang* came down with great violence, missing the head, glancing off the cartilaginous armour, bucking the turtle, throwing up water and pebbles. The head retracted. Dana crouched, waiting. Some ten minutes later, the turtle once more began to look cautiously for its escape. Out came the head, inch by inch. With one blow, Dana severed the neck. The head rolled, quizzically, a little way across the sand.

After a lunch of rice and Sebarau, Dana and Leon heaved the turtle on to its back, slit open its white belly, and threw its guts to the fish. The meat was cut into strips, salted, and stowed away in a basket on the boat. The empty shell, the blood drying, we left on the shingle.

T he river twisted and turned and grew narrower, and the great creepers, tumbling down in profusion from two hundred feet above our heads, edged closer. The rapids and cascades became more frequent. We had to jump out into the river more often, sometimes to our waists, sometimes to our armpits, pushing the dugout up the shallows, guiding it into a side-channel away from the main crash of the water.

'*Saytu, dua, tiga—bata!*' sang Dana, which even we could reconstruct as one, two, three, and push.

The Iban gripped the round, algae-covered stones on the river-bottom easily with their muscled, calloused, spatulate toes. Our boots slipped into crevices, slithered away in the current, threatened to break off a leg at the ankle or at the knee. It was only really possible to push hard when the boat was still, stuck fast, and then Headmaster Dana would shout '*Badas!*' 'Well done!' But the most welcome cry became '*Npan! Npan!*': an invitation to get back in, quick.

Crossing one such deep pool, collapsed in the boat, the engine restarted, we found ourselves staring at a gigantic Bearded Pig sitting quietly on his haunches on the bank. Completely white, an old and lonely male, he looked at us with his piggy eyes. Dana, throwing his pole into the boat, snatched up his shotgun; Leon, abandoning the rudder, followed suit. Inghai shouted a warning, the canoe veered

sideways into the current, the shotguns were discarded, the boat re-
aligned, and the pig, no longer curious, ambled off into the jungle, his
enormous testicles swaying along behind him.

We entered a wide reach of foaming water. The choppy river-
waves, snatching this way and that, had ripped caves of soil out of the
banks, leaving hundreds of yards of overhang on either side. There
was an ominous noise of arguing currents ahead. The rapids-
preamble—the white water, the moving whirlpools, the noise
ahead—was longer and louder than it ought to have been.

With the canoe pitching feverishly, we rounded a sweeping bend;
and the reason for the agitated river became obvious. The Green
Heave ahead was much higher than any we had met. There was a
waterfall to the left of the river-course, a huge surging over a ledge.
The way to the right was blocked by thrown-up trees and piles of
roots that had been dislodged upstream, torn out in floods, and
tossed aside here against a line of rocks. There was, however, one
small channel through; a shallow rapid, dangerously close to the
main rush of water, but negotiable. It was separated from the torrent
by three huge boulders.

Keeping well clear of the great whirlpool beneath the waterfall,
Leon brought the boat to the base of this normal-size rapid. Dana,
James and I made our way carefully up with the bow-rope.

Dana held the lead position on the rope; I stood behind him and
James behind me. We pulled, Leon and Inghai pushed. The boat
moved up and forward some fifteen feet and then stuck. Leon and
Inghai walked up the rapid, and, hunching and shoving, rolled small
rocks aside to clear a channel. We waited on the lip of the rock above,
pulling on the rope to keep the long boat straight. At last Leon and
Inghai were ready. But the channel they had had to make was a little
closer to the waterfall. To pull straight we must move to our right.
Dana pointed to our new positions.

It was only a stride or two. But the level of the river-bed suddenly
dipped, long since scooped away by the pull of the main current.
James lost his footing, and, trying to save himself, let go of the rope. I
stepped across to catch him, the rope bound round my left wrist,
snatching his left hand in my right. His legs thudded into mine,
tangled, and then swung free, into the current, weightless, as if a part
of him had been knocked into outer space. His hat came off, hurtled

past his shoes, spun in an eddy, and disappeared over the lip of the fall.

His fingers were very white; and slippery. He bites his fingernails; and they could not dig into my palm. He simply looked surprised; his head seemed a long way from me. He was feeling underwater with his free arm, impossibly trying to grip a boulder with his other hand, to get a purchase on a smooth and slimy rock, a rock polished smooth, for centuries, by perpetual tons of rolling water.

His fingers bent straighter, slowly, edging out of mine, for hour upon hour—or so it felt, but it must have been seconds. His arm rigid, his fingertips squeezed out of my fist. He turned in the current, spread-eagled. Still turning, but much faster, he was sucked under; his right ankle and shoe were bizarrely visible above the surface; he was lifted slightly, a bundle of clothes, of no discernible shape, and then he was gone.

'Boat! Boat!' shouted Dana, dropping the rope, bounding down the rocks of the rapid at the side, crouched, using his arms like a baboon.

'Hold the boat! Hold the boat!' yelled Leon.

James's bald head, white and fragile as an owl's egg, was sweeping round in the whirlpool below, spinning, bobbing up and down in the foaming water, each orbit of the current carrying him within inches of the black rocks at its edge.

Leon jumped into the boat, clambered on to the raised outboard-motor frame, squatted, and then, with a long, yodelling cry, launched himself in a great curving leap into the centre of the maelstrom. He disappeared, surfaced, shook his head, spotted James, dived again, and caught him. Inghai, too, was in the water, but he faltered, was overwhelmed, and swept downstream. Leon, holding on to James, made a circuit of the whirlpool until, reaching the exit current, he thrust out like a turtle and they followed Inghai down-river, edging, yard by yard, towards the bank.

Obeying Dana's every sign, I helped him coax the boat on to a strip of shingle beneath the dam of logs. James, when we walked down to him, was sitting on a boulder. Leon sat beside him, an arm round his shoulders.

'You be all right soon, my friend,' said Leon, 'you be all right soon-lah, my very best friend. Soon you be so happy.'

James, bedraggled, looking very sick, his white lips an open *O* in his black beard, was hyper-ventilating dangerously, taking great rhythmic draughts of oxygen, his body shaking.

'You be OK,' said Leon. 'I not let you die, my old friend.'

Just then little Inghai appeared, beaming with pride, holding aloft one very wet straw boater.

'I save hat!' said Inghai, 'Jams! Jams! I save hat!'

James looked up, smiled, and so stopped his terrible spasms of breathing.

He really was going to be all right.

Suddenly, it all seemed funny, hilariously funny. 'Inghai saved his hat!' We laughed and laughed, rolling about on the shingle. We giggled together until it hurt. 'Inghai saved his hat! Ingy-pingy saved his hat!' It was, I am ashamed to say, the first (and I hope it will be the last) fit of genuine medically-certifiable hysterics which I have ever had.

D ana, looking at James, decided that we would camp where we were. Finding a level plateau way above flood level on the bank behind us, the pole hut and the pole beds were soon built. I had a soap and a swim, re-covered myself in SAS super-strength insect repellent and silky crutch powder, re-filled our water bottles from the river and dosed everyone with water-purifying pills, took a handful of vitamin pills myself, forced James and the Iban to take their daily measure too, and then settled down against a boulder with my pipe (to discourage further mosquitoes), a mess-mug full of arak, and the third edition of Smythies' *The Birds of Borneo*.

James, covered in butterflies, was reading *Les misérables* and looking a little miserable himself.

'How are you feeling?'

'Not too good, Redmond. I get these palpitations at the best of times. I've had attacks ever since Oxford. I take some special pills for it but they're really not much help. In fact the only cure is to rest a bit and then be violently sick as soon as possible.'

'Can I do anything?'

'No,' said James, pulling on his umpteenth cigarette and concentrating on Victor Hugo.

He was, I decided, an even braver old wreck than I had imagined. Looking fondly at his great bald head I was really fairly pleased with

Leon for helping the future of English literature; for preventing the disarrangement of all those brain cells; for denying all those thousands of brightly-coloured little fish in the shallows the chance to nibble at torn fragments of cerebellum tissue, to ingest synapses across which had once run electrical impulses carrying stored memories of a detailed knowledge of literatures in Greek and Latin, in German and French, in Spanish and Italian. But all the same, I wondered, what would we do if an accident befell us in the far interior, weeks away from any hospital, beyond the source of the Baleh, marching through the jungle towards the Tiban range and well away, even, from the stores in the boat?

Dana took his single-barrelled shotgun, held together with wire and strips of rattan, and set off to find a wild pig. Leon and Inghai went fishing with their harpoons. My Balkan Sobranie tobacco, as ninety-per-cent humid as everything else, tasted as rich and wet as a good gravy.

The sky grew black suddenly. There was an odd breeze. Everyone—insects, monkeys, birds, frogs—stopped making a noise. Dana, Leon and Inghai ran to the dugout and re-tied it, bow and stern, with long ropes leading to trees on the high bank. Huge globules of water began to fall, splashing star-burst patterns on the dry hot rocks along the shore. We made for our bashas, changed fast, and slipped inside. Rain splattered on the tree canopy two hundred feet above, a whispery noise growing duller and increasing in volume to a low drumming. Drops hit our canvas awnings and bounced off; a fine spray came sideways through the mosquito net. A wind arrived; and we heard the first tree start its long crashing fall far off in the forest. Thunder rumbled nearer, and, every few seconds, the trunks of the trees immediately in view through the triangular gap at the foot of the basha were bright with lightning flashes. The reflected power from sheets and zig-zags of light picked out the clumps of lichen on the bark and tendrils of fungus with startling clarity: the stalks of spore-bodies looked like heads of unkempt hair.

I fell asleep and I dreamed of James's sister Chotty. She was coming at me with a particular knife she uses to make her beef stews, her pheasant pies. 'It's quite all right,' she said, 'it doesn't matter now that he's drowned. There's no need to apologize. I don't want to hear your explanations.'

BRUCE CHATWIN
A COUP

The coup began at seven on Sunday morning. It was a grey and windless dawn and the grey Atlantic rollers broke in long even lines along the beach. The palms above the tide-mark shivered in a current of cooler air that blew in off the breakers. Out at sea—beyond the surf—there were several black fishing canoes. Buzzards were spiralling above the market, swooping now and then to snatch up scraps of offal. The butchers were slaughtering, even on a Sunday.

We were in a taxi when the coup began, on our way to another country. We had passed the Hôtel de la Plage, passed the Sûreté Nationale, and then we drove under a limply-flapping banner which said, in red letters, that Marxist-Leninism was the one and only guide. In front of the Presidential Palace was a road-block. A soldier waved us to a halt, and then waved us on.

'Pourriture!' said my friend, Domingo, and grinned.

Domingo was a young, honey-coloured mulatto with a flat and friendly face, a curly moustache and a set of dazzling teeth. He was the direct descendant of Francisco-Félix de Souza, the Chacha of Ouidah, a Brazilian slaver who lived and died in Dahomey, and about whom I was writing a book.

Domingo had two wives. The first wife was old and the skin hung in loose folds off her back. The second wife was hardly more than a child. We were on our way to Togo, to watch a football game, and visit his great-uncle who knew a lot of old stories about the Chacha.

The taxi was jammed with football-fans. On my right sat a very black old man wrapped in green and orange cotton. His teeth were also orange from chewing cola nuts, and from time to time he spat.

Outside the Presidential Palace hung an overblown poster of the Head of State, and two much smaller posters of Lenin and Kim Il-Sung. Beyond the road-block, we took a right fork, on through the old European section where there were bungalows and balks of bougainvillaea by the gates. Along the sides of the tarmac, market-women walked in single file with basins and baskets balanced on their head.

'What's that?' I asked. I could see some kind of commotion, up ahead, towards the airport.

'Accident!' Domingo shrugged, and grinned again.

Then all the women were screaming, and scattering their yams and pineapples, and rushing for the shelter of the gardens. A white Peugeot shot down the middle of the road, swerving right and left to miss the women. The driver waved for us to turn back, and just then, we heard the crack of gunfire.

'C'est la guerre!' our driver shouted, and spun the taxi round.

'I knew it.' Domingo grabbed my arm. 'I knew it.'

The sun was up by the time we got to downtown Cotonou. In the taxi-park the crowd had panicked and overturned a brazier, and a stack of crates had caught fire. A policeman blew his whistle and bawled for water. Above the rooftops, there was a column of black smoke, rising.

'They're burning the Palace,' said Domingo. 'Quick! Run!'

We ran, bumped into other running figures, and ran on. A man shouted 'Mercenary!' and lunged for my shoulder. I ducked and we dodged down a sidestreet. A boy in a red shirt beckoned me into a bar. It was dark inside. People were clustered round a radio. Then the bartender screamed, wildly, in African, at me, and at the boy. And then I was out again on the dusty red street, shielding my head with my arms, pushed and pummelled against the corrugated building by four hard, acridly-sweating men until the gendarmes came to fetch me in a jeep.

'For your own proper protection,' their officer said, as the handcuffs snapped around my wrists.

The last I ever saw of Domingo he was standing in the street, crying, as the jeep drove off, and he vanished in a clash of coloured cottons.

In the barracks guardroom a skinny boy, stripped to a pair of purple underpants, sat hunched against the wall. His hands and feet were bound with rope, and he had the greyish look Africans get when they are truly frightened. A gecko hung motionless on the dirty whitewash. Outside the door there was a papaya with a tall scaly trunk and yellowish fruit. A mud-wall ran along the far side of the compound. Beyond the wall the noise of gunfire continued, and the high-pitched wailing of women.

A corporal came in and searched me. He was small, wiry, angular, and his cheekbones shone. He took my watch, wallet, passport and notebook.

'Mercenary!' he said, pointing to the patch-pocket on the leg of my khaki trousers. His gums were spongy and his breath was foul.

'No,' I said, submissively. 'I'm a tourist.'

'Mercenary!' he shrieked, and slapped my face—not hard, but hard enough to hurt.

He held up my fountain-pen. 'What?'

'A pen,' I said. It was a black Mont-Blanc.

'What for?'

'To write with.'

'A gun?'

'Not a gun.'

'Yes, a gun!'

I sat on a bench, staring at the skinny boy who continued to stare at his toes. The corporal sat cross-legged in the doorway with his sub-machine-gun trained on me. Outside in the yard, two sergeants were distributing rifles, and a truck was loading with troops. The troops sat down with the barrels sticking up from their crotches. The colonel came out of his office and took the salute. The truck lurched off, and he came over, lumpily, towards the guardroom.

The corporal snapped to attention and said, 'Mercenary, Comrade Colonel!'

'From today,' said the colonel, 'there are no more comrades in our country.'

'Yes, Comrade Colonel,' the man nodded; but checked himself and added, 'Yes, my Colonel.'

The colonel waved him aside and surveyed me gloomily. He wore an exquisitely-pressed pair of paratrooper fatigues, a red star on his cap, and another red star in his lapel. A roll of fat stood out around the back of his neck; his thick lips drooped at the corners; his eyes were hooded. He looked, I thought, so like a sad hippopotamus. I told myself I mustn't think he looks like a sad hippopotamus. Whatever happens, he mustn't think I think he looks like a sad hippopotamus.

'Ah, monsieur!' he said, in a quiet dispirited voice. 'What are you doing in this poor country of ours?'

'I came here as a tourist.'

'You are English?'

'Yes.'

'But you speak an excellent French.'

'Passable,' I said.

'With a Parisian accent I should have said.'

'I have lived in Paris.'

'I, also, have visited Paris. A wonderful city!'

'The most wonderful city.'

'But you have mistimed your visit to Benin.'

'Yes,' I faltered. 'I seem to have run into trouble.'

'You have been here before?'

'Once,' I said. 'Five years ago.'

'When Benin was Dahomey.'

'Yes,' I said. 'I used to think Benin was in Nigeria.'

'Benin is in Nigeria and now we have it here.'

'I think I understand.'

'Calm yourself, monsieur.' His fingers reached to unlock my handcuffs. 'We are having another little change of politics. Nothing more! In these situations one must keep calm. You understand? Calm!'

Some boys had come through the barracks' gate and were creeping forward to peer at the prisoner. The colonel appeared in the doorway, and they scampered off.

'Come,' he said. 'You will be safer if you stay with me. Come, let us listen to the Head of State.'

We walked across the parade-ground to his office where he sat me in a chair and reached for a portable radio. Above his desk hung a photo of the Head of State, in a Fidel Castro cap. His cheeks were a basketwork of scarifications.

'The Head of State,' said the colonel, 'is always speaking over the radio. We call it the journal parlé. It is a crime in this country *not* to listen to the journal parlé.'

He turned the knob. The military music came in cracking bursts.

Citizens of Benin . . . the hour is grave. At seven hours this morning, an unidentified DC-8 jet aircraft landed at our International Airport of Cotonou, carrying a crapulous crowd of mercenaries. . . black and white. . .

financed by the lackeys of international imperialism. . . .

A vile plot to destroy our democratic and operational regime.

The colonel laid his jowls on his hands and sighed, 'The Sombas! The Sombas!'

The Sombas came from the far north-west of the country. They filed their teeth to points and once, not so long ago, were cannibals.

'. . . launched a vicious attack on our Presidential Palace. . .'

I glanced up again at the wall. The Head of State was a Somba — and the colonel was a Fon.

'. . . the population is requested to arm itself with stones and knives to kill this crapulous. . .'

'A recorded message,' said the colonel, and turned the volume down. 'It was recorded yesterday.'

'You mean. . .'

'Calm yourself, monsieur. You do not understand. In this country one understands nothing.'

Certainly, as this morning wore on, the colonel understood less and less. He did not, for example, understand why, on the nine o'clock communiqué, the mercenaries had landed in a DC-8 jet, while at ten the plane had changed to a DC-7 turbo-prop. Around eleven the music cut off again and the Head of State announced a victory for the Government Forces. The enemy, he said, were retreating en catastrophe for the marshes of Ouidah.

'There has been a mistake,' said the colonel, looking very shaken. 'Excuse me, monsieur. I must leave you.'

He hesitated on the threshold and then stepped out into the sunlight. The hawks made swift spiralling shadows on the ground. I helped myself to a drink from his water-flask. The shooting sounded further off now, and the town was quieter. Ten minutes later, the corporal marched into the office. I put my hands above my head, and he escorted me back to the guardroom.

I t was very hot. The skinny boy had been taken away and, on the bench at the back, sat a Frenchman.

Outside, tied to the papaya, a springer spaniel was panting and straining at its leash. A pair of soldiers squatted on their hams and were trying to dismantle the Frenchman's shotgun. A third soldier, rummaging in his game-bag, was laying out a few brace of partridge and a guinea-fowl.

'Will you please give that dog some water?' the Frenchman asked.

'Eh?' The corporal bared his gums.

'The dog,' he pointed. 'Water!'

'No.'

'What's going on?' I asked.

'The monkeys are wrecking my gun and killing my dog.'

'Out there, I mean.'

'Coup monté.'

'Which means?'

'You hire a plane-load of mercenaries to shoot up the town. See who your friends are and who are your enemies. Shoot the enemies. Simple!'

'Clever.'

'Very.'

'And us?'

'They might need a corpse or two. As proof!'

'Thank you,' I said.

'I was joking.'

'Thanks all the same.'

The Frenchman was a water-engineer. He worked up-country, on artesian wells, and was down in the capital on leave. He was a short, muscular man, tending to paunch, with cropped grey hair and a web of white laugh-lines over his leathery cheeks. He had dressed himself en mercenaire, in fake python-skin camouflage, to shoot a few game-birds in the forest on the outskirts of town.

'What do you think of my costume?' he asked.

'Suitable,' I said.

'Thank you.'

The sun was vertical. The colour of the parade-ground had bleached to a pinkish orange, and the soldiers strutted back and forth in their own pools of shade. Along the wall the vultures flexed their wings.

'Waiting,' joked the Frenchman.

'Thank you.'

'Don't mention it.'

Our view of the morning's entertainment was restricted by the width of the doorframe. We were, however, able to witness a group of soldiers treating their ex-colonel in a most shabby fashion. We wondered how he could still be alive as they dragged him out and bundled him into the back of a jeep. The corporal had taken the colonel's radio, and was cradling it on his knee. The Head of State was baying for blood—'Mort aux mercenaires soit qu'ils sont noirs ou blancs. . . .' The urchins, too, were back in force, jumping up and down, drawing their fingers across their throats, and chanting in unison, 'Mort-aux-mercenaires! . . . Mort-aux-mercenaires! . . .'

Around noon, the jeep came back. A lithe young woman jumped out and started screeching orders at an infantry platoon. She was wearing a mud-stained battledress. A nest of plaits curled, like snakes, from under her beret.

'So,' said my companion. 'The new colonel.'

'An Amazon colonel,' I said.

'I always said it,' he said. 'Never trust a teenage Amazon colonel.'

He passed me a cigarette. There were two in the packet and I took one of them.

'Thanks,' I said. 'I don't smoke.'

He lit mine, and then his, and blew a smoke-ring at the rafters. The gecko on the wall hadn't budged.

'My name's Jacques,' he said.

I told him my own name and he said, 'I don't like the look of this.'

'Nor I,' I said.

'No,' he said. 'There are no rules in this country.'

Nor were there any rules, none that one could think of, when the corporal came back from conferring with the Amazon and ordered us, also, to strip to our underpants. I hesitated. I was unsure whether I was wearing underpants. But a barrel in the small of my back convinced me, underpants or no, that my trousers would have to come down—only to find that I did, after all, have on a pair of pink-and-white boxer shorts from Brooks Brothers.

Jacques was wearing green string pants. We must have looked a pretty couple—my back welted all over with mosquito bites, he with his paunch flopping over the elastic, as the corporal marched us out, barefoot over the burning ground, and stood us, hands up, against the wall which the vultures had fouled with their ash-white, ammonia-smelling droppings.

'Merde!' said Jacques. 'Now what?'

What indeed? I was not frightened. I was tired and hot. My arms ached, my knees sagged, my tongue felt like leather, and my temples throbbed. But this was not frightening. It was too like a B-grade movie to be frightening. I began to count the flecks of millet-chaff embedded in the mud-plaster wall. . . .

I remembered the morning, five years earlier, my first morning in Dahomey, under the tall trees in Parakou. I'd had a rough night, coming down from the desert in the back of a crowded truck, and at breakfast-time, at the café-routier, I'd asked the waiter what there was to see in town.

'Patrice.'

'Patrice?'

'That's me,' he grinned. 'And, monsieur, there are hundreds of other beautiful young girls and boys who walk, all the time, up and down the streets of Parakou.'

I remembered, too, the girl who sold pineapples at Dassa-Zoumbé station. It had been a stifling day, the train slow and the country burnt. I had been reading Gide's *Nourritures terrestres* and, as we drew into Dassa, had come to the line, 'Ô cafés—où notre démence s'est continuée très avant dans la nuit. . . .' No, I thought, this will never do, and looked out of the carriage window. A basket of pineapples had halted outside. The girl underneath the basket smiled and, when I gave her the Gide, gasped, lobbed all six pineapples into the carriage, and ran off to show her friends—who in turn came skipping down the tracks, clamouring, 'A book, please? A book? A book!' So *out* went a dog-eared thriller and Saint-Exupéry's *Vol de nuit,* and *in* came the 'Fruits of the Earth'—the real ones—pawpaws, guavas, more pineapples, a raunch of grilled swamp-rat, and a palm-leaf hat.

'Those girls,' I remember scribbling in my notebook, 'are the ultimate products of the lycée system.'

And now what?

The Amazon was squawking at the platoon and we strained our ears for the click of safety catches.

'I think they're playing games,' Jacques said, squinting sideways.

'I should hope so,' I muttered. I liked Jacques. It was good, if one had to be here, to be here with him. He was an old Africa hand and had been through coups before.

'That is,' he added glumly, 'if they don't get drunk.'

'Thank you,' I said, and looked over my shoulder at the drill-squad.

'No look!' the corporal barked. He was standing beside us, his shirt-front open to the navel. Obviously, he was anxious to cut a fine figure.

'Stick your belly-button in,' I muttered in English.

'No speak!' he threatened.

'I won't speak.' I held the words within my teeth. 'But stay there. Don't leave me. I need you.'

Maddened by the heat and excitement, the crowds who had come to gawp were clamouring, 'Mort-aux-mercenaires! . . . Mort-aux-mercenaires!' and my mind went racing back over the horrors of Old Dahomey, before the French came. I thought, the slave-wars, the human sacrifices, the piles of broken skulls. I thought of Domingo's other uncle, 'The Brazilian', who received us on his rocking-chair dressed in white ducks and a topee. 'Yes,' he sighed, 'the Dahomeans are a charming and intelligent people. Their only weakness is a certain nostalgia for taking heads.'

No. This was not my Africa. Not this rainy, rotten-fruit Africa. Not this Africa of blood and laughter. The Africa I loved was the long undulating savannah country to the north, the 'leopard-spotted land', where flat-topped acacias stretched as far as the eye could see, and there were black-and-white hornbills and tall red ter-mitaries. For whenever I went back to that Africa, and saw a camel caravan, a view of white tents, or a single blue turban far off in the heat haze, I knew that, no matter what the Persians said, Paradise never was a garden but a waste of white thorns.

'I am dreaming,' said Jacques, suddenly, 'of perdrix aux choux.'

'I'd take a dozen Belons and a bottle of Krug.'

'No speak!' The corporal waved his gun, and I braced myself, half-expecting the butt to crash down on my skull.

And so what? What would it matter when already I felt as if my skull were split clean open? Was this, I wondered, sunstroke? How strange, too, as I tried to focus on the wall, that each bit of chaff should bring back some clear specific memory of food or drink?

There was a lake in Central Sweden and, in the lake, there was an island where the ospreys nested. On the first day of the crayfish season we rowed to the fisherman's hut and rowed back towing twelve dozen crayfish in a live-net. That evening, they came in from the kitchen, a scarlet mountain smothered in dill. The northern sunlight bounced off the lake into the bright white room. We drank akvavit from thimble-sized glasses and we ended the meal with a tart made of cloudberries. I could taste again the grilled sardines we ate on the quay at Douarnenez and see my father demonstrating how his father ate sardines à la mordecai: you took a live sardine by the tail and swallowed it. Or the elvers we had in Madrid, fried in oil with garlic and half a red pepper. It had been a cold spring morning, and we'd spent two hours in the Prado, gazing at the Velasquezes, hugging one another it was so good to be alive: we had cancelled our bookings on a plane that had crashed. Or the lobsters we bought at Cape Split Harbour, Maine. There was a notice-board in the shack on the jetty and, pinned to it, a card on which a widow thanked her husband's friends for their contributions, and prayed, prayed to the Lord, that they lashed themselves to the boat when hauling in the pots.

How long, O Lord, how long? How long, when all the world was wheeling, could I stay on my feet. . . ?

How long I shall never know, because the next thing I remember I was staggering groggily across the parade-ground, with one arm over the corporal's shoulder and the other over Jacques's. Jacques then gave me a glass of water and, after that, he helped me into my clothes.

'You passed out,' he said.

'Thank you,' I said.

'Don't worry,' he said. 'They *are* only playing games.'

It was late afternoon now. The corporal was in a better mood and allowed us to sit outside the guardroom. The sun was still hot. My head was still aching, but the crowd had simmered down and fortunately, for us, this particular section of the Benin Proletarian Army had found a new source of amusement—in the form of three Belgian ornithologists, whom they had taken prisoner in a swamp, along with a Leica lens the shape and size of a mortar.

The leader of the expedition was a beefy, red-bearded fellow. He believed, apparently, that the only way to deal with Africans was to shout. Jacques advised him to shut his mouth; but when one of the subalterns started tinkering with the Leica, the Belgian went off his head. How dare they? How dare they touch his camera? How dare they think they were mercenaries? Did they look like mercenaries?

'And I suppose they're mercenaries, too?' He waved his arms at us.

'I told you to shut your mouth,' Jacques repeated.

The Belgian took no notice and went on bellowing to be set free. *At once! Now! Or else! Did he hear that?*

Yes. The subaltern had heard, and smashed his fist into the Belgian's face. I never saw anyone crumple so quickly. The blood gushed down his beard, and he fell. The subaltern kicked him when he was down. He lay on the dirt floor, whimpering.

'Idiot!' Jacques growled.

'Poor Belgium,' I said.

The next few hours I would prefer to forget. I do, however, remember that when the corporal brought back my things I cursed, 'Christ, they've nicked my traveller's cheques,'—and Jacques, squeezing my arm very tightly, whispered, 'Now *you* keep your mouth shut!' I remember 'John Brown's Body' playing loudly over the radio, and the Head of State inviting the population, this time, to gather up the corpses. Ramasser les cadavres is what he said, in a voice so hoarse and sinister you knew a great many people had died, or would do. And I remember, at sunset, being driven by minibus to the Gezo Barracks where hundreds of soldiers, all elated by victory, were embracing one another, and kissing.

Our new guards made us undress again, and we were shut up, with other suspected mercenaries, in a disused ammunition shed. 'Well,' I thought, at the sight of so many naked bodies, 'there must be some safety in numbers.'

It was stifling in the shed. The other whites seemed cheerful, but the blacks hung their heads between their knees, and shook. After dark, a missionary doctor, who was an old man, collapsed and died of a heart-attack. The guards took him out on a stretcher, and we were taken to the Sûreté for questioning.

Our interrogator was a gaunt man with hollow temples, a cap of woolly white hair and bloodshot slits for eyes. He sat sprawled behind his desk, caressing with his fingertips the blade of his bowie-knife. Jacques made me stand a pace behind him. When his turn came, he said loudly that he was employed by such and such a French engineering company and that I, he added, was an old friend.

'Pass!' snapped the officer. 'Next!'

The officer snatched my passport, thumbed through the pages and began blaming me, personally, for certain events in Southern Africa.

'What are you doing in our country?'

'I'm a tourist.'

'Your case is more complicated. Stand over there.'

I stood like a schoolboy, in the corner, until a female sergeant took me away for fingerprinting. She was a very large sergeant. My head was throbbing; and when I tried to manoeuvre my little finger onto the inkpad, she bent it back double; I yelled 'Ayee!', and her boot slammed down on my sandalled foot.

That night there were nine of us, all white, cooped up in a ramshackle office. The President's picture hung aslant on a bright blue wall and, beside it, were a broken guitar and a stuffed civet cat, nailed in mockery of the Crucifixion, with its tail and hindlegs together, and its forelegs splayed apart.

In addition to the mosquito-bites, my back had come up in watery blisters. My toe was very sore. The guard kicked me awake whenever I nodded off. His cheeks were cicatrized, and I remember thinking how remote his voice sounded when he said, 'On va vous fusiler.' At two or three in the morning, there was a burst of machine-gun fire close by, and we all thought, This is it. It was only a soldier, drunk or trigger-happy, discharging his magazine at the stars.

None of us was sad to see the first light of day.

It was another greasy dawn and the wind was blowing hard onshore, buffeting the buzzards and bending the coco palms. Across the compound a big crowd was jamming the gate. Jacques then caught sight of his houseboy and when he waved, the boy waved back. At nine, the French Vice-Consul put in an appearance, under guard. He was a fat, suet-faced man, who kept wiping the sweat from his forehead and glancing over his shoulder at the bayonet points behind.

'Messieurs,' he stammered, 'this situation is perhaps a little less disagreeable for me than for you. Unfortunately, although we do have stratagems for your release, I am not permitted to discuss your liberty, only the question of food.'

'Eh bien!' Jacques grinned. 'You see my boy over there? Send him to the Boulangerie Gerbe d'Or and bring us sandwiches of jambon, paté and saussisson sec, enough croissants for everyone, and three petits pains au chocolat for me.'

'Oui,' said the Vice-Consul weakly.

I then scribbled my name and passport number on a scrap of paper, and asked him to telex the British Embassy in Lagos.

'I cannot,' he said. 'I cannot be mixed up in this affair.'

He turned his back, and waddled off the way he'd come, with the pair of bayonets following.

'Charming,' I said to Jacques.

'Remember Waterloo,' Jacques said. 'And, besides, you may be a mercenary!'

Half an hour later, Jacques' bright-eyed boy came back with a basket of provisions. Jacques gave the guard a sandwich, spread the rest on the office table, sank his teeth into a petit pain au chocolat, and murmured, 'Byzance!'

The sight of food had a wonderfully revivifying effect on the Belgian ornithologist. All through the night the three had been weepy and hysterical, and now they were wolfing the sandwiches. They were not my idea of company. I was left alone with them, when, around noon, the citizens of France were set at liberty.

'Don't worry,' Jacques squeezed my hand. 'I'll do what I can.'

He had hardly been gone ten minutes before a big German, with a red face and sweeps of fair hair, came striding across the compound, shouting at the soldiers and brushing the bayonets aside.

He introduced himself as the Counsellor of the German Embassy.

'I'm so sorry you've landed in this mess,' he said in faultless English. 'Our ambassador has made a formal protest. From what I understand, you'll have to pass before some kind of military tribunal. Nothing to worry about! The commander is a nice chap. He's embarrassed about the whole business. But we'll watch you going into the building, and watch you coming out.'

'Thanks,' I said.

'Anyway,' he added, 'the Embassy car is outside, and we're not leaving until everyone's out.'

'Can you tell me what *is* going on?'

The German lowered his voice: 'Better leave it alone.'

The tribunal began its work at one. I was among the first prisoners to be called. A young zealot started mouthing anti-capitalist formulae until he was silenced by the colonel in charge. The colonel then asked a few perfunctory questions, wearily apologized for the inconvenience, signed my pass, and hoped I would continue to enjoy my holiday in the People's Republic.

'I hope so,' I said.

Outside the gate, I thanked the German who sat in the back of his air-conditioned Mercedes. He smiled, and went on reading the *Frankfurter Zeitung*.

It was grey and muggy and there were not many people on the street. I bought the government newspaper and read its account of the glorious victory. There were pictures of three dead mercenaries—a white man who appeared to be sleeping, and two very mangled blacks. Then I went to the hotel where my bag was in storage.

The manager's wife looked worn and jittery. I checked my bag and found the two traveller's cheques I'd hidden in a sock. I cashed a hundred dollars, took a room, and lay down.

I kept off the streets to avoid the vigilante groups that roamed the town making citizens' arrests. My toenail was turning black and my head still ached. I ate in the room, and read, and tried to sleep. All the other guests were either Guinean or Algerian.

Around eleven next morning, I was reading the sad story of Mrs Marmeladov in *Crime and Punishment*, and heard the thud of gunfire coming from the Gezo Barracks. I looked from the window at the palms, the hawks, a woman selling mangoes, and a nun coming out of the convent.

Seconds later, the fruit-stall had overturned, the nun bolted, and two armoured cars went roaring up the street.

There was a knock on the door. It was the manager.

'Please, monsieur. You must not look.'

'What's happening?'

'Please,' he pleaded, 'you must shut the window.'

I closed the shutter. The electricity had cut off. A few bars of sunlight squeezed through the slats, but it was too dark to read, so I lay back and listened to the salvoes. There must have been a lot of people dying.

There was another knock.

'Come in.'

A soldier came into the room. He was very young and smartly turned out. His fatigues were criss-crossed with ammunition belts and his teeth shone. He seemed extremely nervous. His finger quivered round the trigger-guard. I raised my hands and got up off the bed.

'In there!' He pointed the barrel at the bathroom door.

The walls of the bathroom were covered with blue tiles and, on the blue plastic shower-curtain, was a design of tropical fish.

'Money,' said the soldier.

'Sure!' I said. 'How much?'

He said nothing. I glanced at the mirror and saw the gaping whites of his eyes. He was breathing heavily.

I eased my fingers down my trouser pocket: my impulse was to give him all I had. Then I separated one banknote from the rest, and put it in his outstretched palm.

'Merci, monsieur!' His lips expanded in an astonished smile. 'Merci,' he repeated, and unlocked the bathroom door. 'Merci,' he kept repeating, as he bowed and pointed his own way out into the passage.

That young man, it struck me, really had very nice manners.

The Algerians and Guineans were men in brown suits who sat all day in the bar, sucking soft drinks through straws and giving me dirty looks whenever I went in. I decided to move to the Hôtel de la Plage where there were other Europeans, and a swimming-pool. I took a towel to go swimming and went into the garden. The pool had been drained: on the morning of the coup, a sniper had taken a pot-shot at a Canadian boy who happened to be swimming his lengths.

The frontiers of the country were closed, and the airport.

That evening I ate with a Norwegian oil-man, who insisted that the coup had been a fake. He had seen the mercenaries shelling the palace. He had watched them drinking opposite in the bar of the Hotel de Cocotiers.

'All of it I saw,' he said, his neck reddening with indignation. The palace had been deserted. The army had been in the barracks. The mercenaries had shot innocent people. Then they all went back to the airport and flew away.

'All of it,' he said, 'was fake.'

'Well,' I said, 'if it was a fake, it certainly took me in.'

It took another day for the airport to open, and another two before I got a seat on the Abidjan plane. I had a mild attack of bronchitis and was aching to leave the country.

On my last morning I looked in at the 'Paris-Snack', which, in the old days when Dahomey was Dahomey, was owned by a Corsican called Guerini. He had gone back to Corsica while the going was good. The bar-stools were covered in red leather, and the barman wore a solid gold bracelet round his wrist.

Two Nigerian businessmen were seated at lunch with a pair of whores. At a table in the corner I saw Jacques.

'Tiens?' he said, grinning. 'Still alive?'

'Thanks to you,' I said, 'and the Germans.'

'*Braves* Bosches!' He beckoned me to the banquette. 'Very intelligent people.'

'*Braves* Bosches!' I agreed.

'Let's have a bottle of champagne.'

'I haven't got much money.'

'Lunch is on me,' he insisted. 'Pierrot!'

The barman tilted his head, coquettishly, and tittered.

'Yes, Monsieur Jacques.'

'This is an English gentleman and we must find him a very special bottle of champagne. You have Krug?'

'No, Monsieur Jacques. We have Roerderer. We have Bollinger, and we have Mumm.'

'Bollinger,' I said.

Jacques pulled a face: 'And in Guerini's time you could have had your oysters. Flown in twice a week from Paris. . . Belons. . . Claires. . . Portugaises. . . .'

'I remember him.'

'He was a character.'

'Tell me,' I leaned over. 'What *was* going on?'

'Sssh!' his lips tightened. 'There are two theories and, if I think anyone's listening, I shall change the subject.'

I nodded and looked at the menu.

'In the official version,' Jacques said, 'the mercenaries were recruited by Dahomean emigrés in Paris. The plane took off from a military airfield in Morocco, refuelled in Abidjan. . .'

One of the whores got up from her table and lurched down the restaurant towards the Ladies.

' '66 was a wonderful year,' said Jacques, decisively.

'I like it even older,' I said, as the whore brushed past, 'dark and almost flat. . . .'

'The plane flew to Gabon to pick up the commander. . . who is supposed to be an adviser to President Bongo. . . .' He then explained how, at Libreville, the pilot of the chartered DC-8 refused to go on, and the mercenaries had to switch to a DC-7.

'So their arrival was expected at the airport?'

'Precisely,' Jacques agreed. 'Now the second scenario . . .'

The door of the Ladies swung open. The whore winked at us. Jacques puushed his face up to the menu.

'What'll you have?' he asked.

'Stuffed crab,' I said.

'The second scenario,' he continued quietly, 'calls for Czech and East German mercenaries. The plane, a DC-7, takes off from a military airfield in Algeria, refuels at Conakry. . . you understand?'

'Yes,' I said, when he'd finished. 'I think I get it. And which one do you believe?'

'Both,' he said.

'That,' I said, 'is a very sophisticated analysis.'

'This,' he said, 'is a very sophisticated country.'

'I know it.'

'You heard the shooting at Camp Gezo?'

'What was that?'

'Settling old scores,' he shrugged. 'And now the Guineans have taken over the Secret Police.'

'Clever.'

'This is Africa.'

'I know and I'm leaving.'

'For England?'

'No,' I said. 'For Brazil. I've a book to write.'

'Beautiful country, Brazil.'

'I hope so.'

'Beautiful women.'

'So I'm told.'

'So what is this book?'

'It's about the slave-trade.'

'In Benin?'

'Also in Brazil.'

'Eh bien!' The champagne had come and he filled my glass. 'You have material!'

'Yes,' I agreed. 'I do have material.'

Paul Theroux
Subterranean Gothic

New Yorkers say some terrible things about the subway— that they hate it, or are scared stiff of it, or that it deserves to go broke. For tourists, it seems just another dangerous aspect of New York, though most don't know it exists. 'I haven't been down there in years,' is a common enough remark from a city dweller. Even people who ride it seem to agree that there is more Original Sin among subway passengers. And more desperation, too, making you think of choruses of 'O dark dark dark. They all go into the dark....'

'Subway' is not its name because, strictly-speaking, more than half of it is elevated. But which person who has ridden it lately is going to call it by its right name, 'The Rapid Transit'? It is also frightful-looking. It has paint and signatures all over its aged face. The graffiti is bad, violent and destructive, and is so extensive and so dreadful it is hard to believe that the perpetrators are not the recipients of some enormous foundation grant. The subway has been vandalized from end to end. It smells so hideous you want to put a clothes-pin on your nose, and it is so noisy the sound actually hurts. Is it dangerous? Ask anyone and he or she will tell you there are about two murders a day on the subway. It really is the pits, people say.

You have to ride it for a while to find out what it is and who takes it and who gets killed on it.

It is full of surprises. Three and a half million fares a day pass through it, and in the first nine months of last year the total number of murder victims on the subway amounted to six. This half-dozen does not include suicides (one a week), 'man-under' incidents (one a day), or 'space-cases'—people who get themselves jammed between the train and the platform. Certainly the subway is very ugly and extremely noisy, but it only *looks* like a death-trap. People ride it looking stunned and holding their breath. It's not at all like the BART system in San Francisco, where people are constantly chattering, saying, 'I'm going to my father's wedding,' or 'I'm looking after my mom's children,' or 'I've got a date with my fiancée's boyfriend.' In New York, the subway is a serious matter—the rackety train, the silent passengers, the occasional scream.

We were at Flushing Avenue, on the GG line, talking about rules for riding the subway. You need rules: the subway is like a complex—and diseased—circulatory system. Some people liken it to a sewer and others hunch their shoulders and mutter about being in the bowels of the earth. It is full of suspicious-looking people.

I said, 'Keep away from isolated cars, I suppose.'

And my friend, a police officer, said, 'Never display jewellery.'

Just then, a man walked by, and he had Chinese coins—the old ones with a hole through the middle—woven somehow into his hair. There were enough coins in that man's hair for a swell night out in old Shanghai, but robbing him would have involved scalping him. There was a woman at the station, too. She was clearly crazy, and she lived in the subway the way people live in railway stations in India, with stacks of dirty bags. The police in New York call such people 'skells' and are seldom harsh with them. 'Wolfman Jack' is a skell, living underground at Hoyt-Schermerhorn, also on the GG line; the police in that station give him food and clothes, and if you ask him how he is, he says, 'I'm getting some calls.' Term them colourful characters and they don't look so dangerous or pathetic.

This crazy old lady at Flushing Avenue was saying, 'I'm a member of the medical profession.' She had no teeth, and her plastic bags were taped around her feet. I glanced at her and made sure she kept her distance. The previous day, a crazy old lady just like her, came at me and shrieked, 'Ahm goon cut you up!' This was at Pelham Parkway, on the IRT-2 line in the Bronx. I left the car at the next stop, Bronx Park East, where the zoo is, though who could be blamed for thinking that in New York City, the zoo is everywhere?

Then a Muslim unflapped his prayer mat—while we were at Flushing Avenue, talking about rules—and spread it on the platform and knelt on it, just like that, and was soon on all fours, beseeching Allah and praising the Prophet Mohammed. This is not remarkable. You see people praying, or reading the Bible, or selling religion, on the subway all the time. 'Hallelujah, brothers and sisters,' the man with the leaflets says on the BMT-RR line at Prospect Avenue in Brooklyn. 'I love Jesus! I used to be a wino!' And Muslims beg and push their green plastic cups at passengers, and try to sell them copies of something called *Arabic Religious Classics*. It is December and Brooklyn, and the men are dressed for the Great Nafud Desert, or Jiddah or Medina—skullcap, gallabieh, sandals.

'And don't sit next to the door,' the second police officer said. We were still talking about rules. 'A lot of these snatchers like to play the doors.'

The first officer said, 'It's a good idea to keep near the conductor. He's got a telephone. So does the man in the token booth. At night, stick around the token booth until the train comes in.'

'Although...token booths,' the second officer said. 'A few years ago, some kids filled a fire extinguisher with gasoline and pumped it into a token booth at Broad Channel. There were two ladies inside, but before they could get out the kids set the gas on fire. The booth just exploded like a bomb, and the ladies died. It was a revenge thing. One of the kids had got a summons for Theft of Service—not paying his fare.'

Just below us, at Flushing Avenue, there was a stream running between the tracks. It gurgled and glugged down the whole length of the long platform. It gave the station the atmosphere of a sewer—dampness and a powerful smell. The water was flowing towards Myrtle and Willoughby. And there was a rat. It was only my third rat in a week of riding the subway, but this one was twice the size of rats I've seen elsewhere. I thought, *Rats as big as cats*.

'Stay with the crowds. Keep away from quiet stairways. The stairways at 41st and 43rd are usually quiet, but 42nd is always busy—that's the one to use.'

So many rules! It's not like taking a subway at all; it's like walking through the woods—through dangerous jungle, rather: Do this, Don't do that....

'It reminds me,' the first officer said. 'The burning of that token booth at Broad Channel. Last May, six guys attempted to murder someone at Forest Parkway, on the J line. It was a whole gang against this one guy. Then they tried to burn the station down with Molotov cocktails. We stopped that, too.'

The man who said this was six-feet four, and weighed about twenty stone. He carried a .38 in a shoulder holster and wore a bullet-proof vest. He had a radio, a can of Mace and a blackjack. He was a plain-clothes man.

The funny thing is that, one day, a boy—five-feet six, and about ten stone—tried to mug him. The boy slapped him across the face while the plain-clothes man was seated on a train. The boy said, 'Give

me your money,' and then threatened the man in a vulgar way. The
boy still punched at the man when the man stood up; he still said,
'Give me all your money!'

The plain-clothes man then took out his badge and his pistol and
said, 'I'm a police officer and you're under arrest.'

'I was just kidding!' the boy said, but it was too late.

I laughed at the thought of someone trying to mug this well-armed
giant.

'Rule one for the subway,' he said. 'Want to know what it is?' He
looked up and down the Flushing Avenue platform, at the old lady
and the Muslim and the running water and the vandalized signs. 'Rule
one is—don't ride the subway if you don't have to.'

A lot of people say that. I did not believe it when he said it,
and, after a week of riding the trains, I still didn't. The
subway is New York City's best hope. The streets are impossible, the highways are a failure, there is nowhere to park. The
private automobile has no future in this city whatsoever. This is
plainest of all to the people who own and use cars in the city; they
know, better than anyone, that the car is the last desperate old-
fangled fling of a badly-planned transport system. What is amazing is
that back in 1904 a group of businessmen solved New York's
transport problems for centuries to come. What vision! What
enterprise! What an engineering marvel they created in this
underground railway! And how amazed they would be to see what it
has become, how foul-seeming to the public mind.

The subway is a gift to any connoisseur of superlatives. It has the
longest rides of any subway in the world, the biggest stations, the
fastest trains, the most track, the most passengers, the most police
officers. It also has the filthiest trains, the most bizarre graffiti, the
noisiest wheels, the craziest passengers, the wildest crimes. Some New
Yorkers have never set foot in the subway; other New Yorkers
actually live there, moving from station to station, whining for
money, eating yesterday's bagels and sleeping on benches. These
'skells' are not merely down-and-out. Many are insane, chucked out
of New York hospitals in the early 1970s when it was decided that
long-term care was doing them little good. 'They were resettled in
rooms or hotels,' Ruth Cohen, a psychiatric social-worker at

Bellevue, told me. 'But many of them can't follow through. They get lost, they wander the streets. They're not violent, suicidal or dangerous enough for Bellevue—this is an acute-care hospital. But these people who wander the subway, once they're on their own they begin to de-compensate.'

Ahm goon cut you up: that woman who threatened to slash me was de-compensating. Here are a few more de-compensating—one is weeping on a wooden bench at Canal Street, another has wild hair and is spitting into a Coke can. One man who is de-compensating in a useful way, has a bundle of brooms and is setting forth to sweep the whole of the change area at Grand Central; another is scrubbing the stairs at 14th Street with scraps of paper. They drink, they scream, they gibber like monkeys. They sit on subway benches with their knees drawn up, just as they do in mental hospitals. A police officer told me, 'There are more serious things than people screaming on trains.' This is so, and yet the deranged person who sits next to you and begins howling at you seems at the time very serious indeed.

The subway, which is many things, is also a madhouse.

When people say the subway frightens them, they are not being silly or irrational. It is no good saying how cheap or how fast it is. The subway *is* frightening. It is also very easy to get lost on the subway, and the person who is lost in New York City has a serious problem. New Yorkers make it their business to avoid getting lost.

It is the stranger who gets lost. It is the stranger who follows people hurrying into the stair-well: subway entrances are just dark holes in the sidewalk—the stations are below ground. There is nearly always a bus-stop near the subway entrance. People waiting at a bus-stop have a special pitying gaze for people entering the subway. It is sometimes not pity, but fear, bewilderment, curiosity, or fatalism; often they look like miners' wives watching their menfolk going down the pit.

The stranger's sense of disorientation down below is immediate. The station is all tile and iron and dampness; it has bars and turnstiles and steel grates. It has the look of an old prison or a monkey cage.

Buying a token, the stranger may ask directions, but the token booth—reinforced, burglar-proof, bullet-proof—renders the reply incoherent. And subway directions are a special language: 'A-train…Downtown…Express to the Shuttle…Change at Ninety-sixth for the two…Uptown…The Lex…CC…LL…The Local…'

Most New Yorkers refer to the subway by the now-obsolete forms 'IND', 'IRT', 'BMT'. No one intentionally tries to confuse the stranger; it is just that, where the subway is concerned, precise directions are very hard to convey.

Verbal directions are incomprehensible, written ones are defaced. The signboards and subway maps are indiscernible beneath layers of graffiti. That Andy Warhol, the stylish philistine, has said, 'I love graffiti' is almost reason enough to hate it. One is warier still of Norman Mailer, who naively encouraged this public scrawling in his book *The Faith of Graffiti*. 'Misguided' seems about the kindest way of describing Mailer who, like Warhol, limps after the latest fashions in the hope of discovering youthfulness or celebrity in colourful outrage. That Mailer's judgement is appalling is clear from his bluster in the cause of the murderer and liar Jack Abbot, who brought about a brief, bloody New York run of *Mr Loveday's Little Outing*. Mailer admires graffiti.

Graffiti is destructive; it is anti-art; it is an act of violence, and it can be deeply menacing. It has displaced the subway signs and maps, blacked-out the windows of the trains and obliterated the instructions. *In case of emergency*—is cross-hatched with a felt-tip. *These seats are for the elderly and disabled*—a yard-long signature obscures it. *The subway tracks are very dangerous: if the train should stop, do not*—the rest is black and unreadable. The stranger cannot rely on printed instructions or warnings, and there are few cars out of the six thousand on the system in which the maps have not been torn out. Assuming the stranger has boarded the train, he or she can feel only panic when, searching for a clue to his route, he sees in the map-frame the message, *Guzmán—Ladrón, Maricón y Asesino*.

Panic: and so he gets off the train, and then his troubles really begin.

He may be in the South Bronx or the upper reaches of Broadway on the Number 1 line, or on any one of a dozen lines that traverse Brooklyn. He gets off the train, which is covered in graffiti, and steps on to a station platform which is covered in graffiti. It is possible (this is true of many stations) that none of the signs will be legible. Not only will the stranger not know where he is, but the stairways will be splotched and stinking—no *Uptown*, no *Downtown*, no *Exit*. It is also possible that not a single soul will be around, and the most dangerous stations—ask any police officer—are the emptiest. Of course, the passenger might just want to sit on a broken bench and, taking Mailer's word for it, contemplate the *macho* qualities of the graffiti; on the other hand, he is more likely to want to get the hell out of there.

This is the story that most people tell of subways fear. In every detail it is like a nightmare, complete with rats and mice and a tunnel and a low ceiling. It is manifest suffocation, straight out of Poe. Those who tell this story seldom have a crime to report. They have experienced fear. It is completely understandable—what is worse than being trapped underground?—but it has been a private horror. In most cases, the person will have come to no harm. He will, however, remember his fear on that empty station for the rest of his life.

When New Yorkers recount an experience like this they are invariably speaking of something that happened on another line, not their usual route. Their own line is fairly safe, they'll say; it's cleaner than the others; it's got a little charm, it's kind of dependable; they've been taking it for years. Your line has crazy people on it, but my line has 'characters'. This sense of loyalty to a regularly-used line is the most remarkable thing about the subway passenger in New York. It is, in fact, a jungle attitude.

In any jungle, the pathway is a priority. People move around New York in various ways, but the complexities of the subway have allowed the New Yorker to think of his own route as something personal, even *original*. No one uses maps on the subway—you seldom see any. Most subway passengers were shown how to ride it by parents or friends. Then habit turns it into instinct, just like a trot down a jungle path. The passenger knows where he is going because he never diverges from his usual route. But that is also why, unless you are getting off at precisely his stop, he cannot tell you how to get where you're going.

In general, people have a sense of pride in their personal route; they may be superstitious about it and even a bit secretive. Vaguely fearful of other routes, they may fantasize about them—these 'dangerous' lines that run through unknown districts. This provokes them to assign a specific character to the other lines. The IRT is the oldest line; for some people it is dependable, with patches of elegance (those beaver mosaics at Astor Place), and for others it is dangerous and dirty. One person praises the IND, another person damns it. 'I've got a soft spot for the BMT,' a woman told me, but found it hard to explain why. 'Take the A train,' I was told. 'That's the best one, like the song.' But some of the worst stations are on the (very long) A line. The CC, 8th Avenue local, was described to me as 'scuzz'—disreputable—but this train, running from Bedford Park Boulevard, the Bronx, via Manhattan and Brooklyn, to Rockaway Park, Queens, covers a distance of some thirty-two miles. The fact is that for some of these miles it is pleasant and for others it is not. There is part of one line that is indisputably bad; that is the stretch of the 2 line (IRT) from Nostrand to New Lots Avenue. It is dangerous and ugly and when you get to New Lots Avenue you cannot imagine why you went. The police call this line 'The Beast'.

But people in the know—the police, the Transit Authority, the people who travel throughout the system—say that one line is pretty much like another.

No line is entirely good or bad, crime-ridden or crime-free. The trains carry crime with them, picking it up in one area and bringing it to another. They pass through a district and take on the characteristics of that place. The South Bronx is regarded as a high risk area, but seven lines pass through it, taking vandals and thieves all over the system. There is a species of vandalism that was once peculiar to the South Bronx: boys would swing on the stanchions—those chrome poles in the centre of the car—and, raising themselves sideways until they were parallel with the floor, they would kick hard against a window and break it. Now this South Bronx window-breaking technique operates throughout the system. This business about one line being dependable and another being charming and a third being dangerous is just jungle talk.

The most-mugged man in New York must be the white-haired creaky-looking fellow in Bedford-Stuyvesant who has had as many as thirty mugging attempts made on him in a single year. And he still rides the subway trains. He's not as crazy as he looks: he's a cop in the Transit Police, a plain-clothes man who works with the Mobile Task Force in the district designated 'Brooklyn North'. This man is frequently a decoy. In the weeks before Christmas he rode the J and the GG and the 2 lines looking like a pathetic senior citizen, with two gaily-wrapped parcels in his shopping bag. He was repeatedly ambushed by unsuspecting muggers, and then he pulled out his badge and handcuffs and arrested his attackers.

Muggers are not always compliant. Then the Transit Police Officer unholsters his pistol, but not before jamming a coloured headband over his head to alert any nearby uniformed officer. Before the advent of headbands many plain-clothes men were shot by their colleagues in uniform.

'And then we rush in,' says Sergeant Donnery of the Mobile Task Force. 'Ninety per cent of the guys out there can kick my ass, one on one. You've got to come on yelling and screaming. "You so-and-so! You so-and-so! I'm going to kill you!" Unless the suspect is deranged and has a knife or something. In that case you might have to talk quietly. But if the guy's tough and you go in meek you get sized up very fast.'

The Transit Police has three thousand officers and thirteen dogs. It is one of the biggest police forces in the United States and is altogether independent from the New York City Police, though the pay and training are exactly the same. It is so independent the men cannot speak to each other on their radios, which many Transit Police find inconvenient when chasing a suspect up the subway stairs into the street.

What about the dogs? 'Dogs command respect,' I was told at Transit Police Headquarters. 'Think of them as a tool, like a gun or a nightstick. At the moment it's just a test programme for high-crime stations, late-night hours, that kind of thing.'

I wondered aloud whether it would work, and the reply was, 'A crime is unlikely to be committed anywhere near one of these dogs.'

The Canine Squad is housed with a branch of the Mobile Task Force at the underground junction of the LL and GG lines: Lorimer Street—Metropolitan Avenue. The bulletin board on the plain-clothes men's side is plastered with unit citations and merit awards, and Sgt Donnery of the Task Force was recently made 'Cop of the Month' for a particularly clever set of arrests. Sgt Donnery is in charge of thirty-two plain-clothes men and two detectives. Their motto is 'Soar with the Eagles.' A sheaf of admiring newspaper clippings testifies to their effectiveness. As we talked, the second shift was preparing to set out for the day.

'Morale seems very high,' I said. The men were joking, watching the old-man decoy spraying his hair and beard white.

'Sure, morale is high,' Sgt Donnery said. 'We feel we're getting something accomplished. It isn't easy. Sometimes you have to hide in a porter's room with a mop for four days before you get your man. We dress up as porters, conductors, motormen, track-workers. If there are a lot of robberies and track-workers in the same station, we dress up as track-workers. We've got all the uniforms.'

'Plain-clothes men' is something of a misnomer for the Task Force that has enough of a theatrical wardrobe to mount a production of *Subways are for Sleeping*.

And yet, looking at Howard Haag and Joseph Minucci standing on the platform at Nassau Avenue on the GG line, you would probably take them for a pair of physical-education teachers on the way to the school gym. They look tough, but not aggressively so; they are healthy and well-built—but some of that is padding: they both wear bullet-proof vests. Underneath the ordinary clothes the men are well armed. Each man carries a .38, a blackjack and a can of Mace. Minucci has a two-way radio.

Haag has been on the force for seventeen years, Minucci for almost seven. Neither has in that time ever fired his gun, though each has an excellent arrest-record and a pride in detection. They are funny, alert and indefatigable, and together they make Starsky and Hutch look like a pair of hysterical cream-puffs. Their job is also much harder than any City cop's. I had been told repeatedly that the average City cop would refuse to work in the conditions that the Transit Police endure every day. At Nassau Avenue, Minucci told me why.

'Look at the stations! They're dirty, they're cold, they're noisy. If you fire your gun you'll kill about ten innocent people—you're trapped here. You stand here some days and the cold and the dampness creep into your bones and you start shivering. And that smell ‹—smell it?›—it's like that all the time, and you've got to stand there and breathe it in. Bergen Street Station, the snow comes through the bars and you freeze. They call it "The Ice-Box". Then some days, kids recognize you—they've seen you make a collar—and they swear at you, call you names, try to get you to react, smoke pot right under your nose. "Here come the DT's"—that's what they call us. It's the conditions. They're awful. You have to take so much crap from these schoolkids. And your feet are killing you. So you sit down, read a newspaper, drink coffee, and then you get a rip from a shoofly—'

Minucci wasn't angry; he said all this in a smiling, ironical way. Like Howie Haag, he enjoys his work and takes it seriously. A 'shoofly', he explained, is a police-inspector who rides the subway looking for officers who are goldbricking—though having a coffee on a cold day hardly seemed to me like goldbricking. 'We're not supposed to drink coffee,' Minucci said, and he went on to define other words in the Transit Police vocabulary: 'lushworker' (a person who robs drunks or sleeping passengers); and 'Flop Squad' (decoys who pretend to be asleep, in order to attract lushworkers).

Just then, as we were talking at Nassau, the station filled up with shouting boys—big ones, aged anywhere from fifteen to eighteen. There were hundreds of them and, with them, came the unmistakable odour of smouldering marijuana. They were boys from Automotive High School, heading south on the GG. They stood on the platform howling and screaming and sucking smoke out of their fingers, and when the train pulled in they began fighting towards the doors.

'You might see one of these kids being a pain in the neck, writing graffiti or smoking dope or something,' Howie Haag said. 'And you might wonder why we don't do anything. The reason is we're looking for something serious—robbers, snatchers, assault, stuff like that.'

Minucci said, 'The Vandalism Squad deals with window-kickers and graffiti. Normally we don't.'

Once on the train the crowd of yelling boys thinned out. I had seen this sort of activity before: boys get on the subway train and immediately bang through the connecting doors and walk from car to car. I asked Minucci why this was so.

'They're marking the people. See them? They're looking for an old lady near a door or something they can snatch, or a pocket they can pick. They're sizing up the situation. They're also heading for the last car. That's where they hang out on this train.'

Howie said, 'They want to see if we'll follow them. If we do, they'll mark us as cops.'

Minucci and Haag did not follow, though at each stop they took cautious looks out of the train, using the reflections in mirrors and windows.

'They play the doors when it's crowded,' Minucci said.

Howie said, 'School-kids can take over a train.'

'Look at that old lady,' Minucci said. 'She's doing everything wrong.'

The woman, in her late sixties, was sitting next to the door. Her wristwatch was exposed and her handbag dangled from the arm closest to the door. Minucci explained that one of the commonest subway crimes was inspired by this posture. The snatcher reached through the door from the platform and, just before the doors shut, he grabbed the bag or watch, or both; and then he was off, and the train was pulling out, with the victim trapped on board.

I wondered whether the plain-clothes men would warn her. They didn't. But they watched her closely, and when she got off they escorted her in an anonymous way. The old woman never knew how well protected she was and how any person making a move to rob her would have been hammered flat to the platform by the combined weight of Officers Minucci and Haag.

There were men on the train drinking wine out of bottles sheathed in paper bags. Such men are everywhere in New York, propped against walls, with bottle and bag. A few hours earlier, at Myrtle-Willoughby, I had counted forty-six men hanging around outside a housing project, drinking this way. I had found their idleness and their stares and their drunken slouching a little sinister.

Minucci said, 'The winos don't cause much trouble. It's the kids coming home from school. They're the majority of snatchers and robbers.'

Minucci went on, 'On the LL line, on Grant Street, there's much more crime than before, because Eastern District High School relocated there. It's mostly larceny and bag snatches.'

It was a salutary experience for me, riding through Brooklyn with Officers Minucci and Haag. Who, except a man flanked by two armed plain-clothes men, would travel from one end of Brooklyn to the other, walking through housing projects and derelict areas, and waiting for hours at subway stations? It was a perverse hope of mine that we would happen upon a crime, or even be the victims of a mugging-attempt. We were left alone, things were quiet, there were no arrests; but for the first time in my life I was travelling the hinterland of New York City with my head up, looking people in the eye with curiosity and lingering scrutiny and no fear. It is a shocking experience. I felt at first, because of my bodyguards, like Haile Selassie; and then I seemed to be looking at an alien land—I had never had the courage to gaze at it so steadily. It was a land impossible to glamourize and hard to describe. I had the feeling I was looking at the future.

'It's not the train that's dangerous—it's the area it passes through.'

The speaker was a uniformed Transit Police Officer named John Burgois. He was in his mid-thirties and described himself as 'of Hispanic origin'. He had four citations. Normally he worked with the Strike Force out of Midtown Manhattan in areas considered difficult: 34th and 7th, 34th and 8th, and Times Square. Officer Burgois told me that the job of the uniformed cop is to reassure people by being an obvious presence that someone in trouble can turn to. The Transit cop in uniform also deals with loiterers and fare evaders, assists injured people and lost souls, keeps a watch on public toilets ('toilets attract a lot of crime') and as for drunks, 'We ask drunks to remove themselves.'

I asked Officer Burgois whether he considered his job dangerous.

'Once or twice a year I get bitten,' he said. 'Bites are bad. You always need a tetanus shot for human bites.'

One of the largest and busiest change-areas on the subway is at Times Square. It is the junction of four lines, including the Shuttle, which operates with wonderful efficiency between Times Square and Grand Central. This, for the Christmas season, was John Burgois's beat. I followed him and for an hour I made notes, keeping track of how he was working.

4.21—Smoker warned (smoking is forbidden in the subway, even on ramps and stairs).

4.24—Panicky shout from another cop. There's a woman with a gun downstairs on the platform. Officer Burgois gives chase, finds the woman. She is drunk and has a toy pistol. Woman warned.

4.26—'Which way to the Flushing Line?'

4.29—'How do I transfer here?'

4.30—'Is this the way to 23rd street?'

4.37—'Donde esta Quins Plaza?'

4.34—'Where is the A train?' As Officer Burgois answers this question, a group of people gathers around him. There are four more requests for directions. It occurs to me that, as all maps have been vandalized, the lost souls need very detailed directions.

4.59—*Radio call:* there is an injured passenger at a certain token booth—a gash on her ankle. Officer Burgois lets another cop attend to it.

5.02—'Where ees the Shuffle?' asks a boy carrying an open can of beer. 'Over there,' Officer Burgois says, 'and dispose of that can. I'm watching you.'

5.10—*Radio call:* a man whose wallet has been stolen is at the Transit Police cubicle on the Times Square concourse. Officer Burgois steps in to observe.

Man: What am I going to do?

Officer: The officer-in-charge will take down the information.

Man: Are you going to catch him?

Officer: We'll prosecute if you can identify him.

Man: I only saw his back.

Officer: That's too bad.

Man: He was tall, thin, and black. I had twenty-two dollars in that wallet.

Officer: You can kiss your money goodbye. Even if we caught him he'd say, 'This is my money.'

Man: This is the first time anything like this has ever happened to me.

5.17—Seeing Officer Burgois, a member of the public says, 'There's two kids on the train downstairs snatching bags—go get them!' Officer Burgois runs and finds the boys hanging over the gate between trains, the favourite spot for snatching bags from passengers on the platform. Officer Burgois apprehends them. The boys, named Troy and Sam, are from the Bronx. They can't remember when they were born; they seem to be about fourteen or fifteen. They deny they were snatching bags. Each boy has about thirty-five dollars in his pocket. They are sullen but not at all afraid. Officer Burgois gives them a YD form and says, 'If I catch you again, your mother's going to pick you up from the station....'

5.28—'Hey, Officer, how do I get to...?'

At this point I stopped writing. I could see that it would be repetitious—and so it was, dreary questions, petty crime and obstinate sneaks. But no one-bit officer Burgois. He has been doing this every hour of every working day for twelve and a half years, and will go on doing it, or something very much like it, for the rest of his working life.

It costs twenty-five dollars or more to go by taxi from Midtown to Kennedy Airport. For five dollars it is possible to go by subway, on 'The JFK Express' and the forty minutes it takes is the same or less than a taxi. But it is rumoured that this service will soon be withdrawn, because so few people use it. If that happens, there is another option—the express on the A line to Howard Beach, which takes under an hour and costs seventy-five cents.

There are ducks at Howard Beach, and herons farther on at Jamaica Bay, and odd watery vistas all the way from Broad Channel to Far Rockaway. The train travels on a causeway past sleepy fishing villages and woodframe houses, and it's all ducks and geese until the train reaches the far side of the bay, where the dingier bungalows and the housing projects begin. Then, roughly at Frank Avenue station, the Atlantic Ocean pounds past jetties of black rocks, not far from the tracks; and at Mott Avenue is the sprawling two-storey town of Far Rockaway, with its main street and its slap-happy architecture and its ruins. It looks like its sister-cities in Ohio and Rhode Island, with just enough trees to hide its dullness, and though part of it is in a state of decay, it looks small enough to save.

That was a pleasant afternoon, when I took the train to the Rockaways. I had spent the whole week doing little else except riding the subway. Each morning I decided on a general direction, and then I set off, sometimes sprinting to the end of the line and making my way back slowly; or else stopping along the way and varying my route back. I went from Midtown to Jamaica Estates in Queens, and returned via Coney Island. There are white Beluga whales at the

Aquarium at Coney Island, and Amazonian electric eels that produce six hundred and fifty volts (the Congo River electric catfish is punier at three hundred and fifty volts), and the African lungfish which drowns if held underwater but can live four years out of water. There are drunks and transvestites and troglodytes in the rest of out-of-season Coney, and the whole place looks as if it has been insured and burned. Though it is on Rockaway Inlet, it is a world away from Rockaway Park. It is also the terminus for six lines.

Never mind the dirt, ignore the graffiti—you can get anywhere you want in New York this way. There are two hundred and thirty route miles on the system—twice as many as the Paris Métro. The trains run all night—in London they shut down at midnight. New York's one-price token system is the fairest and most sensible in the world; London's multi-fare structure is clumsy, ridiculous and a wasteful sop to the unions; Japan's, while just as complicated, is run by computers which spit tickets at you and then belch out your change. The Moscow Metro has grandiose chandeliers to light some stations, but the New York subway has hopeful signs, like the one at 96th and 7th Ave: 'New Tunnel lighting is being installed at this area as part of a Major Rehabilitation Programme. Completion is expected in the summer of 1980.' They are over a year late in finishing, but at least they know there's a problem. In most of the world's subway trains, the driver's cab occupies the whole of the front of the first car. But on the New York system you can stand at the front of the train and watch the rats hurrying aside as the train careers towards the black tilting tunnel and the gleaming tracks.

The trains are always the same, but the stations differ, usually reflecting what is above ground: Spring Street is raffish, Forest Hills smacks of refinement, Livonia Avenue on the LL looks bombed. People aspire to Bay Ridge and say they wouldn't be caught dead in East Harlem—though others are. Fort Hamilton turns into the amazing Verrazano-Narrows Bridge and the 1 into a ferry landing. By the time I had reached 241st Street on the 2, I thought I had got to somewhere near Buffalo, but returning on the 5 and dropping slowly through the Bronx to Lexington Avenue and then to Lower Manhattan and across on the 4 to Flatbush, I had a sense of unrelieved desolation.

No one speaks on the subway except to the person on his

immediate right or left, and only then if they are very old friends or else married. Avoiding the stranger's gaze is what the subway passenger does best: there is not much eye-contact below ground. Most passengers sit bolt upright, with fixed expressions, ready for anything. A look of alertness prevails. As a New York City subway passenger you are J. Alfred Prufrock—you 'prepare a face to meet the faces that you meet.' Few people look relaxed or off-guard. Those new to the subway have the strangest expressions, like my English friend, who told me there was only one way to survive the subway: 'You have to look as if you're the one with the meat cleaver. You have to go in with your eyes flashing.'

In order to appear inconspicuous on the subway, many people read. Usually they read *The Daily News*—and a few read—*Nowy Dziennik,* which is the same thing; the *Times* is less popular, because it takes two hands to read it. But the Bible is very popular, along with religious tracts and the Holy Koran and Spanish copies of *The Watchtower*; lots of boys study for their Bar-Mitzvah on the F line in Queens. I saw *The Bragg Toxic-less Diet* on the B and *La Pratique du Français Parlé* on the RR. All over the system riders read lawbooks—*The Interpretation of Contracts, The Law of Torts, Maritime Law.* The study of law is a subway preoccupation, and it is especially odd to see all these lawbooks in this lawless atmosphere—the law student sitting on the vandalized train. The police officers on the vandalized trains create the same impression of incongruity. When I first saw them, they looked mournful to me, but after I got to know them I realized that most of them are not mournful at all, just dead-tired and overworked and doing a thankless job.

Not long ago, *The Daily News* ran a series about the subway called 'The Doomsday Express'. It was about all the spectacular catastrophes that are possible on the New York system—crashes and nuclear disasters and floods with heavy casualties. 'Doomsday' has a curious appeal to a proud and vaguely religious ego. One of the conceits of modern man is his thinking that the world will end with a big bang. It is a kind of hopeful boast, really, the idea that it will take destruction on a vast scale for us to be wiped out.

It is easy to frighten people with catastrophes; much harder to convince them that decay and trivial-seeming deterioration can be inexorable. The New York subway system is wearing out, and parts of it are worn out; all of it looks threadbare. No city can survive without people to run it, and the class divisions which have distinct geographical centres in New York make the subway all the more necessary.

There is a strong political commitment to the subway, particularly among down-market Democrats. But only money can save it. To this end there is a plan afoot called 'The Five-Year Capital Programme' of $7.2 billion dollars. It remains to be seen whether this programme is instituted. If it isn't, New York will come even closer to looking like dear old Calcutta. There will be no big bang.

Anyway, I am a supporter of the whimper theory—the more so after my experience of the subway.

The subway is buried and unspectacular-looking. Its worst aspects are not its crime or its dangers, but the cloudy fears it inspires, and its dirt and delay. It ought to be fixed, and very soon.

PATRICK MARNHAM
IN SEARCH OF AMIN

The journey started uneventfully with an application to the appropriate Ministry. The earliest letter is dated 5 October 1973. 'Dear Permanent Secretary,' it begins.

> On the advice of the press officer at the Uganda High Commission here in London I am writing to you directly to request an interview with the President of Uganda, His Excellency General Idi Amin Dada. I have been commissioned by *Esquire*, one of the most prominent and influential magazines in America, to seek this interview. I found on a recent visit to New York that there was a great deal of interest among Americans, especially the young people . . .

Extraordinary what one will say in order to earn a living.

Something went wrong with my plans after that. In November there was a letter from an editor at *Esquire*. 'I regret terribly that after I talked to you I was informed that we already *have* an Amin assignment out to Auberon Waugh.' Unknown to the editor, I shared an office with Auberon Waugh at that time and it did not take very long to establish that Mr Waugh had long since told *Esquire* that he had no further interest in this project. For some reason I continued with it.

Before Christmas I set out for Africa having heard nothing from the President, who was preoccupied at that time with a purge of opponents in the northern tribal areas. I wrote three further letters from Nairobi and made several telephone calls, without success. During the next three months it was not difficult to forget about Uganda. I travelled all over Kenya and Tanzania and flew to Zaire, the Ivory Coast, Senegal, Mauritania, Mali, Upper Volta and Ghana before preparing to return to London. In those days the English papers were richer and more interested in abroad. They were happy to pay the expenses of travelling correspondents. Before returning to London, I called for the last time at my post office box in Nairobi. There was one letter in it from Economy Tours and Travel, *'re Visitors Pass IM/2128/71'*: 'We have been requested by the Uganda Tourist Development Corporation to arrange for your transport. We would like to request you to contact us as soon as you arrive. Assuring you of our attention . . .' Still, I was perfectly safe. I didn't have a commission, so I couldn't afford to go. But in due course another letter reached me. It was from *Oui* magazine of Chicago, Illinois, offering £500 for an interview with President Amin. I think I may have been a little overwrought after three months of travelling around Africa because these courteous invitations now read to me like a judgement.

A t Entebbe airport, two weeks later, there was a banner over the building saying 'Uganda Welcomes Tourists' just where Courtney Fitch had tied it up. Courtney Fitch had, until the previous year, been the Englishman responsible for running the country's tourist industry. On the instructions of General Amin he had arranged for a large party of East African travel agents to go to Uganda for a reconnaissance. As they disembarked, in some trepidation, they saw Courtney Fitch being escorted to the plane they had just left. He was being deported. Since then the Immigration Office had virtually closed down. None of the ministries wanted to take responsibility for admitting a foreigner. At the airport I had to surrender my passport.

In those days Kampala seemed like a model city. Laid out around its seven hills it possessed one of everything, like Toytown. There was a scenic golf course and a park, a bandstand, a sports stadium, a Salvation Army hostel, the RSPCA dog kennels, the Animal Clinic, the caravan site, the Police Sports Club, the Masonic Hall, the campus of Makerere University and the leafy grounds of Mulago Teaching Hospital. There was a Vehicle Testing Centre and a Domestic Science College. Perhaps they are still there; such details tend to survive even civil wars.

By February 1974 Amin had completed his massacres of the Lango and Acholi tribes, who were Christian and thought to be faithful to Obote, and had started to move against the Lugbara army officers. The tribal killings in the countryside had stopped for the time being; the murder squads—called the 'Public Safety Unit' and the 'Bureau of State Research'—were concentrating on Amin's other main enemy, the educated people of Uganda. But Kampala appeared reasonably quiet. After looking round for a day or so I set out to contact those who had so mysteriously provided me with the means of entering Uganda. The Immigration Department knew nothing about it so I went to the Uganda Tourist Development Corporation. It seemed sensible to do everything as conspicuously as possible. There was less chance, then, of being accused of spying and more chance of somebody noticing if I went missing. I don't know what I thought anyone could do in either case. I telephoned the managing director of the Uganda Tourist Development Corporation, who was astute enough to require me to make an appointment. When I kept it he was out. This meant that his deputy had to sign the letter of introduction which I was to carry. Neither of them, however, had my Visitor's Pass. That was still with Economy Tours and Travel. They sent the document, via an elderly messenger, to my hotel. On reading the letter of introduction I found that I was now travelling under a false identity. Although I had entered the country as an emissary of *Oui* magazine, this letter stated that I was a travel writer with *African Encounter*. I had never heard of this publication.

The next person to call on was the man who had proved more evasive than anyone else, the man who was supposed to have provided me with a special visa in the first place, the Permanent Secretary. When I walked into his office he was clearly surprised to see me. 'How did you get in to the country?' he asked. Not very polite. When I told him, he said that there must have been some mistake. Still, deportations were not his responsibility. He certainly wasn't going to do anything about it. He had never heard of *Oui* magazine so I told him that it was owned by *Playboy*. He looked appalled. He himself was a Christian and unphased by the First World's obsession with saucy photographs, but the President was a Moslem. The possible juxtapositions worried him. I told him that *Oui* was actually quite different from *Playboy*. I described a paper that was somewhere between the *New York Review of Books* and *Encounter*. Then I asked the Permanent Secretary why he had failed to answer all my letters. He said that there was no point in replying if one had nothing to say. He asked me why I wanted to see the President. Why did I not interview Kenyatta or Nyerere? Weren't they also well-known in North America? He was completely unimpressed by my explanation—'a new style of leadership, question of the Middle East' and so on. He was confident that he knew what I was going to write.

The Permanent Secretary was a threatened species in Uganda: a serious, highly-educated and efficient civil servant trying to run a government ministry. He was rude to me because I had complicated his life and possibly placed him at some risk merely by my arrival. In the circumstances, rudeness was a moderate response.

I suppose I must have realized that it was tactless to go on pressing him, and I met him only once more: in the hallway of the Ministry, late on a Friday afternoon. He was in a bad-tempered hurry. We smiled at each other with our teeth. The next day's headlines explained his bad temper. He had been rebuked before his assembled staff by the Minister, an upstart illiterate from Amin's 'home district'. Men like Amin were much easier to understand than men like the Permanent Secretary. Ambition might have explained why he stayed on, or the chance to earn an unofficial fortune. But he did not seem a corrupt man, and it needed more than ambition to explain why an intelligent person should risk his life and the lives of his family for some short-term advantage. Men like him were killed every week.

The next official I saw was an under-secretary who left me alone in his room for some time. 'Have you been reading the papers on my desk?' he asked when he came back.

'No'.

'You should. Some of them are marked *confidential*. I haven't read them either. There are so many and I can't find anything interesting. Go out and do some research. And then some sight-seeing. You will have the place to yourself. Don't forget to count the dead bodies you will see on the street corners.' Very dry.

There were then various theories about 'the General'. The English expatriates offered the first clear view, although in this, as in much else, they were behind the times. You find the expatriates in several places. One was the Kampala Rugby Club, with its white members and black caddies—it was actually on the golf course. The members were a curious assortment of unidealistic teachers who had chosen the wrong African country, old colonials and slightly dubious businessmen. The atmosphere in the club was deteriorating with the African members picking quarrels for no reason, resentful perhaps that the club's protective aura, the white aura, had begun to disperse. The whole place was a bit threadbare. There was another British club which had been turned into a hotel, but there was something colonial, paramilitary, about it still: the bare flagpole, the neat white lines on the tarmac outside, the bougainvillaea hedge, now out of control. Inside, the old clock with its brass pendulum still occupied the stained wooden case on the wall; the breeze crept through the open French window and rustled the faded chintz curtains; and a businessman told me that Amin was 'Not nearly as black as he is painted . . . Always found him quite charming, terribly pro-Scottish, loves the bagpipes and plays the accordion himself quite well. Twice played rugby for Uganda . . . extremely brave . . . terrific energy . . . natural leader . . . stopped all the freelance armed robbery . . . tourists have gone but so have the beggars.' Such men, of course, had lost virtually everything they had. They wanted it to be true, they were shipwrecked, washed up. They were reassured when Amin played the big buffoon.

This picture of the bluff, black Highlander, an over-promoted pipe-major, was not assisted by the true story of how Amin had come to power. About that there had been nothing essentially African at all. Before Obote was overthrown, his regime had been accused of gold-smuggling across the Zairean border. One of the leading participants in this activity was Colonel Amin. Later Brigadier Amin came under suspicion of stealing £1.2 million from the Defence budget and of murdering a fellow Brigadier. On the night of 25 January 1971, Amin was due to be arrested and charged with these crimes. But the telephone call issuing the order to loyal officers was connected by an *effendi* of Amin's tribe, Sergeant Musa. Amin was duck shooting. Musa seized the armoury and sent for 'the Boss'. By the time of my visit Sergeant Musa had become Colonel Musa, officer commanding the Fifth Mechanized Regiment.

These facts did not illuminate the Palestinian view of Amin either. Their representative was living in an abandoned colonial villa, too dilapidated to be suburban. He told me: 'No matter what people might say about the General, he is a true friend of the Palestinian people.' Nor did gold-smuggling square with the Libyan picture of Amin as a devout Moslem, nor with the Second World's view of Amin as an effective African ally. The Russians, who supplied Amin with tanks and planes, saw their protégés dumped in the Nile with everyone else. The coffee crop continued to go to the United States. East Germany sent one of their best men to Uganda, Gottfried Lessing, unusual among Second-Worlders in being an experienced Africa-hand. His name adorns hundreds of thousands of books all over the world because his former wife writes under it. There is a memorable picture of a young man like him in her early African books, an ideologue living in a colony, a hardliner. This man, who should have been famous, was killed during the 'liberation' of Kampala by the Tanzanian army when Amin was overthrown. He and his family died when their car was set alight by a flame-thrower; an obscure death during a political non-event. Palestinians, Russians, East Germans, British—all were eventually made to look foolish by Amin, all were as thoroughly duped as the sodden, shifty expats in their run-down club.

One day I took a taxi over the pot-holes and under the trees and up the hill to the former palace of the Kabakas of Uganda, now a deserted tourist resort. There was a recent name in the Visitors' book, 'Stokely Carmichael, Conakry, Guinea'. Mr Carmichael had just completed a triumphal visit to Uganda in his capacity as leader of the All African People's Party in the United States. On leaving he had assured Amin that 'what he had seen in Uganda had encouraged him very much and that he was going to do everything possible to represent Uganda very well'. The reports of his speech appeared under a photograph of Mrs Kay Amin clasping the hand of the wife of the Yugoslav ambassador. Mrs Amin died later that year. Her dismembered body was taken to the city mortuary. Amin, by then divorced from her, took their children to visit her and abused their mother's corpse. 'Your mother was a bad woman,' he shouted, 'see what has happened to her.' These children, like Svetlana Stalin, were brought up with a privileged insight into the brutal use of power. Unlike Svetlana, they were also trained as future rulers. When Amin attended the Pan-Moslem conference in Pakistan he took one of his sons with him. The entire conference, packed with heads of state, and locked behind impenetrable security, sat there listening to the burblings of little Mwanga.

In order to discover what was really happening in Toytown I sought out 'the Opposition'. They didn't have an office of course, not even an underground newspaper, but they weren't hard to find.

I applied for an interview with the Archbishop of Kampala, E.K. Nsubuga, now a Cardinal. He refused to see me. He is a very canny man, a skilful politician, a protector of the various Catholic tribes of Uganda, and a survivor. He was reported at that time to have had an unusually frank exchange with the General. While thanking Amin for donating 50,000 shillings for the completion of a shrine to Uganda's early Christian martyrs, the Archbishop asked him to stop opening his incoming and outgoing letters. The exchange took place on the site of the Martyrs' shrine. The previous time the Archbishop visited it the General had not been there but an army patrol had: four members of the Archbishop's family were abducted. Today, Cardinal Nsubuga is still in his palace and has become one of the most influential political leaders in Uganda, a mediator between the guerrillas and the government. He has the right stuff, whatever that is, to survive as a prominent, unarmed Ugandan under Amin, the Tanzanians, Obote (twice) and Okello. His Anglican counterpart, a brave but less subtle man whom I spoke to at length, was eventually shot in the back of the head, and mourned by Amin as 'the victim of a road accident'.

The sites of such atrocities were not always remote. From my hotel it was only a stroll down the Queen's Road to the High Court. Down these steps the Lord Chief Justice of Uganda, Benedicto Kiwanuka, was dragged to his death in his socks one working morning by unidentified men. Incredibly, the High Court continued to function, and while I was there an army corporal, Bahemuka from the West Nile region, Amin's homeland, was sentenced to six years prison for encouraging cannibalism. He had cut off the ears of a man suspected of witchcraft and forced the poor fellow to eat them. On the same day, another known cannibal, Lieutenant Colonel Isaac Malyamungu, was reported merely to have harangued Magamaga shopkeepers for overcharging. The High Court was at the mercy of some of the most brutal men in the county and yet continued to condemn them, and yet not all of them. It was easy to parody this reality from London, easy to simplify it even in Kampala. At times it *was* simple enough. When Amin seized the armoury, then the barracks, then the capital, he needed to show that he had support. The Inspector-General of Police, Wilson Oryema, was photographed with him, posed in a friendly handshake. In due course Oryema joined Amin's cabinet as Minister of Mineral and Water Resources. His son was selected for training as a military pilot in West Germany. On the day that this pilot returned to his country, trained to fight for it, he was abducted and shot. That was during my visit. Oryema's usefulness was exhausted in 1977. He was taken from a meeting of diplomats and Ugandan notables, with the Anglican Archbishop and the Minister for Internal Affairs, by Malyamungu, the same Lieutenant Colonel; all three were murdered. Amin no longer cared who saw his men at work. He needed to frighten everyone and the more prominent the witnesses were the better.

For most Kampalans life continued to run its familiar, haphazard course. Setting out on one visit to the Ministry, near a corner on Speke Road, I came across a man lying on the pavement. He was having a fit. He was an old man, his hair was grey and he was wearing a brown suit. His shirt had ridden up and as he rolled and jerked across the pavement one could see that underneath his trousers he was wearing tight, elasticated, nylon bathing shorts. They did not look comfortable. This man was in danger of swallowing his tongue. He was experiencing muscular contractions which caused his back to arc up in a curve, lifting his torso five or six inches into the air. His suit was soon covered in dust, there was dust on his face and the black grit on the ground was mixed with the bubbling foam from his mouth. His eyelids were open, his eyeballs immobile, rolled up beneath his brow, just the bulging whites exposed. One wondered, as he jerked over onto his face, that his eyes were not crushed by the weight of his head as it banged onto the pavement. A girl picked up his brown trilby hat, other people stepped out of his way. There was a feeling among those watching him that might shortly express itself in laughter. They were nervous. The girls put their hands up to cover their mouths. One could use the listless reaction to illustrate the general fear of Amin—the fear of making oneself prominent by taking the initiative—but it would not be true. Such scenes and such reactions can be seen in all the cities of Africa. The particular effects of Amin's rule were not usually so public.

There was a consultant surgeon at Mulago Teaching Hospital, a Scotsman, who invited me into his house and gave me a list of prominent men who had recently been murdered. He had good Scotch whisky and plenty of ice, but he had to check both the door and the window for eavesdroppers; he didn't trust his own 'houseboy'. I took notes of our conversation which omitted all the

119

names and then posted the names, without notes, to my post office box in Nairobi. It was melodramatic but essential. Two years before there had been another reporter from London who had taken notes in the usual way, with names. He had been arrested on his way out to Entebbe airport, his notebooks had been examined and several of the Ugandans he had spoken to had subsequently been murdered. In all this, the curious visitor to Toytown had one excellent camouflage; the routine confusion of life in Africa. In a country which could admit a foreign journalist by mistake, where even a Permanent Secretary was too cautious to implement a deportation order, it was more than likely that the visitor would have left before any hostile inquiry had been organized. So often in Africa the danger arises not by intention but by chance; the drunken sentry at the road block, the once faithful servant who has been denied a bag of old clothes.

And so, I am convinced, was it by chance that I was denied my interview with His Excellency General Idi Amin Dada. I had been to see another 'permanent' secretary, Peter Ucanda, who ran the President's office, and who was subsequently to flee the country. I was also on speaking terms with Juma, the illiterate minister, who happened to be Amin's current favourite. They told me that it was just a matter of the president 'fitting me into his schedule'. And then something quite unexpected occurred.

The news-stand on Speke Road received a consignment of *Oui* magazine. A city which was short of bread, beer, sugar, and a country which no longer had the foreign currency to buy toothpaste or shoes, had managed to import about one hundred copies of a not very recent issue and display them along the pavement. There was the usual cover picture, not the sort favoured by either *Encounter* or the *New York Review of Books*.

After that, my interview became less and less likely. The President was reported to be taking spiritual instruction from the Chief Kadhi before attending the Pan-Moslem conference. The ministry adopted a much friendlier attitude to my visits; they were no longer worried about me.

In the time left to me in Uganda there was a crowded official schedule to cover. I never met the Archbishop's future murderer, the cannibal Malyamungu, but I did meet Ali Towelli, the head of the

Public Safety Unit at a diplomatic cocktail party. This was followed by an International Medical Conference, which Amin addressed. His speech was devoted to the problems of 'disabled children in rural areas' to which he intended to devote the President's charity fund. One of the administrators of the conference disappeared on the morning that it opened. Then there was the downfall of the foreign minister, Lieutenant Colonel Ondoga: it started with a newspaper report that Amin thought his ministry 'the most inefficient he had ever seen'; then came the announcement that Ondoga had been 'assigned to other duties', then the appointment of his successor, Princess Elizabeth of Toro—'Miss Bagaya' as Amin called her. The Princess accepted my congratulations with a trill in her voice. Two weeks later Ondoga's body was found in the Nile, by members of the Public Safety Unit. Miss Bagaya's good fortune was made public on the campus of Makerere University. Everyone was there, students and faculty. Amin was frightened of this audience; he felt ignorant and foolish. The professors sucked their pipes and looked at the ground. There is a special horror for people who think clearly in the realization that they are living in a country where to think clearly is to risk your life. Looking back on the Amin days it was his fear and hatred of educated people that were both the most characteristic and unpredictable aspects of his tyranny. He was not the only African leader who carried out tribal massacres; the advantage of such behaviour is that it identifies those at risk. They may be able to avoid the danger. But Amin also attacked people for being good at their jobs. The better you served him the more likely you were to attract his resentment.

At my last meeting with Juma, the General's favourite son, he said: 'Do not worry that you have not seen the Head of State. You just came at the wrong time.' Then he chuckled, 'Heh, heh, heh.' But he was wrong about that. I *had* seen Amin. I had seen him in the way Juma fingered the telephone receiver and opened his eyes wide while he listened to the 'Effendi' on the telephone. I had seen Amin in the fear shown by those who were queueing in the corridor outside Juma's office. This was a fear which men who were frightened of Amin instilled in men who could be made dependent on *them*; fear in this way becoming a burden to be more equally shared. I had seen Amin in the clumsy buffoonery of the leader, as imitated by anyone who wished to evade an inquisitive question.

'Not quite as black as he's painted!' Oh very good, a joke from the sergeant's mess, appropriate in a country which was being drilled by an evil-tempered sergeant. And I had watched Amin himself, sweating with fear into his Savile Row suit, before starting a speech to an educated audience; the almost hapless victim of Uganda's post-colonial plight, a man trained to kill by the King's African Rifles, who used his single professional skill to keep himself in power.

'You just came at the wrong time,' Juma said. 'Anyway I hope you will come back. Anyway you have seen a lot. I think you will go away quickly. Oh yes.' Yes. I went away quickly—on the flight before the one I said I was going on, to be exact. No one had violated my notebooks, no one would be blamed for admitting me. Almost all the evidence of my visit disappeared with my departure. From Nairobi, in delighted relief, I sent a long telex to the *Sunday Times* dealing with the topical information. It was prominently used in that week's issue. Then I set out for London, looking forward to writing the real story, the complicated truth about Uganda, for *Oui* magazine. Sabena had a flight from Nairobi to Brussels, with connections to London. Nobody mentioned that it called at Entebbe.

And so it was that, with my completed records, names and all, and a copy of my telex to the *Sunday Times*, and my all-too-familiar appearance, I found myself back in Uganda, sitting in a Sabena plane in the middle of the night and refusing to join the other passengers in the transit lounge of Entebbe airport. A hard-faced Belgian stewardess told me that it was a rule at Entebbe that *all* passengers had to leave the plane. I told her that in my case that would be inadvisable. She said that Ugandan security men always boarded the plane to enforce the rule. I told her that I had a high fever and must not be moved. She looked extremely irritated but brought me a blanket. It was not difficult to look ill, running with sweat, teeth chattering, grey skin, when the security men passed down the plane. The stewardess explained. The security men passed on.

In due course *Oui* magazine rejected my article, on the grounds that it was not an interview, and declined to pay most of my expenses. It had turned out to be rather a costly adventure. The

African correspondents of Fleet Street continued to write about Uganda as one more piece on the world chessboard, and to press for the return of the legitimate ruler, the moderate Dr Obote. Today, when the appalling Obote has been overthrown for the second time, they continue to report Uganda in terms of ideologies and 'spheres of East-West influence'; the word 'tribalism' rarely appears in their copy, and they don't seem to have noticed that *they* may have got Dr Obote wrong.

They got Field-Marshall Amin wrong too. The Western view of Uganda, the view which is formed by 'interviews', makes no sense at all. It fails to explain how a 'simple buffoon' could rule so many sophisticated men for so long. Nor does it explain how such a man could dominate Uganda's complicated mixture of tribal and religious groups, Muslim and Christian, Catholic and Protestant, Bantu and Nilotic, Bantu and Bantu. Perhaps the truth was that nobody in the West wanted to read that Amin was more than a buffoon, or that he was extremely popular in parts of Uganda, or that the return of Obote would be a disaster. In Chicago and London the men who had never been to Amin's Uganda already knew what they thought. An eye-witness account only served to confuse them.

They preferred the *Punch* view of an illiterate oaf, straight down from the trees, who spoke in phrases like 'Who am dat?' *Punch* ran a highly successful parody along those lines for several years. If you had been to Uganda it read like a weekly lesson in the limitations of popular humour.

Amin was a shrewd man who played an old trick on those who opposed him. He encouraged them to underestimate him. He knew what expatriates thought of him so he fed their prejudices and clowned about. He had another role to play for Gadaffi, another for the Yugoslavs, another for Kenyatta. To have interviewed a man who could disguise himself so successfully would have been interesting, but it was not essential. There was more to be learned by watching him sweating with fear before he spoke to a room full of unarmed doctors.

Salman Rushdie
Eating the Eggs of Love

I first read Omar Cabezas's book, *Fire from the Mountain*, on the plane from London to Managua. (The English title is much less evocative, though shorter, than the Spanish, which translates literally as *The Mountain is something more than a great expanse of green*.) Now, on the road to Matagalpa, travelling towards the mountains about which he'd written, I dipped into it again. Even in English, without any of the 'Nica' slang that had helped make it the most successful book in the new Nicaragua (its sales were close to 70,000 copies), it was an enjoyable and evocative memoir of 'Skinny' Cabezas's recruitment by the FSLN, his early work for the Frente in León, and his journey up into the mountains to become one of the early guerrillas. Cabezas managed to communicate the terrible difficulty of life in the mountains, which were a hell of mud, jungle and disease (although one of his fans, a young Nicaraguan soldier, thought he had failed to make it sound bad enough because he had made it too funny). But for Cabezas the mountains were something more than a great expanse of unpleasantness. He turned them into a mythic, archetypal force, The Mountain, because during the Somoza period hope lay there. The Mountain was where the Frente guerrillas were; it was the source from which, one day, the revolution would come. And it did.

Nowadays, when it was the Contra that emerged from The Mountain to terrorize the *campesinos*, it must have felt like a violation; like, perhaps, the desecration of a shrine.

Forested mesas flanked the road to Matagalpa; ahead, the multiform mountains, conical, twisted, sinuous, closed the horizon. Cattle and dogs shared the road with cars, refusing to acknowledge the supremacy of the automobile. When the trucks came, however, everybody got out of the way fast.

Tall cacti by the roadside. Women in fatigues carried rifles over their shoulders, holding them by the barrels. Moss hung in clumps from the trees and even from the telephone wires. Children pushed wooden wheelbarrows full of wood. And then, as we neared Matagalpa, we came upon a sombre procession carrying a distressingly small box: a child's funeral. I saw three in the next two days.

It had begun to rain.

I was pleased to be getting out of Managua again. Matagalpa felt like a real town, with its church-dominated squares, its town centre. It was like returning to normal, but normality here was of a violent, exceptional type. The buildings were full of bullet-holes left over from the insurrection years, and dominating the town was a high, ugly tower which was all that remained of the National Guard's hated command post. After the revolution, the people had demolished the Guardia's fearsome redoubt.

The ice-cream shop had no ice-cream because of the shortages. In the toy shop the evidence of poverty was everywhere; the best toys on display were primitive 'cars' made out of a couple of bits of wood nailed together and painted, with Coca-Cola bottle tops for hub-caps. There were, interestingly, a number of mixed-business stores known as 'Egyptian shops', boasting such names as 'Armando Mustafa' or 'Manolo Saleh', selling haberdashery, a few clothes, some toiletries, a variety of basic household items—shampoo, buckets, safety-pins, mirrors, balls. I remembered the Street of Turks in *One Hundred Years of Solitude*. In Matagalpa, Macondo did not seem so very far away.

The faces in the Egyptian shops didn't look particularly Egyptian but then neither did the Orientally-named Moisès Hassan, mayor of Managua. In the cafés, I met some more familiar faces. Posters of the Pope and of Cardinal Obando y Bravo were everywhere, the Cardinal's scarlet robes rendered pale pink by the passage of time. Sandinistas, unconcerned about the company they were keeping, drank hideously sweetened fruit squashes, including the bright purple *pitaya*, and munched on the glutinous kiwi-like *mamón*, beneath the watching Cardinal. I talked to Carlos Paladino, who worked in the office of the *delegado* or governor of Matagalpa province, about the regional resettlement policy.

Large areas of the mountainous and densely jungled war zone in the north-eastern part of Jinotega province had been evacuated, and the population relocated in southern Jinotega, and Matagalpa province, too. It had been a 'military decision'—that is, compulsory. The army had been having trouble fighting the Contra because the scattered civilian population kept getting in the way. The people were also in danger from the Contra, who regularly kidnapped *campesinos*, or forced them to grow food for the counter-revolutionary soldiers, or killed them. But wasn't it also true, I asked, that many people in those areas sympathized with the Contra? Yes, Paladino replied, some men had gone to join them, leaving many women with children behind. The large number of one-parent families of this type had become quite a problem. But in many cases the men would return, disillusioned, after a time. The government offered a complete amnesty for any *campesino* who returned in this way. 'We don't hold them responsible,' Paladino said. 'We know how much pressure the Contra can exert.'

Resettlement brought problems. Apart from the single-parent issue—how were these women to be involved in production when they had to look after their children?—the resettled northerners were people who were utterly unfamiliar with living in communities. They had led isolated lives in jungle clearings. Now they were being put into clusters of houses built close together. Their animals strayed into their neighbours' yards. Their children fought. They hated it. Many of them were racially different from the local *mestizos*: they were Amerindians, Miskito or Sumo, with their own languages, their own culture, and they felt colonized. 'We made many mistakes,' Carlos Paladino admitted.

The plan was to have child-care centres at each co-operative settlement, but so far they had only been able to put in eleven such centres in over fifty communities. They had also managed to build some schools, some health-care facilities; but there was still a lot of resentment in the air.

The lack of resources (and, no doubt, the haste with which the operation had been carried out) had meant that in some places the authorities had been unable to provide the resettled families with completed houses. The 'roof only policy,' as it was called, offered the uprooted families exactly what its name suggested: a roof. They had to build the walls out of whatever materials they could find. It was not a policy calculated to win hearts and minds. But, Paladino insisted, the state was doing its best, and international volunteer brigades and relief agencies were helping, too. There were even some unexpected individual initiatives. 'A few days after the mine blew up and killed the thirty-two bus passengers,' he told me, 'a tall, fair-haired man appeared in the area, a foreigner, with fifteen hundred dollars to give away. He was just carrying it in his pockets, and looking for the families of the thirty-two, to hand over the money. It was his savings.'

Progress remained slow. 'It isn't easy,' Carlos said. 'Eight new communities have been destroyed by the Contra in the last six months. Hundreds of *campesinos* die in the attacks every year.'

Our best defence is the people in arms. 'The people are more and more able to undertake their own defence. In November 1985 at Santa Rosa hundreds of Contra were killed. Since then, in the attacks on the new co-operatives, hundreds more.'

But the Contra were doing damage, all right. For a country in Nicaragua's position, the loss of an estimated forty percent of the harvest was a crippling blow.

When Carlos Paladino came to work in Matagalpa, he was highly critical of the way the revolution had handled the resettlements, and won the approval of the regional *delegado*, Carlos Zamora, for his new approach. He went into the jungle with his staff, and lived with the peasants for months, to learn about their way of life and their needs before attempting any resettlement. This altered the layout of the new settlements, and greatly increased the officials' sensitivity to the people's wishes. Paladino became an expert on Miskito Indian culture, and had started writing about it. In his spare time (!) he was doing a history degree. Not for the first time, I felt awed by the amount people were willing to take on in Nicaragua.

After I'd been talking to him for more than an hour, I discovered that Paladino had been in hospital twenty-four hours earlier, having a .22 bullet removed from his lung. It had been there since before the 'triumph', the result of an accident: he had been shot in training by a careless cadet. He opened his shirt, after I had bullied him into it, and showed me the scar. It was an inch away from his heart.

I stayed in a wooden chalet in the mountains high above Matagalpa, and that night the *delegado*, Carlos Zamora, and his deputy, Manuel Salvatierra, dropped by to inspect the *escritor hindú*. Zamora was small, slight, moustachioed; Salvatierra of much bigger build. They were old college friends. We sat down to a dinner of beef in hot pepper sauce, squash with melted cheese, and banana chips.

The week before on the seventh anniversary of the revolution, Zamora volunteered, the Contra had moved a thousand men into Jinotega province. Their plan had been to attack one of the two hydro-electric stations and cut the power cable. They had also intended to ambush *campesinos* on their way to Estelí. 'They failed completely,' he said with satisfaction. 'Our intelligence was good enough. But 700 of them are still in the region, still in Nicaragua. The rest have returned to Honduras.'

Salvatierra stressed the Contra's morale problem. 'They're scared of us,' he said. 'Dollars won't help that.'

I changed the subject. Was it true that it cost six head of cattle to get your car serviced?

They laughed. 'Or ten hectares of maize,' said Carlos Zamora.

So, then, I said, if prices are that high, tell me about corruption.

They looked embarrassed, not unexpectedly, but they didn't refuse to answer. Yes, Zamora said, there was, er, some. 'About the car service,' he said. 'You see, a mechanic will tell you that a certain part is unavailable, or can be ordered for crazy money, but he just happens to have one at home, for a price.'

The black market accounted for maybe forty percent of the country's liquid assets. 'Anything that can be bought can be sold down the road for more,' Salvatierra said. 'There is an old woman who hitch-hikes from Matagalpa to León every day, with a suitcase full of beans, mangoes and rice. She earns 5,000 cordobas a day. I earn around 3,000.'

Zamora and Salvatierra had been 'bad students' in Managua when the FSLN recruited them. Zamora's father was a garage mechanic. (I had accidentally hit on the right subject when I talked about servicing motor cars.) 'He wasn't against the revolution, but he wasn't for it, either.' I said that it seemed at times that the revolution had been a struggle between the generations—the Frente's *muchachos*, kids, against the older generation of Somocistas and cautious, conservative *campesinos*. No, no, they both hastened to correct me. But the impression stuck.

'How old are you?' I asked them. They giggled prettily.

'Thirty,' Carlos Zamora said. He had fought a revolution and was governor of a province, and he was nine years younger than me.

Later, when a little Flor de Caña Extra Seco had loosened things up, the old stories came out again: of the battle of Pancasán in 1974, at which the Sandinistas suffered a bloody defeat, but after which, for the first time, the *campesinos* came to the Frente and asked for arms, so that the defeat was a victory after all, the moment at which the *muchachos* and the peasants united; and of the local boy, Carlos Fonseca, who was born in Matagalpa. Sandino and Fonseca were both illegitimate, they told me.

'So what's the connection between bastards and revolutions?' I asked, but they only laughed nervously. It wasn't done to joke about the saints.

I tried to get them to open up about the period in the seventies during which the Frente had split into three 'tendencies', after a bitter dispute about the correct path for the revolution. (The 'Proletarian faction', led by Jaime Wheelock, believed that a long period of work with the *campesinos*, to politicize and mobilize them, was the way forward, even if it took years. The faction that favoured a prolonged guerrilla war, and based itself in the mountains, included Carlos Fonseca himself; and the third faction, the *terceristas*, which believed in winning the support of the middle classes and proceeding by a strategy of large-scale urban insurrection, was led by Daniel Ortega and his brother. The factions united, in December 1978, for the final push to victory, and it was the *tercerista* plan that carried the day.)

Zamora and Salvatierra denied that there had been any internal power struggles, claiming that the division had been tactical and not a real split.

'I've never heard of a revolution without a power struggle in the leadership,' I said. 'Wasn't it true that Jaime Wheelock was accused of being responsible for the split? Wasn't it true that Daniel Ortega became President because the *tercerista* faction won the internal fight?'

No, they said, anxiously. Not at all. 'The directorate has always been very united.'

That simply wasn't true. Where had they spent the insurrection years, I asked them.

'I was in the cities,' Zamora replied, and Salvatierra nodded. So they had belonged to the urban-insurrectionist, *tercerista* faction, the winning team. They didn't want to seem to be gloating over the victory.

To stir things up, I said that the case of Edén Pastora suggested that the divisions were deeper than they cared to admit. After all, Pastora had been a *tercerista* himself, he had been the famous

'Commander Zero', glamorous and dashing, who had led the sensational attack on the Palácio Nacional, taken the entire Somocista Chamber of Deputies hostage, and obtained the release of fifty jailed Sandinistas plus a half-million dollar ransom; and there he was today, in exile in Costa Rica, having tried to lead a counter-revolutionary army of his own... He had been defeated by the Sandinistas, but surely his break with the revolution he helped to bring about was significant?

There were grins and embarrassed laughs from the *delegado* and his deputy. 'Edén Pastora wanted personal glory,' Salvatierra said. 'He joined the wrong army in the first place.'

The next day I drove up into the north. I knew that the road I was on, the one that went up past Jinotega and headed for Bocay, was the one on which the Contra mine had exploded, killing 'the thirty-two', and even though that had happened a good deal further north than I was going, I felt extremely fearless as we went over the bumps. 'How do you protect the roads?' I asked the army officer who was accompanying me.

'It's impossible to guarantee total safety,' he replied.

'I see,' I said. 'Yes. By the way, how do you know when there's a mine in the road?'

'There's a big bang,' came the straight-faced reply.

My breakfast of rice and beans—*gallo pinto*, it was called, painted rooster—began to crow noisily in my stomach.

There were vultures sitting by the roadsides. Low clouds sat among the mountains. The road-signs were punctured by bullet-holes. In the jeep, the driver, Danilo, had a radio, or rather a 'REALISTIC' sixteen-band scanner, on which he picked up Contra transmissions. We passed co-operatives with resolutely optimistic names: *La Esperanza. La Paz.* The mountains thickened and closed: walls of tree and cloud. There was a flash of electric-blue wings; then, suddenly, a peasant shack surrounded by trees and hedges clipped into cones, domes, rectangles, spheres, all manner of geometric shapes. To be a topiarist in a jungle, I reflected, was to be a truly stubborn human being.

Then there was a tree lying across the road, blocking our way. Was this it? Was this where Contra fiends with machetes between

132

their teeth would burst from the foliage, and goodbye *escritor hindú*? It was just a tree across the road.

The Enrique Acuña co-operative was named after a local martyr, who had been murdered by a wealthy local landowner after Somoza's fall. (The killer got away, fleeing the country before he could be arrested.) It was a CAS, a Cooperativa Agricola Sandinista, that is, a proper co-op, with all the land held and farmed collectively. Elsewhere, in areas where there had been resistance to the co-operative idea, the government had evolved the CCS, the Co-operative of Credits and Services. In a CCS the land was owned and farmed by individuals, and the government's role was limited to supplying them with power, water, health care and distribution facilities. There was no doubt that the *campesinos* were encouraged to adopt the CAS structure, but the existence of the alternative was an indication of the authorities' flexibility; this was not, surely, the way a doctrinaire commune-ist regime would go about its business.

The houses were built on the 'mini-skirt' principle: metal roofs stood over walls that were made of concrete up to a height of three feet, and of wood above that height. This had become the *campesinos*' favourite building method. The Contra couldn't set fire to the roofs, or shoot the occupants through the walls while they lay sleeping. The houses were arranged around wide avenues, with plenty of space between them. Pigs were snoozing in the shade. There was a tap with running water, and even a shower. In a ramshackle shed, a play school was in progress: clapping games and songs. In the next room, there was a baby care centre with instructions for the care and diagnosis of diarrhoea pinned up on the wall, written out and illustrated by the children themselves. The disease was the main child-killer in the rural areas.

All around the co-operative's residential area was a system of trenches. The *campesinos* did guard duty on a rota basis, and many of the men were familiar with the workings of the AK-47 automatic rifle. They were also geniuses with the machete. The *campesino* who had hacked to pieces the tree that had held us up could have shaved you without breaking your skin. Alternatively, he could have sliced you like a loaf.

Last November, the Contra had attacked the Acuña co-operative, by daylight and in force: around 400 of them against thirty-two armed defenders. Arturo, the burly young man who was in charge of the defence committee, told me proudly that they had held out for three hours until help arrived from a neighbouring co-operative. In the end the Contra were beaten off, with thirteen dead and around forty wounded. 'We lost nobody,' Arturo boasted. Since then, the Contra had been seen in the neighbourhood twice, but had not attacked.

A thought occurred to me: if the opposition were correct, and the Sandinistas were so unpopular, how was it that they could hand out all these guns to the people, and be confident that the weapons would not be turned against them? There wasn't another regime in Central America that would dare to do the same: not El Salvador, not Guatemala, not Honduras, not Costa Rica. While in Nicaragua, which the US was calling tyrannical, 'Stalinist', the government armed the peasantry, and they in turn pointed the guns, every one of them, against the counter-revolutionary forces.

Could this mean something?

I got talking to a group of five *campesinos* during their lunch break. They parked their machetes by hacking them into a tree-stump, but brought their AKs along. Did they know anyone who had joined the Contra? They knew of kidnaps, they said. But how about someone who had joined voluntarily? No, they didn't. The people were afraid of the Contra.

One of the *campesinos*, Humberto, a small man with a big-toothed smile, was an *indígena*, but he wasn't sure what sort. He wasn't Miskito or Sumo, he knew that. 'I'm trying to find out what I am.' He had lived in the north, in the area now evacuated. The Contra, he said, had kidnapped him, threatened to kill him, but he had escaped. A while later he heard that they were still after him, and intended to recapture him. 'This time they'd have killed me for sure.' So he was delighted to be resettled. 'It was hard at first, but for me it was a blessing.' He sat close to a matchstick-thin man with wiry black hair sticking out sideways from beneath his peaked cap.

'The same happened to me,' this man, Rigoberto, said. 'Just the same story. Me, too.'

Another of the quintet came from a coastal fishing community, where there had been no possibility of getting any land. The other two were locals. 'So do you think of this as your home now?' I asked. 'Or does it seem like just some temporary place?'

Arturo, the defence organiser, answered. 'What do you mean? We've put our sweat into this earth, we've risked our lives for it. We're making our lives here. What do you mean? Of course it's home.'

'It's our first home,' the fisherman said, the oldest of the five at around fifty. He was called Horacio, and as I listened to him, the penny dropped. What he had said, and what the *indígena* Humberto had told me—'I'm trying to find out what I am'—were both connected to an idea I had heard before in Managua: that one's own country can be a place of exile, can be Egypt, or Babylon. That in fact Somocista Nicaragua had literally *not been* these people's country, and that the revolution had really been an act of migration, for the locals as well as the resettled men. They were inventing their country, and, more than that, themselves. It was by belonging here that Humberto might actually discover what he was.

I said: 'You're lucky.' The idea of home had never stopped being a problem for me. They didn't understand that, though, and why should they? Nobody was shooting at me.

The co-operative's day began at five a.m., when the workers assembled to hear the day's work rota from the representatives of the various (annually elected) committees. Then they went home, breakfasted on tortillas and beans, and were in the fields (coffee, rice) at six, working for around eight hours. After work there were adult education classes. Three of the five men I spoke to had learned to write since arriving here—Humberto, he confessed, 'not very well.' The classes went up to the fourth grade.

What did they do for fun? Cock-fighting, cards, guitar music, the occasional social call at the neighbouring co-op, the odd trip into Jinotega or Matagalpa, and of course the various fiestas. But they seemed awkward talking about fun. 'In spite of the men lost to the war effort'—Arturo insisted on getting the conversation back to the serious stuff—'we have kept up our levels of production.'

With the generosity of the poor, they treated me to a delicacy at lunch. I was given an egg and bean soup, the point being that these eggs were the best-tasting, because they had been fertilized. Such eggs were known as 'the eggs of love'. When people had so little, a fertilized hen's egg became a treat.

As I ate my love-eggs, which really did taste good, there were children playing in the shack next door to the kitchen hut. Their playing-cards were made out of rectangles of paper cut out of an old Uncle Scrooge comic book. *Waak! My money! You dratted...* Pieces of Huey, Dewey and Louie fled from the rage of the billionaire American duck. While on a radio, I promise, Bruce Springsteen sang 'Born in the USA'.

The Germán Pomares field hospital, on the road back to Jinotega, was named after the FSLN leader who had been killed in May 1979, just two months before the 'triumph'. Pomares had been a great influence on Daniel Ortega, and one of the most popular Sandinista leaders.

'He was so loved,' my interpreter told me, 'that his death wasn't even announced on the news for six months.' I added this to my collection of depressing sentences, alongside the one about the 'cosmetic' nature of press freedom, the justification offered me earlier in Managua to explain the recent closing of *La Prensa*, the only opposition paper.

At the sentry-box at the hospital gate everybody was supposed to hand in their weapons, but our driver, Danilo, hid his pistol under a sweatshirt I'd taken off as the day grew hotter. Stripping in the heat was one thing, but he would have felt under-dressed, he agreed when I discovered his deception, without some sort of gun.

The hospital was just two years old. 'We have had to develop it quickly,' said the director, Caldera, an Indian-looking man with a shell-picture of Che on his office wall. 'Never in the history of our nation have we had so many wounded.' The specialist staff were all Cubans. Nicaraguan doctors were gradually being trained to take over, but at present simply didn't have the skills required for this kind of surgery.

The average age of the patients was twenty-one. Ten percent of them were regular soldiers, thirty percent came from the peasant militias, and no less than sixty percent were youngsters doing their military service.

'That's astonishing,' I said. 'Why so many military service casualties?'

The reason, Caldera said, was that these kids were the main components of the BLI forces, the small commando units that would pursue the Contra deep into the jungle, into the Mountain. Military service in Nicaragua was no joy-ride.

In recent months, many of the hospital's patients had been mine-blast victims, and almost all of these had died. Otherwise the main injuries were from bullet wounds. 'Eighty-three percent heal completely,' said director Caldera, who knew his statistics. 'Six to seven percent survive with disabilities.' That left ten percent. I didn't ask what happened to them.

By chance, I visited the Pomares hospital when there were quite a few empty beds, and very few amputees. Usually, Caldera said, things were different. 'If it was always this way I could write poetry.' Another poet. There was no escape from the fellows.

I asked if they had to import blood. No, he said, the national blood donation programme provided enough. That struck me as fairly remarkable. It was a small country, and it had been losing a lot of blood.

The young men in the wards were all gung-ho, all volubly starry-eyed about the revolution—'Since my injury,' one teenager told me, 'I love this revolutionary process even more' —and all super-keen to return to the fray. I met a nineteen-year-old youth who had been fighting for six years. I met a shamefaced seventeen-year-old who had shot himself accidentally in the foot. I met an eighteen-year-old with wounds all over his body. 'First I was hit in the leg,' he said, 'but I could keep firing. Then the shrapnel, here'—he indicated his bandaged forehead—'and my vision blurred. I passed out, but only for a moment.' I asked about the alarming gash above his right knee. 'I don't know,' he said. It looked too large to have arrived without being noticed, but he shook his head. 'It's funny, but I just don't know how I got it.'

They were all very young, yet already so familiar with death that they had lost respect for it. That worried me. Then, as I was leaving, I met a young woman in a wheelchair. She had been shot in the groin, and her face was glassy, expressionless. Unlike the boy soldiers, this was someone who knew she'd been shot, and was upset about it.

'And what do you think about the revolution?' I asked her.

'I've got no time for that junk,' she replied.

'Are you against it?'

'Who cares?' she shrugged. 'Maybe. Yes.'

So there were people for whom the violence was too much, and not worth it. But it also mattered that she had been entirely unafraid. She had been in the presence of several officers of the state, and it hadn't bothered her a bit.

When I was back in my chalet, the mountains looked so peaceful in the evening light that it was hard to believe in the danger they contained. Beauty, in Nicaragua, often contained the beast.

COLIN THUBRON
A FAMILY IN NANJING

Weigi, a Chinese acquaintance, was separated by his job from his wife and parents, and had asked me to visit them when I travelled to Nanjing. So one evening, carrying his gift of clothes for them, I groped down a dark street in a district of shabby blocks of flats. I felt vaguely misused and prepared myself for an evening of courtesies.

Weigi's parents lived in rooms of a kind by now familiar to me: bare-floored, crudely furnished, and stark with the signs of modest privilege—a television, a refrigerator. A huge, fragmentary family had assembled to meet me: children of absent aunts, wives of husbands still at work. I could not sort them all out. They massed across the sitting-room in a wavering crowd of hesitating hands and smiles and greetings, sabotaged by an undertow of yelling babies.

The old couple were formal and reticent. They had joined the Revolution from Nanjing in the mid-1940s, and had now entered a decent retirement, cushioned by six children. Of their two daughters-in-law, one was a pert-faced girl from Suzhou, a city famous for its women's beauty. Her delicately-lashed eyes looked as if they had been surgically widened, and she chattered with steely brightness.

But the second woman, Weigi's wife Hua, was extraordinary. Whereas the others were dressed in workaday shirts and trousers, she wore an evening dress, flamboyant white, and her neck dangled a quartz pendant-watch. She was darkly imposing. She intentionally eclipsed them all—seemed not to notice them. She clasped my hand and stared at me with a face not beautiful but oddly arresting: a feral power about the heavy slope of her cheeks and bow-shaped mouth. In another society she would have been a sexual predator. Here she emanated a black charge of frustration and contempt. She seized the parcel I had brought from her husband to his parents, pulled it open, then tossed it derisively onto a sofa. 'Just men's things.'

The old people had prepared a banquet for me—an extravagant spread of cold meats and dumplings which we ate with the prestige television blaring, and nobody watching it. I had always thought of the Chinese family as a stereotype of unity and closeness, but here mother-in-law and daughter-in-law were soon waging war in iron silences. Compared to the old couple—conservative peasants—Hua was the daughter of a once-discredited bourgeoisie: voluble, raw, overbearing.

The Suzhou girl was different again. She could scarcely bear the sight of her three-year-old son, an electric urchin with a sprout of chimney-brush hair. 'I think he's mad. He never stops. Not even at night. I don't think he sleeps. He just wears me to death.' Her pretty face never smiled as he sprawled yelling across her knees. She pushed him away. He came back. She pushed him away again. 'Do you have a word for this in English?'

'Hyperactive, I think.'

She thought about this word, and said softly 'Hypercti,' as if it held some solution.

'Hypercti! Hypercti!' the boy screamed. He dashed the chopsticks out of her hands. She pushed him away. He thrust a fist into her rice. She elbowed him back.

At last, he reached into his pants—which with Chinese children are conventionally slit for excreting—discovered his penis, plucked it out and waved it derisively round the table. For a few seconds everybody pretended not to notice. The old couple developed an important conversation together. The women's gaze shuddered into their laps, and the foreigner concentrated on his dumplings. The cabaret ended only with a furious slap from the boy's mother—the first and last time that I saw a child hit in China—and a volley of laughter from Hua.

I turned tactfully away. On my other side sat a shrimpy, thirteen-year-old girl with long, hoydenish legs and plaits, who promised to be beautiful. She wormed against me and started practising her English. Hua tried to shut her up, but she only said loudly: 'I like *Weigi*. He's nice.'

I asked: 'Is the little boy your brother?'

'No. I'm Yulong. My parents aren't here. I haven't got any brothers or sisters, and I'm glad.' She rotated her bony shoulders. 'It means I get all the love.'

Around me, then, were a mother who hated her son, a niece who despised her aunt and a bullying daughter-in-law. Almost everybody was competing for my attention. I felt amused but uneasy. Hua tried to monopolize me with a sexual tyranny which seemed second nature to her. 'I'm a singer,' she said. 'I sing for factory workers. But I'm studying Western opera too.' Her head tilted back in a silent High C. 'You'll come to my home afterwards and I'll sing for you.'

141

Her home, in this confused family, turned out to be that of an absent sister, a divorcee whose daughter was the skinny nymphet Yulong. It was still early when the three of us wandered there along a muddy lane. In their tenth-storey flat the signs of prerogative multiplied—a Hitachi cassette-player, an electric fan, an old Chinese-made piano, central heating—but when I mentioned hot water they laughed.

Over this eyrie presided Hua's mother. She had been half paralysed by a series of strokes a decade before, and she looked even older than her eighty-eight years. Her hand, when I took it, was a cold hook. Her hair was coiled in a grey pigtail, clipped to the back of her head by a huge iron paper-clip, and her nose sank so flat that its bridge completely vanished, and seemed to place her eyes on collision course. Almost immobile, she navigated the tiny rooms by premeditated shuffles, often clutching the shoulder of a daughter or granddaughter in front, and heaved one dead leg after her like a club.

'I can't grip,' she said, staring at her hand in disgust. 'I'm sorry. Often... often I can't speak either. There are days... when I can't say anything at all. My voice goes. But today I can... say things.' The fingers of her live hand circled her throat. 'I should talk Russian with you. I used to teach Russian in... in Harbin. But I can't speak it now. All those consonants... I can't express anything any more...'

She settled watchfully on the sofa, smoking out of a box of two hundred cigarettes, while Hua sat at the piano in her astonishing dress as if this were a concert hall. Her voice was so good, she said, that her academy teacher had hoped she might represent China at international festivals, and she had rehearsed six show arias for over a year. She longed to go abroad; she craved Western dresses and make-up, which she called the good things of life. But the factories had refused to release her.

She turned back the lid of the piano. 'Shall I play "I love you, China"?'

Her voice was a deep contralto: astonishingly strong and sure, harshly expressive, unlovely. It drowned the untuned piano and lingered sentimentally over selected phrases, with swooping portamenti. She sang on and on: Bach's 'Qui Sedes', the 'Habanera' from *Carmen*, Strauss's 'Zueignung'. After each one she would ask: 'You like it? Really? *Really*?' She was exultant that I knew these

142

songs. And all the time her voice grew louder and fuller. She trilled at the bare wall in front of her as if a vast auditorium lay beyond. I wondered what the neighbours thought. And now the cramped bareness of the room and the crippled woman hunched in the dim light had ceased to exist for her. Her face was burning with self-love. She was creating a first-night audience, an ocean of idolaters applauding her arpeggios or legatos, her shimmering white dress, her fierce, momentary, masculine beauty—a clapping Festspielhaus, a cheering Carnegie Hall, a whole Scala. But her shoes on the pedals were caked with suburban mud; one of the piano ivories had gone dead, and her old mother was suddenly, uncontrollably laughing. She rocked up and down on the sofa with short, guttural, mocking coughs.

'When I laugh I can't stop . . . I don't know why.' She massaged her throat. 'I just can't stop.'

Hua took no notice. She launched into *Les Huguenots*. The nymphet came in from the bedroom looking wronged and defiant, and flung out again with a groan. The old woman's laughter guttered into coughing. The last coloratura bars of 'Nobles Seigneurs' rolled dreamily from Hua's lips, and for a few seconds, while the badly-tuned piano's notes survived her own, she went on gazing at the wall plaster. Then: 'You liked it? *Really*? You really did?' She was darkly radiant, touching, preposterous. 'My husband hates my singing.'

The old woman spluttered like a fire-cracker.

Hua said: 'Do you want to see the clothes I'm going to sing in? You'll tell me what you think.' She vanished into the bedroom and reappeared with an olive-green jacket. 'I sing in this for the workers. What do you think?'

I said it was smart, a bit stiff perhaps.

'I hate it. I long to get rid of it. I want to dress as a woman!' She disappeared back into the bedroom.

I sat down by her mother, and in the sudden quiet we started to talk.

The old lady was bitter. Her parents had been educated people from Harbin university in Manchuria, she said. They'd spoken Russian, and she'd become a teacher. But Hua, she implied, had married into a family of village farmers, and that class—in post-

Mao China—carried no dignity on the old lady's lips.

'Do you know what sort of clothes Weigi sent with you? Hua told me. Just men's clothes. Poor quality shirts. Cheap ones.' She cracked into laughter, then abruptly stopped. 'He sent things for his parents, but nothing for anyone else. I suppose he hasn't any money.'

Hua emerged suddenly from the bedroom in a black *cheongsam* garnished with a brooch of artificial pearls. 'How does it look?' She twisted her hips outrageously. Her fingers trickled over her breasts and down her thighs. Her raven hair and black eyes shone above the black curves below. My own gaze was drawn irresistibly down to her broad hips and up again to her cheeks and mouth. 'You really like it? You do?'

Her mother went on ignoring her, trickling cigarette-ash on to the floor with the ceaseless tapping of her liver-spotted hand. Hua vanished again.

'I don't like living here,' the old woman said. 'Yulong is always weeping and complaining. I hate her.' The people she hated were many. Her eldest daughter had divorced, and this had rankled for years. It was proof that the world was rotting. 'Such things weren't done by my generation. That man still comes to visit me at the New Year Festival, I don't know why.' She stared bitterly at the window. 'I hate him.'

Most of the time she sat gazing in front of her, brooding in the narcotic halo of her smoke, but then she would suddenly turn her face to me and I would see a kaleidoscope of slyness, humour and cynicism. These expressions alternated unpredictably, so I lost confidence that I was reading them right, and I did not always understand why she laughed or why the ancient eyes, undivided in their plain of noseless flesh, should sometimes narrow into theatrical distrust. 'I hate Hua.' She lit a new cigarette from another barely started. 'She's got a pile of money but she never shares it.' She added: 'I shouldn't have had daughters.'

In 1938, during the Japanese invasion, she said, she and her husband had retreated with the Nationalists to Chongqing, the temporary capital, and there she'd borne her children. 'My husband died when the youngest was three.'

'In an accident?'

'No. I think he was just tired out with so many children. I think he just gave up.'

'So you brought them up yourself?'

'It was very hard. Those times.'

'You must be proud of them.'

'No,' she said stubbornly, angrily. 'I'm not proud. They're all monkeys. Just a lot of monkeys. They have no education. None of them. They don't know a thing. And none of them is pretty.'

At this moment Hua reappeared in wine-red velvet. 'Yes? No? What do you think?'

'Just monkeys,' the old woman said.

Hua spun round. She drew the cloth in tighter at the waist, letting her hips fall into languorous disequilibrium.

'My children keep going away. They're nearly all gone. I had one son and five daughters, but two died in Chongqing as tiny girls.' The old woman wedged her dwindling cigarette between the fingers of her dead hand, and pulled a sprig of dirty grapes out of her pocket. 'They all leave me on my own. And now Hua wants to leave me too. She wants to go to Beijing—'

Hua was grimacing down at her dress. Its faint shimmer dissatisfied her. 'It spoils everything. Look, look!' She plucked at the material, setting off a rippling sheen. Once or twice she grasped my hand to emphasize some point. Our fingers twined. The old lady was stuffing grapes into her mouth. Hua said: 'Weigi doesn't care about my dresses. Sometimes he's like a peasant.'

'—She just wants to get away to Beijing,' the old woman said. 'A week after Weigi went she realized she was pregnant, so what does she do? She goes to the doctor and gets it aborted. She doesn't want to have a baby here. Not here.' She bolted down the last grapes. 'Not with her old mother.'

They asked me to stay the night with them. The buses had stopped and it was starting to rain in light, scuttling gusts. Hua ushered me into the bedroom. 'You'll sleep here,' she said.

But nobody slept yet. I became the object of an obscure, half-conscious duel. On the dressing-table were Hua's music sheets and cassette-recorder, on which she played me operatic arias. Her cultural isolation was formidable. She owned four classical cassettes, acquired at random: she had never heard of Callas or Sutherland.

Then Yulong barged into the room, and Hua flounced out.

Yulong had changed into a black, bare-shouldered night-dress dotted with pink flowers and her hair was loosed down her back in a glossy torrent. She stretched out on my bed in delectation, coddling a Japanese cassette-player and a pair of earphones. She sang tunelessly to herself.

'Have I taken your bed?' I asked. 'Is this your room?'

'Yes,' she said resentfully. 'But it's Hua's now. It *used* to be mine.' She clipped her earphones gently over my head. I was surprised to hear a tinny Beethoven piano sonata. 'That's what I like,' she said. She edged closer to me, spreading her homework possessively over Hua's dressing-table, and opened an English exercise book. I read: 'Mary likes to go to lessons every week...'

But now Hua was back. 'I'd like you to help me with my French diction.' She lowered the score of 'Claire de lune' on my knee, displacing Yulong's book. 'Listen. Is this right? Listen:

Votre âme est un paysage choisi
Que vont charmants masques...'

The words whispered and fluted through her pouts. 'We can't afford proper English tuition, you see. Weigi's so poor. We've been married seven years, and look!' She extended empty fingers. 'No ring! He can't even afford that. So poor, but always working. Even when he's here he comes home late, and it's work, work, work. We never talk. No time any more. Not any more. *Au calme claire de lune triste et beau...*'

Before the evening was out she had metamorphosed twice more—first into a crimson ball gown and finally into an unbecoming mini-skirt in which she eventually went to bed. She could only have acquired such clothes in the privileged Friendship Stores, but there was no opportunity for her to wear them, except in secret. Hers, I felt, was the narcissism of the emotionally deprived, an enforcement of self.

I slept in the bedroom, alone, while the three women lay in the sitting-room on sofas and camp-beds. Outside, the rain steadied, thickened. I fell into a dream haunted by the wife of Mao Zedong's ex-president, Liu Shaoqi: the Red Guards had attempted to break her by decking her out in the trappings of a grotesque femininity—a necklace of ping-pong balls.

By dawn the verandahs of the blocks of flats opposite were a commotion of hanging birds cages and onions and suspended bedrolls violently swinging. Potted plants were rolling along the balustrades. I woke to rain and wind beating through the mosquito meshing of my window, its flimsy curtains billowing. When I peered into the sitting-room, only Yulong was awake; she lay indolently with her dress thrown up above her thighs, staring at the ceiling. Half an hour later Hua lumbered out of her camp-bed. The glow of the night before had gone. She looked heavy and ordinary.

The old woman was sitting at the piano. 'Years ago I had another piano,' she said, 'better than this one. I bought it by scraping together a few *kwai* from my salary over years. But it was smashed in the Cultural Revolution, so my children wasted money by buying me this one.' Her face had softened. She lifted her dead hand fruitlessly onto the keys. 'Wasted.'

For all I knew, she was proud of her children, or even loved them.

Martha Gellhorn
Cuba Revisited

The first morning in Havana, I stood by the sea-wall on the Malecon, feeling weepy with homesickness for this city. Like the exile returned; and ridiculous. I left Cuba forty-one years ago, never missed it and barely remembered it. A long amnesia, forgetting the light, the colour of the sea and sky, the people, the charm of the place.

The Malecon is a nineteenth-century jewel and joke. Above their arcade, the mini-mansions rise three storeys, each house exuberantly different from the next: windows garlanded with plaster roses, Moorish pointy windows of stained glass, caryatids, ornate ironwork balconies, huge nail-studded carved doors. The paint on the stone buildings is faded to pastel, a ghostly reminder of former brilliance: pink trimmed with purple, blue with yellow, green with cobalt. Whoever lived here, when Cuba was my home from 1939 to May 1944, had departed: fluttering laundry suggested that their rich private houses were now multiple dwellings.

A delightful little black kid bounced out of somewhere, in spotless white shirt and royal blue shorts. He smiled up at me with a look of true love and undying trust. '*Rusa?*' he asked. I was mortally offended. Russian women of a certain age, seen in Moscow, had bodies like tanks and legs like tree trunks.

'No,' I said crossly, '*Americana.*' I should have said '*Norteamericana.*' South of the US border, people do not accept Americans' exclusive ownership of the continent.

The loving smile did not change. '*Da me chicle,*' he said. Give me chewing-gum. Cuba does not manufacture chewing-gum. In due course, I gathered that kids admire gum chewing as seen in American movies, still the most popular.

The Prado is a stylish old street with a wide central promenade: live oak trees, big light globes on wrought iron lamp-posts, benches. The benches were occupied by old women knitting and gossiping, old men reading papers and gossiping, poor people by our standards, looking comfortable and content. Now in the lunch-hour, groups of school children—from gleaming black to golden blonde—romped about the promenade, healthy, merry and as clean as if emerged from a washing-machine. The little ones wear a uniform of maroon shorts or mini-skirts, short-sleeved white shirts and a light blue neckerchief; the secondary school children wear canary yellow long pants or mini-skirts and a red neckerchief. The neckerchiefs show that they are Pioneers, blue for the babies, like Cubs and Scouts in my childhood.

Before, street boys would have drifted around here, selling lottery tickets or papers, collecting cigarette butts, offering to shine shoes, begging. They were funny and talkative, barefoot, dressed in dirty scraps, thin faces, thin bodies, nobody's concern. They did not attend school. Nor were they Afro-Cubans.

I had never thought of Cubans as blacks, and could only remember Juan, our pale mulatto chauffeur. Eventually I got that sorted out. A form of apartheid prevailed in central Havana, I don't know whether by edict or by landlords' decision not to rent to blacks. Presumably they could not get work either, unless as servants. But of course there were blacks in Cuba as everywhere else in the Caribbean, descendants of African slaves imported for the sugar-cane plantations. In my day, they must still have been concentrated in the eastern provinces, still cutting cane. Roughly one third of Cubans are of African or mixed blood, two thirds Caucasian.

Calle Obispo, formerly my beat for household supplies, had been turned into a pedestrian street. At one of the cross streets I saw the only cops I noticed in Havana, trying to disentangle a jam of trucks, motorcycles and hooting cars. The shops were a surprise: bikinis and cosmetics, fancy shoes, jewellery, a gift shop with china and glass ornaments. Not high fashion, but frivolous. And many bookstores, a real novelty; I remembered none. And a neighbourhood store-front clinic.

Faces looked remarkably cheerful, unlike most city faces, and the street was enveloped in babble and laughter. Men met women, kissed them on the cheek, talked, moved on. That public friendly cheek-kissing astonished me; I had never seen it in a Latin American country, and never here in my day. Most of the women wore trousers made of a stretch material called, I think, crimplene; and most women were amply built. Their form-hugging pants were lavender, scarlet, emerald green, yellow, topped by blouses of flowered nylon. The young, boys and girls, wore jeans and T-shirts. T-shirts printed with Mickey Mouse, a big heart and LUV, UNIVERSITY OF MICHIGAN. Presents from relatives in the US? Grown men wore proper trousers of lightweight grey or tan material and white shirts. These people were much better dressed than average Cubans before, and much better nourished.

At the top of this street, Salomon, a very small tubercular man of no definite age but great vitality, sold lottery tickets. Salomon was a communist and lived with the certainty of a glorious communist future, when everyone would eat a lot and earn their keep by useful work. I remembered him out of nowhere, and hoped with all my heart that he lived to see his dream come true, but doubted it; Salomon didn't look then as if he had the necessary fifteen years left.

I was staying at the Hotel Deauville, a post-war, pre-Revolución blight on the Malecon. It is a plum-coloured cement Bauhaus-style tower. I came to dote on the hideous Deauville because of the staff, jokey and friendly with each other and the guests. The Deauville is classed as three-star, not suitable for rich dollar tourists. My room with bath cost $26. Like all tourist hotels, the Deauville has its own Duty-Free Shop. Tourists of every nationality pay for everything in US dollars. You are given your change, down to nickels and dimes, in American money. For practical purposes one dollar equals one Cuban peso, a parallel economy for natives and tourists. President Reagan has tightened the permanent US economic embargo to include people. Cuba is off limits to American tourists. But that year, 1985, 200,000 capitalist tourists, from Canada, Europe, Mexico, South America, uninterested in or undaunted by communism, had caught on to the idea of the cheapest Caribbean holiday.

At the Deauville, I had my first view of the amusing and economical national mini-skirt: above-the-knee uniform for women employees, different colours for different occupations. And was also plunged into the national custom of calling everyone by first names, beginning with Fidel who is called nothing else. I was rather testy, to start, hearing 'Marta' from one and all and the intimate *tu* instead of *usted*, a disappearing formality. But I quickly adjusted and was soon addressing strangers as *compañero* or *compañera*. You cannot say comrad (American) or comraid (British) without feeling silly, but *compañero* has the cosy sound of companion.

I wanted to be on my way. I had not come to Cuba to study communism but to snorkel. At the Cuban Embassy in London, I found some tourist bumf, describing a new glamorous hotel at

Puerto Escondido, which included the magic word, snorkelling. I was going to Nicaragua, serious business, and meant to treat myself *en route* to two weeks mainly in the lovely turquoise shallows off the Cuban coast. A couple of days in Havana, to retrace my distant past; then sun, snorkelling, thrillers, rum drinks: my winter holiday.

You can go anywhere you want in Cuba, except to the American naval base at Guantanamo on the eastern tip of the island—an extraordinary piece of property which most foreigners do not know is held and operated by the United States. You can hire, with or without driver, a small Russian Lada sedan belonging to INTUR, the Ministry of Tourism. The Lada is as tough as a Land Rover, Third World model, with iron-hard upholstery and, judging by sensation, no springs. I asked INTUR for a car with driver, intending to look over the hotel at Puerto Escondido, the goal of my Cuban trip.

The driver, rightly named Amable, said that Puerto Escondido was half an hour from Havana; my introduction to Cuban optimism. 'No problem' might be the national motto; it is the one English phrase everyone can say. We drove through the tunnel under Havana harbour, new to me, and along the superhighway, adorned with billboards, very depressing: progress. The billboards are exhortations, not advertisements. A light bulb, with ENERGÍA in huge letters and a plea to save it. A bag of coins and a single-stroke dollar sign for the peso, recommending the public to bank their money at two-and-a-half percent interest. Many patriotic billboards: 'WE WOULD DIE BEFORE WE GIVE UP OUR PRINCIPLES.' Two hours from Havana found us bumping on a mud road through lush jungle scenery. A solitary soldier stopped us where the track ended. Puerto Escondido was not finished; it would be ready next year. More Cuban optimism. The soldier suggested a tourist resort at Jibacoa further on.

Amable managed to find Jibacoa—small brick houses, newly landscaped—and a bar and a restaurant. At the bar two Canadian girls, secretaries from Toronto who had arrived yesterday, were full of enthusiasm and information. They had a nice double room; the food was 'interesting'; rape was punished by shooting; Cubans were lovely people; and they looked forward to a night out at the Tropicana, Havana's answer to the Paris Lido. Goody, but what about snorkelling? A man in a wet-suit was coming up from the beach; the girls said he was Luis, in charge of water sports. Luis guaranteed that the snorkelling was fine and we both stared to the north where clouds like solid black smoke spread over the sky.

'*Un norte?*' I asked with dismay. I remembered only perfect winter weather.

'Yes, come back in a few days when it is passed.'

But it did not pass.

By morning, the sea was greenish black, matching the black sky. Waves smashed across the Malecon, closed to traffic, and drove sand and pebbles up the side streets. The wind was at gale force; it rained. A gigantic storm and worsening. I was cold and slumped into travel despair, an acute form of boredom. With no enthusiasm, I arranged to fill time, meeting people and seeing sights, until the storm ended.

T he distinguished Afro-Cuban poet and I talked in the crowded lobby of the Hotel Nacional, an old four-star hotel. Suddenly she made a sound of disgust and said, 'I hate that stupid out-of-date stuff.' She spoke perfect American. The object of her disgust was a wedding party: bride in white with veil, groom in tuxedo, flower girls, bridesmaids, beaming parents and guests, headed for the wedding reception. I was pleased that the out-of-date could be freely practised by those who wanted it.

I had an important question to ask her but was very unsure of my ground. 'Something puzzles me,' I said. 'Fidel made a decree or whatever, as soon as the Revolución started, forbidding racism. I mean, he said it was over; there wouldn't be any more. And there isn't. Surely that is amazing?' It sure is. Even more amazing, it seems to work.

'Of course you can't change people's prejudices by law; you can't change what they feel in their hearts. But you can make any racist acts illegal and punish them. We hope that as we live together more and know each other better as human beings, the prejudices will disappear.'

We had no racist problem, she and I, just the wrong vibes. She thought me too light; I thought her too heavy.

I was interested in how writers earned their livings. Very few of the 600 members of the Writers' Union can live by books alone, like us. There are many publishing houses, state-owned but managed by distinct staffs for a varied public. You submit your manuscript; if accepted, you get sixty percent of the retail price of the first edition, whether the books are sold or not; then forty percent of further editions. Cubans love poetry, so poets abound and are widely read.

Feeling dull but dutiful, I went to look at Alamar—a big housing estate, white rectangular factories for living spread over the green land off the highway outside Havana.

'Marta, why do you say you do not like such a place? I have friends there. They have a very nice apartment.' Today's driver, called Achun, part Chinese, had served in Angola. He said he was truly sorry for those Africans; they were a hundred years behind Cuba.

I asked, 'How big?'

'Two bedrooms, three, four, depending on the number of the family.'

I told him about vandalism as we know it. Achun was dumbfounded.

'Why would people ruin their own homes?'

Close-up, Alamar was not bad; no graffiti on the white walls, no broken windows—on the contrary, shined and curtained—a skimpy fringe of flowers around each building, and thin new trees. The buildings are four storeys high, widely separated by lawn.

'The cinema is behind those buildings,' Achun said.

Here the bus stopped; a few weary people were piling out. The forty-minute ride to and from Havana in the always overcrowded buses has to be a trial. (Havana is about to get a needed metro system.) This central shopping area reduced me to instant gloom. I thought at first it was filthy. The impression of grime was not due to dirt but to unpainted cement. Of course Cuba is poor and needs many things more vital than paint, yet it distresses me that these people, who adore bright colour, must be denied it.

The bookstore was attractive because of the gaudy book covers. A soldier and a child were the only customers in the middle of a chilly grey weekday afternoon. A corner of the room had been set aside for children's books. The paper is coarse, the covers thin, but books cost from forty-five to seventy-five cents.

'Every year we have a quota,' said the middle-aged saleslady. 'And every year we exceed it.'

'How can you have a quota? You can't force people to buy books, can you?'

'Oh no, it is not like that. Every year we are sent a quota of books and every year we must ask for more, because they are sold. All ages buy books. Fidel said "Everything basic to the people must be cheap. Books are basic."'

'What is most popular?'

'Detectives and romantic novels.'

I drove around Havana, sightseeing, half-curious, and wholly sick of the miserable weather. I chatted in the dingy main market where the toy counter and meat and poultry counter were the busiest. I asked about fares at the jammed railroad station, learning that the best fast train to the other end of the island costs $10.50. I cruised through the stylish section of Vedado with the big hotels, airline offices, shops, restaurants, movies and the large Edwardian houses. I peered at the Miramar mansions. The rich departed Cubans left a bountiful gift to the Revolución, all their grand homes and classy apartment buildings. The big houses are clinics, kindergartens, clubs for trade unions, and whatever has no public use is portioned off for private living space.

Then I decided I needed some action and barged into a secondary school, announcing that I was a foreign journalist and would like to sit in on a class and see how they taught their students. This caused extreme confusion. (As it probably would if I barged into the Chepstow comprehensive.) The school sent me to the local Poder Popular office where I met the very cornerstone of bureaucracy: the woman at the door. Behind a desk/table/counter in every government office is a woman, preferably middle-aged; her job is to keep people out. Poder Popular sent me to the Ministry of Education. There the woman at the door said that Public Relations at INTUR, the Ministry of Tourism, must write to Public Relations at the Ministry of Education. I reported this to INTUR, decrying it as an absurd fuss about nothing. INTUR promised that a school visit would be arranged. 'Be patient, Marta,' said Rosa, an INTUR director. 'Everything is done through organizations here.'

To their credit, the Ministry of Education sent me to a very modest school in a poor suburb. The Secondary School of the Martyrs of Guanabacoa. The driver could not find it. We were twenty minutes late. I got out of the Lada and saw school kids in canary yellow lined up along the path to the front door and a greeting committee of adults. I apologized unhappily for keeping everyone waiting and walked past the honour guard, feeling absurd. Instead of a twenty-one-gun salute, I got a shouted slogan. On the school steps a little Afro-Cuban girl stepped from the ranks, shouted something and behind her the official chorus shouted an answer. This went on for several minutes but I could not decipher a single shouted word. I was then presented with a sheaf of gladioli and lilies in cellophane and began to feel as if I were the Queen Mother.

The man in charge, whose position I never understood, presented the school principal, a large shy Afro-Cuban woman in dark blue crimplene trousers and white blouse. I was shown the school bulletin board with its smiling photographs of the 'martyrs'— handsome girls and boys, not much older than the children here, killed by Batista's police for their clandestine work in the Revolución. Asked what I would like to visit, I said the English class. The school was unpainted cement inside and out, built on the cheap in 1979.

The English teacher was nervous and nice and desperately eager for his class to perform well. Each child read aloud a sentence from their textbook, dealing with Millie's birthday party. Offhand, I could not think of a deadlier subject. '"Toothbrush" and "toothpaste"' (Millie's birthday presents!) 'are very hard for them to say; also "room."' His own accent was odd; the kids were choked with stage fright, rivalling mine.

A bell blessedly rang. Here, the children stay in one room, the teachers move. It was the history hour in another classroom. The children—the top form, aged fifteen—rose to their feet and shouted a slogan, led by the elected class prefect who was always a girl. Hard to understand, but it sounded like promising Fidel to study and be worthy of the Revolución. Each class devised its own slogan, a new one every month, and five times a day, at the start of their class periods, they shouted this at the teacher. The history teacher was a thin intense shabbily-dressed young man who described the sugar

157

crisis of 1921, when prices fell and the people suffered despair and starvation though their work had enriched the bourgeoisie and the American capitalists. I wanted to say that American workers suffered too in times of depression and unemployment, but didn't feel that speech-making was part of my new role.

Biology was taught by a stout mulata compañera in lavender pants, and taught brilliantly. The subject for the day was the renal system, up to that moment a total mystery to me. All the kids raised their hands, competing to answer. This subject—their bodies—clearly interested them much more than history or English. After class, the teacher explained that by the end of the term they would have studied the sexual organs, the nine months of pregnancy and birth. To finish, they would discuss 'the human couple, and the need for them to be equals and share the same ideals and interests.' She showed me their laboratory, a small room with a few bunsen burners. Her only teaching-aid was a plaster human torso, open at the front, with all the brightly-coloured alarming organs in place.

There were 579 children, more caucasian than Afro-Cuban, and fifty teachers, about equally divided as to colour and sex. School is compulsory through the ninth grade, age fifteen. After that, children can choose to continue for three years in pre-university studies or technical schools, according to their grades. At eighteen, the boys do military service, but university students are exempt since Cuba needs all the professionals it can train.

Snacks had been laid out in the principal's office. I looked at these poorly-dressed men and women and grieved to think of them chipping in for this party. They were so excited about me because the school had never received a visitor before, no Cuban personage, let alone a foreigner. They spoke of their students with pride; it must feel good to teach such lively and willing children. Never mind that they had no library, no workshop, no gym, no proper laboratory in this bleak building. The staff invented substitutes and got on with the job. I asked to meet the Head Prefect, elected by her peers. She was a lovely tall slim girl, almost inaudible from shyness, blonde with grey eyes. She said that the entire school went on two camping weekends a year and for a week to Varadero, Cuba's famous beach. The top student (this girl) joined all the other secondary school top-graders for a whole summer month at Varadero. Fun and sport as a reward for work. I remember winning a school prize, a richly-bound uninteresting book.

I liked everyone and told them they had a fine school, meaning it, and thanked them for the visit. In the Lada, returning to Havana, I gave my character a shake and became again a normal, not a Very Important, person.

That night, on the thirteenth floor of the Deauville, I listened to the howling wind. The storm had renewed itself with spiteful vigour and would never end. Snorkelling was a dead dream. I gave up. I had no choice; there was nothing left to do except cramp myself into a Lada, drive around the country and get a general idea of how communism works in Cuba.

For transport on this journey to the Cuban hinterland, I went to Rosa at INTUR, my sole contact with the Cuban government. She is small, brunette, very pretty, very bright and kind and patient above and beyond the call of duty. My manners to her were abominable and in no way deserved. I was rudely determined that nobody was going to show or tell me anything; I would see and question for myself. Rosa assigned Rafael as my driver. Rafael is grey-haired, mid-forties, overweight, racked by a cigarette cough, intelligent, good and a charmer. We drank a lot of delicious ice-cold Cuban beer and he laughed at my disrespectful jokes.

Rafael's story is one example of how the Revolución has changed lives. His wife works as an accountant in some ministry. Rafael is an official of the drivers' trade union, bargaining on his members' behalf with another ministry. 'Whoever gets home first cooks the dinner.' One son is reading English at Havana University. Another, having failed his exams, is doing military service and expects a place in medical school afterwards. Rafael pays thirty-five dollars monthly rent for an apartment in Vedado, formerly the chic section of Havana, and soon will own it. Rents pile up like down payments year after year, until the sale price of the flat is reached, whereupon bingo, you become an old-fashioned capitalist owner. Mrs Thatcher's vision of a home-owners' society coming true in communist Cuba.

Rafael left me strictly alone whenever we stopped. I stayed in several sumptuous hotels; these were the Mafia's legacy to Cuban tourism, built with Mafia money because they included casinos, now closed. It was all new to me; I had never bothered to travel in Cuba when I lived here and had no sense of its size—730 miles long by an average of fifty miles wide—or of the variety of the towns and the landscape. We drove without any previously arranged plan—wherever I felt like going—and covered 1,500 miles in the back-breaking Lada, a partial look at about a third of the country. Our first stop was Trinidad.

Trinidad is a beauty; Cubans are very proud of it. It is an unspoiled colonial town, most of it late eighteenth- and early nineteenth-century, but inhabited from the sixteenth century. The streets are cobbled, the houses one storey high, with vast, handsome wood doors, wide enough for a carriage, and bowed iron grille-work on the front windows. Every house is painted, and paint makes the difference—pale green, pink, blue, yellow. The Cathedral, at the top of the town, is yellow trimmed in white, and fronts a flowery square that descends in steps to the houses.

The Museo Historico was the home of a nineteenth-century sugar baron. The enchanting girl in charge, aged around twenty, with blonde hair in a pony tail, wore the museum uniform, immaculate white shirt, dark blue jacket and mini-skirt. 'He had thirty slaves,' she said. *'Thirty.* They lived in that one big room at the back.' The idea of slaves horrified her. Earlier, when she had collected my entry centavos, she said, 'Cuba was under Spanish domination for three centuries, until 1899. After that, it was under American domination until 1959.' It had sounded pat and off-putting, straight Party line, until I thought it over and decided it was true, no matter how it sounded.

The US actually ruled Cuba twice, and the Marines had been around in the usual Monroe Doctrine way. Until 1934, the United States government had the right by law to interfere in internal Cuban affairs. But American domination was mainly felt through its support of whatever useless Cuban government protected American investments. In my time, no one ever talked politics or bothered to notice which gang was in office and robbing the till. I cannot remember any elections, though I think the government did change, perhaps by palace coup. One day driving in to Havana, I heard shooting and Salomon or the street boys advised me to settle in the Floridita and drink frozen daiquiris until it was over; the noise was farther down towards the harbour. This was taken lightly as a joke:

160

who cared which crooks got in, the results would be the same. The poor would stay poor; the rich would stay rich; a different bunch of politicians would grow richer. After World War Two, during the Batista dictatorship, apart from the standard horrors of such rule—arrest, torture, executions—corruption must have been out of control, thanks to Batista's faithful friends, the Mafia.

At the Museo Romantico, said to be the former home of a Count, a bunch of noisy young people was clattering up the stairs to the salons and bedrooms. In the hall, a white-garbed nun waited, saying that she had seen it before. 'If you have lived in Spain,' said the little dark Spanish nun, 'there is nothing to look at in this country.' She seemed about thirty years old and had a sharp, severe face. She had come to Trinidad from Cienfuegos with the young people to attend the cathedral wedding of two of them, tomorrow. Her order has two houses, in Cienfuegos and Havana. There are eight Spanish, three Mexican and three Cuban nuns in all.

'People must be very brave to go to Mass,' she told me. 'We do not go out in the street with the young for fear of compromising them. There is much fear.'

'Fear? You mean fear of prison, fear for their lives?'

'No, no,' she said impatiently. 'Fear of losing their jobs or not getting a good one, if they are seen to be practising Catholics.' Mass is celebrated here in the Cathedral and in another church 'down there,' twice on Sundays and that is all. She felt outraged by this. 'No, nuns are not molested in any way but we are not allowed to do our pastoral work in the streets.' As far as I was concerned, that was great: I don't want anyone of any religion, secular or spiritual, haranguing me in the streets. 'Still, people do talk to us.'

I pointed out that she had come here with these young people, a whole band of them, to take part in a church wedding.

'Yes, they are very loyal,' she said.

The stern Afro-Cuban museum lady, the ticket collector, stared at us with plain dislike. The nun remarked on it. 'She does not want me to talk to you.' Even so, it did not stop the nun from talking to me, an obvious foreigner.

Cuba is awash with museums. Museums for everything, past and present. The museums are scantily furnished—no great art treasures—and are visited with interest by all kinds of Cubans, young and old. I don't think I've ever raced through so many anywhere and I think I understand them. This is consciousness-raising on a national scale. The mass of Cubans had no education and no real sense of identity. Being Cuban meant being somebody else's underling, a subordinate people. I knew a few upper-class Cuban sportsmen; they spoke perfect English, had been educated abroad, and were considered honorary Americans or Europeans, not in words, nor even in thought, but instinctively: they were felt to be too superior to be Cubans. Now, through these innumerable museums, Cubans are being shown their history, how their ruling class lived and how the people lived, the revolts against Spanish 'domination', and everything about the Revolución. They are being told that they have been here a long time: they are a nation and they can be proud to be Cubans.

Between Trinidad and Sancti Spiritus, the country looked like Africa: hump-backed, bony cattle, like Masai cattle; palms and ceibas, the handsomer Cuban form of the African baobab tree; jungle-green hills; brown plains; but where were we going to sleep? We had been turned away at two hotels, full up with Cubans, who travel joyfully and constantly. We set out again, hunting for rooms.

Suddenly loud horns and sirens. Motorcycle cops pushed the traffic to the roadside. Ten first-class buses flashed past, filled with excited kids, singing, shouting, waving. 'Pioneers,' Rafael said. They were primary school children, the baby Pioneers of the light-blue neckerchief. 'They are going to camp at Ismaela. They go for a week with their teachers and continue with their lessons.'

Not that bunch, far too elated for lessons.

'Fidel started the idea of camping,' Rafael went on. 'Nobody in Cuba ever did that, live in a tent, cook over a fire. Now everybody does it. It is very popular.' Cubans have two paid vacations a year, two weeks each, and alternate full weekends. Besides camping, many new beach resorts dot the coasts. These resorts are simple, rudimentary—I don't want to give the impression of places like luscious photos in travel brochures—and so inexpensive that most Cubans must be able to afford them. And there are town parks with children's playgrounds, swimming pools, sports grounds. I like the government's decision in favour of pleasure: Cuba's Revolución is not puritanical. Outlawing drugs, gambling and prostitution eradicated crime as big business, hardly a bad idea. But there remain the delicious beer and rum, flowing freely, and cigarettes and cigars, since Cubans haven't yet heard of the horrors of smoking. But I think that the main cause of a different, open, pleasurable life-style is the change in women. The old Hispanic and Catholic custom of the women at home—isolated, the daughter guarded, the stiffness of that relation between men and women—is truly gone. Women are on their own at work, feeling equal to men, and showing this new confidence. Girls are educated equally with boys and chaperonage is dead. There is a feeling that men and women, girls and boys are having a good time together, in a way unknown before.

Bayamo, said the tourist map, offered historical sights; the church where the national anthem was first sung and other episodes of heroism against the Spanish overlords. I was not interested; I was interested in food. The food is ghastly, apart from breakfast. If Cuba means to earn millions of tourist dollars, it will have to make a culinary Revolución. On a corner of the main square, I saw an ice-cream parlour and bought a huge helping of delicious chocolate ice-cream.

I was enjoying this feast at an outside table when a boy came up, said his name was Pépé, shook hands, sat down and asked my name and where I came from. I thought he was eighteen; he was twenty-four, good-looking with light brown hair, blue eyes and a summery smile. He wanted to buy a pack of my cigarettes, Kools from a hotel Duty-Free; I said he could share mine. He wanted to see what a dollar looked like; I showed him. He wanted to know the price of cigarettes, gas lighters, dark glasses and trousers in England. He then brought out of his wallet a small colour print of a beautiful little bejewelled and bedecked doll, the Virgen de la Caridad de Cobre, patron of Cuba. He handed me this as if he were giving me a family photo.

A young Afro-Cuban in a dark business suit lurked nearby, listening. I said, 'Why do you stand there with a look of suspicion? Sit with us.' His presence at first annoyed Pépé, then he ignored the newcomer.

Pépé wished to talk about religion, absolutely not my subject.

'Are you a believer? Do you go to Mass? Do you believe in Jesus Christ?' By now we had another member of the seminar—an older Afro-Cuban—and slowly the waitresses pulled up chairs around our table.

Hoping to bring an end to this topic, I said, 'In our country, people are Protestants.' Easy misinformation.

'What religion is that?' said Pépé. *'Protestante?'*

'They are not loyal to the Pope,' the older Afro-Cuban said.

'But you believe?' Pépé insisted.

As an untroubled unbeliever, I could not go into a long thing about Jesus as a man and a teacher, so I said, *'De vez en cuando'*—which comes out as 'sometimes' and satisfied Pépé.

'There are churches in Bayamo?' I asked.

'Four,' they said in unison.

'People go to Mass?'

In unison, 'Yes.'

'They have trouble if they go to Mass?'

Again in unison, 'No.'

'I want to see a capitalist country,' Pépé said. 'I want to go to France. I met some Frenchmen here.'

'You want to leave?' the business suit asked, scandalized.

'No, not leave,' Pépé said. 'Visit. To see. But they will never give me a passport. Only to the socialist countries.'

The older Afro-Cuban said, 'Artists can go. Musicians, people like that.'

I didn't want Pépé to cherish hopeless golden dreams and could imagine the Frenchmen talking about France as the French do. 'You know, Pépé, everything is not perfect in our capitalist countries. We are not all rich and happy. We have great unemployment. There is also much crime.'

'There is no crime here,' said both Pépé and the business suit.

'No unemployment,' said the others.

Cubans believe that there is no crime in Cuba. They feel safe in their homes and on their streets. You see very small unaccompanied children going about their business in Havana, and women walking alone at night wherever they wish to go. No one fears mugging. Rape is too unimaginable to think about. But of course there are crimes since there are gaols for common criminals.

We were now talking about education and the main members of the seminar, Pépé and the business suit, agreed that education was very good here. 'And free,' Pépé added, 'everything is free, even universities.'

Business suit, who was a serious young man employed as health inspector for hotel and restaurant kitchens, now departed: end of the lunch-hour. The rest of the seminar drifted back to work.

Pépé, it developed, was a night-watchman at a cement factory, scarcely a demanding job, and had only completed two years of secondary school. I began to realize that he was twenty-four going on sixteen, but no less sweet and interesting for that. 'Do people have servants in England? Not here, there are no servants here. Could I come to England and be your servant, chauffeur or something? I wouldn't want any money.' How he longed to see the mysterious capitalist world. 'If I was going about in France, just looking, doing nothing wrong, would they give me difficulties?' Cuban police are notably absent everywhere, and as Pépé had talked openly in front of his compatriots, strangers to him, he must have picked up some ominous news about police in the free world.

By now we were great friends and he said confidentially, 'I don't like dark girls.' I thought: gentlemen prefer blondes. But no. 'I only like girls with light skin.' He now produced two photographs from his wallet, almost identical Caucasian Cubans with a lot of brunette hair.

'Two *novias*, Pépé, isn't that one too many?'

He grinned, then said in a low voice, 'I have a brother who is a racist. He told me.'

I imagined an older brother and said, 'There is nothing much he can do about it, is there? You don't have to marry a dark girl. You aren't obliged to make any friends you don't want, are you?'

'No. Clearly no.'

'Well then. How old is your brother?' I disliked this tedious dummy brother, a bad example for young Pépé, and remembered the Afro-Cuban poet and the prejudices of the heart.

'Thirteen,' said Pépé. I shouted with laughter. At first he was bewildered; racism is no joke, an offence in law; then gradually he understood and the summery smile appeared.

165

I wandered into the square: live oaks, Ali Baba flower jars, benches of bright patterned tile, a design in the paving bricks— the Cubans had luck, architecturally, to be colonized by Spain. No sign of Rafael, so I sat on a bench in the shade, and an elderly lady sat beside me. She wore a neat, rather prissy cotton dress and a hat, unheard-of, a proper lady's hat; I felt she should have gloves. She said her husband had gone to the 'office' to speak about their pension. 'We are retired. Our pension is fifty-two pesos monthly. What can you do with that? Some people get seventy pesos. If you have children, they could help. Or else you must do work at home, little work.' She was very worried and indignant. 'Ridiculous,' she said. 'Impossible. I hope they listen to my husband.'

In the car I asked Rafael about this. He said that pensions depended on how long you had worked. His mother got sixty pesos a month, from her dead father's pension. I pointed out that his brother lived in the same village and would help her and so would he. 'Surely it is a bad system, Rafael, if people must depend on their children for money in their old age. It would be a reason to have as many children as possible.'

'But people do not want many children; they want few and to give them more. People do not have big families now. Every woman, girl, can get birth control assistance, whether married or not. There is no sense in big families.'

I abandoned pensions.

'Stop, Rafael. I want to take a photo.' This was a picture of rural poverty. Everywhere, in the villages, along the roads, the sign of new private prosperity was paint. If they could afford no more, people painted their door a brilliant colour and painted a band to outline their windows. Here three small, crumbling, unpainted wood houses stood on bare treeless ground in the middle of nowhere. They were typical peasants' homes; painted, beflowered, they would be picturesque cottages. They are box-shape, one room wide, with a porch on wood pillars. If very poor, the roof is palm thatch, less poor, it is corrugated tin. I chose the worst of the three.

'Did you see that?' Rafael pointed.

I had not. Each of the houses had a TV aerial.

'Marta,' Rafael said, 'have you seen anyone without shoes?'

'No.'

'You say everyone is too fat. When you lived here, how did the *campesinos* look?'

How did the *campesinos*, the peasants, look; how did everyone look? They looked abjectly poor or just everyday poor. Except for us, the narrow top layer. You could live in princely comfort on very little money in Cuba.

There was a farmhouse, barely visible beyond our land, east of the driveway. It was a bit larger than these houses, with peeling paint. The farmer was a bone-thin, unsmiling man; he kept chickens. If I saw him I said good morning. That is all I knew about him; I don't even know if the cook bought eggs there. The village below our place was a small cluster of houses like these; I knew nothing about the village except that it had a post office. The children waved when I drove by, I waved back, lots of smiles. They were in rags, barefoot, and everyone was unnaturally thin.

I did not say to myself: it isn't my country, what can I do? I didn't think about Cuba at all. Everything I cared about with passion was happening in Europe. I listened to the radio, bought American newspapers in Havana, waited anxiously for letters from abroad. I wrote books, and the minute I could break free, I went back to the real world, the world at war. Rafael had asked the wrong question. The right question would be: who looked at the *campesinos*? Who cared? Nobody, as far as I knew; including me.

'I know, Rafael. They were hungry and miserable.'

'Those people own their houses and prefer to stay there, not move themselves to a new co-operative building which is like an apartment block.'

'So would I.'

'Good, if they prefer television to making their houses beautiful, that is their business. When they get more money, maybe they will improve their homes. My mama lives in a house like that. I was born in a house like that. Clearly it is better repaired.'

'**W**hat is that thing, Rafael?'

He slowed the car.

'Back there, a sort of monument.'

It looked like a little cement obelisk, standing by the empty road among the hills, not a house in sight. I got out to read the inscription. MARTYR OF THE REVOLUCIÓN. TEACHER. KILLED IN 1960. All those who were killed in the years of rebellion against Batista are called Martyrs of the Revolución.

'How can this be, Rafael? The Revolución won in 1959.'

'He would have been a volunteer teacher in the literacy campaign. Killed by the *campesinos* who had crazy ideas, maybe from propaganda by the priests. The *campesinos* thought the literacy campaign would take their daughters away and ruin them. Many young volunteers were killed at that time. It is very sad, very stupid.'

We were on a winding road, in pleasing green tree-covered hill country, that led down to a hotel by the sea. This hotel was post-Revolución, built for Cubans and lesser tourists. The site, on a bay surrounded by mountains, was lovely and the architects merit high marks. Otherwise, it had little to recommend it. The manager was always absent at Party meetings. They ran out of bread, and never had butter; when I ate the fish, I knew I was doomed. The bath towels had been washed to fragility. The front fell off the unwanted air-conditioning and barely missed my Russian vodka, the only booze I had left.

I settled grumpily at the snack bar which had nothing to offer except Cuban soft drinks, far too sweet, and had a heart-to-heart with the Afro-Cuban lady in charge. We shouted at each other over the din of the whiney-sugary anti-music that Cubans love. She was thirty with three children, divorced. The oldest, aged fourteen, was at school in Havana with his father, the others at school here. 'Oh compañera, life has changed much, much. We have things we never had before. Furniture, frigidaire, television, and the right to work which women never had. We work, we have our own money.' And the pay? 'Women are paid equal to men, *igual, igual.*'

At lunch, a group of Polish tourists murmured to each other in whisper voices. They were the only non-capitalist tourists I saw. They looked bemused and pitiful, dressed in shades of grey, a non-colour, with grey skin. Lunch finished, their guide-nanny, a young, pretty Cuban woman, came to talk to them in Polish, no doubt the day's agenda; she raised a timid laugh. She had well cut and well set black shoulder-length hair and wore tight yellow pants, a brilliant poncho, big gold loop ear-rings, and lots of make-up. What on earth could these sad Poles think of communism, Cuban-style?

A man was watching TV in the hall; Fidel on the box. At this time, Fidel had been giving one of his marathon interviews to the *Washington Post* and it was broadcast like a serial on TV. The front desk receptionist beckoned to me. 'You should talk to him, Marta, the doctor on horseback.'

A fair-haired young man, with specs and a beard, tweed jacket, jeans, was telephoning. I waited and latched on to him. He had just finished his medical training, six years, and was now stationed in the mountains. 'They asked for volunteers, for two years. It is very dynamic work.' He lives alone in the Sierra Maestra and visits patients on horseback if they cannot come to his *consultorio*, a room in his three-room house. He is in charge of 117 families. This is a new idea, a doctor who stays in close touch with the same families over years, urban as well as rural preventive medicine. 'The main complaint is high blood pressure; maybe too much salt, maybe over-weight. There is no tuberculosis, no cancer, no diabetes. Sometimes parasites. My work is to teach hygiene.' The people raise coffee and cattle in the mountains. The children go to primary school up there and come down to rural boarding schools for secondary education. I had seen a few of these, large buildings planted in the fields.

'Older women had as many as twelve children. Now women have two or three at most. There is every form of birth control, it is the physician's task to find what is best for each woman.'

'Don't you think the women are much too fat?'

'Yes, but it is the custom of the country and men like women to be fat. It is slow education, to teach them to eat less starch and sweets. They enjoy eating; you know, to be fat here was a sign of wealth. No, I am not lonely. I have many books and I like the people very much.'

Fidel announced somewhere, sometime, that he wished Cuba to be 'the greatest medical power in the world.' I dislike the form of words but applaud the ambition. The rule-of-thumb gauge of public health is the nation's infant mortality rate. I am using the figures given in the World Health Organisation Statistics Annual for 1985. These figures are their estimates, arguably more accurate than the figures supplied by the nations concerned, and more recent. In 1985, Cuba's infant mortality rate was 19 per 1,000 live births. (Great Britain's was 11 per 1,000 live births.) No other country in

Latin America compares with Cuba by this standard: Mexico, 47; Guatemala, 57; Argentina, 32; El Salvador, 60; Chile, 36.

For a population of almost ten million, there are 260 hospitals, of which fifty-four are rural. Public health depends on preventive medicine and quick early care, so they have 396 polyclinics—an out-patient service. General practitioners, neurologists, gynaecologists and paediatricians work in polyclinics, with X-ray machines and laboratory facilities in the building. There are 158 rural medical sta-tions (the type I had seen in the villages) and 143 dental clinics. Most of the doctors and dentists, middle-class professionals, emigrated after the Revolución, but the number of physicians had tripled from 1958 to 1983 (increasing every year), the number of dentists quad-rupled and nursing staff, less than a thousand in 1958, numbered over 30,000 in 1983.

Apart from the grandiose hospital in Havana, which is Fidel's monument, hospitals and clinics are basic like everything else, but they are there, fully and willingly manned. They have eradicated malaria, polio and diphtheria; no deaths from tuberculosis since 1979 and the incidence of the disease in 1983 down to 0.7 per 100,000 population. Maybe they have finished it off by now. Tuber-culosis, a poverty disease, is endemic in this part of the world. In health, as a single indicator of progress, Cuba is unique in Latin America. Ordinary people, which means the vast majority, from Mexico south to Tierra del Fuego, would weep with joy to have the medical care that is free and routine for Cubans. Millions of North Americans would feel the same.

For a quarter of a century, everybody has heard how communism works in Cuba from successive American administrations. I do not believe anything that any govern-ments say. Judge them by their deeds, by results, by what you can observe yourself and learn from other unofficial observers. Apart from Jimmy Carter, all American presidents have hated Fidel Cas-tro as if he were a personal enemy. They have done their varied powerful best to destroy him, and failed. Since it was politically impossible to accept that the monster Castro might be popular, even loved by his people, he had to be oppressing ten million cowed Cubans.

Whatever it is, Cuba is not a police state ruled by fear. You can sense fear at once, anywhere, whether the police are communist or fascist, to use the simplified terms. Fear marks the faces and manners of the people. It makes them suspicious, especially of strangers. And it is catching; fear infects the visitor. I know, for I have never been more frightened than in El Salvador, and I was shaking with relief to be safe inside the airplane leaving Moscow. No government could decree or enforce the cheerfulness and friendliness I found around me in Cuba. I haven't space to describe all the people I met in all the places but this is what matters: none of them was afraid to talk to a foreigner, to answer my questions, and they spoke their minds without hesitation.

The undeniable shame of the Cuban government is political prisoners. Sources that I trust estimate about one hundred men in jail for political reasons. The trials were secret, neither charges nor evidence published. The sentences, dating back to the early years of the Revolución, were crushing, twenty years and more. These prisoners call themselves *plantados,* firmly and forever planted in their loathing of Castro communism. They refuse to wear prison uniforms or be 're-educated' politically. Defiant to the end of their tremendous jail terms, released *plantados*—now abroad—have reported atrocious prison conditions, brutality from jailers, denial of family visits and mail, appalling malnutrition, periods of solitary confinement and barbarous medical neglect. These are terrible accusations and there is no reason to doubt them.

A book called *Against All Hope* by a former *plantado,* Armando Valladares, has recently appeared. Valladares served twenty-two years in prison and is now happily alive and well in Madrid. His charges against the Cuban prison regime are frightful, including torture, biological experiments, lightless cells and murder. The book should be studied with dispassionate care, especially by medical experts. The immediate question is: why did none of the many freed *plantados*—among them writers—provide such information earlier?

Amnesty has this year adopted five Cuban prisoners of conscience. Apparently four are long-term prisoners and one, a teacher of adult education, was arrested in 1981. Three of them are dissident Marxists; I don't know about the others. Amnesty is absolutely reli-

171

able. But whatever the remaining political prisoners are, I cannot understand why Fidel Castro does not release them all and allow them to go abroad. Or publish the charges and evidence that would justify the sentences. The secrecy about the *plantados* and the conditions of their imprisonment damage Cuba irreparably in world opinion. And, in the end, the *plantados* are released anyway. So what is the point? What is the Cuban government's need for this self-multilation? The Revolución has triumphed. It has gone far beyond the threatened inexperienced violent early years. It has made an admirable record in social reform, in education, in public health; and, in its own way, it is an upwardly-mobile society where anyone can better his life through individual ability. Why spoil that record, why disgrace the Revolución by holding political prisoners?

You can name in minutes the few governments which hold no political prisoners. This ugly fact does not condone Cuba but puts it into perspective. My sources did not suggest that political arrests were a continuing frequent process in Cuba. But a small country existing under a relentless state of siege, persecuted by the strongest nation on earth, is not in the best shape for flourishing freedom. If any American administration truly cared about Cuban political prisoners and Cuban civil liberties, it would let up on Cuba, leave Cuba alone, give Cuba a chance to breathe for a while and feel secure enough to afford more and more freedom. I hope for the arrival, one day, of a sensible US administration which will come to sensible live-and-let-live terms with Cuba. I hope this for the sake of both America and Cuba.

I returned to Havana from Santiago de Cuba by air; the Lada had destroyed me. As I was about to leave Cuba, the sky cleared. On a sunny morning I collected Gregorio and we went to visit my former home, the Finca Vigía, fifteen miles outside Havana, now a museum or indeed a shrine. Gregorio is eighty-seven years old, the only link to my Cuban past and the only Cuban repository of Hemingway lore, as he was the sailor-guardian of Hemingway's boat, the *Pilar*, for twenty-three years. People come from far and wide to hear his verbatim memories, which he quotes like Scripture. Hemingway and he were the same age. His devotion to his patron-hero is genuine and time has added lustre to that devotion. The

Pilar years were surely the best for Gregorio. He is a tall thin weather-beaten man, with calm natural dignity. He was liked and respected—thought, typically, to have the finest qualities of a Spaniard. Not that anybody troubled about his separate existence; I had never seen his house.

The Museo Hemingway, temporarily closed to the public for repairs, is wildly popular with Cubans. They come again and again, bringing picnics to spend the day, after a respectful tour of the house. The long driveway is flanked by towering royal palms and sumptuous jacaranda trees. I couldn't believe my eyes; I remembered nothing so imposing. The driveway curved to show the house, now glaring white and naked. 'It looks like a sanatorium,' I said. 'What did they do to the ceiba?'

Forty-six years ago, I found this house through an advertisement and rented it, for one hundred dollars a month, indifferent to its sloppiness, because of the giant ceiba growing from the wide front steps. Any house with such a tree was perfect in my eyes. Besides, the terrace beyond the steps was covered by a trellis roof of brilliant bougainvillaea. Flowering vines climbed up the wall behind the ceiba; orchids grew from its trunk. All around the house were acres of high grass, hiding caches of empty gin bottles, and rusty tins, and trees. The house was almost invisible but painted an unappetizing yellow; I had it painted a dusty pale pink; the Museo changed it to glaring white. The great tree was always the glory of the finca.

'The roots were pulling up the floor of the house. The Museo had to cut it down,' Gregorio said.

'They should have pulled down the house instead.'

I never saw a ceiba like it, anywhere. The enormous trunk, the colour and texture of elephant hide, usually dwarfs the branches of a ceiba. But this one had branches thick as other tree trunks, spreading in wide graceful loops; it was probably several hundred years old. The house is a pleasant old one-storey affair of no special style; the six rooms are large and well proportioned, full of light.

The members of the museum staff have their office in the former garage; they are earnest, devout keepers of the shrine. I recognized all the furniture I had ordered from the local carpenter, and lapsed into giggles over the later addition of stuffed animal heads

and horns on every wall. In the master's bedroom, the biggest buffalo head I had ever seen, including hundreds on the hoof, glowered
over the desk. True, I had never been so close to any buffalo, living
or dead. 'He did not write here,' said one of the staff. He wrote *For
Whom The Bell Tolls* at this desk, but that was pre-buffalo.

The house depressed me; I hurried through it, eager to get back
to the trees. How had I taken for granted this richness? Then it
struck me: time, the years of my life at last made real. The trees had
been growing in splendour for forty-one years—the immense mangoes and flamboyantes and palms and jacarandas and avocates were
all here before, but young then like me.

I had definitely forgotten the size and the elegant shape of the
swimming-pool. Gregorio was interested in two large cement cradles, placed where the tennis court used to be. The *Pilar* was his
inheritance, he had cared for it and given it to the state, and it was
to be brought here and placed on these cradles.

'Like the *Granma*,' I said, and everyone looked slightly
shocked at the irreverence. The *Granma* is the large cabin cruiser
that bore Fidel and his followers from Mexico to Cuba in 1956: the
transport of the Revolución. It is enshrined in a glass case in a small
park in Old Havana. As an object of patriotic veneration, a lot jol-
lier than Lenin embalmed. It seems that *Granma*, now the name of
a province and of the major national newspaper, is simply a
misspelling of Grandma, which is delightful.

The visit was as fast as I could make it—handshakes, compli-
ments standing under a beautiful jacaranda by the garage—and we
were off to Gregorio's house in the fishing village of Cojimar. The
visit to the Museo had been a duty call; it was expected. I wanted to
listen to Gregorio.

In the car, I began to have faintly turbulent emotions. I remembered with what gaiety I had come to this country and how I had left,
frozen in distaste of a life that seemed to me hollow and boring to
die. Looking after the finca ate my time, but was worth it because of
the beauty. Then Cuba became worth nothing, a waste of time.
Cuba now is immeasurably better than the mindless feudal Cuba I
knew. But no place for a self-willed, opinionated loner, which is
what I suppose I am. Never a team-player—though I wish this team,
this people, well, and hope it improves, as it has, year by year.

'Gregorio, it is a comfort that nobody is hungry.'

Gregorio looked at me and smiled. 'You remember that?'

'Yes.'

'Pues sí, Marta, nobody is hungry now.'

Gregorio has owned his small cement house since 1936 and it is freshly painted, sky blue and white. Gregorio was still anxious about his wife, *mi señora* he calls her in the old way, who fell off a ladder weeks ago and broke her thigh. She was waiting for us indoors, in a chair, her leg in plaster. She kissed me, told me I was 'very well preserved', and they both recounted the saga of the leg. They have a telephone; the ambulance came at once; she was taken to hospital and operated on. '"A big operation," the doctor said.' Gregorio's turn: 'Very big. He said at our age the bones are like glass.' She stayed twenty days in hospital, then the ambulance brought her home. The doctor from the local polyclinic came every day to check her condition, now he only comes once a week. 'Not a cent, Marta, you understand. It did not cost even one centavo.'

Gregorio has a monthly pension of 170 pesos (call it pre-inflation dollars); actually a large pension, due to his long work years. Still, I thought this a skimpy sum until they told me the price system: six dollars a month flat for the telephone, which is a luxury; three dollars flat for electricity—and they have an electric fridge and cooker and water heater; the colour TV is bought on the never-never, at ten percent a month of salary or pension. The food ration is extremely cheap.

'Is it enough food?'

'Yes, yes, more than enough, but if you want different things you buy them. It costs more.' Clothes are also rationed and cheap; they would not need or want more than the yearly quota of shoes, shirts, underclothes etc. 'Young people care for clothes, they buy more off rations. And education is free too, Marta.'

His middle-aged daughter now arrived; she is volubly enthusiastic about the new Cuba. Then his grand-daughter appeared with a pink and white baby in her arms, Gregorio's great grandson, on her way to his weekly check-up at the polyclinic. Each generation owns its little house in this village.

I felt that Gregorio was getting a trifle restive among all these females so we moved to the front porch to smoke. He brought out a bottle of Cuban rum. 'As long as I have this,' he said, pouring me a hefty slug, 'and my cigars, I am content.' Now talking soberly he said, 'Marta, all the intelligentsia left, all of them.' I was baffled by that word: what would Gregorio know of intelligentsia? Then I guessed he meant the world he had known with Hemingway, the Sunday parties with the jai-alai players at the finca, parties at the Cojimar pub, the carefree company of the rich and privileged, the big-game fishermen, the members of the pigeon-shooting club, and though I had never seen the Country Club he meant that circle too, since the *Pilar* was berthed there in later years. He may have missed the glamour of a life he shared and did not share. But he had met Fidel. 'I think he is a good man,' Gregorio said. After Hemingway left in 1959, Gregorio returned to his old profession of fisherman, then retired and became unofficial adviser to the Museo Hemingway. 'I have never had any trouble with anyone.'

I asked about the few Cubans I could remember by name; they had all long decamped. I asked about the Basque jai-alai players, exiles from Franco's Spain, who had fought for their homeland and lost. I loved them, brave and high-spirited men who never spoke of the past, not expecting to see their country and families again.

'They left when Batista took power. They did not like dictatorship. There was much killing with Batista, in secret. I heard that Patchi died.'

'Patchi!' I was stunned. 'And Ermua?' Ermua was the great *pelotari* who moved like a panther and was the funniest, wildest of them all.

'Yes, he died too.'

'How could he? Why? So young?'

And suddenly I realized that Patchi was probably my age, Ermua maybe five years younger; they need not have died young.

'Gregorio, I am growing sad. Cuba makes me understand that I am old.'

'I too,' Gregorio laughed. *'Pues, no hay remedio.'*

My bag was packed, my bill paid and I had nothing to do until two a.m. when I took the plane to Nicaragua. I went back to Jibacoa where I had gone in hope of snorkelling on my first day. Now the weather was the way it ought to be, brilliantly blue cloudless sky, hot sun. I went to the Cuban resort, not the foreigners' tourist domain on the hill. There were dozens of small cabins for two or four people, a boat-yard with rentable pleasure craft, an indoor recreation room, ping-pong and billiards, a snack bar to provide the usual foul American white bread sandwiches and a restaurant. The main feature was a beautiful long white sand beach, bracketed by stony headlands. Where there are rocks there are fish. I was loaned a cabin to change in and a towel: No, no, you pay nothing, you are not sleeping here. I could never decide whether I was treated with unfailing kindness because I was a foreigner or because of my age.

There were many people on the beach, looking happy in the lovely weather, all ages, sunbathing, swimming, picnicking. A young man offered me his deck-chair so that I could read and bake comfortably between swims. I put on my mask and plunged in, feeling the water cold after the storm, but bursting with joy to see familiar fish, special favourites being a shoal of pale blue ovoid fish with large smiles marked in black on their faces. In my old Cuban days, I wore motorcyclist's goggles; masks and snorkels had not been invented.

When I returned to my deck-chair at the far end of the beach, I found two small fat white bodies lying face down near me. After a while they worried me, and I warned them in Spanish that they were getting a dangerous burn. A grey-haired man sat up and said, 'Spik Engleesh?' They were 'Greek-Canadians' from the tourist resort above; they liked the place, they even liked the food. He said, 'They work slow. No, lady, I don't think it's the climate. But they're happy. The guy who looks after our group is doing double time. For that, he gets a month off.' He smiled, he shrugged.

From nine to five, the tour guide would be on hand to interpret if needed, to coddle the old if they wanted it, swim with the girls, play table tennis, eat, drink. Maybe he would take them on a day sight-seeing tour of Havana. And then, from five to one in the morning, if anyone was still awake, he would do the same, except he would drink more than swim, and dance with the girls to radio music in the bar, and of course escort them all on the big night out at the Tropicana. The Greek-Canadian's shrug and smile said clearly that he did not consider this to be hardship duty. Here was a small-scale capitalist deriding the easy life of communists. Soft communism, a comic turn-around from the dreaded American accusation: 'soft on communism.' I thought it the best joke yet.

AMITAV GHOSH
THE IMAM AND THE INDIAN

I met the Imam of the village and Khamees the Rat at about the same time. I don't exactly remember now—it happened more than six years ago—but I think I met the Imam first.

But this is not quite accurate. I didn't really 'meet' the Imam: I inflicted myself upon him. Perhaps that explains what happened.

Still, there was nothing else I could have done. As the man who led the daily prayers in the mosque, he was a leading figure in the village, and since I, a foreigner, had come to live there, he may well for all I knew have been offended had I neglected to pay him a call. Besides, I wanted to meet him; I was intrigued by what I'd heard about him.

People didn't often talk about the Imam in the village, but when they did, they usually spoke of him somewhat dismissively, but also a little wistfully, as they might of some old, half-forgotten thing, like the annual flooding of the Nile. Listening to my friends speak of him, I had an inkling, long before I actually met him, that he already belonged, in a way, to the village's past. I thought I knew this for certain when I heard that apart from being an Imam he was also, by profession, a barber and a healer. People said he knew a great deal about herbs and poultices and the old kind of medicine. This interested me. This was Tradition: I knew that in rural Egypt Imams and other religious figures are often by custom associated with those two professions.

The trouble was that these accomplishments bought the Imam very little credit in the village. The villagers didn't any longer want an Imam who was also a barber and a healer. The older people wanted someone who had studied at al-Azhar and could quote from Jamal ad-Din Afghani and Mohammad Abduh as fluently as he could from the Hadith, and the younger men wanted a fierce, black-bearded orator, someone whose voice would thunder from the mimbar and reveal to them their destiny. No one had time for old-fashioned Imams who made themselves ridiculous by boiling herbs and cutting hair.

Yet Ustad Ahmed, who taught in the village's secondary school and was as well-read a man as I have ever met, often said—and this was not something he said of many people—that the old Imam read a lot. A lot of what? Politics, theology, even popular science . . . that kind of thing.

This made me all the more determined to meet him, and one evening, a few months after I first came to the village, I found my way to his house. He lived in the centre of the village, on the edge of the dusty open square which had the mosque in its middle. This was the oldest part of the village: a maze of low mud huts huddled together like confectionery on a tray, each hut crowned with a billowing, tousled head of straw.

When I knocked on the door the Imam opened it himself. He was a big man, with very bright brown eyes, set deep in a wrinkled, weather-beaten face. Like the room behind him, he was distinctly untidy: his blue jallabeyya was mud-stained and unwashed and his turban had been knotted anyhow around his head. But his beard, short and white and neatly trimmed, was everything a barber's beard should be. Age had been harsh on his face, but there was a certain energy in the way he arched his shoulders, in the clarity of his eyes and in the way he fidgeted constantly, was never still: it was plain that he was a vigorous, restive kind of person.

'Welcome,' he said, courteous but unsmiling, and stood aside and waved me in. It was a long dark room, with sloping walls and a very low ceiling. There was a bed in it and a couple of mats but little else, apart from a few, scattered books: everything bore that dull patina of grime which speaks of years of neglect. Later, I learned that the Imam had divorced his first wife and his second had left him, so that now he lived quite alone and had his meals with his son's family who lived across the square.

'Welcome,' he said again, formally.

'Welcome to you,' I said, giving him the formal response, and then we began on the long, reassuring litany of Arabic phrases of greeting.

'How are you?'

'How are you?'

'You have brought blessings?'

'May God bless you.'

'Welcome.'

'Welcome to you.'

'You have brought light.'

'The light is yours.'

'How are you?'

'How are you?'

He was very polite, very proper. In a moment he produced a kerosene stove and began to brew tea. But even in the performance of that little ritual there was something about him that was guarded, watchful.

'You're the *doktor al-Hindi*,' he said to me at last, 'aren't you? The Indian doctor?'

I nodded, for that was the name the village had given me. Then I told him that I wanted to talk to him about the methods of his system of medicine.

He looked very surprised and for a while he was silent. Then he put his right hand to his heart and began again on the ritual of greetings and responses, but in a markedly different way this time; one that I had learnt to recognize as a means of changing the subject.

'Welcome.'

'Welcome to you.'

'You have brought light.'

'The light is yours.'

And so on.

At the end of it I repeated what I had said.

'Why do you want to hear about *my* herbs?' he retorted. 'Why don't you go back to your country and find out about your own?'

'I will,' I said. 'Soon. But right now . . .'

'No, no,' he said restlessly. 'Forget about all that; I'm trying to forget about it myself.'

And then I knew that he would never talk to me about his craft, not just because he had taken a dislike to me for some reason of his own, but because his medicines were as discredited in his own eyes as they were in his clients'; because he knew as well as anybody else that the people who came to him now did so only because of old habits; because he bitterly regretted his inherited association with these relics of the past.

'Instead,' he said, 'let me tell you about what I have been learning over the last few years. Then you can go back to your country and tell them all about it.'

He jumped up, his eyes shining, reached under his bed and brought out a glistening new biscuit tin.

'Here!' he said, opening it. 'Look!'

Inside the box was a hypodermic syringe and a couple of glass phials. This is what he had been learning, he told me: the art of mixing and giving injections. And there was a huge market for it too, in the village: everybody wanted injections, for coughs, colds, fevers, whatever. There was a good living in it. He wanted to demonstrate his skill to me right there, on my arm, and when I protested that I wasn't ill, that I didn't need an injection just then, he was offended. 'All right,' he said curtly, standing up. 'I have to go to the mosque right now. Perhaps we can talk about this some other day.'

That was the end of my interview. I walked with him to the mosque and there, with an air of calculated finality, he took my hand in his, gave it a perfunctory shake and vanished up the stairs.

K hamees the Rat I met one morning when I was walking through the rice fields that lay behind the village, watching people transplant their seedlings. Everybody I met was cheerful and busy and the flooded rice fields were sparkling in the clear sunlight. If I shut my ears to the language, I thought, and stretch the date palms a bit and give them a few coconuts, I could easily be back somewhere in Bengal.

I was a long way from the village and not quite sure of my bearings, when I spotted a group of people who had finished their work and were sitting on the path, passing around a hookah.

'*Ahlan!*' a man in a brown jallabeyya called out to me. 'Hullo! Aren't you the Indian *doktor*?

'Yes,' I called back. 'And who're you?'

'He's a rat,' someone answered, raising a gale of laughter. 'Don't go anywhere near him.'

'Tell me *ya doktor*,' the Rat said, 'if I get on to my donkey and ride steadily for thirty days will I make it to India?'

'No,' I said. 'You wouldn't make it in thirty months.'

'Thirty months!' he said. 'You must have come a long way.'

'Yes.'

'As for me,' he declared, 'I've never even been as far as Alexandria and if I can help it I never will.'

I laughed: it did not occur to me to believe him.

When I first came to that quiet corner of the Nile Delta I had expected to find on that most ancient and most settled of soils a settled and restful people. I couldn't have been more wrong.

The men of the village had all the busy restlessness of airline passengers in a transit lounge. Many of them had worked and travelled in the sheikhdoms of the Persian Gulf, others had been in Libya and Jordan and Syria, some had been to the Yemen as soldiers, others to Saudi Arabia as pilgrims, a few had visited Europe: some of them had passports so thick they opened out like ink-blackened concertinas. And none of this was new: their grandparents and ancestors and relatives had travelled and migrated too, in much the same way as mine had, in the Indian sub-continent—because of wars, or for money and jobs, or perhaps simply because they got tired of living always in one place. You could read the history of this restlessness in the villagers' surnames: they had names which derived from cities in the Levant, from Turkey, from faraway towns in Nubia; it was as though people had drifted here from every corner of the Middle East. The wanderlust of its founders had been ploughed into the soil of the village: it seemed to me sometimes that every man in it was a traveller. Everyone, that is, except Khamees the Rat, and even his surname, as I discovered later, meant 'of Sudan'.

'Well, never mind *ya doktor*,' Khamees said to me now, 'since you're not going to make it back to your country by sundown anyway, why don't you come and sit with us for a while?'

He smiled and moved up to make room for me.

I liked him at once. He was about my age, in the early twenties, scrawny, with a thin, mobile face deeply scorched by the sun. He had that brightness of eye and the quick, slightly sardonic turn to his mouth that I associated with faces in the coffee-houses of universities in Delhi and Calcutta; he seemed to belong to a world of late-night rehearsals and black coffee and lecture rooms, even though, in fact, unlike most people in the village, he was completely illiterate. Later I learned that he was called the Rat—Khamees the Rat—because he was said to gnaw away at things with his tongue, like a rat did with its teeth. He laughed at everything, people said—at his father, the village's patron saint, the village elders, the Imam, everything.

That day he decided to laugh at me.

'All right *ya doktor*,' he said to me as soon as I had seated myself. 'Tell me, is it true what they say, that in your country you burn your dead?'

No sooner had he said it than the women of the group clasped their hands to their hearts and muttered in breathless horror: '*Haram! Haram!*'

My heart sank. This was a conversation I usually went through at least once a day and I was desperately tired of it. 'Yes,' I said, 'it's true; some people in my country burn their dead.'

'You mean,' said Khamees in mock horror, 'that you put them on heaps of wood and just light them up?'

'Yes,' I said, hoping that he would tire of this sport if I humoured him.

'Why?' he said. 'Is there a shortage of kindling in your country?'

'No,' I said helplessly, 'you don't understand.' Somewhere in the limitless riches of the Arabic language a word such as 'cremate' must exist, but if it does, I never succeeded in finding it. Instead, for lack of any other, I had to use the word 'burn'. That was unfortunate, for 'burn' was the word for what happened to wood and straw and the eternally damned.

Khamees the Rat turned to his spellbound listeners. 'I'll tell you why they do it,' he said. 'They do it so that their bodies can't be punished after the Day of Judgement.'

Everybody burst into wonderstruck laughter. 'Why, how clever,' cried one of the younger girls. 'What a good idea! We ought to start doing it ourselves. That way we can do exactly what we like and when we die and the Day of Judgement comes, there'll be nothing there to judge.'

Khamees had got his laugh. Now he gestured to them to be quiet again.

'All right then *ya doktor*,' he said. 'Tell me something else: is it true that you are a Magian? That in your country everybody worships cows? Is it true that the other day when you were walking through the fields you saw a man beating a cow and you were so upset that you burst into tears and ran back to your room?'

'No, it's not true,' I said, but without much hope: I had heard

185

this story before and knew that there was nothing I could say which would effectively give it the lie. 'You're wrong. In my country people beat their cows all the time; I promise you.'

I could see that no one believed me.

'Everything's upside-down in their country,' said a dark, aquiline young woman who, I was told later, was Khamees's wife. 'Tell us *ya doktor*: in your country, do you have crops and fields and canals like we do?'

'Yes,' I said, 'we have crops and fields, but we don't always have canals. In some parts of my country they aren't needed because it rains all the year around.'

'*Ya salám,*' she cried, striking her forehead with the heel of her palm. 'Do you hear that, oh you people? Oh, the Protector, oh, the Lord! It rains all the year round in his country.'

She had gone pale with amazement. 'So tell us then,' she demanded, 'do you have night and day like we do?'

'Shut up woman,' said Khamees. 'Of course they don't. It's day all the time over there, didn't you know? They arranged it like that so that they wouldn't have to spend any money on lamps.'

We all laughed, and then someone pointed to a baby lying in the shade of a tree swaddled in a sheet of cloth. 'That's Khamees's baby,' I was told. 'He was born last month.'

'That's wonderful,' I said. 'Khamees must be very happy.'

Khamees gave a cry of delight. 'The Indian knows I'm happy because I've had a son,' he said to the others. 'He understands that people are happy when they have children: he's not as upside-down as we thought.'

He slapped me on the knee and lit up the hookah and from that moment we were friends.

One evening, perhaps a month or so after I first met Khamees, he and his brothers and I were walking back to the village from the fields when he spotted the old Imam sitting on the steps that led to the mosque.

'Listen,' he said to me, 'you know the old Imam, don't you? I saw you talking to him once.'

'Yes,' I said. 'I talked to him once.'

'My wife's ill,' Khamees said. 'I want the Imam to come to my house to give her an injection. He won't come if I ask him, he doesn't like me. You go and ask.'

'He doesn't like me either,' I said.

'Never mind,' Khamees insisted. 'He'll come if you ask him—he knows you're a foreigner. He'll listen to you.'

While Khamees waited on the edge of the square with his brothers I went across to the Imam. I could tell that he had seen me—and Khamees—from a long way off, that he knew I was crossing the square to talk to him. But he would not look in my direction. Instead, he pretended to be deep in conversation with a man who was sitting beside him, an elderly and pious shopkeeper whom I knew slightly.

When I reached them I said 'Good evening' very pointedly to the Imam. He could not ignore me any longer then, but his response was short and curt, and he turned back at once to resume his conversation.

The old shopkeeper was embarrassed now, for he was a courteous, gracious man in the way that seemed to come so naturally to the elders of the village. 'Please sit down,' he said to me. 'Do sit. Shall we get you a chair?'

Then he turned to the Imam and said, slightly puzzled: 'You know the Indian *doktor*, don't you? He's come all the way from India to be a student at the University of Alexandria.'

'I know him,' said the Imam. 'He came around to ask me questions. But as for this student business, I don't know. What's *he* going to study? He doesn't even write in Arabic.'

'Well,' said the shopkeeper judiciously, 'that's true; but after all he writes his own languages and he knows English.'

'Oh those,' said the Imam. 'What's the use of *those* languages? They're the easiest languages in the world. Anyone can write those.'

He turned to face me for the first time. His eyes were very bright and his mouth was twitching with anger. 'Tell me,' he said, 'why do you worship cows?'

I was so taken aback that I began to stammer. The Imam ignored me. He turned to the old shopkeeper and said: 'That's what they do in his country—did you know?—they worship cows.'

He shot me a glance from the corner of his eyes. 'And shall I tell you what else they do?' he said to the shopkeeper.

He let the question hang for a moment. And then, very loudly, he hissed: 'They burn their dead.'

The shopkeeper recoiled as though he had been slapped. His hands flew to his mouth. 'Oh God!' he muttered. '*Ya Allah.*'

'That's what they do,' said the Imam. 'They burn their dead.'

Then suddenly he turned to me and said, very rapidly: 'Why do you allow it? Can't you see that it's a primitive and backward custom? Are you savages that you permit something like that? Look at you: you've had some kind of education; you should know better. How will your country ever progress if you carry on doing these things? You've even been to the West; you've seen how advanced they are. Now tell me: have you ever seen them burning their dead?'

The Imam was shouting now and a circle of young men and boys had gathered around us. Under the pressure of their interested eyes my tongue began to trip, even on syllables I thought I had mastered. I found myself growing angry—as much with my own incompetence as the Imam.

'Yes, they do burn their dead in the West,' I managed to say somehow. I raised my voice too now. 'They have special electric furnaces meant just for that.'

The Imam could see that he had stung me. He turned away and laughed. 'He's lying,' he said to the crowd. 'They don't burn their dead in the West. They're not an ignorant people. They're advanced, they're educated, they have science, they have guns and tanks and bombs.'

'We have them too!' I shouted back at him. I was as confused now as I was angry. 'In my country we have all those things too,' I said to the crowd. 'We have guns and tanks and bombs. And they're better than anything you have—we're way ahead of you.'

The Imam could no longer disguise his anger. 'I tell you, he's lying,' he said. 'Our guns and bombs are much better than theirs. Ours are second only to the West's.'

'It's you who's lying,' I said. 'You know nothing about this. Ours are much better. Why, in my country we've even had a nuclear explosion. You won't be able to match that in a hundred years.'

So there we were, the Imam and I, delegates from two superseded civilizations vying with each other to lay claim to the violence of the West.

At that moment, despite the vast gap that lay between us, we understood each other perfectly. We were both travelling, he and I: we were travelling in the West. The only difference was that I had actually been there, in person: I could have told him about the ancient English university I had won a scholarship to, about punk dons with safety pins in their mortar-boards, about superhighways and sex shops and Picasso. But none of it would have mattered. We would have known, both of us, that all that was mere fluff: at the bottom, for him as for me and millions and millions of people on the landmasses around us, the West meant only this—science and tanks and guns and bombs.

And we recognized too the inescapability of these things, their strength, their power—evident in nothing so much as this: that even for him, a man of God, and for me, a student of the 'humane' sciences, they had usurped the place of all other languages of argument. He knew, just as I did, that he could no longer say to me, as Ibn Battuta might have when he travelled to India in the fourteenth century: 'You should do this or that because it is right or good or because God wills it so.' He could not have said it because that language is dead: those things are no longer sayable; they sound absurd. Instead he had had, of necessity, to use that other language, so universal that it extended equally to him, an old-fashioned village Imam, and great leaders at SALT conferences: he had had to say to me: 'You ought not to do this because otherwise you will not have guns and tanks and bombs.'

Since he was a man of God his was the greater defeat.

For a moment then I was desperately envious. The Imam would not have said any of those things to me had I been a Westerner. He would not have dared. Whether I wanted it or not, I would have had around me the protective aura of an inherited expertise in the technology of violence. That aura would have surrounded me, I thought, with a sheet of clear glass, like a bullet-proof screen; or perhaps it would have worked as a talisman, like a press card, armed with which I could have gone off to what were said to be the most terrible places in the world that month, to gaze and wonder. And then perhaps I too would one day have had enough material for a book which would have had for its epigraph the line, *The horror! The horror!*—for the virtue of a sheet of glass is that it

189

does not require one to look within.

But that still leaves Khamees the Rat waiting on the edge of the square.

In the end it was he and his brothers who led me away from the Imam. They took me home with them, and there, while Khamees's wife cooked dinner for us—she was not so ill after all—Khamees said to me: 'Do not be upset, *ya doktor*. Forget about all those guns and things. I'll tell you what: *I'll* come to visit you in your country, even though I've never been anywhere. I'll come all the way.'

He slipped a finger under his skull-cap and scratched his head, thinking hard.

Then he added: 'But if I die, you must bury me.'

Ryszard Kapuściński
Stiff

The truck is racing through the dusk, its headlamps, like pupils, searching for the finishing line. It's close: Jeziorany, twenty kilometres. Another half hour, and we'll be there. The truck is pushing hard, but it's touch and go. The old machine wasn't meant for such a long haul.

On the flat-bed lies a coffin.

Atop the black box is a garland of haggard angels. It's worst on bends: the box slides and threatens to crush the legs of those sitting on the side rails. They curse, desecrating the coffin's decomposing contents.

The road bends into blind curves, climbing. The engine howls, rises a few notes, hiccups, chokes and stops. Another breakdown. A smeared figure alights from the cab. That's Zieja, the driver. He crawls under the truck, looking for the damage. Hidden underneath, he swears at the perverse world. He spits when hot grease drips on to his face. Finally he drags himself out into the middle of the road and brushes off his clothes. '*Kaput*,' he says. 'It won't start. You can smoke.'

To hell with smoking. We feel like crying.

Just two days ago I was in Silesia at the Aleksandra-Maria coal mine. The story called for an interview with the director of the workers' dormitory. I found him in his office explaining something to six youngsters. And I listened in.

This was the problem. During blasting a block of coal had fallen and crushed a miner. They managed to dig out the body, but he had died instantly. No one had known the dead man well. He had been working in the mine for barely two weeks. His identity was established. Name: Stefan Kanik. Age: eighteen. His father lived in Jeziorany, in Mazuria. The management contacted the local authorities there by telephone. It turned out that the father was paralysed and could not travel to the funeral. The Jeziorany authorities asked if the remains couldn't be transported to the home town. The management agreed, provided a truck and assigned the director of the workers' dormitory to find six people to escort the coffin.

These are the ones who have been summoned.

Five agree, one refuses. He doesn't want to lose any overtime. So there's a gap.

Can I go as the sixth?

The director shakes his head: a reporter as a pallbearer?

This empty road, this wreck of a truck, this air without a wisp of breeze.

This coffin.

Zieja wipes his oily hands with a rag. 'So what next?' he asks. 'We were supposed to be there this evening.'

We are stretched out on the edge of a ditch, on grass coated with a patina of dust. Our backs ache, our legs hurt, our eyes sting. Sleep, uninvited, introduces itself: warm, companionable, ingratiating.

'I think we all deserve a little nap,' says Wiśnia and curls up into a ball.

'And so?' Zieja says, surprised. 'Are we just going to go to sleep? But what about that other one?'

He shouldn't have mentioned it. Embarrassed by the question, sleep becomes awkward, backs away. We have been lying, tormented by our fatigue, and now feel anxious and uncertain, stare dully into a sky swimming with a school of silver stars.

We have to decide on something. 'What? Perhaps you'll tell me.'

Woś says: 'Let's stay here till morning. In the morning one of us can go to town and borrow a tractor. There's no need to hurry. This isn't a bakery.'

Jacek says: 'We can't wait till morning. It would be better to get this over with quickly, as quickly as possible.'

Kostarski says: 'You know, what if we just picked him up and carried him? He was a little guy, and a good part of him is still underneath that block of coal. It's not much of a load. We'll be finished by noon.'

It's a crazy idea, but it's one everyone likes. Put your shoulder to the wheel. It's early evening, and there aren't more than fifteen kilometres to go. We'll make it for sure. Besides, there is something else. Crouching at the edge of the ditch, having overcome the first temptation of sleep, more and more we begin to feel that with this coffin literally hanging above our heads we are keeping a vigil, here in the deep darkness, amid shadows and bushes and the silent, deaf horizon: the tension of waiting for the dawn would be unbearable. It would be better to go, better to lug him! Take some sort of action, move, talk, destroy the silence of the black box, prove that you belong to the realm of the living—in which he, nailed in, stiff, is an intruder, an alien, resembling nothing at all.

At the same time we find ourselves looking upon the task ahead—this arduous carrying—as a sort of offering to be presented to the deceased, so that he will leave us in peace, freeing us of his stubborn, insistent presence.

This march with the coffin on our backs has got off to a rough start. Seen from the viewpoint beneath it, the world has shrivelled to a small segment: the pendulum legs of the man ahead, a black slice of ground, the pendulum of your own legs. With his vision confined to this meagre prospect, a man instinctively summons imagination to his aid. Yes, the body may be bound, but the mind remains free.

'Anybody that came along now and ran into us would sure make tracks.'

'Know what? The moment he starts moving, we drop him and take off.'

'I just hope it doesn't rain. If it rains, he'll be waterlogged, and then he'll be very, very heavy.'

But there is no sign of rain. The evening is warm and the enormous, clear sky soars above an earth that is asleep now except for the sound of the crickets and the rhythm of our steps.

'Seventy-three, seventy-four, seventy-five'—Kostarski is counting. At 200 steps we change. We switch sides, left to right. Then the other way around. The edge of the coffin, hard and sharp, digs into our shoulders. We turn off the paved road on to a forest track, taking a short cut that passes near the shore of the lake. After an hour we haven't done more than three kilometres.

'Why is it,' Wiśnia wonders, 'that someone dies and instead of being buried in the ground he hangs around and wears everybody else out. Not only that. They all wear themselves out just so that he can hang around. Why?'

'I read somewhere,' Jacek says, 'that in the war, when the snow melted on the Russian battlefields, the hands of the dead would start to show, sticking straight up. You'd be going along the road and all you'd see would be the snow and these hands. Can you imagine, nothing else? A man, when he's finished, doesn't want to drop out of sight. It's people who hide him from their sight. To be left in peace, they hide him. He won't go on his own.'

'Just like this one of ours,' says Woś. 'He'd follow us round the world. All we have to do is take him along. I think we could even get used to it.'

'Why not?' Gruber quips from the back of the coffin. 'Everyone's always bearing some burden. A career for one, rabbits for another, a wife for a third. So why shouldn't we have him?'

'Don't speak ill of him, or he'll kick you in the ear,' Woś warns.

'He's not dangerous,' Gruber says softly. 'He's behaved himself so far. He must have been OK.'

But in fact we don't know what he was like. None of us ever saw him. Stefan Kanik, eighteen, died in an accident. That's all. Now we can add that he weighed around sixty kilos. A young, slender boy. The rest is a mystery, a guess. And now this riddle—boxed up, unseen, unknown—this shape, this alien, this stiff, rules six living men, monopolizes their thoughts, wears out their bodies, and, in silence, accepts their votive sacrifice.

'If he was a good guy, then you don't mind lugging him,' says Woś, 'but if he was a son of a bitch, into the water with him.'

What was he like? Can you establish such facts? Yes, certainly! We've been lugging him for about five kilometres and we've poured out a barrel of sweat. Haven't we invested a great deal of labour, of nerves, of our own peace of mind, into this remnant? This effort, a part of ourselves, passes on to the stiff, raises his worth in our eyes, unites us with him, makes him our brother across the barrier between life and death. The feeling of mutual strangeness dwindles. He has become ours. We won't plop him into the water. Sentenced to our burden, we will fulfill, to the very end, our appointed mission.

The forest trail leads to the edge of the lake. There is a little clearing. Woś calls for a rest and starts to make a bonfire.

The flame shoots up immediately, impudent and playful. We settle down in a circle and pull off our shirts, now wet and sour-smelling. In the glow of the fire we can see each other's sweating face, glistening torso and red, swollen shoulders. The heat spreads from the bonfire in waves. We back away, leaving the coffin by the fire.

'We'd better move that piece of furniture before it starts to roast and begins stinking,' Woś says.

We pull the coffin back, push it into the bushes, where Pluta breaks off some branches and covers it up.

We sit down again. We are still breathing heavily, fighting sleep and a feeling of unease, baking ourselves in the warmth and revelling in a light miraculously conjured from the darkness. We begin to fall into a state of inertia, abandon, numbness. The night has encapsulated us, closed us off from the world, from any other existence.

Just at that moment we hear Wiśnia's high, terrifying whisper: 'Quiet. Something's coming!'

A sudden, unbearable spasm of terror. Icy pins stab into our backs. Against our will, we glance towards the bushes, in the direction of the coffin. Jacek can't take it: he presses his head into the grass and, exhausted, sleep-starved, suddenly afraid, he begins to weep. This brings us all to our senses. Woś comes to himself first and falls upon Jacek, pulling at him and then pummelling him. He beats him fiercely, until the boy's weeping turns to groans, to a low, drawn-out sigh. Woś backs off at last, leans on a stump and ties his shoe.

In the meantime the voices that Wiśnia detected become distinct: they are approaching. We can hear snatches of melody, laughter, shouts. We listen attentively. Amid this dark wilderness our caravan has found traces of mankind. The voices are quite close now. Finally we pick out the silhouettes. Two, three, five.

They're girls. Six, seven.

Eight girls.

The girls—at first afraid, uncertain—end up staying. As the conversation gets off the ground, they start settling down around the fire next to us, so close that we could reach out and put our arms around them. It feels good. After everything we've been through, after a day of hard travelling, an exhausting march, the nerve-wracking tension, after all of this, or perhaps in spite of all this, it feels good.

'Are you coming back from a hike, too?' they ask.

'Yes,' Gruber says, lying. 'Beautiful evening, isn't it?'

'Beautiful. I'm just starting to appreciate it. Like everyone.'

'Not everyone,' Gruber says. 'There are some who don't appreciate anything. Now or ever. Never.'

We're all watching the girls closely. In colourful dresses, their shoulders bare and sun-bronzed—in the flickering light golden and brown by turns—their eyes seemingly indifferent but in fact provocative and vigilant at the same time, accessible and unreachable, they stare into the flames and appear to be surrendering to the strange and somewhat pagan mood that a night-time, forest-bonfire evokes in people. Looking upon these unexpected visitors, we feel that, despite the numbness, sleepiness and exhaustion, we are slowly being filled by an inner warmth: and, while wanting it, we sense the danger that comes with it. The edifice that holds in place the purpose and justification for making this extraordinary effort on behalf of a dead man is suddenly tottering. Why bother? Who needs it, when an opportunity like this presents itself? Only negative feelings link us to the dead man: in our new mood we could break away from the stiff so completely that any further toil of carrying the coffin would strike us as downright idiocy. Why make fools of ourselves?

Woś, however, has remained gloomy after the incident with Jacek, and has not joined in the flirting. He draws me aside.

'There's going to be trouble,' he whispers. 'One or the other of them is sure to go off after a skirt. And if we're a man short, we won't be able to carry the coffin. Then what?'

From this remove, our legs almost touching the sides of the coffin, we watch the scene in the clearing. Gruber will go for sure. Kostarski, Pluta—no. And Jacek? He's a question mark. He is, at heart, a shy boy, and wouldn't initiate a thing unless the girl made the first move: he'd turn tail at her first 'no.' Yet because his character affords him few chances, he would grab avidly if one presented itself.

'It's a dead cert Jacek goes,' Woś says.

'Let's get back to the fire,' I tell him. 'We're not going to solve anything here.'

We return. Pluta has thrown on some more wood. 'Remember,

it was autumn,' the girls are singing. We feel good, and we feel uneasy. No one has breathed a word about the coffin, but the coffin is still there. Our awareness of its existence, of its paralysing participation, makes us different from the girls.

Stefan Kanik, eighteen. Someone who is missing and who at the same time is the most present. Reach out and you can put your arm around a girl; take a few steps and you can lean over the coffin—we are standing between life at its most beautiful and death at its most cruel.

T he stiff came to us unknown, and for that reason we can identify him with every boy we have known. Yes, that was the one, that one for sure. He was standing in the window in an unbuttoned checked shirt, watching the cars drive past, listening to the babble of conversations, looking at the passing girls—the wind blowing out their full skirts, uncovering the whiteness of their starched slips, so stiff that you could stand them up on the floor like haystacks. And then he went out into the street and met his own girl and walked with her, buying her lifesavers and the most expensive lemon soda—'Moorish Delight'—and then she bought him strawberries and they went to the movie *Holiday with Monica,* where an actress with a difficult name undresses in front of an actor with a difficult name, which his girl had never done in front of him, not even once. And afterwards he kissed her in the park, watching from out of the corner of his eye from behind her head, through her careless loose hair, to make sure that a policeman wasn't coming who would take down his name and send him to school, or would want twenty *zloty* when they didn't have more than five between them. And afterwards the girl would say, 'We have to go now,' but she wouldn't get up from the park bench; she would say, 'Come on, it's late,' and she would cuddle against him more tightly, and he would ask, 'Do you know how butterflies kiss?' and move his eyelids close to her cheek and flutter them, which must have tickled her, because she would laugh.

Perhaps he would meet her many more times, but in our minds that naïve and banal image was the only and the final one, and afterwards we saw only what we had never wanted to see, ever, until the last day of our lives.

And when we pushed away that other, bad vision, we felt good again and everything was a joy to us: the fire, the smell of trampled grass, that our shirts had dried, the sleep of the earth, the taste of cigarettes, the forest, the rested legs, the stardust, life—life most of all.

In the end, we went on. The dawn met us. The sun warmed us. We kept walking. Our legs buckled, our shoulders went numb, our hands swelled, but we managed to carry it to the cemetery—to the grave—our last harbour on earth, at which we put in only once, never again to sail forth—this Stefan Kanik, eighteen, killed in a tragic accident, during blasting, by a block of coal.

Translated from the Polish by William R. Brand

BILL BRYSON
FAT GIRLS IN DES MOINES

I come from Des Moines. Somebody had to. When you come from Des Moines you either accept the fact without question and settle down with a local girl named Bobbi and get a job at the Firestone Factory and live there forever and ever, or you spend your adolescence moaning at length about what a dump it is and how you can't wait to get out, and then you settle down with a local girl named Bobbi and get a job at the Firestone factory and live there forever and ever.

Hardly anyone leaves. This is because Des Moines is the most powerful hypnotic known to man. Outside town there is a big sign that says: WELCOME TO DES MOINES. THIS IS WHAT DEATH IS LIKE. There isn't really. I just made that up. But the place does get a grip on you. People who have nothing to do with Des Moines drive in off the interstate, looking for gas or hamburgers, and stay forever. There's a New Jersey couple up the street from my parents' house whom you see wandering around from time to time looking faintly puzzled but strangely serene. Everybody in Des Moines is strangely serene.

The only person I ever knew in Des Moines who wasn't serene was Mr Piper. Mr Piper was my parents' neighbour, a leering, cherry-faced idiot who was forever getting drunk and crashing his car into telephone poles. Everywhere you went you encountered telephone poles and road signs leaning dangerously in testimony to Mr Piper's driving habits. He distributed them all over the west side of town rather in the way dogs mark trees. Mr Piper was the nearest possible human equivalent to Fred Flintstone, but less charming. He was a Shriner and a Republican—a Nixon Republican—and he appeared to feel that he had a mission in life to spread offence. His favourite pastime, apart from getting drunk and crashing his car, was to get drunk and insult the neighbours, particularly us because we were Democrats, though he was prepared to insult Republicans when we weren't available.

Eventually, I grew up and moved to England. This irritated Mr Piper almost beyond measure. It was worse than being a Democrat. Whenever I was in town, Mr Piper would come over and chide me. 'I don't know what you're doing over there with all those Limeys,' he would say. 'They're not clean people.'

'Mr Piper, you don't know what you're talking about,' I would reply in my affected British accent. 'You are a cretin.' You could talk like that to Mr Piper because (one) he *was* a cretin and (two) he never listened to anything that was said to him.

'Bobbi and I went over to London two years ago and our hotel room didn't even have a *bathroom* in it,' Mr Piper would go on. 'If you wanted to take a leak in the middle of the night you had to walk about a mile down the hallway. That isn't a clean way to live.'

'Mr Piper, the English are paragons of cleanliness. It is a well-known fact that they use more soap per capita than anyone else in Europe.'

Mr Piper would snort derisively at this. 'That doesn't mean diddly-squat, boy, just because they're cleaner than a bunch of Krauts and Eye-ties. My God, a *dog's* cleaner than a bunch of Krauts and Eye-ties. And I'll tell you something else: if his Daddy hadn't bought Illinois for him, John F. Kennedy would never have been elected President.'

I had lived around Mr Piper long enough not to be thrown by this abrupt change of tack. The theft of the 1960 presidential election was a long-standing plaint of his, one that he brought into the conversation every ten or twelve minutes regardless of the prevailing drift of the discussion. In 1963, during Kennedy's funeral, someone in the Waveland Tap punched Mr Piper in the nose for making that remark. Mr Piper was so furious that he went straight out and crashed his car into a telephone pole. Mr Piper is dead now, which is of course one thing that Des Moines prepares you for.

When I was growing up I used to think that the best thing about coming from Des Moines was that it meant you didn't come from anywhere else in Iowa. By Iowa standards, Des Moines is a Mecca of cosmopolitanism, a dynamic hub of wealth and education, where people wear three-piece suits and dark socks, often simultaneously. During the annual state high school basketball tournament, when the hayseeds from out in the state would flood into the city for a week, we used to accost them downtown and snidely offer to show them how to ride an escalator or negotiate a revolving door. This wasn't always so far from reality. My friend Stan, when he was about sixteen, had to go and stay with his cousin in some remote, dusty hamlet called Dog Water or Dunceville or some such improbable spot—the kind of place where if a dog gets run over by a truck everybody goes out to have a look at it. By the second week, delirious with boredom, Stan insisted that he and his cousin drive the fifty miles into the county town, Hooterville, and find something to do. They went bowling at an alley with warped lanes and chipped balls and afterwards had a chocolate soda and looked at a *Playboy* in a drugstore, and on the way home the cousin sighed with immense satisfaction and said, 'Gee thanks, Stan. That was the best time I ever had in my whole life!' It's true.

I had to drive to Minneapolis once, and I went on a back road just to see the country. But there was nothing to see. It's just flat and hot, and full of corn and soybeans and hogs. I remember one long, shimmering stretch where I could see a couple of miles down the highway and there was a brown dot beside the road. As I got closer I saw it was a man sitting on a box by his front yard in some six-house town with a name like Spiggot or Urinal, watching my approach with inordinate interest. He watched me zip past and in the rear-view mirror I could see him still watching me going on down the road until at last I disappeared into a heat haze. The whole thing must have taken about five minutes. I wouldn't be surprised if even now he thinks of me from time to time.

He was wearing a baseball cap. You can always spot an Iowa man because he is wearing a baseball cap advertising John Deere or a feed company, and because the back of his neck has been lasered into deep crevasses by years of driving a John Deere tractor back and forth in a blazing sun. (This does not do his mind a whole lot of good either.) His other distinguishing feature is that he looks ridiculous when he takes off his shirt because his neck and arms are chocolate brown and his torso is as white as a sow's belly. In Iowa it is called a farmer's tan and it is, I believe, a badge of distinction.

Iowa women are almost always sensationally overweight—you

see them at Merle Hay Mall in Des Moines on Saturdays, clammy and meaty in their shorts and halter-tops, looking a little like elephants dressed in children's clothes, yelling at their kids, calling names like Dwayne and Shauna. Jack Kerouac, of all people, thought that Iowa women were the prettiest in the country, but I don't think he ever went to Merle Hay Mall on a Saturday. I will say this, however—and it's a strange, strange thing—the teenaged daughters of these fat women are always utterly delectable, as soft and gloriously rounded and naturally fresh-smelling as a basket of fruit. I don't know what it is that happens to them, but it must be awful to marry one of these nubile cuties knowing that there is a time bomb ticking away in her that will at some unknown date make her bloat out into something huge and grotesque, presumably all of a sudden and without much notice, like a self-inflating raft from which the stopper has been abruptly jerked.

Even so, I don't think I would have stayed in Iowa. I never really felt at home there, even when I was small. In about 1957, my grandparents gave me a Viewmaster for my birthday and a packet of discs with the title 'Iowa—Our Glorious State'. I can remember thinking, even then, that the selection of glories was a trifle on the thin side. With no natural features of note, no national parks or battlefields or famous birthplaces, the Viewmaster people had to stretch their creative 3D talents to the full. Putting the Viewmaster to your eyes and clicking the white handle gave you, as I recall, a shot of Herbert Hoover's birthplace, impressively three-dimensional, followed by Iowa's other great treasure, the Little Brown Church in the Vale (which inspired the song whose tune nobody ever quite knows), the highway bridge over the Mississippi River at Davenport (all the cars seemed to be hurrying towards Illinois), a field of waving corn, the bridge over the Missouri River at Council Bluffs and the Little Brown Church in the Vale again, taken from another angle. I can remember thinking even then that there must be more to life than that.

Then one grey Sunday afternoon when I was about ten I was watching TV and there was a documentary on about movie-

205

making in Europe. One clip showed Anthony Perkins walking along some venerable old city street at dusk. I don't remember now if it was Rome or Paris, but the street was cobbled and shiny with rain and Perkins was hunched deep in a trench coat and I thought: 'Hey, *c'est moi!*' I began to read—no, I began to consume—*National Geographic*s, with their pictures of glowing Lapps and mist-shrouded castles and ancient cities of infinite charm. From that moment, I wanted to be a European boy. I wanted to live in an apartment on a tree-lined street across from a park in the heart of a city, and from my bedroom window look out on a vista of hills and roof-tops. I wanted to ride trams and understand strange languages. I wanted friends named Werner and Marco who wore short pants and played soccer in the street and owned toys made of wood. I cannot for the life of me think why. I wanted my mother to send me out to buy three-foot-long loaves of bread from an aromatic shop with a wooden pretzel hung above the entrance. I wanted to step outside my front door and *be* somewhere.

As soon as I was old enough I left. I left Des Moines and Iowa and the United States and the War in Vietnam and Watergate, and settled across the world. And now when I come home it is to a foreign country, full of serial murderers and sports teams in the wrong towns (the Indianapolis Colts? the Toronto Blue Jays?) and a personable old fart who is President. My mother knew that personable old fart when he was a sportscaster called Dutch Reagan at WHO Radio in Des Moines. 'He was just a nice, friendly kind of dopey guy,' my mother says.

Which, come to that, is a pretty fair description of most Iowans. Don't get me wrong. I am not for a moment suggesting that Iowans are mentally deficient. They are a decidedly intelligent and sensible people who, despite their natural conservatism, have always been prepared to elect a conscientious, clear-thinking liberal in preference to some cretinous conservative. (This used to drive Mr Piper practically insane.) And Iowans, I am proud to tell you, have the highest literacy rate in the nation: 99.5 per cent of grown-ups there can read. When I say they are kind of dopey, I mean that they are trusting and amiable and open. They are a tad slow, certainly—when you tell an Iowan a joke, you can see a kind of race going on between his brain and his expression—but it's not because they're incapable of high-speed mental activity, it's only that there's not much call for it. Their wits are dulled by simple, wholesome faith in God and the soil and their fellow man.

Above all, Iowans are friendly. You go into a strange diner in the south and everything goes quiet, and you realize all the other customers are looking at you as if they are sizing up the risk involved in murdering you for your wallet and leaving your body in a shallow grave somewhere out in the swamps. In Iowa you are the centre of attention, the most interesting thing to hit town since a tornado carried off old Frank Sprinkel and his tractor last May. Everybody you meet acts like he would gladly give you his last beer and let you sleep with his sister. Everyone is strangely serene.

The last time I was home, I went to Kresge's downtown and bought a bunch of postcards to send back to England. I bought the most ridiculous ones I could find—a sunset over a feedlot, a picture of farmers bravely grasping a moving staircase beside the caption: 'We rode the escalator at Merle Hay Mall!'—that sort of thing. They were so uniformly absurd that when I took them up to the check-out, I felt embarrassed by them, as if I were buying dirty magazines and hoped somehow to convey the impression that they weren't really for me. But the check-out lady regarded each of them with great interest and deliberation—just like they always do with dirty magazines, come to that.

When she looked up at me she was almost misty-eyed. She wore butterfly eyeglasses and a beehive hairdo. 'Those are real nice,' she said. 'You know, honey, I've bin in a lot of states and seen a lot of places, but I can tell you that this is just about the purtiest one I ever saw.' She really said *'purtiest'*. She really meant it. The poor woman was in a state of terminal hypnosis. I glanced at the cards and to my surprise I suddenly saw what she meant. I couldn't help but agree with her. They *were* purty. Together, we made a little pool of silent admiration. For one giddy, careless moment, I was almost serene myself.

My father liked Iowa. He lived his whole life in the state, and indeed is even now working his way through eternity there, in Glenview Cemetery in Des Moines. But every year he became seized with a quietly maniacal urge to get out of the state and go on vacation. Every summer, without a whole lot of notice, he would load the car to groaning, hurry us into it, take off for some distant point, return to get his wallet after having driven almost to the next state, and take off again for some distant point. Every year it was the same. Every year it was awful.

The big killer was the tedium. Iowa is in the middle of the biggest plain this side of Jupiter. Climb on to a roof-top almost anywhere in the state and you are confronted with a featureless sweep of corn as far as the eye can see. It is 1,000 miles from the sea in any direction, 600 miles from the nearest mountain, 400 miles from skyscrapers and muggers and things of interest, 300 miles from people who do not habitually stick a finger in their ear and swivel it around as a preliminary to answering any question addressed to them by a stranger. To reach anywhere of even passing interest from Des Moines by car requires a journey that in other countries would be considered epic. It means days and days of unrelenting tedium, in a baking steel capsule on a ribbon of highway.

In my memory, our vacations were always taken in a big blue Rambler station wagon. It was a cruddy car—my dad always bought cruddy cars, until he got to the male menopause and started buying zippy red convertibles—but it had the great virtue of space. My sister and I in the back were yards away from my parents up front, in effect in another room. We quickly discovered during illicit forays into the picnic hamper that if you stuck a bunch of Ohio Blue Tip matches into an apple or hard-boiled egg, so that it resembled a porcupine, and casually dropped it out the back window, it was like a bomb. It would explode with a small bang and a surprisingly big flash of blue flame, causing cars following behind to veer in an amusing fashion.

My dad, miles away up front, never knew what was going on or could understand why all day long cars would zoom up alongside him with the driver gesticulating furiously, before tearing off into the distance. 'What was that all about?' he would say to my mother in a wounded tone.

'I don't know, dear,' my mother would say mildly. My mother only ever said two things. She said: 'I don't know, dear.' And she said: 'Can I get you a sandwich, honey?' Occasionally on our trips she would volunteer other bits of information like 'Should that dashboard light be glowing like that, dear?' or 'I think you hit that dog/man/blind person back there, honey,' but mostly she kept quiet. This was because on vacations my father was a man obsessed. His principal obsession was trying to economize. He always took us to the crummiest hotels and motor lodges—the sort of places where there were never any coat-hangers because they had all been used by abortionists. And at the roadside eating houses, you always knew, with a sense of doom, that at some point before finishing you were going to discover someone else's congealed egg yolk lurking somewhere on your plate or plugged between the tines of your fork. This, of course, meant cooties and a long, painful death.

But even that was a relative treat. Usually we were forced to picnic by the side of the road. My father had an instinct for picking bad picnic sites—on the apron of a busy truck stop or in a little park that turned out to be in the heart of some seriously deprived ghetto so that groups of Negro children would come and stand silently by our table and watch us eating white people's foods like Hostess Cupcakes and crinkle-cut potato chips—and it always became incredibly windy the moment we stopped so that my mother spent the whole of lunchtime chasing paper plates over an area of about an acre.

In 1957 my father invested $19.98 in a gas stove that took an hour to assemble and was so wildly temperamental that we children were always ordered to stand well back when it was being lit. This always proved unnecessary, however, because the stove would flicker to life for only a few seconds before spluttering out, and my father would spend many hours turning it this way and that to keep it out of the wind, simultaneously addressing it in a low, agitated tone normally associated with the chronically insane. All the while my sister and I would implore him to take us some place with air-conditioning and linen table-cloths and ice cubes clinking in glasses of clear water. 'Dad,' we would beg, 'you're a successful man. You make a good living. Take us to a Howard Johnson's.' But he wouldn't have it. He was a child of the Depression and where capital outlays were involved he always wore the haunted look of a fugitive who has just heard bloodhounds in the distance.

Eventually, with the sun low in the sky, he would hand us hamburgers that were cold and raw and smelled of butane. We would take one bite and refuse to eat any more. So my father would lose his temper and throw everything into the car and drive us at high speed to some roadside diner where a sweaty man with a floppy hat would sling hash while grease fires danced on his grill. And afterwards, in a silent car filled with bitterness and unquenched basic needs, we would mistakenly turn off the main highway and get lost and end up in some no-hope town with a name like Draino, Indiana, or Tapwater, Missouri, and get a room in the only hotel in town, the sort of rundown place where if you wanted to watch TV it meant you had to sit in the lobby and share a cracked leatherette sofa with an old man with big sweat circles under his arms. The old man would almost certainly have only one leg and probably one other truly arresting deficiency, like no nose or a caved-in forehead, which meant that although you were sincerely intent on watching *Laramie* or *Our Miss Brooks*, you found your gaze being drawn, ineluctably and sneakily, to the amazing eaten-away body sitting beside you. You couldn't help yourself. Occasionally the man would turn out to have no tongue, in which case he would try to engage you in a lively conversation.

On another continent, 4,000 miles away, I am quietly seized with that nostalgia that overcomes you when you have reached the middle of your life and your father has recently died and it dawns on you that when he went he took a part of you with him. I want to go back to the magic places of my youth—to Mackinac Island, Estes Park, Gettysburg—and see if they were as good as I remember them. I want to hear the long, low sound of a Rock Island locomotive calling across a still night, and the clack of it receding into the distance. I want to see lightning bugs, and hear cicadas shrilling, and be inescapably immersed in that hot, crazy-making August weather that makes your underwear scoot up every crack and fissure and cling to you like latex, and drives mild-mannered men to pull out handguns in bars and light up the night with gunfire. I want to look for Ne-Hi Pop and Burma Shave signs and go to a ball game and sit at a marble-topped soda fountain and drive through the kind of small town that Deanna Durbin and Mickey Rooney used to live in in the movies. It's time to go home.

NORMAN LEWIS
ESSEX

Essex is the ugliest county. I only went there to be able to work in peace and quiet and get away from the settlers from London south of the river. It was flat and untidy and full of water with the Colne and the Crouch and the Blackwater and all their tributaries fingering up from the sea and spreading vinous tendrils of water into the flat land. For half the year, the wind blew in from the east, over shingle, mud-flats, saltings and marshes: even twenty miles inland, where I first set up house, gulls drove the crows out of the fields.

In the late 1960s I found an empty farmhouse called Charmers End in the village of Long Crendon, took a three-year lease and settled in. Many of the farms and villages had odd, even poetic names—Crab's Green, Sweet Dew, Blythe Easter, Fantail and Honey Wood—although on the whole, the more fanciful the name the more dismal the place. When I moved in, there were black-and-white cows in a shining field at the bottom of the garden. The cows were responsible for my decision to take the place. Otherwise this part of Essex reminded me of the southern tip of South America, where the trees are deformed, a cold wind combs the grass and glum Indians, reserved and off-hand like the country people of Essex, are muffled in their clothes against the grey weather.

The farmer who had lived here had grown old alone and sold his land. One day he hauled himself to the top of the tallest tree in the garden, drank a quarter of a bottle of Lysol, shoved the barrel of a German pistol collected in the war into his mouth, and pulled the trigger. This man had also liked the cows. The new owner did not, and so they disappeared soon after.

The house was surrounded by a great moat, and all along its banks stood big white leafless trees which, stripped of their bark and dying, eventually fell into the water. It was like the Amazon. Some of the trees in the moat had lost their branches, and little remained but their trunks, turned grey and slimy like submerged alligators showing only the tips of their snouts above the surface. Those still standing provided an annual crop of an uncommon oyster fungus, collected by an Italian from Chelmsford. He called with a present of a bottle of Asti Spumante shortly after I moved in.

The Post Office found me a woman to clean up four days a week. She arrived on a horse, charging up the lane and across the moat, black hair streaming in the wind, another contribution to the Latin American aspect of this corner of Essex. With her fine, aquiline features and almond eyes she could easily have been an Indian of the plains under the eastern slope of the Andes, where the natives are tall and slender.

Dorothea was thirty-seven, handsome if not quite beautiful, with a partially disabled husband and a pretty daughter of twelve.

She immediately took control. She persuaded the pump to emit a dribble of water, removed the mummified jackdaw from the chimney, dropped a pebble to test the black and silken surface of the fluid in the septic tank, and nodded with satisfaction. She then went with me in the car to point out the bakers, the man who might agree to cut the grass and mow the lawn, and the one who could fix up a television aerial. We passed two men in baseball caps, chatting outside a pub. One wore dark glasses and a lumberjack shirt. 'Americans?' I asked.

'No, locals. Carpenters up at the base.'

'They look like Yanks.'

'Well, they want to, don't they? Most of the fellows work on the base these days. If you can call it work.'

Long Crendon was a long, narrow street straggling over the best part of a mile, hence its name. There was a bad smell at one end from a rubbish dump that looked like a collapsed volcano that had been smouldering for several years, and at the other from a pig farm. The houses were simple and plain, with white plastered fronts. The poorer and smaller ones were thatched, and some still had leaded lights. A substantial mansion standing in gardens back from the road had suffered brutal modernization, and the garden was now enclosed with a ranch-style fence. Until the previous month it had been named Hill Top, said Dorothea. Now, with a new owner who had been in property development, it had become Rancho Grande. It was the only evidence that money had been spent in the village, either on preservation or ornament.

We passed three depressing pubs and a grey little school with children squabbling in the playground. The church was the only building of note, with a Norman door, good stained glass and tombstones packed close in separate familial groups as if to carry earthly associations beyond the grave.

The tour ended with a passing glance at the village hall. 'That's where I go dancing with my friend Mr Short on Saturday night,' Dorothea said.

'Your friend?'

'Well, not my *boyfriend*. Actually I don't like him all that much. We just go dancing together. Otherwise I don't find him all that interesting. I expect you heard all about Dick's accident?'

'Doesn't Dick mind?'

Dorothea saw no reason why he should. 'He doesn't dance and he realizes I have to have some sort of break. Well, I mean it's only normal, isn't it?'

Later, I heard the gossip: that she was the target of village adulterers, who were encouraged by Dick, her complaisant husband.

I asked Dorothea why she had to ride. I mentioned that village opinion considered the horse a bad one, with the habit of tripping over its legs.

'It's an old jumper,' she said. 'It's not so much its legs as its back. It's hit the deck a few times.'

'They were telling me you were a member of one of the Cloate families, whatever they mean by that.'

'It's a sort of clan,' she said. 'The thing they have in Scotland. Dick and I belong to it. About half the village used to be Cloates, but there's only five families left now. They say only the Cloates were allowed to ride in the old days.'

'What else do you do besides ride horses?'

'Well, nothing really. We're supposed to help each other, but that's a laugh. Really, it's more a question of keeping in touch. You sometimes get Cloate people who've gone overseas writing home. I suppose they feel lonely out there. Maybe you write two or three letters and then it drops.'

'Nothing else?'

'We have a sort of get-together in August. There used to be about fifty of us, but now it's down to half that. A lot of these things are dying out.' She said times changed.

One interesting aspect of the Cloate personality was its attitude to education. For men, schooling was only a means to an end—usefulness and self-sufficiency—and the boys, having taken what the primary school had to offer, moved on as soon as possible to the education provided by life. In the old days, Dorothea had heard, a Cloate would always build his own house. The function of a girl, however, was to please. If she was plain and dull, there was nothing to be done, but if she showed promise—in beauty, even wit—no sacrifice was too great to develop her potential. Then she would be packed off to a boarding school—of an unassuming, yet rather special kind—in Woodford, London E11, where a village girl would be subjected to a process of transformation so great that at its end she was hardly recognizable, even to her own family.

First impressions often mislead. My original view of Long Crendon was of a poverty-stricken, backward Essex village, of the kind often described as 'unspoilt' because there was no money for necessary improvements. While every roof, thatched or otherwise, carried a television aerial, only a quarter of the houses had bathrooms, or even inside lavatories, and less than half were connected to the mains water supply or the sewer. Two buildings, the Rancho Grande and a pub, the Pied Bull, had central heating; otherwise coal fires burned, as ever, in small grates. The locals pretended contempt for luxuries city-dwellers everywhere took for granted, and there were villagers who boasted of leaving their windows open through the interminable Essex winter. That Long Crendon remained on the surface unchanged was a matter of stubborn conservatism and resistance to change rather than economics. Yet a hidden transformation was in progress. In 1943 the Americans had built an important base at Effingham, some five miles away, and since then, despite all local claims to a preference for the hard but worthy life, self-indulgence and luxury were making a stealthy appearance.

The Americans offered to employ every civilian capable of holding down a job. They paid well and were considerate, almost over-tolerant employers. Dorothea's Dick was one of the many who benefited. He had been considered unemployable after his accident, but as soon as he was able to get about he was taken on at

217

the base as a timekeeper, an occupation for which nimbleness was not required. For some time Dorothea had kept him out of sight, but one day she brought him to see me. He was prematurely wizened and sat askew on a pony he controlled with one arm. The story was that while he was working twelve years before in an agricultural smithy, the prototype of a new combine harvester had run amok, snatched him up, neutered him, torn off a forearm, an ear and most of one foot. He and Dorothea had been married a matter of weeks when the accident occurred, and their daughter, Jane, had been conceived just in time.

I got to like Dick. According to the villagers, working for the Americans was like being on paid holiday. The main problem was finding a place to sleep undisturbed, because of the noise of the planes. Dick put his endless leisure to good use. He liked people, and limped about the place getting to know everybody and picking up useful gossip. He was a treasure house of village information, a holder of strong opinions and interested in religion.

'But you don't go to church, Dick?'

'Well, no. Most people round these parts don't.'

'And yet you're a believer?'

He gave a sly grin. 'When it suits me, I am. In the resurrection of the body, for instance. Now that's something I believe in. And I've every right to. It gives anybody like me a second chance, doesn't it? If the Bible says God can put back my missing bits, who am I to argue about it?' This, I supposed, was meant to be a joke.

In my second year at Long Crendon the new farmer moved in. The black-and-white cows had long gone, and the farmer now ploughed up the field and planted horse-beans, the most hideous of crops. My neighbour was thorough. The trees across the moat were on his land, and they all came down, whether dead or alive, and were cut up. He rode round on a tractor painted in astonishing psychedelic colours, like Sennacherib in his chariot, dealing death and destruction to nature. One of the big chemical firms was encouraging farmers to experiment with its sprays. He sprayed the banks of the moat and killed off a vast colony of frogs. The resident mallards, feeding on the frogs, also died. I watched them seized by a kind of paralysis, trying to take off. After splashing about in desperate fashion for a while they subsided and swam in slow tightening circles. In the end they could no longer hold their heads up, and finally drowned. In a single year this man changed everything in my Essex landscape. What looked in summer like the southern, treeless edge of the Argentine *pampas* became Siberia in winter. Nothing held back the east wind as it blew in from the North Sea. Six inches of snow lay in the ploughed fields. The wind plucked up the snow like feathers from a moulting goose and dropped it in the hollows of the land. When spring came there were still yard-deep pockets of frozen snow lying between the bare banks at the bottom of the lanes.

Every penny Dorothea and Dick scraped together was saved to send Jane to Woodford, but Jane was already thirteen and they were becoming desperate. Dorothea worked three days a week at the Rancho Grande, now owned by a man who had made a fortune from laundromats. Her beloved horse was for sale but there were no takers. She got permission to build on her garden and sold most of it to a speculator. This was a sacrifice indeed: endlessly enriched with the night soil from their cesspit, the garden produced vegetables of spectacular size and quality. Henceforth, she said, they would live on Cornish pasties with the occasional addition of sugar-beet leaves. These, which the farmers threw away, looked and tasted like spinach of an inferior kind. 'Are you really sure,' I asked, 'that what you're doing is for the best?'

But Dorothea insisted that Jane be given a proper start. She mentioned her cousins the Broadbents, accepted as the leading Cloate family. Bill and Emily Broadbent's daughter Patricia had just finished four years at Woodford, had gone straight from it to one of the leading schools for models and faced the prospect of a dazzling future. Pictures of her had begun to appear in the Essex newspapers, and there was talk of contracts. I made no attempt to dampen Dorothea's enthusiasm. But it was hard to believe that Jane—slouching about the village with rounded shoulders, pretty but vapid, burdened with a nasal and moaning Essex accent—could ever hope to imitate her cousin.

A few days later Dorothea cut several inches from Jane's lifeless hair, tidied up her finger-nails and took her to Woodford for an interview with Mrs Amos, headmistress of Gladben's Hall.

Mrs Amos was formidable, smooth-skinned, immaculate and precise. She unnerved Dorothea by the combination of her penetrating stare and an almost excessively sympathetic manner. There was something spiderish about her. 'But there you are,' Dorothea said. 'She gets the results.'

Jane, however, had been at her worst: fidgeting, embarrassed and tongue-tied. 'She couldn't have been more stupid,' Dorothea said.

'I want to know all about you,' Mrs Amos had said. 'Are you a sporty girl? Does music appeal to you, or do you like to curl up with a book?'

But Jane just sat there, Dorothea explained. 'She wouldn't utter. She wouldn't even look Mrs Amos in the face. There was a picture on the wall of a German battleship going down after some battle—was it the Battle of the Plate?—and she was hypnotized by it. "I'm sorry," I said to Mrs Amos. "It's just her nerves. It'll pass in a minute." I have to say Mrs Amos was very understanding. Full marks to her for that. She asked Jane what she wanted to do with her life and Jane told her she didn't know, and Mrs Amos said that was quite normal—most young people didn't. She was trying to draw Jane out,' Dorothea said, 'and so then she asked her what she did in the evening. Jane said she looked at the telly, but she didn't have any favourite programme: she just watched anything that happened to be on; it was all the same. Otherwise she went down to the bus shelter. That's what the kids do when there's nothing on the box. They just sit there.'

'So what was the outcome?' I asked.

'You won't believe this,' Dorothea said. 'She was accepted.'

'That's really tremendous news,' I said. 'You must be very happy and relieved.'

She was, and was worried now only about how she was going to come up with the money. But I was curious about what was taught at this school beside charm.

'Well,' Dorothea said, 'there's much more to it. I'll tell you exactly what Mrs Amos said to me. She said, "Here we introduce them to pride. Often when a girl first comes to us she has no ego, and therefore no personality, and we set out to change that. When she leaves us we expect her to be full of herself, and that in a woman is the Open Sesame to success.'''

With the coming of spring there were great changes in the neighbourhood. The Americans expanded the base, doubling their military personnel and building accommodation for families brought in on long-term postings. Once again, as it had been back in the forties, there were Americans everywhere. They were young, smartly uniformed and outstandingly polite, and local men who had sucked in humility with their mothers' milk were now amazed to be addressed as 'sir'.

The village began to smarten up. Essex had been discovered by the frontiersmen from London who paid dearly for arriving late on the scene. Charmers End, not worth £5,000 when I moved in, was expected to fetch at least five times that sum by the time my lease ran out. A half-dozen rather sombre-looking lath-and-plaster Jacobean buildings were snapped up. The newcomers stripped away plaster to expose ancient beams, knocked out partition walls to join up poky little rooms, put in cocktail bars and usually found a place somewhere for a wrought-iron Spanish ornamental gate. There was nothing to be done about a cesspit except lift the iron cover, peer in and drop it hastily back in place. The settlers from London cut down old diseased fruit trees to turn gardens into paddocks, and sometimes made the mistake of buying local horses on the cheap. They rose early to exercise fashionable dogs. For the first time the Pied Bull had vodka on sale, and the village shop now stocked yoghurt in various flavours.

A paternalistic US government assured military personnel volunteering for overseas service that the comforts awaiting them were no less complete than those they had come to expect at home, and so air transports began to fly in to Effingham laden with deep-freezers, washing-machines, pressure- and microwave cookers, hi-fi equipment, Hoovers, electric organs and even Persian carpets. Many of those for whom this flood of goods were destined had become accustomed to an annual trade-in, replacing old models with new, and a major disadvantage to the life overseas was that no regular outlets existed for discarded equipment. Thus, the efficient turnover of the entire system was threatened and a surplus built up, for the houses on base were small and soon glutted with gear.

Dick was everybody's friend. When consulted by the Americans about their quandary, he immediately discussed it with the local shopkeepers and affluent villagers such as the Broadbents; a number agreed to do what they could to ease the log-jam of consumer durables. It was the commitment to Jane's future that turned Dick into a salesman. First he accepted small gifts, then a trifling commission, then finally obliged American friends by giving them a price for some article for which there was no immediate sale and keeping it until a customer could be found. Thus trade developed. Dick was a reluctant and therefore good salesman, a little troubled about the legality of his enterprise, and there was a melancholic religiosity about him that reassured both seller and buyer.

Dorothea and Dick continued to live on Cornish pasties and sugar-beet tops. Dick did not like to talk about finance, but Dorothea told me that in the first few months of operations they added enough to the cache of money somewhere under the floor to pay for a year's schooling at Woodford. It was arranged that Jane would enter Gladben's in the coming September.

These mildly illicit activities brought Dick close to others of a more dangerous kind. He was approached by a senior sergeant newly arrived in the country with what sounded at first a tempting proposition. The sergeant had heard of Dick's connections and said that a source of supply of goods of a better kind had opened up. He showed Dick a Sears Roebuck catalogue and said that most of the items listed could be made available at about half price.

The feeling I had was that he had already half-committed himself, but something was clearly worrying him.

'The first thing you have to do is to find out where the stuff's coming from,' I told him.

'I have. It got sent here instead of to Germany and they're stuck with it up at the base.'

'Why don't they send it back?'

'He says there's no laid-down procedure. If it's here, it's here. They've got to get shot of it as best they can or it'll stay here forever.

All they want to do is recover the cost price.'

'Nobody will believe a story like that,' I told him. 'Where is it now?'

'In Warehouse 8. I've seen some of it.'

'How does this man strike you? Do you get the feeling he's a crook?'

'He's like any sergeant. A bit tough. They get used to ordering people about.'

I told Dick that I hoped he was not involved already, but that, if he was, he should get out of it as fast as he could. And so Dick went back and told the sergeant he wanted a day or two to think about it. The sergeant told him to keep his mouth shut.

A few days later Dick returned, full of excitement and alarm. He had been out fishing in a flooded gravel-pit at six in the morning when something happened that made him suspicious, and he asked me to come and see the place.

The site was where a company had been taking out gravel, pebbles and sand for as long as anybody could remember, and then suddenly had dropped everything and pulled out. This had happened ten or fifteen years before. In true Essex style there had been no attempt to tidy up before departure, and so now a half-dismantled pump protruded from the water and rails carried several shattered trucks down to the bullrushes sprouting on the verge of what was now a small lake. There were old breeze-blocks, oil barrels, a wheel-less vehicle sitting on its springs, and iron gates that opened wide upon further devastation. All these objects were host to the rank but vigorous creeping plants that would eventually muffle their outlines with coarse leaves and insignificant flowers.

Dick, very jumpy, insisted that we should pretend to fish, and we had taken rods with us. I fixed up my line and helped him to fix his. We then clambered down the bank and waded into the shallows among the bullrushes. A moorhen scuttled away dragging splashes across the water, and I breathed in the heavy odour of decaying vegetation and mud. It was a school holiday and two small boys were hacking with knives at the bushes and seedling trees. Part of a large brick and corrugated iron building showed among the elder trees on the far bank. It was reached, Dick said, by an overgrown track from the main road that he had seen a few days before. He had been down in the bushes by the water baiting his hook when a big US Air Force truck came down the track and stopped outside the building. Three US servicemen got out. Dick recognized one of them as the top sergeant. They unlocked the door of the building and began to unload packing cases from the truck and carry them in. It took them half-an-hour. Then they drove off.

'And what do you imagine it was all about?' I asked him.

'Stuff nicked from the base,' he said. 'I was shit-scared.'

'Why?'

'The sergeant. He'd have cut my throat if he saw me and thought I was spying on them.'

Dick explained how the racket worked. There was a fix back in the States with whoever handled the air schedules. Transports flying in always landed after the warehouses had been locked up for the night. The C-Van containers, unloaded and left in the parking bays—theoretically under armed guard—were promptly opened and up to a quarter of their contents spirited away. The consignment sheets corresponding to the abstracted goods were simply torn from the shipping documents and next morning the chief storeman cheerfully signed everything as OK.

'Why come to me about it?' I asked Dick.

'What do you think I ought to do?'

'Steer clear of it,' I said. I told him he should tell the sergeant anything he wanted and then keep away from him. I told him he should go somewhere else to fish.

Most of the married American servicemen and their families were content to stay on base, and the base did its best, with considerable success, to provide those things that made home sweet to them. England remained largely unknown. Only young servicemen ventured out, and when they did it was usually in search of female company. They were a godsend to the girls of Essex, which had become a sad backwater for young people. The Essex girls found the Americans more polite, considerate and enthusiastic than the English boys. In approaches to the opposite sex, the Americans often displayed an outmoded gallantry, which sometimes evoked pretended amusement but was always well received. Apart from drinking sessions in the pubs, Saturday night discos were about the only form of entertainment surviving in country places. A girl escorted to one by a local lad had to resign herself to a loutish rather than romantic experience. By contrast the weekend dances at the base offered a model of propriety and good order.

The calm, homely and rather formal atmosphere of the social club at the base seemed to exert a tranquillizing effect upon even the most unruly and pugnacious English males. Finding it impossible to pick a quarrel with their urbane American hosts, they soon gave up trying. Drinks at the base were better and much cheaper; the music was good and played on the very latest system; and the décor was tasteful and relaxing, and avoided cheap effects. No one was ever over-charged, and the old, sly trick practised in so many local clubs of turning up the heat to increase thirst and consumption was unnecessary, since American hospitality was not perverted by the profit-motive.

Above all, it was the servicemen themselves who impressed. The story had gone around that before arriving in Britain they had been issued with a booklet telling them how to behave. This struck all those who came into contact with them as absurd. These, the girls decided, were nature's gentlemen: handsome, clean-cut in both appearance and motive, sophisticated and rich. In the most discreet fashion, careful always not to provoke the rivalry of their English counterparts, the Americans showed photographs of themselves in their civilian days, often at the wheels of enormous cars, in the glamorous environment of their homeland: Santa Barbara and Beverly Hills, the Rocky Mountains, Yellowstone Park, Miami Beach and Disneyland. Few impressionable young girls could resist such an emotional assault. It was an experience that turned many a head. To Dorothea's horror, her daughter Jane was among them. Any girl under the age of seventeen, unless accompanied by her mother, was excluded from the magical Saturday night at the base. Jane—tall for her age—was dressed and made up by her friends to look at least eighteen and smuggled past the scrutiny at the door. She came home at midnight, defiant and smelling of alcohol; and Dorothea feared that, after this brief glimpse of paradise, Jane would never settle for the monotony of Long Crendon again. But it was July, and the dangerous weeks were coming to an end. 'Only a couple of months to go and she'll be safely out of harm's way at Woodford,' Dorothea said. 'My feeling is we're just in time.'

After our visit to the old gravel pit, Dick was under a cloud. He could not shake himself free from the attentions of the sinister sergeant, who refused to allow him to break what he claimed was an agreement, and began to adopt a threatening posture. Then suddenly the man dropped out of sight. The English detectives on permanent duty with the base police toured the village with his photograph, and took statements, including one from Dick, but there the matter was dropped. Dick learned that the sergeant had been arrested and packed off in handcuffs back to the States. The transports ceased to land after dark, and the volume of American luxury goods in circulation went into steep decline. Some time later, as a matter of curiosity, Dick visited the old shed where he had seen the crates unloaded and found it open and empty.

'It has all been a bit of a fright,' Dick said. Now, suddenly, he was nervous about his involvement in the disposal of the base families' surplus gear. Dick had learned that such imported items were for personal use only. Somebody had broken a law, but Dick was not sure whose law it was, and who had done the breaking. The visits of the detective occasioned further unease. The villagers interviewed would have been crafty enough to keep him out of the kitchens where any piece of machinery of American origin would certainly be on view. Still, one never knew. A man like that was trained to use his eyes. Despondently, Dick decided to play safe and pull out of the business, and then, just as his hopes for Jane's future began to recede, new prospects for commerce opened up.

The idea of status had hardly reached Long Crendon at the time of my arrival, and the alterations made by the newcomers to the houses they bought were seen by the natives as unreasoning and eccentric. Why, the villagers argued, should a man enclose his garden with a fence that kept nothing out? Why, instead of spending a hundred or two on renovating a barn, should he have it rebuilt in Norman style at a cost of £2,000?

Slowly an inkling of what was behind this madness began to seep in. Here and there a villager became infected with it. The problem was how, in their gentle and unassertive manner, could village people acquire the magical property that enabled a man to stand out from his fellows? Nothing a man could do to alter his house—by a lick of paint on the outside or a glass front door or a chiming bell—could conceal the stark facts, known to all, of pump-water and outside privy. Almost every employable male worked at the base for a similar salary: village life was one of total equality; all were at the bottom of the pyramid. Humility had been inherited from the feudal servility of a not too distant past. Now suddenly the idea was abroad that a man could be 'different'—command a little more than average respect. Nothing could be done about the house, but, as Dick pointed out, the possession of a good car, for example, could set a man apart, and by cutting down expenses, such a prize could come within reach.

American servicemen normally arrived in the country for a three-year tour of duty, and often brought their cars with them. When the time came to move on, they were quite ready to part with the vehicle at a reasonable price. Dick had discovered this and acted accordingly. He came to an agreement with the Customs over the matter of excise duty, and after some trial and error, was able to cope with the paperwork required. Everyone knew Dick and knew that they would get value for money. Within a few months many of Long Crendon's cottages had a shining American car parked outside.

After Christmas and Easter the third most important feast celebrated in Long Crendon was the ancient secular one of August Bank Holiday. At this the Cloates, for all their slow loss of power and influence, appeared together as a clan, and assisted by alcohol the old defiant spirit flickered strongly.

On the bank holiday the people of Long Crendon who normally preferred to stay inside when not working felt suddenly and briefly the mysterious call of the open, and gathered up their families to go to the sea-shore or on picnics amid the few trees that remained where there once had been woods. It was almost a point of honour to escape from confining walls. The local pubs which normally served, at best, a sandwich at the bar provided full-scale lunches. The traditional holiday dish was eel pie, although Long

Crendon was possibly the last place in Essex where it could be tasted. It was not what it had been, since the eels were no longer caught in the Blackwater or Crouch, but imported frozen from Holland. Nevertheless, eel pie was not to be avoided on this occasion.

Several tables had been reserved for the Cloates in the pleasant garden at the back of the Pied Bull. Some of the family had moved away from the area but made the effort to be present at the annual reunion. Of these family members I knew nothing at all. Nor had I had contacts with the Cloates living in the village who were notorious for keeping to themselves. I knew only Dorothea and Dick, and their cousins the Broadbents.

For both families this was an exceptional occasion. Both Jane and Patricia would soon be saying goodbye to the village for a while: Jane to face whatever Mrs Amos had in store for her; Patricia, having completed with distinction her course at the school for models, to join a party of them visiting Brazil, where they were to be photographed wearing the creations of a famous couturier against that pageant of water, the Iguazu Falls.

I drove Dick down to the Pied Bull and we had a drink in the bar while waiting for the others. Soon Dorothea came into sight with Emily and Bill Broadbent, all on horseback. Patricia broke with the custom. She was dropped off at the pub by the Cambridge-educated son of a local landowner who drove her in his Porsche.

Dick left me. I walked to the door of the bar to stand for a moment. A faint scent of eel pie was in my nostrils, and I looked down on this gathering of the clans. At this level success made itself felt, and Bill Broadbent, a once handsome saloon-bar joker, now prematurely aged by the good life his asset-stripping had provided, was surrounded by family toadies who had not done so well, a single gin and tonic held in every hand. These men were less prosperous than the average villager. Some were too old to be employed at the base, and some declined the opportunity, speaking of private means. Apart from Bill, only two had come on horseback. The Essex historian Stephen Maudsley, writing at the end of the last century, had mentioned the great-grandfathers of these men. 'Scant heed was paid to law and order in these remote parts. Scarcely a score of years have passed since the notorious Cloates of Crendon's

End raided a nearby village which had given them some offence.'
This seemed like the end of the road.

Jane and Patricia had moved out of the crowd and were
walking together. They were fond of each other. Patricia, described
by Mrs Amos as possibly her most finished product, floated,
drifted, seeming at times almost to be airborne, while Jane plodded
at her side as if carrying a sack of potatoes on her shoulders.
Patricia's svelte body was clad to perfection. By comparison Jane
appeared outlandish, almost tribal, as so many village girls were. In
defiance of Dorothea's protests, she had applied bleach to her hair,
followed by a bizarre attack with scissors. Patricia was pleasant and
gracious, fluttering the tips of her fingers at anyone greeting her
who could not easily be reached. Jane ignored these gestures. Both
girls were smiling, and studying them as they came close I
understood that Patricia's smile was part of Mrs Amos's art—an
asset, an accomplishment which matched the other ingredients of
her beauty. Jane's smile, for all her lumpishness, was human—
fallible, but sweet.

Soon after, a project took me to the Far East, off and on for
nearly four years. I felt involved in Long Crendon and its
problems, and before leaving I tried to secure a base there by
buying Charmers Green, but the asking price was beyond my
means. Nevertheless I kept in touch with Dorothea. We exchanged
letters two or three times a year. Things continued to go fairly well
for them. Her first letter informed me that she had sold her horse,
and that she and Dick now owned a veteran but serviceable MG.
After that, their gracious but shattered house, with the remnant of
its incomparable vegetable patch and its cracked rear wall, went to
a buyer from London and they moved into a brand-new bungalow.
The view was of other bungalows.

Dick had been treated, and was now able to stand up straight
and had taken a course in public speaking. But most of her news
concerned Jane. 'It's just as they told us it would be,' she said. 'The
year's not up yet and you can hardly believe the difference. It's
wonderful what they can do.'

By the next year Jane's speech had been dealt with to
everybody's satisfaction. 'You remember the way she used to

mumble? I could hardly understand what she was saying myself. Now she speaks as clear as anybody. But she doesn't sound too la-di-da with it if you know what I mean. Which is rather nice.'

Letters in the third year indicated that Jane might have started to think for herself. 'She's been awarded a prize for social awareness, whatever they mean by that,' Dorothea wrote. 'I suppose we're the tiniest bit disappointed because modelling's out. She says it's not for her. Mrs Amos says she's clever enough to do anything she wants, but we shouldn't attempt to sway her. While we're on the subject, did you hear about Patricia? She's always in the papers these days. Do you remember when she was just off to Brazil? Well, she married a Brazilian landowner with an estate the size of Essex. The paper said he was the seventh richest man in the world.' The latest story was that the marriage was on the rocks. Money wasn't everything, Dorothea noted.

By the time of her last letter, Dorothea's disappointment with her daughter seemed to have deepened. 'Mind you,' she wrote, 'whatever we've done for her, we'd do it all over again. Her father and I have written to suggest that she might consider being something like a personal secretary to an MP, or a television presenter. She says we'll talk about it when she comes home for the holidays. She hasn't had much to say about herself, which doesn't seem a good sign. The news of Patricia isn't so good. I sent you a cutting about her divorce from the Brazilian. Now she's married a French count with a castle in Angoulême. He's more than twice her age. Sometimes I wonder. Her mother can't see this one lasting long either. I always say happiness is what counts.'

I found myself once more in Long Crendon. The changes, although more radical than expected, had not been unforeseen. It was remarkable that so dramatic a face-lift could have been achieved in so short a time. The villagers had done whatever they could to make the place ugly within their resources, adding a little raw red brick here, an atrocious plastic ornament there, but it was the newcomers who had set to work to strip every vestige of character. There were many newcomers now. In their total isolation they formed an ethnic minority. They searched for the picturesque and were able to finance change from limitless funds.

Certain iniquities had been suppressed. The smouldering refuse dump had been removed and the health authorities had curbed the smellier operations at the pig farm. Main drainage had come to the long street at last, thus—except in the case of outlying houses—putting an end to the collection of night soil which had produced so many superb vegetables in the past. All three austere old pubs had been tarted up. I stayed at the Pied Bull. Its simple façade was tricked out with coloured lights and a sign of Pre-Raphaelite inspiration had been hung, showing a bull without testicles. In the past, narrow, straight-backed wall benches had enforced dignity upon the patrons. Now they lounged in armchairs upholstered in buttoned pink plastic. At Charmers End the moat had been sanitized and given a concrete landing stage, to which a black gondola with a lamp on its prow was tied. The house had statuary and a double garage, and it could only be glimpsed through the sombre foliage of the *Cupressus leylandii*, now to be seen everywhere in Long Crendon.

My conviction that the village was destined to become a cultural colony of the United States had proved well founded, but the process had been swifter than I would have thought possible. Two cars were parked outside many of the village houses, some of them fish-tailed monsters. Matters of fundamental custom, such as mealtimes, had been revolutionized. For centuries, country people everywhere had sat down at twelve-thirty prompt to stuff themselves with the main meal of the day, and had then risen from the table to burn off the stodgy food by hard physical work in the field.

Such work was now a thing of the past, and gone with it was the traditional midday meal. Men employed at the base no longer wished to consume a pound and a half of potatoes every lunchtime, and had fallen in with the American system of a quick and easily digested meal, followed by something more substantial in the evening. Chilli con carne was the current favourite. A few of the more advanced families joined with American friends to celebrate Thanksgiving: butterball turkey and all the trimmings flown in from the US. The local English, apart from the newcomers, were becoming less reclusive. Even in the recent past they had lived their private, separate lives behind tightly drawn curtains. Now they organized get-togethers in the American fashion. Pabst and Schlitz beer were drunk from cans. Pre-cooked, containerized foods from Indian and Chinese take-aways were served on cardboard plates and eaten with plastic cutlery. These accessories were smuggled out with little difficulty from the base. The memory in Long Crendon of poverty once endured was fading fast.

Dorothea and Dick were in their bungalow. They were no longer under a strain. A bungalow—with furniture polished and in place, the comforting sound of the toilet's flush and no major cracks in the wall—can act as a tranquillizer. Dick's nervous tic, which had once surfaced every few minutes in the wrinkles round his mouth, was gone, and the doctors, in straightening him out, had added an inch to his height. Dorothea had put on a few pounds and was all the better for it, and a hairdresser had brought life to the lank black Indian hair of old.

Dick was as busy as ever. Within minutes of my arrival he was summoned by telephone. He was running a little agency affair of his own, Dorothea said. Accommodation was very short in a rapidly expanding area, and he was doing what he could to help out. He had at last found the Lord. Many of his friends from the States were Baptists, and he had become one as well. Dorothea put in a few hours most days, as ever, at Charmers End, not because they needed the money with Jane now more or less off their hands, but because she liked having something to do.

Jane had been home for three months. 'Isn't that earlier than intended?' I asked.

'We had a long talk with Mrs Amos,' she said, 'after which there didn't seem much point in going any further.'

'In what direction? You told me Jane had decided against modelling. What about the other possibilities? It sounded as though Mrs Amos had high hopes for her.'

'According to Mrs Amos, Jane was exceptionally gifted. She was attractive and intelligent, and she could have done anything she wanted to.' Dorothea gestured resignation.

'But she didn't want to be a television presenter or anybody's personal secretary?'

'It was her whole attitude. That kind of thing didn't seem to mean anything to her. In one way, Mrs Amos said, she'd turned out better than hoped, and in another year she could have had the world at her feet. But it all left her cold.'

I told Dorothea that I was beginning to suspect she was to be congratulated. She had an interesting daughter.

'Mrs Amos said you sometimes come across people you thought you could change, and they fooled you by pretending to go along, but really underneath they were going their own way all the time.'

So Jane had beaten the system, I said; she had survived.

'I suppose that's one way of looking at it,' Dorothea said. 'Anyway, we brought her home.'

I asked what she was going to do.

'She's filling in time in the accounts office at the base.'

'And after that?'

'She'll take up nursing.'

'What could be better?'

'You won't be surprised to hear she has an American boyfriend.'

'Why should I be surprised? What is he—a pilot, or a navigator?'

'No,' she said. 'He's on the catering side. An assistant cook.'

I was struck by inspiration and asked: 'Would he by any chance be coloured?'

'How on earth did you guess?'

It was just something that had occurred to me. I said, 'We're getting to know Jane. Both of us. What time do you expect her home? I'm much looking forward to seeing her.'

Nicholas Shakespeare
In Pursuit of Guzmán

Lima

I arrived in Lima, having forgotten what a vile city it is.

I arrived in the middle of a police strike, and the streets were crowded with hooded officers. They were shooting guns in the air, and some had commandeered buses. They were protesting against a regulation requiring them to supply their own uniforms and practice ammunition. They held aloft their symbol, a worn-out boot.

That night I counted seventeen explosions—not from the police but from guerrillas. The next evening the restaurant around around the corner was machine-gunned and then blown up with dynamite. There was a curfew, and each morning I discovered new graffiti on the walls, slogans painted in red celebrating the guerrillas, Sendero Luminoso, the 'Shining Path'. The slogans also celebrated the man who led Sendero. They called him *Presidente* Gonzalo, but his name was Abimael Guzmán. I had come to Lima to find Guzmán, although I knew I wouldn't succeed. I didn't. But that was the reason I was here.

In fact, Guzmán hadn't been spotted since 1981, and not much was known about him. He had been pictured with a Devil's tail: they said he taught his young initiates to murder and then forced them to drink the blood of their victims. They said he was in league with drug-traffickers, that he was dying or that he was dead or that he was abroad—in Bolivia, New York, London. I read one newspaper with the headline, 'ABIMAEL VISITS HARRODS?'

For that matter, not much was known about his followers, the Senderistas. They gave no interviews, issued few statements and did not claim responsibility for their bombings. They accepted no funds from abroad; their weapons were stolen or hand-made: beer-can bombs hurled from slings made of llama hair. Most people believed their story began eight years ago in the village of Chuschi.

Eight years ago, in 1980, Peru held the presidential election that returned Fernando Belaúnde. Belaúnde had been removed twelve years before: in October 1968, the military had entered the presidential palace through a guard-room lavatory and carried him out, still wearing his pyjamas. On his return,

Belaúnde found plenty of unfinished business—the single achievement of his previous Minister of Agriculture had been to sign a permit allowing a dog into the country—and the events in a little Andean village went unnoticed.

Chuschi is near a source of the Amazon. Three hundred families live there, growing maize on the terraces overlooking the Río Pampas Valley and tending a few animals. Once a year the priest succeeds in getting members of the village to clean out the irrigation ditches; occasionally, they tidy the church. On 18 May 1980, the day of Peru's elections, the village of Chuschi was visited by strangers. They had come to burn the ballot boxes. 'The old dead-end votes,' the visitors announced, served only to preserve the old order. 'A new path of arms' would lead Peru towards a transformed society that served the people.

The date of the ballot-burning was interesting. Peru's last great Indian revolt was nearly 200 years before led by a man named José Gabriel Condorcanqui who called himself the Inca Túpac Amaru II. He wore his hair long, in ringlets, and carried a grey blunderbuss with a mouth the size of an orange. He was captured by the Spanish in Cuzco in 1781 and was led to the main square where his tongue was cut out, and his body was pulled apart by horses. His limbs were then packed in leather bags and sent by mule for exhibition in the provinces of Chumbivilcas, Lampa and Carabaya. But there was a legend among Peruvian Indians that José Gabriel Condorcanqui did not die in 1781, and that his limbs were re-growing underground. One day, it was believed, the pieces of his body would be joined together, and Inca Túpac Amaru II would rise up to liberate his people.

Inca Túpac Amaru II was executed on 18 May 1781. It was the same day, 199 years later, 18 May 1980, that Sendero arrived in Chuschi, bearing, for the first time, the news of President Gonzalo.

About two months after the ballot-burning, on Independence Day, dynamite was thrown into the ranks of a procession in Ayacucho—the 'capital' of the Andes—and an army captain trod out the fuse. The next day, in the city of Arequipa, 275 miles south of Ayacucho, an electricity pylon was blown up, and the city was left without light. In August, there were nineteen different bombings, finally prompting a statement from the Minister of the Interior: there were no guerrillas in Peru, but there appeared to be a problem with 'delinquents'.

In the following month, September, delinquents seized 2,000 sticks of dynamite from a mine in Huancayo. On 5 November, twenty delinquents invaded the town of Vischongo, and raised a red flag in the square. On 23 December, in San Agustín de Ayzcara, a land-owner was killed. Three days later, the day after Christmas, delinquents had hung dead dogs from the traffic lights in Lima, with dynamite stuffed in their mouths and placards tied round their necks identifying them as the Chinese leader Deng Xiaoping, whose 'fascist dictatorship' had betrayed the world revolution. It was a mystifying spectacle. Leaflets explained that a dead dog was the Indian symbol of a tyrant condemned to death by his people.

The government was unconcerned; 'narco-terrorists', according to Belaúnde: there was no need for alarm; after all, he had experience with terrorists, including his successful containing of the Castro-inspired revolt of Luis de la Puente and Hector Bejar in 1965. In this instance, however, the terrorists had no identifiable leaders and no manifesto, only their own head of state: *Presidente* Gonzalo.

Finally, in early June 1981, the Minister of the Interior announced a 'decisive battle' had broken out between police and what was finally acknowledged to be the 'Shining Path'.

But the attacks continued.

Sendero had grown so sophisticated that it was able to subject Lima to a complete electrical black-out on New Year's Eve or during the Pope's visit: the only light came from the hills across the city, where huge bonfires burned in the shape of the hammer and sickle. One day saw the bombing of the American Embassy and the Chinese Embassy ('Dogs who betrayed the Cultural Revolution') and the Indian Embassy and the embassies of Italy and Chile and the Cultural Centre of the Soviet Union ('Filthy Revisionists'). There was a joke. Only two things worked in Peru: the women's volley-ball team and Sendero Luminoso.

And still the attacks continued—in Ayacucho, dogs ran through the streets with bombs strapped to their backs; in a market crowd at Huanta, a donkey exploded; in Lima's Crillón Hotel, a child walked into the foyer and blew up; in Chimbote a telephone exchange was damaged by an explosive attached to a duck—until finally, on 29 December, Belaúnde finally declared a state of emergency in the three Andean regions of Ayacucho, Huancavelica and Apurímac.

Suddenly in Ayacucho soldiers were seen in the streets wearing round their necks the mutilated corpses of dogs. In Chuschi, a soldier fixed a stick of dynamite to a peasant, noting afterwards that, 'This is how terrorists die.' In Soccos thirty-four villagers were machine-gunned and then set alight with incendiary grenades. One survivor lay in a hole beside her husband, watching him burn 'like a roast pig'.

Belaúnde did not stand in the elections of 1985.

B elaúnde's successor was Alan García, thirty-seven years old, head of the American Popular Revolutionary Alliance. García had been elected, confident that his centre-leftist policies would appease the Senderistas. He was wrong. They saw him as just another bourgeois politician. By the end of 1987, Sendero assassins were killing an average of four officials each day. Military intelligence maps revealed that Sendero could launch assaults at any point along the spine of the Andes, from Jaen in the north to Puno in the south. Several areas of the Upper Huallaga, where Sendero had reportedly come to an understanding with the region's drugs-traffickers, had simply passed out of government control. Over 11,000 people had been killed. García himself had nearly died, once in a mortar attack and once when an old peasant woman pushed forward to embrace him, concealing several sticks of dynamite beneath her skirt.

In May 1987, García offered a reward of $80,000 to anyone whose efforts would lead to the arrest of Julio Mezzich, Osman Morote, and, the most wanted of all, Abimael Guzmán.

W hen I arrived in Lima last summer, I discovered at least five journalists writing books on Sendero, among them Manuel Granados, formerly a student at the university at Ayacucho. His bachelor's thesis, completed eight years ago, was a study of Sendero's early history—perhaps the most thorough study

237

if only because Granados knew personally the people he was writing about.

But there were only three copies of Granados's thesis, and on seeing one I understood why there were no more. At the time, Granados said, Sendero 'seemed to have no future, and I criticized everything they were doing in Ayacucho.' He criticized Sendero to such an extent that the three professors assigned to mark his thesis all resigned. The next three nominations also refused. Sendero had an effect on people, and Granados was warned that his thesis would be held against him, 'when the time comes to send me to Heaven.' Granados's nails had been bitten down, and, throughout our meeting, his eyes moved constantly, flicking, flicking. It was the first time I had seen this kind of nervousness. Later I would see it frequently.

Granados pointed out that the full name was not Sendero Luminoso, the 'Shining Path', but the 'Peruvian Communist Party for the Shining Path of José Carlos Mariátegui'. Mariátegui, a morose cripple with a falsetto voice, was the founder of the Peruvian Socialist Party in the twenties. Like many of his subsequent Sendero followers, Mariátegui had hoped to become a priest—the Roman Catholic Church remains the only institution left untroubled in Peru—but ended up as a journalist, his most influential work being the polemical *Seven Interpretive Essays on Peruvian Reality*. In this, his followers claimed, he became the first to understand the reality of Peruvian society: that it was a land of Indians whose position as underdogs had remained unchanged since Pizarro's Conquest. The Spanish had destroyed an impressive society—the Incas—and had not replaced it, and for Mariátegui and his disciples the pre-Conquest Inca empire of Twantinsuyo represented a kind of primitive communist society. The future would combine revolutionary Marxism with the society of the Incas.

Like Mariátegui, who described Peru as a 'semi-feudal and semi-colonial country', Senderistas saw around them the same conditions that characterized China before Mao. They hoped, in following Mariátegui's Shining Path, to introduce the thoughts of Chairman Mao to a Peru of the Incas, and arrive at a New Democracy.

The proponent of the 'New Democracy', Abimael Guzmán, was born, illegitimate, on 4 December 1934—an anniversary regularly commemorated by Sendero in Lima with a blackout. He was born with the Old Testament name of his father, Abismael, later dropping the letter 's' to assume the name of one of the Horsemen of the Apocalypse.

The Guzmán family doctor lived in Lima in a house near the sea, and, although now eighty-nine, he remembered Abimael's father as a small, square man who didn't drink or dance. His weakness was women. Sometimes he had three at the same time. One of them was Abimael's mother, Berenice Reynoso. After Abimael's birth, his father moved to Mollendo, a port fifteen miles away. The doctor said, 'He had a shop on the corner of Arequipa in front of the market where he sold rice and sugar. He lived above it with his "official" woman—a Chilean. She was a better class of woman than Abimael's mother.'

But Berenice Reynoso followed, also moving to Mollendo and living with her son 150 yards away in a yellow-wood house consisting of two rooms and a patio where they cooked. The father visited at night. When his mother died in 1939, Abimael, the bastard, was moved in with his Chilean step-mother. A picture was starting to emerge. I decided to fly south to Arequipa, about 450 miles, to the town where Guzmán grew up.

Arequipa

Arequipa is one of the most dramatic cities in Peru. Its buildings are made of white stone, and the snow-capped volcano Misti can be seen from every street. It was here that Guzmán attended secondary school. I spent several days in Arequipa. While there, I met by chance a man who had been at the the same school at the same time. When I mentioned Guzmán's name, however, the classmate showed the familiar apprehensions: Guzmán, he assured me, would kill him if his name was known.

I promised several times not to reveal it, but nothing I said seemed to help. He was terrified.

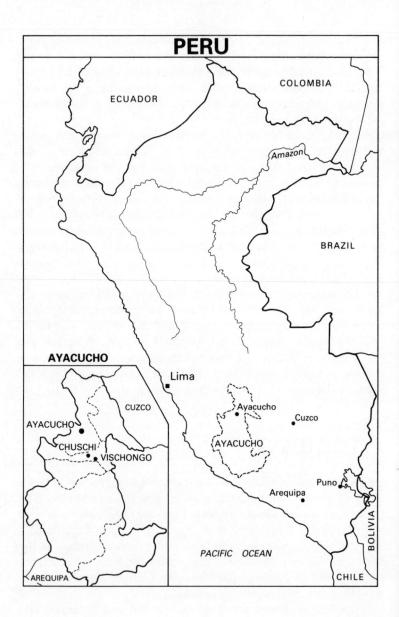

'*Es un loco,*' he repeated, '*un loco.*'

Slowly some details emerged.

For instance, I learned that Guzmán had won a prize for *good* conduct. It wasn't much, admittedly. I learned that Guzmán was religious—'very religious'—introspective, and virtually impenetrable. I learned that he never drank, never went to parties, never played games, never had girl-friends. 'None of us,' the class-mate said, 'could ever have imagined that Guzmán would grow up to be what he is now: Peru's most wanted assassin.'

The class-mate opened a school magazine from 1952, which included reports on each student's performance. Guzmán was not exceptional and I saw little to support the myth surrounding him— of the genius whose childhood was spent exclusively with books. He was, in almost every respect, average, distinguishing himself in only Spanish and the history of Peru. The 1952 report also showed his mug-shot: handsome, with gleaming hair and dark, blank eyes. He looked like a dandy, Spanish rather than Indian.

I looked at the picture for some time, and then flipped through the pages until I came across a mention of Guzmán and then an article by him. His first words in print, an account of how Guzmán had succeeded in organizing students into a number of extra-curricular groups devoted to the study of culture, sport, religion, journalism and economics. 'At the head of each group there will be a leader. The group leader will appoint four assistants . . . there will be a central committee made up of nine members.'

It was not much, but its logic had an appeal: Guzmán, at seventeen, already organizing.

I asked the class-mate if he could remember anything else about Guzmán—a detail, an event.

'No. No incidents. He was . . . he was—' he said, shaking his head, searching for the appropriate word, 'he was an *anonymity.*'

In the following year, 1953, Guzmán would have been nineteen, about the time he dropped the 's' from his Christian name and went to Arequipa's University of San Agustín, where he studied philosophy and law. I learned that the current rector was in fact Guzmán's former teacher. I got an appointment by mentioning a mutual acquaintance in Lima, and the Rector was delighted to see me, until I mentioned Guzmán's name and his face suddenly went flat. It was, again, the fear. It was difficult to get him to resume talking.

Could he remember anything about Guzmán?

He could remember that Guzmán was one of his best students.

I see. Perhaps some detail? His character?

A long pause. 'Yes. Guzmán was quiet.'

Quiet?

'Yes, very quiet.'

I see.

'He was not fiery, not at all. He was not an original thinker.' And again: 'It would have been hard to believe that he wanted to change the processes of history.'

And so we sat.

'Perhaps,' the Rector said, finally, rising from his chair, 'perhaps, you should see Dr Garaycochea. Yes, it's Dr Garaycochea whom you should see.'

D r Walter Garaycochea lived on the other side of town, and so, following the Rector's advice, I made an appointment. Garaycochea was a lecturer in philosophy, and the buildings nearby were sprayed with crimson graffiti, accusing the García government of fascism and genocide. Garaycochea was remarkably forthcoming.

Garaycochea met Guzmán in 1953, the year he began studying at the university. Together they founded an institution to promote 'cultural activities', a group that met every Saturday to talk about Kant, Heidegger, Hegel, Russell, Husserl. The group also started a magazine, *Hombre y Mundo* (**Mankind** and the World), but it collapsed after three issues, and Guzmán's contribution to it was one article, a review of Pascual Jordán's *Physics in the Twentieth Century*. It was unexceptional stuff—as was true of most of Guzmán's contributions to the group. Being the youngest, he spoke the least. 'He heard everything but he didn't participate.'

I urged Garaycochea to remember something further about Guzmán, something more revealing—a detail, an incident. I asked Garaycochea, in short, the same question I had asked everyone else who knew Guzmán.

Nothing.

Then, suddenly, he remembered something—in fact, a story.

The event took place in 1959. Garaycochea and Guzmán had gone to a party, a graduation party given by Páquita Valladores. 'At about ten p.m. Abimael and I left the party and we went to a bar. At the bar we drank a lot. This was rare because Abimael hardly ever drank. We then went to another bar in Alto de la Luna on the other side of the market, where we talked until six in the morning.'

Dr Garaycochea looked pleased.

But what did you talk about?

Dr Garaycochea scratched his head. 'I don't know.'

Then suddenly, Dr Garaycochea grew animated again. There was another story—he was able to remember another incident. Perhaps it would help.

This was the story: 'Guzmán once went with my wife and me to see the film of *Porgy and Bess*. Afterwards we visited the Café Paris in Mercedares where we praised the film and said how lovely Gershwin's music was. Abimael disagreed. "It's a primitive film," he said. "The Americans don't understand the first thing about music."'

There was a pause.

'I see,' I said, 'that is what you remember Guzmán to have said.'

'Yes,' Dr Garaycochea said, 'about Gershwin.' He looked pleased.

Garaycochea had been one of the five men marking Guzmán's first dissertation in January 1961, a work on the Kantian theory of space. 'I think it's slightly elementary,' said Garaycochea.

It must have been original in some way. It is popularly held to be outstanding.

'Not at all. Really, it's quite remarkable that he was destined to be a political leader.'

I decided the next morning to read Guzmán's dissertation, and discovered that a copy, bound in grey, was locked in a cabinet in the Faculty of Letters. To borrow it, I had to leave my passport.

'So many people try to steal it,' said the librarian. The 178-page essay was dedicated to Dr Miguel Angel Rodríguez Rivas. Dr Garaycochea had spoken a great deal about Rivas. He had been the leader of the weekly philosophy group. According to Garaycochea, Rivas, a Marxist, was an imposing man and an attractive orator, and he described him as Guzmán's mentor. On the dedication page, Guzmán himself describes Rivas as 'dear friend and master'.

Guzmán's thesis consists of thirty-seven conclusions arguing that Kant's theory of space has been superseded by advances in modern physics. I had reached conclusion twenty-seven (a), when the librarian leaned over, put his hands on my desk, and told me that he had run into Guzmán in Puno in 1964.

Was I interested?

Of course.

It was, the librarian said sitting down, rather peculiar. 'I couldn't understand why he was there.'

I asked him to explain.

Guzmán had been on a honeymoon—in the Andes. On meeting the librarian, Guzmán introduced him to his new wife.

'But why are you in Puno?' the librarian had asked again: it was so cold there.

Guzmán had replied: 'In Peru there's much to know and much to do. I want to know this part of Peru because I won't have another chance.' The librarian remembered him saying just those words, whereupon he asked Guzmán to join him for a glass of beer. Guzmán accepted only a mineral water.

I thanked the librarian and left, feeling increasingly frustrated. I was not sure what I expected to find of Guzmán. I knew, however, that I had expected more than a pedestrian autodidact who drank mineral water on his honeymoon and whose only distinguishing feature was a dislike for *Porgy and Bess*.

I wandered over to one of Guzmán's old haunts, La Dalmacía in San Juan de Dios, and ordered a beer, and sat reading through some of the material I had accumulated. In one magazine there was a mention of a song that Guzmán liked to sing to himself: '*Pepito de mi Corazón*'—Little Pepe of my Heart.

I tried several record shops. No one had heard the song, but, in one, I met a man and his wife who hummed what they thought were the opening lines. They couldn't remember the rest. The man was a Christadelphian who believed in the pure Gospel of the first century. He promised to send me the lyrics.

The lyrics of *Pepito de mi Corazón* arrived a few weeks later.

> *Ay, Pepito, yo te ruego,*
> *Si, si, si, si es que aún me quieres*
> *Como yo te quiero. Ven hacia mi,*
> *Pepito de mi corazón.*

> (Oh, my little Pepe, I beg you,
> If, if, if, if you still love me
> As I love you. Come to me,
> Little Pepe of my heart.)

I read them and imagined the young Kantian philosopher after a night at the Dalmacía, drinking mineral water. Afterwards he would walk home through the streets of Arequipa, looking at the cloudless sky and humming the refrain of his favourite song: 'Oh, my little Pepe, I beg you—'

The morning I left I walked down the Calle Ejericios, where Guzmán had lived in Arequipa. His father, that industrious womanizer, must have come up in the world to move his family into number 307. It was a large, old, elegant house. Fine wrought-iron grilles protected the windows. Two secretaries worked in the front office. They had never heard of Guzmán. The building, they explained, was now used as a primary and secondary school: the College of the Divine Master.

Lima

I returned to Lima to meet Guzmán's 'dear friend and master', Dr Miguel Angel Rodríguez Rivas, and found the city recovering from the first anniversary of the prison massacres.

The year before, after a night of rioting, 257 suspected members of Sendero Luminoso had been killed in the prisons at Lurigancho, El Frontón and Santa Bárbara. A nun who had heard the shooting told me it was like the popping of grilled maize. Those responsible for the killing, led by the megaphone-wielding Brigadier Rabanal Portilla, had been given total, albeit unwritten, authority to crush the riot. President García had promised: 'Either all the culprits go or I go.' They remain unpunished. At three p.m. on the afternoon of the anniversary, a Friday, the Minister of the Interior appeared on television and alerted the nation to expect Sendero attacks that night. By late afternoon the city was dead. It turned out to be one of the few nights of the year when nothing happened. Sendero had none the less brought the country to a standstill.

I met Rivas in a garden where there was a parrot that shrieked at the mention of 'Mao'.

Rivas and Guzmán had been friends since the fifties. Following the earthquake in 1960, Rivas had organized a group of 200 to take an inventory of the damage. Guzmán led one of the teams. He entered the barrios—possibly for the first time—and the misery he saw had a profound effect. One evening Guzmán returned to report on a house near the Bolognesi bridge. The family lived in cold, horrible conditions, without help from the authorities, with no hope of work. 'He said only an organized people could do something, and he saw the necessity of organizing them,' Rivas remembered.

Rivas last saw his former pupil in Lima in 1972. They had talked about Mao [the parrot shrieked] and of Ayacucho, where Guzmán had gone to teach. Guzmán spoke of his intention to start a subversive movement, one that, according to Rivas, was different from the terrorist groups of Argentina or Colombia. 'Sendero,' he said, 'is an ethnic, cultural movement, señor. It recognizes that we are a fundamentally Indian republic with a fundamentally Indian outlook. It will win and its triumph will be its death and it will disappear. It will win because it is fighting an unlosable war.'

Was Guzmán alive?

'Yes,' Rivas said, without hesitation. He mentioned a pamphlet that had appeared in his office a year ago, written in a style and advancing an argument that could only be Guzmán's. The pamphlet, entitled 'Develop the People's War To Serve The World Revolution', 110 pages long, commemorates the six-year struggle. It draws on Mao and Mariátegui, and charts the progress since the

246

burning of the ballot boxes at Chuschi: it describes how, guns in hand, the poor peasants of Peru are now about to storm the heavens, bringing about a new dawn, 'towards which fifteen billion years of matter . . . have been inevitably and irresistibly heading.' It makes, it must be admitted, for rather turgid reading. And it ends, finally, with a detailed catalogue of the atrocities allegedly committed by the armed forces. The last words are 'Long Live Chairman Gonzalo'.

Rivas had been living in Lima since 1961, when he had to leave Arequipa owing to a political dispute at the university. Following Rivas's departure, Guzmán appears to have been isolated, unable to secure a university post. It was finally Dr Efraín Morote Best, rector of the newly re-opened University of San Cristóbal de Huamanga in Ayacucho, who offered a good position to anyone from Rivas's group who was prepared to go to Ayacucho. In 1962, Guzmán had accepted.

For the Spanish-speaking Limeños, Ayacucho is part of a region referred to as *La Mancha India*, the Indian Stain. Its population of Quechua-speaking Indians has long been ignored by the central government. Life expectancy is forty-five years, with most of the population surviving barely above subsistence level. The annual income is fifty dollars, roughly the price of a Peruvian passport. In Quechua, Ayacucho means 'Corner of the Dead'.

Ayacucho

There are thirty-three churches in Ayacucho, most of them padlocked. The new buildings are the barracks near the airport. At night you can hear soldiers splashing in a pool with the prostitutes. Ayacucho is not listed in the tourist brochures. And while there are fewer bombings than before, the army is in control, and outsiders, especially journalists, are mistrusted. Journalists have been killed in Ayacucho.

I told the officer at the airport that I was a tourist.

Leaving, I was uncomfortable. No one looked at me. Women giggled as I passed. Somebody said something. And later I heard the same thing again. And again. At last I realized what they were saying: '*pistaco*'.

I ordered a meal in a café. The chicken was lukewarm and cooked in lumpy black grease. I left a large tip and as I walked away the cook appeared from the kitchen. He spat and said, '*Pistaco*'.

I climbed into the back of a pick-up to get a lift into town. 'Let the *pistaco* walk,' said a woman.

Another woman, with gold teeth and a pony-tail like a string of garlic, pointed at the ink spots on my jacket where a pen had run. 'Indian blood,' she said and pushed her hand inside my jacket. She said she was looking for a knife.

Pistaco.

In the local paper *Ahora!*, I read an article, 'Ayacucho lives in terror', and from it I learned that a *pistaco* was a tall white foreigner who slept by day, drank a lot of milk and carried a long white knife under his coat. He used the knife to cut up Indians. He chopped off heads and limbs, and kept their trunks for the human grease with which he oiled his machines. Europe's industrial revolution had been lubricated with the lard made from helpless Indians. So had been the Vietnam and Korean wars. The space shuttle Challenger, I learned, had blown up because it lacked this '*aceite humano*'.

Another word for *pistaco* is *nakaq*, which comes from the Quechua *nakay*, to strangle, and references to it occurred as early as 1571. I discovered a paper on the subject written in 1951 by Dr Morote in which he lists the *pistaco*'s characteristics:

1. He is semi-human, wild and cruel.
2. He lives alone in inaccessible places.
3. He is white or mestizo with a long beard, dishevelled hair and a fearsome face.
4. His weapons are a knife and a lasso made from human skin.
5. He waits on roads and bridges.
6. He attacks by night.
7. He strangles.
8. He extracts human grease.
9. He makes his victims disappear.
10. He uses the grease to melt down bells.
11. He is mortal. He has one son who takes his place when he dies.

I had a long conversation with a grim man wearing a Coca-Cola baseball cap. *Pistacos*, he told me, had recently hacked the limbs off 30,000 Indians.

I said I was a little sceptical. Had he any evidence?

Oh, no, but he'd seen it in the press. Most *pistacos* were government mercenaries employed by President García to pay off his $15 billion debt. The blood he sold to the blood banks, the oil to western industry. The man thought García's *pistacos* were Argentinian.

But he is wrong, a taxi-driver told me later. They were not Argentinian. They were Swiss.

No, insisted another, later that same day. They came from Cangallo, two hours away.

At night, there were large groups walking the streets, blowing whistles, thumping pan lids, pushing lanterns into the face of anyone they met, convinced their children were in danger. I had heard what had happened to the last white man to visit Ayacucho, two weeks before. He was Luis Angel Calderón, who, after returning from a brothel in the Avenida Cuzco, was set upon by a crowd. Luis Calderón's head was crushed by stones, because you cannot shoot a *pistaco*, and his eyes were pulled out by hand. His body was then dragged through the Victoria district until the bones showed. Luis Calderón had been a commercial traveller from Huancayo.

A lecturer from the university told me that some believed the *pistaco* myth had been revived by Sendero to make things difficult for the army. He argued that the myth was the Indian way of explaining the Spanish domination, and that the present manifestation was not organized but spontaneous: the community, under fire from both the military and Sendero, had turned against all.

I had sought out the lecturer, hoping he would illustrate the extent of Sendero's influence in Ayacucho. I made him uncomfortable, because people were always uncomfortable whenever Sendero was mentioned and also because I was white: many of his colleagues at the university believed the *pistaco* myth. He invited me that evening to see a film of the funeral of Edith Lagos. She was the Ayacucho regional chief—nineteen years old, with long dark hair and a convent education—who died 'heroically in battle' in 1982.

The lecturer explained. 'Twice we were told she was dead and she wasn't. The third time no one believed it, so the government said the body had to be displayed.' The film showed a crowd of 30,000, so tightly packed the people had to clap with hands above their heads. The coffin moved out of the cathedral and someone arranged a red flag on the coffin. The flag bore a hammer and sickle.

'The armed people will win!' shouted the mourners. 'The people will never forget spilled blood.'

'Who killed her?'

'Belaúnde!'

'Who will avenge her?'

'The people!' roared the crowd.

The lecturer said this was the Robin Hood phase for Sendero: more people turned up for Lagos's funeral than for the Pope's visit. The film jumped to the house of Edith Lagos's parents, where medical students were examining the body. They discovered a bullet near the kidney and a knife thrust in the pelvis. Her bloody shirt was held to the camera.

I walked to the cemetery on the outskirts of the town. I met the boy who painted the names on the headstones. He showed me the headstone of Luis Angel Calderón, the *pistaco*; there was only one date, 10 September 1987. He took me to Lagos's tomb, where there was a vase of yellow and red roses. The boy asked my name. I told him.

'Hamlet,' he said. He knew the grave-digger's scene. He told me about Edith Lagos's burial. Sendero had been there with guns. So had *Presidente* Gonzalo. 'I didn't know it was him till I saw his photo in a newspaper a few days later.'

I met two white priests who had worked around Ayacucho for twenty years. They belonged to a denomination founded by a Boston cardinal determined to save South America from communism. 'Lima only starts caring about the Indians when the food is spoiling in the freezer,' said one, who had a frizzy scrub of hair and smoked a black pipe.

'Round here, there's one doctor for every 39,000 people. About fifty per cent of all children die before the age of five—and it's getting worse. The people are Stone Age up here. They sit in a field watching a cow. That's what they do all day. I used to think they were contemplative. In fact they're so lacking in self-awareness that I'm sure they find it difficult to distinguish between themselves and their environment. There is no point talking about political consciousness, about Mao or Mariátegui; they wouldn't have a clue. They don't know what's going on.'

In 1985 the priest had asked one of the men working in his church how he was going to vote. 'Belaúnde,' said the man, because Belaúnde was a *'muy bien caballero'*. Belaúnde wasn't even standing.

'They're so simple it's unbelievable,' the priest went on. 'They've never seen newspapers. They don't know where Lima is. If they do go to Lima, they're never seen again. The move from *campo* to city has been compared to moving from the age of the Pharaohs to modern New York in four days. That's the length of their bus journey. And yet the strange thing about Sendero is that they don't make any attempt to woo these people. They'll even slaughter their animals—which is anathema to the campesinos. The animals are all they've got. They can't even afford to eat them.'

The other priest began to talk. He had a beard and his neck was burnt red by the sun. He said, 'Sendero will arrive one day. They'll pick up someone in the outskirts and ask who the authorities are. I'm not talking about powerful vested interests but a piddling little town of 200 people and the guy who maintains the church. To save ammunition they then crush him with rocks. I saw two kids who'd been killed in this way. You couldn't tell one from the other. Their mother identified them by their clothes.'

'Tell him about Cabana,' said the one with the pipe.

'Cabana,' said the other. 'A town of 220 people. Sendero arrived at five in the afternoon. They herded the authorities into the square—a grassy area with a school and a playing field. They lined them up inside the goal-posts. The mayor, the magistrate, the government representative, the chap who held the key to the graveyard. Six altogether. Their heads were jerked back by the hair and their throats were cut like chickens. It was a teenage girl doing it. She was the leader. She held a bucket beneath their necks to collect the blood. It was used to daub communist slogans on the walls. Their feet and heads were then cut off and sewn on backwards.

'It's an Andean tradition. The heads, so the dead won't recognize you; the feet, so they won't follow. Not that Sendero need worry. Nobody will talk. No one will give away any information at all. It's not called terrorism for nothing.'

This was not the first time I had heard about Sendero's women leaders. I asked about Edith Lagos. According to the bearded priest, Edith Lagos was being taught to drive by her common-law husband; needing a vehicle for the lesson, they stole a truck, but the truck developed engine trouble. About that time, another truck appeared, coming round the corner, which they both felt was more suitable for finishing the lesson. The other truck was being driven by prison police, on their way to Ocobamba in seach of an escaped prisoner. They opened fire and Lagos was killed. Her body was dragged away by her companion and hidden. A child who witnessed this told the police who took it into the hospital in Andahuaylas. A finger-tip was cut off and sent to Lima for prints. Meanwhile the body lay for two days without anyone claiming it.

'She had been living in the rough for so long that her hair was riddled with lice. Eventually a social worker called on me to say they wanted to get the body out of the morgue. No one was going to claim it.'

Huanta

From Ayacucho, Huanta was a three-hour drive through the mountains. Some of the most extreme violence in the war between Sendero and the armed forces had taken place here. I travelled there on the flatbed of a truck. My companions were women. It was a curious journey. I could not hear entire conversations, but I could hear phrases, parts of sentences. '*Pistaco*,' I heard again, first from children by the roadside and later a woman in the truck, although by the time we arrived she was smiling. I heard 'PIP', the word for the plain clothes police, and I heard the broken details of a machete killing committed by Sendero. There was mention of women disappearing and a child taken from the streets.

I had travelled to Huanta because it was the day of the great regional fair. In the past Sendero had actively discouraged these traditional *ferias*, arguing that they fed the urban capitalist system at a time when it must be starved, though for the really poor the fairs remained the only chance to earn money for paraffin and salt. This time, the night before the fair, Sendero had attacked the town with dynamite, and there were soldiers everywhere. They sat in Jeeps and open trucks. They stood at street corners in black tunics with yellow skulls on their shoulders. They strolled through the crowds of people who pretended not to notice and instead played hula-hoop for prizes of Carnation Milk.

A procession began. There were red velvet banners, a bad brass band and the cross of Our Lord of Mainay. There were dancers and a man with a red violin. In one dance, the dancers wore masks and pith helmets representing Spanish overlords. Another dance was quite different and featured a man in an orange cap and green jacket, carrying a plastic machine-gun that he jabbed into the backs of five men with painted black faces, who cowered, then approached, and all at once rushed and tossed him into the air.

'Sendero!'

And the following day they attacked.

The bingo announcer appealed for calm, and the crowd scattered, leaving behind the corpse of a nineteen-year-old soldier. A twelve-year-old boy was wounded in the cross-fire, and you could hear his crying.

I caught a pick-up back to Ayacucho along with two young boys. Ten miles out of Huanta the vehicle was flagged down by ten men in ponchos, their faces covered by black Balaclavas, except that of the leader, who wore a camouflage cowboy hat. One carried a cassette recorder. All had guns. They were not interested in me. Instead they crowded round the youngest boy and began a fierce interrogation. He was wearing a blue track-suit and could not have been more than nine, the age that Sendero begin recruiting. I heard their questions.

'Who are you?'

'Where are you from?'

'Where are you going?'

The boy answered with remarkable calm, and the man in the cowboy hat hammered the roof of the truck and led his men down.

'Gracias,' shouted the driver, ironically.

The men filed up a narrow path on the dry hill and disappeared among the paddle-shaped cacti. They were members of a military intelligence unit, and I assumed they were operating from Huanta, the main base in the area.

Later I met a former member of one of the intelligence units, an articulate, well-dressed and mild man, who described how the units worked, trapping the Senderistas while they recruited from the villages. 'Collaborators in the villages would inform us that a meeting was to be held at such and such a time and place, and we would drive part of the way and walk the rest until we reached the house where the meeting was taking place, which we would then surround and ask those inside to come out with their hands up. If they began firing, we fired back, usually with grenades.'

He said that he personally had killed five people. He had been taught to kill with a knife, he said, so people would believe that the killing had been done by Sendero. 'It was common to convince them that they'd be freed if they told us everything, and afterwards we'd escort them to their homes, and along the way, usually in open country, we'd kill them. It was easier this way. After all, it's a war. They were campesinos. They didn't know why they were fighting.'

What did the people think of Abimael Guzmán?

'They thought he and Mao were liberators—like San Martín and Bolognesi—who were fighting to make the country free.' Although the Peruvian military had used less brutal tactics (for instance, General Huamán's 'Hearts and Minds Campaign' in 1984), the young man's views were shared by many others—shared for instance by the senior air force officer I met later at a reception in Lima: 'The Argentine solution,' he whispered approvingly. 'Go in and kill them. When an apple has a rotten core, cut it out.' He leaned closer. 'Everyone knows who they are. It's only the law which prevents us from solving the problem.'

Ayacucho

When I returned to Ayacucho, the cocks, for reasons no one understood, were crowing relentlessly. They sounded like dogs howling. On my return, I intended to visit Guzmán's old house on Calle Libertad, and had an introduction to see Juan Granda, the professor who now lived there.

Walking there, I passed a row of old women, sitting in the shade beside heaps of coca leaves, who hissed at me as I went by.

Guzmán would have arrived here twenty-four years ago, one year before the city's first telephone was installed. Ayacucho would have seemed remote, provincial. Yet it is in the urban centres that thought evaporates; there are too many distractions. In a place like Ayacucho you can go to bed with a book by a lamp that then goes out. You are cut off; your thoughts become more extreme and, if put into action, more effective. Kant, the subject of Guzmán's thesis, had constructed an elaborate metaphysical critique while rarely leaving Koenigsberg.

Guzmán worked initially in the Faculty of Social Sciences. Following the Sino-Soviet split in 1964, Guzmán turned from Stalinism to Maoism—a realignment which explains his lukewarm attitude to Peru's Castro-inspired uprisings in 1965 (Che Guevara 'was a chorus girl'). In the same year he married one of his pupils, Augusta de la Torre, the middle-class daughter of local left-wing activists who introduced him to a network of contacts in the region. One person who knew her described Augusta as a militant with a nice figure: 'She was small, like him, and *absolutamente seria*. She didn't respond or acknowledge your presence—ever. It was as if you were nothing.'

In January 1965, Guzmán made the first of three visits to China.

Most of Sendero's leadership and support came from the classrooms of San Cristóbal de Huamanga, from provincial academics who had little in common with the *serranos* from the mountains and did not even speak Quechua. By the 1970s, Guzmán's students controlled most of the university, and slowly began a systematic infiltration of the peasant communities.

255

When I finally met Juan Granda, he was in what was once Guzmán's kitchen. Granda had arrived in Ayacucho in 1970, by which time Guzmán was at the height of his power in the university. Guzmán was responsible for the hiring and firing all those who came to the university. 'This house,' Granda said, 'was the Kremlin. Only very close friends were allowed here. And with Guzmán you were either a close friend or a servant.'

The Guzmán Granda described was different from the one I learned about in Arequipa. The mountains of Ayacucho had changed him. Guzmán, was now wearing a dark suit. There was no smoking in class. There was no interruptions. There was no conversation until ten minutes before the end when there were questions. He never smiled. Like his wife, he never spoke to anyone in the streets. He wore thick-rimmed glasses and saw everything as a battle between Democracy and Authority or Idealism and Materialism. He spoke well, gesticulating, and writing his arguments 'one, two, three, four, five' on the blackboard. He was a schematic thinker.

He did not have an impressive intellect, but it was effective among his students, the poor campesinos, the sons of peons from haciendas, who had come to the modern world of the city. 'He understood their way of life. They didn't have to think. This was how he had got his nickname.'

His nickname?

'Shampoo,' said Juan Granda. 'Because he brain-washed people.'

Juan Granda last saw Guzmán in 1976, when he resigned from the university. By that time, Sendero, dominating the university, had infiltrated the community. They tilled the fields, and several important Senderistas had married into Indian families. When Guzmán resigned from the university in 1976, it was because, by then, Sendero were ready for a revolution.

Huancayo

Sendero have not yet created a 'liberated zone', an identifiable area capable of reproducing itself. They have, however, established an effective presence in sparsely populated areas like the northern jungle region of the Upper Huallaga. I was unable to visit the northern jungles, but I met a man who had, a photographer, Victor Chacón Vargas, who was one of the very few people also to have visited a Sendero base. In 1987, working for the weekly magazine *Caretas*, he was captured twice by Sendero. During our conversation, the lights went out; there had been an attack on the pylons in Huancayo.

Chacón had travelled to Uchiza, a small town 350 miles north of Ayacucho following a report that Sendero had attacked a police station, killing seven policemen, gouging out the eyes and testicles of one officer. He had been in Uchiza a matter of minutes when three Indians appeared, each about twenty years old, wearing jeans with pistols shoved down their belts. They pushed him and several other journalists into a car and drove to the end of the airstrip. Their documents were taken away; they were interrogated one by one; and finally they were moved out of the town, awaiting orders from 'higher up'.

They waited all day, and, when it grew dark, they were led across the river. Chacón said, 'We walked through the jungle and were presented to a man with a Korean machine-gun on his back—it had been taken from one of the policemen. Mosquitoes were everywhere, and he began a political lecture that would go on for two hours: Mao says . . . Mariátegui says . . . President Gonzalo says . . . All jargon. I tried to look as if I was concentrating, but I was thinking of the mosquitoes, my house in Lima, my wife.'

There was no need to be afraid, they were told. If they were spies, they would be killed. If not, not. Sendero had a thousand eyes. A thousand ears.

Chacón was asked why he didn't join the struggle, and he said it was because he was married with two children.

'So am I,' said the Senderista. 'But if I am told to kill my mother, I will kill her. We need people like you. People who know how to speak to the people.'

They spent the night singing revolutionary slogans, and Chacón was released.

And then he was captured again at the end of August, and actually invited to take photographs of the camps.

Chacón's visits were unprecedented. Part of Sendero's success has been attributed to the secrecy of its operations—presupposing a degree of organization and efficiency traditionally so alien to the Peruvian character that President Belaúnde originally concluded that the Sendero could only be foreigners. Even today there are few clear ideas as to how the leadership operates. James Anderson, probably the leading expert on Sendero, describes a rigidly vertical organization in which a 'co-ordination committee' presides over regional committees that preside over regional sub-committees that preside over cells of between five and nine members. Only one member of a cell will have any communication with the layer of leadership above him.

Lima

Sendero's hermetic secrecy derives from the guerrilla campaign of 1965 when everybody seemed to know everything. Hector Bejar was involved in the 1965 campaign. He led the National Liberation Army, one of the two revolutionary movements at the time. He was captured and sent to prison. Today he works as a doctor in Puno and as a lecturer in Lima's San Marcos University. I met him on my return to Lima. He was one of the last people to have seen Abimael Guzmán—in 1979, when they shared a prison cell after a round-up of prominent left-wingers. Their fellow inmates numbered sixty people, all kept in one small room, and included the ten academics from Ayacucho university who are now the main leaders of Sendero, most notably Osman Morote, son of Dr Efraín Morote who hired Guzmán in the sixties.

'We were,' Bejar said, 'sixty people, co-existing in the same small space day and night, but divided into two groups—Guzmán's and mine. Guzmán's regarded me as a member of the opposition—a petit bourgeois defector. For instance, for Guzmán, Cuba, our inspiration, was an example of one of the most advanced bourgeois democracies in Latin America.

'Guzmán was very formal and dogmatic. He disciplined his group in a calm voice, making them study and memorize Mariátegui in the way one might study the Bible. His level was very elementary, very provincial. *Muy Jesuítico.*'

A photograph taken during Guzmán's brief imprisonment shows that the dandy from La Salle had fattened out, his unshaven face weighed down by jowls, his hair still swept back, but without its sheen.

On 3 December 1979, soon after Guzmán's release, it was proposed that the Armed Struggle begin, or in Sendero's inimitable words, it was proposed 'to forge the First Company in Deeds.' The formal decision was made on 17 March 1980. Guzmán appears to have cited a treatise by Washington Irving on Mohammed. He then gathered the members of his group round him and instructed them to read from the first two acts of *Macbeth*. These acts illustrated, it seems, 'how treason is born.' Two months later Sendero entered the sleepy town of Chuschi and Abimael Guzmán disappeared.

There is a wide gap between the Quechua and the Spanish mind. For the Indian, goals do not have to be accomplished in the five-year cycle of a presidential term. For President Gonzalo it does not matter whether his revolution takes five, twenty-five or seventy-five years. It will take place, that's what matters.

But Guzmán was also said to be dying. Of leukaemia, a serious kidney infection, cancer of the lymph glands and Hodgkinson's disease. But few informed people believed Abimael Guzmán to be dead. And if the armed forces had killed him, they would certainly have produced the body.

Perhaps Guzmán was alive but unwell, and had therefore delegated his responsibilities. Perhaps he had left the country, disappeared. In myth, the hero departs for the unknown, and becomes a hero. Guzmán's secret was his invisibility. It didn't matter whether Abimael Guzmán was alive or dead. He had done enough. On reaching the point where the trail vanished, I found myself indifferent. I had looked forward to an encounter with the 'universal genius' who had created Sendero Luminoso. I had argued that if by some chance he was leading a movement that could successfully challenge both Russia and the United States, then his words would be seen as oracle. At the least, I had hoped to resurrect the persona he had left behind. Now I felt thwarted. Perhaps, I found myself reasoning, if one got to the heart of Stalin and Trotsky one would also find a vacant core, a banality. Perhaps people like that are like that, made of straw.

I remained in no doubt that Sendero Luminoso possessed a shaping character, a dominating personality. Yet the character of Abimael Guzmán seemed so insubstantial: the loather of Gershwin, the lover of *Pepito de mi corazón*, the pedestrian thinker, the 'anonymity', a man with whom it was possible to spend seven whole years and remember nothing.

When I returned to Lima, however, I talked to a friend, who had bought the house once owned by Dr Efraín Morote in Ayacucho. 'Speak to Dr Efraín Morote Best,' my friend said. 'He will make you uncomfortable. He will mentally undress you as you sit before him. He will make you laugh simply out of nervous fear. He is filled with brilliant hatred.'

What did he hate? 'Everything,' said my friend. 'Except Chinese cashew nuts and Albanian olive oil.'

I knew little about Dr Efraín Morote Best. I knew that he had been the rector at the university at Ayacucho, the one who had recruited Guzmán. I knew that he was an eminent anthropologist; that at Cuzco University he had been a famous joker and party-goer—an extrovert—until the early 1950s when he suffered a complete change of character. 'He avoided all engagements,' said a colleague. 'He joined the Communist Party and dressed like a Mormon in a lace cravat.' I knew, finally, that one of Morote's sons was imprisoned as a suspected Senderista, that his son Osmán was considered to be one of Sendero's most important leaders.

I discovered more. I learned that General Clemente Noel, the first military commander in Ayacucho, had always believed that Morote was the true leader, 'the high priest of Sendero'.

But Morote did not give interviews, and no one knew where he lived.

I discovered the number of Morote's sister. I rang her, a few days after the security forces had captured Morote's daughter Katia. She was suspected of an arson attack in the Lima suburb of Pueblo Libre.

The sister was polite. And early the next morning I received a call from Morote himself. I was surprised. He spoke an elegant,

Castilian Spanish. He agreed to see me, giving an address in Chaclacayo, twenty miles north of Lima.

In Chaclacayo, there was no Lima mist, and the sky was a cloudless blue. I walked up a street named Eucalyptus. Mountain dust covered the lawns and rose bushes. Half-way up on the right was a large yellow house. There was a man kicking a ball. Otherwise no one was about.

Dr Morote came down the steps to greet me, unlocking the gate. He was a small man, in a black cardigan, black trousers and a white shirt open at the neck. His hair was greyer than his moustache and swept back from his face. It was difficult to judge whether he is Spanish or mestizo.

We went up to a room of books, and Morote made idle chat—about the weather in Chaclacayo, how much more pleasant it was than in Lima—and his niece brought me coffee. She then went over to his desk and began fiddling. It was a tape-recorder. I, the interviewer, was being taped. I began sweating, something that had never happened during any other interview I could remember.

I mentioned the increasing European interest in Sendero Luminoso, lamenting the impossibility of finding anyone to speak for the movement. I said that I had been to Ayacucho and that if I had been born a poor *serrano* in those hills, I would be sympathetic to Sendero. I said all this to encourage Morote, but I also meant it.

'Sendero Luminoso is a political party,' Dr Morote said, with a superior smile. 'The Marxist-Leninist-Maoist Communist Party of Peru. Its objectives are to transform the dialectics of Peru, no matter how long this takes.'

I drew a comparison with the architects of Europe's cathedrals, who did not live to see their work complete.

'If you like, politics are today's equivalent to the Church.' But more than anything else it was a very intense battle between two classes. On the one side was the Peruvian Communist Party, and on the other the bourgeois state with its army, its police, its bureaucracy. 'The man who governs Peru and calls himself Pérez— I refer to him by his mother's name because he has a mother's mind—doesn't recognize there's a war on. And it is a war. There is no place for neutrals. Those in the centre will be killed by the cross-fire. It was a historical necessity to take a position, a law of history and a law of nature.' For Morote, García was the last hope of the Peruvian bourgeois democracy. 'But a monkey who dresses in silk remains a monkey.'

He mentioned that there were now only two or three regions in Peru that had not witnessed Sendero activitity. The movement's methods of advance and retreat resembled those of the communists in China, where Morote spent four years working on the Spanish translation of Mao's works. Throughout our conversation, Morote referred to China and its leaders. Later, when I expressed regret that the Peruvian novelist José María Arguedas is not translated more into English, Morote said, as if in answer, that, 'in China there are translations.'

'The China of 1911 is very similar to the present epoch in Peru,' Morote said. 'But then again, this isn't a movement for Peru, this is a movement for the whole of Latin America.'

'What do you see happening in Peru?'

'It will be the same fight, only more intense, more radical, more triumphant.'

'And the violence? How does the Sendero condone that?'

'Violence is part of the human condition. Violence in politics is not only necessary, it is indispensable. We are discussing a new birth, and a new birth is always produced in blood. As in a Caesarian operation, the child insists on living.'

And, by analogy I assumed, the mother might die. The day I met Morote, two officials from García's party were killed in a car bomb, the newspaper reproducing their mangled bodies on the front page. As his niece was preparing coffee, a bus was stopped on the road to Ica in which Sendero discovered two Guardia Civil among the passengers and later shot them in the head outside on the tarmac.

I asked Morote whether he seriously believed that the Peruvian peasant understood a thing about Mao or Mariátegui.

'Life is a permanent contradiction between those who know and those who don't. The people can understand, in their fashion, that the problem of this country is an unfeeling bourgeoisie incapable of changing the situation, either by reason or by force.' The reply, simple and polished, was terrifying. I remembered a sentence from Conrad: 'He would have been a splendid leader of an extreme party.'

I asked about those who were simply indifferent.

'When one has a bottle of whisky, one doesn't drink it all at the same time. One drinks it little by little. The same with indifferent, neutral people. Each day, they will be less indifferent. Each day the badly informed will be less badly informed. It's a question of time. It's part of the philosophy of both China and the Peruvian Indian.'

There was the Sendero patience.

I mentioned Guzmán. Morote smiled. I wondered if I had met the king-maker.

'Guzmán is important but not indispensable. I worked with him for seven years. He was a person of the utmost intelligence, culture and sensitivity. A man who knows as much of Shakespeare as of Cervantes, who understands the music of Liszt as well as the music of Schumann, who began by understanding Marx, Lenin, Stalin.'

I asked if Guzmán was political when Morote first met him, when Guzmán first came to Ayacucho.

'Yes. Because he is *Homo sapiens*.'

But how did he make the change from being a quiet introverted student of philosophy to a terrorist, a proponent of the Armed Struggle?

'The mind is always capable of great leaps. I haven't got Abimael Guzmán's, and I can't know the leaps it took. But it's clear that without the Armed Struggle, the situation wouldn't change.'

'Is Guzmán alive?'

Morote's expression doesn't change. 'When one dies, one lives. Life continues. Marx has been dead many years, but today he is more alive than ever.'

We talked of other things, of Cervantes, Vargas Llosa and Hong Kong, 'a turbulent, congested city'. Morote revealed that he was ill and that he now worked only on a book about the mythologies, legends and religions of Peru. I told him of my experience in Ayacucho, and he brought down from the shelf a folder containing information on the *pistacos* for the last four centuries. It included Cristóval de Molina's reference in 1571:

> For in year 1560 and not before, it was held and believed
> by the Indians that an ointment from the bodies of the
> Indians had been sent for from Spain to cure a disease
> for which there was no medicine there.

I asked why the myth had resurfaced now.

'Because of the killing of campesinos by the armed forces.'

'Doesn't Sendero kill them too?'

'Yes, but always in public, and after a people's trial.'

'What about reports of women who cut men's throats like chickens?'

'Absolute propaganda,' he said.

My mind was full of questions. I asked why Sendero refused to speak to the government.

'What for? So they can be destroyed by them? When García Pérez says he wants a dialogue—that's what *he* wants.'

And journalists? Why did Sendero never speak to journalists?

Morote said journalists were killed here. I thought he was joking. Kill journalists? I said.

'A journalist is never objective. He takes sides. He is a man who lives in the present. I live for the future.'

I felt uneasy. 'Why have you agreed to see me?'

'My sister said you sounded nice on the phone.'

There was a silence: *because I sounded nice on the phone*? The tape continued recording. His niece, sitting behind the desk, stared at me. There was the sound of a shoe tapping. Morote cleared his throat and said, 'You haven't finished your coffee.'

I swallowed. The coffee was cold. I was thinking of Morote, how he revealed nothing about Sendero and nothing about his relationship to it, and yet displayed complete familiarity with its activities.

I asked one last question.

'Do you know the words of *Pepito de mi corazón*?'

The author gratefully acknowledges the information and assistance provided by James Anderson, whose pamphlet 'Sendero Luminoso: A New Revolutionary Model?' is published by the Institute for the Study of Terrorism.

IAN JACK
UNSTEADY PEOPLE

On 6 August last year a launch overturned in the River Ganges near Manihari Ghat, a remote ferry station in the Indian state of Bihar. Many people drowned, though precisely how many will never be known. The district magistrate estimated the number of dead at around 400, the launch-owner at fourteen. The first estimate was reached by subtraction: 529 tickets had been sold and only a hundred passengers had swum ashore. The second estimate came from the number of bodies the launch-owner said he had counted stretched out on the bank. But then the river was in flood; hundreds of bodies could have been swept far downstream; scores may still be entangled in the wreckage or buried in the silt. The launch-owner had good reason to lie.

It was, in its causes and consequences, an accident which typified the hazards of navigating the River Ganges. Monsoon rains had swollen the river and changed its hydrography, cutting new channels and raising new shoals. The launch was overcrowded. Licensed to carry 160, it seems to have set out with at least three times that number, nearly all of whom were fervent Hindu pilgrims travelling from their villages in north Bihar to a shrine which lies south of the river. Devotees of Lord Shiva, the destroyer, they wore saffron robes and carried pots of sacred Ganges water on their shoulders. Eyewitnesses said the launch left the north bank to the chanting of Shiva's name, the chorus *'bol bam'* rising from the massed saffron on the upper deck; until, hardly a hundred metres from the shore, the chants turned into screams.

According to a survivor quoted in the Calcutta newspapers, what happened was this. As the launch moved off, its stern got stuck in the shallows near the bank. The skipper decided to redistribute his vessel's weight, to lighten the stern by weighing down the bow. He asked his passengers to move forward; the stern bobbed up and the launch surged forward, head down and listing badly, to run a few hundred feet into a submerged sandbank and capsize.

In Bihar a revengeful clamour arose which sought to identify the guilty and exact punishment. The Bihar government and its servants blamed the launch-owner and charged him with murder. The opposition blamed government corruption and the conduct of the police. According to Ajit Kumar Sarkar, a Marxist member of the Bihar Legislative Assembly, the launch took six hours to sink, and many victims could have been saved had not the police beaten back agitated crowds of would-be rescuers on the shore. According to the police, corruption had made their job impossible; almost every Ganges ferry flouted safety legislation because the ferry-owners organized 'gangs to protect their interest.' Bihar had a 'steamer mafia' whose profits had perverted the political administration. Chief among this mafia was Mr Bachcha Singh, the 'steamer tycoon of Bihar' and owner of the launch that had gone down at Manihari Ghat.

Some days after the accident another of Mr Singh's vessels approached the wreck, ostensibly with the task of dragging it off the sandbank and on to the shore. Watchers on the bank, however, saw something different. They saw the second vessel pressing down on the wreckage of the first. It seemed to them that the other ship had come to bury the launch and not to raise it, thus destroying the evidence and, in the words of the *Calcutta Telegraph*, 'obscuring the gravity of the tragedy.' In the face of public protest the second ship backed off.

Where, meanwhile, was the steamer tycoon, Mr Bachcha Singh? Nobody could say. The Chief Minister of Bihar promised 'stern action', charges of murder and negligence were registered in the courts and some of Mr Singh's property was seized. But the police said they could not find Singh himself. He was, in the English of official India, 'absconding' and so the courts declared him an 'absconder'.

Thereafter public interest evaporated with the monsoon rains. Manihari Ghat became just another Ganges launch disaster. The people who had died were poor. None had relatives influential enough to secure the lasting attention of the press or the government, both of which in any case were soon preoccupied with other problems.

What was the precise truth of the affair? Nobody could say. Truth in its least elevated and most humble sense, truth as detail, truth as times and numbers, truth arrived at by observation and deduction—this kind of truth left the scene early. Like Mr Singh, it absconded. Unlike Mr Singh, it did not reappear.

S ix months later I met the steamer tycoon at his house in Patna, the state capital. To European eyes, the house looked like something a Nazi cineaste might have built. It had the smooth curves of a pre-war suburban Odeon and a large tower with two large swastikas etched high up in the concrete; they were visible from my cycle rickshaw long before the mansion itself swung into view. Mr Singh had called it 'Swastika House'—the name was on the gate—but only because he was a devout Hindu and the swastika is an ancient Hindu symbol of good fortune.

Fortune had been good to Mr Singh. It was manifest in his living arrangements, the dozens of domestic servants, his house's fifty bedrooms and thirty bathrooms, the superior quality of his tipped cigarettes. All of this (and a good deal else—apartments in Calcutta, real estate in the USA) derived from Mr Singh's role as the Ganges' principal ferryman. But his person as opposed to his surroundings seemed untouched by wealth. He was a small old man with heart trouble who wore loose Indian clothes and tapped ash from his Gold Flake King Size into an old spittoon.

We sat on his terrace and drank tea from mugs. I wondered about the murder charge. What had happened to it?

Nothing, said Singh, the case would never come to court. Did I understand the caste system? In Bihar caste was the key to everything. The murder charge had been instigated by the then Chief Minister, who was a Brahmin. Singh belonged to the Rajput caste, and Rajputs were the Brahmins' greatest political rivals. The charge had been politically inspired.

And now?

'Now the Chief Minister is a Rajput. He is known to me. Case finish.'

He apologized for his English and called for his son, who, he said, would be more intelligible to me. This proved to be only partly true. The younger Singh was reading Business Administration at Princeton University, ferry profits having dispatched him to the United States when he was an infant, and his English crackled with the abrasive nouns of the new capitalism. 'Cash-burn . . . acquisition and diversification . . . buy-out.' It was strange to hear these words in Bihar, still governed by ancestry and feudal law, but they completely matched the younger Singh's appearance. In

T-shirt, shorts and sneakers, he might have stepped out of a college tennis game. The sight of son next to father, crouched beside his spittoon, was a testament to the transforming power of money.

The father had recalled his son to Patna soon after what both referred to, opaquely, as 'the tragedy'. The son looked at his new surroundings with cold eyes. Corruption, poverty, ignorance, tradition—they ruled life here. It was sickening. Outside the family, nobody could be trusted. Did I know, for example, that after the tragedy peasants from adjacent villages had brought newly-dead relatives to the river, so that their bodies could be discreetly inserted among the launch's victims and compensation claimed?

I hadn't heard that, but maybe it was true; Bihar can sometimes be a desperate place. But what did he think had caused the accident?

'Panic and stupidity,' said the younger Singh. He thought for a moment. 'Basically these people weren't willing to make the smart move and analyse the situation.'

Of course these were ludicrous words; passengers packed on a tilting motor launch cannot be expected to plan their next five minutes like Wall Street commodity brokers. But the longer I travelled through Bihar, squashed on trains and river boats, the more I recognized the younger Singh's detachment as an indigenous sentiment rather than an American import.

Certain facts about Bihar were undeniable. The launch-owners were greedy and their craft decrepit and dangerous; the police were corrupt and tended to enforce the law of the highest bidder—the younger Singh said himself that his family had put off police inquiries with a few thousand rupees; and covert supplies of money moved through the system at every level—an honest police-officer could have his orders countermanded by a corrupt district administrator, an honest district administrator could be transferred or demoted by a corrupt politician. To behave dutifully and honestly in this amoral environment involved great courage and sacrifice. It was no surprise that the safety of the travelling public, especially a public so lacking in clout, did not figure highly in the minds of their appointed guardians.

My fellow-travellers would talk quite frankly about all this—humbug is not a Bihari vice—but then they also echoed the younger Singh: people in Bihar, they would say, did not know how to behave. They were 'uneducated' and 'ignorant' and, most of all, 'backward'. The populations of western democracies hesitate—still—to describe their fellow-citizens so bluntly, at least in public. But Biharis have no such inhibitions. The ancient social pyramid of caste enables those at the top to look down at those below with a dispassionate prejudice, at an inferior form of human life.

'I'm afraid we are not a *steady* people,' an old man said to me one day, and I could see exactly what he meant. Often the unsteadiness was frightening. The resources of transportation are scarce all over India; there is a continual press and scramble for tickets and seats wherever you go. But young Biharis travel on the roofs of trains even when the compartments below are empty and rush listing ferries like a piratical horde. Even the old and lame press forward as though fleeing some imminent disaster.

Towards the end of my journey in Bihar I met another Singh, a relative of the steamer tycoon, who operated a couple of old steamboats just upriver from Manihari Ghat. In an interval between crossings he took me up on to the bridge of his ferry, which was berthed at the foot of a steep bank, glistening and slippery with unseasonal rain. At the top of the slope men with staves, Singh's employees, were restraining a crowd of waiting passengers. Then the steamer's whistle gave two hoots; the men with staves relented; and the crowd, with its bicycles and milk-churns, came rushing down the bank towards us, slithering and whooping.

Singh looked down at his customers as they milled across the gangplank and then laughed like a man in a zoo. 'Crazy people. What can you do with them?'

On 15 April this year ninety-five people were crushed to death on the terraces of a football stadium in Sheffield, northern England. Most of the dead came from Liverpool, and all of them were supporters of Liverpool football club, who that day were to play Nottingham Forest in the semi-final of English football's premier knock-out competition, the Football Association

Cup. The deaths came six minutes after the kick-off. The match was then abandoned.

I read about the disaster in Delhi on my way back to London. Newspaper reports speculated on the possible causes and recalled that the behaviour of Liverpool fans had prompted the crush which killed thirty-nine people at the European Cup Final in Brussels in 1985, all of them Italian supporters of the other finalists, Juventus of Turin. It seemed something similar had happened in Sheffield. Liverpool fans had swept into the ground and pressed their fellow-supporters forward until they were squashed against the barriers and fences which had been erected some years before to prevent unruly spectators rushing on to the pitch and interfering with the game.

All that winter in India I'd heard about death in Britain. Planes fell to earth and trains left the rails, and Mrs Thatcher's face appeared on Indian television talking of her sympathy and concern. There were shots of disintegrated fuselages, body bags, shattered railway coaches. Indian friends tutted at the carnage, and I recognized in their reaction the momentary interest—the shake of the head, the small ripple of fascination—that passes through a British living-room when news of some distant tragedy flits before it; say, of the last typhoon to strike Bengal.

Meanwhile, the India I saw reported every day on the news—orderly, calm, soporific—looked more and more like the country I came from—or at least as I had once thought of it. Accidents such as Manihari Ghat were certainly reported, but rarely filmed. We watched the prime minister greeting foreign delegations at the airport, men in good suits addressing seminars and shaking hands, women cutting tapes and accepting bouquets. Indian news, or what India's government-controlled television judged to be news, took place indoors in an atmosphere notably free of dust, flies and mess. There was a lot of cricket. The mess—grief and ripped metal under arc lights—came from abroad, imported by satellite and shiny film-cans—they were like luxury items, a new spice trade going the other way—which the makers of Indian bulletins slotted in between the hand-shaking and the seminars as if to prove that disaster could overtake the foreign rich as well as the native poor, and that it was not confined to terrorism in the Punjab or the chemical catastrophe at Bhopal.

There were two train crashes in the southern suburbs of London (forty dead); a Pan Am Jumbo which exploded over Lockerbie (270 dead); a Boeing forced to crash-land on a motorway (forty-seven dead). All of them had specific and identifiable causes—a bomb, signal failure, faulty engines—though the roots (what caused the cause?) led to a vaguer territory: under-investment in public utilities, 'international terrorism', the collapse of civic feeling under a political leader who has said she cannot grasp the idea of community. This kind of worry—the cause of the cause—had bobbed to the surface of British life like old wreckage ever since the Channel ferry *Herald of Free Enterprise* turned over at Zeebrugge in 1987, the first in a series of large accidents which has marked Britain out as a literally disastrous country. But from the distance of India, Sheffield looked different. It seemed to turn on the behaviour of a fervent crowd; there was, in that sense, something very Indian about it.

When my landlord in Delhi said he thought football in England must have assumed 'a religious dimension', it was difficult to resist the parallel: saffron pilgrims struggling to board their launch at Manihari Ghat, the mass of Liverpudlian red and white which surged into the stadium at Sheffield. And the parallels did not end there. In fact the nearer I got to home the closer they became.

Changing planes in Paris, I bought a newspaper and read about M. Jacques Georges, the French president of the European Football Association. An interviewer on French radio had asked M. Georges if he thought Liverpool was peculiar in some way, given its football club's recent history of violent disaster. Well, said Georges, Liverpool certainly seemed to have 'a particularly aggressive mentality'. The crowd that had stormed into the ground at Sheffield had scorned all human feeling. 'I have the impression—I am distressed to use the expression—but it was like beasts who wanted to charge into an arena.'

The English are not a steady people. Today all Europe knows that. None the less M. Georges's words had scandalized England. At Heathrow the papers were full of him, even though he had said little more than the Sheffield police. According to Mr Paul Middup, chairman of the South Yorkshire Police Federation, there was 'mass drunkenness' among the 3,000 Liverpool supporters, who turned up at the turnstiles shortly before the kick-off: 'Some of them were uncontrollable. A great number of them had obviously been drinking heavily.' According to Mr Irvine Patrick, a Sheffield MP, the police had been 'hampered, harassed, punched, kicked and urinated on.'

But then the police themselves had behaved ineptly. Seeking to relieve the crush outside the stadium, they had opened a gate and sent an excited crowd—drunks, beasts or otherwise—into a section of the terracing which was already filled to capacity. And then, for some minutes at least, they had watched the crowd's desperate attempt to escape over the fences and mistaken it for hooliganism. They had hardly made a smart move and analysed the situation.

It would have all been familiar to any citizen of Bihar. An underclass which, in the view of the overclass, did not know how to behave. 'Drunks . . . beasts . . . uneducated . . . ignorant.' An antique and ill-designed public facility. A police force which made serious mistakes. Clamorous cross-currents of blame.

At home, I watched television. The disaster excited the medium. For several days it replayed the scene at Sheffield and then moved on to Liverpool, where the football ground was carpeted with wreaths. Funeral services were recorded, football players vowed that they might never play again and political leaders in Liverpool demanded the presence in their city of royalty—a prince, a duke—so that the scale of the 'national tragedy' might be acknowledged. When members of Liverpool's rival team turned up at a burial, the commentator spoke reverently of how the disaster had 'united football', as though the French and Germans in Flanders had stopped bombardment for a day to bury their dead. One football official said he hoped that ninety-five people had not 'died in vain.' Another said that they had 'died for football.'

Nobody in Bihar would have suggested that the dead of Manihari Ghat had made such a noble sacrifice. Nobody would have said: 'They died to expunge corruption, caste and poverty.' Whatever their other faults, Biharis are not a self-deluding people.

Graham Swift
Looking for Jiří Wolf

t the beginning of December 1988, I visited Czechoslovakia
for the first time. I knew then about the case of Jiří Wolf,
though it was not the prime reason for my visit. A month
before, I had been in Stockholm, where my publisher, Thomas von
Vegesack, is president of the International PEN Writers in Prison
Committee. I told him that I had been invited to Czechoslovakia
for the publication of a Slovak translation of one of my books, and
he reminded me that Jiří Wolf was a prisoner 'adopted' by both the
Swedish and English Committees. Perhaps I could ask some
discreet questions.

I got some information on Wolf from the PEN Committee in
London and did indeed ask questions during my visit. I
discovered, rapidly enough, that the opportunity to ask questions
was limited by the general constraints on talking freely. Also, for
most of my visit I was in Bratislava, the Slovak capital, while Wolf
was a Czech from Bohemia. I spent just a couple of days in Prague.
The fact remains that when I did ask questions, I got the same
response: genuine, not simulated, ignorance. No one seemed to
have heard of him.

My visit made a strong impression on me, in part because I
had read the dossier on Wolf, and some of Wolf's own words, just
before my departure. Frankly, the country depressed me. I
encountered a great deal of individual kindness, above all from my
Slovak translator, Igor, a reservedly humorous man and a good
friend, but I felt that I was in a land that had gone into internal
emigration. It was cut off from its own best resources, and even the
things that could be simply admired, like the beautiful buildings of
Prague, seemed false and irrelevant.

Much of this may be the standard Western reaction. I felt a
mixture of gladness and guilt on returning home, and for some
while I was haunted by my impressions and in particular—though
here I had only imagination to go on—by thoughts of Jiří Wolf. I
wrote letters on his behalf. I heard from the British Embassy in
Prague that his case had been raised during the Vienna meeting of
the Conference on Security and Co-operation in Europe, though to
no apparent avail. It was only to be hoped that he would at least
survive the remainder of his prison sentence, which was due to end
during 1989.

I did not know if and when I might return to Czechoslovakia. I certainly felt, from my limited knowledge and from what I had picked up on the spot, that despite Gorbachev the situation in the country was unlikely to improve. It might even worsen. A typical joke at the time of my first visit ran:

Karel: This perestroika is getting real bad.

Pavel: Yes, soon we Czechoslovaks will have to send tanks into Russia.

But we have all been surprised by the events of the last year. And, almost a year to the day after I had left it, I found myself returning to a Prague in the grip of what was variously called, depending on your translator, a 'smiling', a 'gentle' or a 'tender' revolution. My chief purpose, with some five days to achieve it, was to find Jíří Wolf.

Wolf's case may be as unexceptional as it is awful. His is a history of harassment, imprisonment and maltreatment which has been documented—largely self-documented—and which seized my interest. There are many other documented cases, and time has yet to reveal, if it ever will completely, the extent of undocumented cases. Prisons are often the last sections of society to be touched by political reform and though, as I write, Czechoslovakia has a new government, it would be a mistake to suppose that the country no longer has institutions and personnel accustomed to the regular abuse of human rights.

Wolf was born in 1952. The facts I knew of his life were these. An orphan, he was brought up in state homes. He is of Jewish origin, with no living relatives save one half-sister. He married, has a son, but was divorced in 1978. He has worked in the uranium mines at Pribram, also as a driver and stoker. Apart from his writings in and about prison, he has written an autobiographical work, *Mrtvá cesta* ('Dead Journey') and a novel, *Čěrné barety* ('Black Berets'). In 1977 he signed the Charter 77 declaration and in 1978 was arrested for possessing 'anti-State', 'anti-Party' and 'anti-Socialist' documents, and subsequently sentenced to three years' imprisonment for 'subversion of the Republic'. He was committed to Minkovice prison.

At his trial Wolf complained that he had been forced to admit guilt under physical and psychological pressure, and his sentence was extended by six months for 'false accusations'. He was transferred from Minkovice to Valdice, a prison of the harshest category and perhaps the most notorious prison in Czechoslovakia, and released in 1981. He remained active and was subject to harassment and arrest. In May 1983 he was charged with 'subversion in collusion with foreign agents' and 'divulging official secrets' for allegedly passing information to the Austrian Embassy about conditions in Minkovice. He was sentenced to six years' imprisonment and in 1984 found himself again in Valdice.

Wolf's prison writings, covering a ten year period of imprisonment, are grim and harrowing. His 'regime' was one of terror, cold, hunger, isolation and deprivation. Prisoners are allowed one visit, of one hour only, and one parcel every ten months, though these minimal rights are often denied. They are exploited as cheap labour. They are denied clothing sent to them. They are subject to indiscriminate beatings, some of which prove fatal, and to medical neglect. They are forced to eat food off the floor, food which is in any case inadequate, as prisoners are known to cut their wrists in order to drink their blood. Or just to cut their wrists. In 1988 Wolf was permitted a brief visit by two American doctors. They found him in poor shape but were not allowed to leave vitamins or medicines for ulcer treatment. Wolf told them he contemplated suicide.

I arrived in Prague with little more than a list of possibly useful names and telephone numbers. I had established from the PEN Committee in London that Wolf had indeed been released, in bad health, on 17 May 1989, but his whereabouts were unknown and information unforthcoming. I had recommendations and promises of help from various sources and, via a BBC unit in Prague, the name of a man, Miloš, who might act, if needed, as interpreter and co-searcher. I had phoned him from London, along with a number of other people in Prague. Miloš knew nothing of Wolf but, with only limited free time, was ready to help. Other responses, where there was not an immediate language problem, were co-operative, but no one, just as a year ago, seemed to have more than a dim notion of Wolf.

I had phoned Igor in Bratislava, who was prepared to meet me in Prague the following Saturday; also an editor in Prague, who again knew nothing of Wolf but promised to do what she could and in any case to arrange some meetings with other Czech writers. All these phone calls I prefaced with a wary 'Please tell me if I should not discuss certain matters on the phone.' This met with varying reactions, from 'Say what you like' to 'It's probably bugged but what the hell?' It was hard to tell if this was bravado or if a real barrier of caution had been lifted.

I arrived on Wednesday, 6 December. The 'gentle revolution', if it was to be dated from the ungentle night of 17 November, when police brutality had ignited the will of the people, was barely two weeks old. The opposition group Civic Forum was locked in intense negotiation with a government that still held a firm communist majority. The last big demonstration had been on Monday the fourth. A general strike was threatened for the following Monday.

It has to be said that on the streets the general impression was one of calm normality—if normality is not an ambiguous term for Czechoslovakia. The Czechoslovak flag was everywhere. Unostentatious red, white and blue tags adorned hats and lapels. In the central part of the city posters and information sheets, many of them hand-written and seemingly modest, were thick on walls and shop fronts. On *Staroměstské náměstí*, Old Town Square, a huge Christmas tree vied with a vigil of striking students beneath the statue of Jan Hus.

'Gentle revolution' seemed appropriate. But the gentleness was deceptive as well as touching. Optimism was being undermined by a jitteriness at the extreme fragility of the situation. This was a week when things might go either way. The 'smiling' revolution might lose its smile or show its teeth. People admitted to violent swings of mood from euphoria to depression. Little things told a lot: a confusion in the use of the pronouns 'we' and 'they'; the tiredness in people's eyes; the hoarseness in their voices. They had been doing a lot of shouting, a lot of talking, aware of never before having been able to talk so much. But old habits die hard: a sudden glance over the shoulder or to the side would be followed by a self-reproachful but still worried laugh.

I made a round of phone calls, including one to Miloš, and arranged to meet the editor, Alžběta, that evening. She had done a great deal of homework since my call from London and had fixed meetings for me with the writers Ludvík Vaculík and Ivan Klíma, with the possibility of meeting other writers and dissidents. She had found out nothing further about Wolf but she had made her own list of contacts to compare with mine. My priority was to find Wolf, but, viewing things pessimistically, I wanted to keep my options open. If there was no trail to follow, I didn't want my time to be empty.

I confess to more complex motives. What drew me to Wolf was, in part, that he was unknown (in more ways than one, it seemed). He was a writer, but he appeared to have no standing in contemporary Czechoslovak literature. Quite possibly, he was not an exceptionally good writer, although very brave, and his literary career had simply been eclipsed by his activist and prison experience.

A certain myth of the 'Czechoslovak Writer' seems to have arisen, at least in Western eyes: a figure automatically martyred and ennobled—banned, exiled—for the very act of writing. There may be both truth and justice in this sanctification: Václav Havel is a genuine intellectual hero who has won the spontaneous following of a people. But I suspected that the elevation of prominent writers into political symbols had obscured many 'unknowns'—writers and non-writers—and that it was perhaps unfair to the individuality of the prominent figures themselves. I wanted to test the myth, to discover whether writers resented or accepted their politicization and how they viewed a future which might restore their freedom but also remove some of their politically conferred cachet. To all this, Wolf's case would lend a rigorous perspective.

I met Alžběta at six. I gave her a copy I had of the PEN dossier on Wolf (unsure whether this was still a risky document to carry around), and we went to make inquiries at Civic Forum's new headquarters, a short distance from Alžběta's office. I anticipated the problem that, given the hectic pace of events, people who might otherwise be able to help would be too busy. I placed strong hopes on contacting members of the unofficial network VONS—the Committee for the Unjustly Prosecuted—which worked to monitor and publish details of such cases as Wolf's and included many ex-prisoners itself. The VONS network was inextricably connected with the Charter 77, and as both were now involved in the opposition movement, I did not expect to make much practical headway at Civic Forum.

I was surprised by the relaxed and low-key atmosphere of the Civic Forum office. I had imagined a throng of inquirers: there was a small knot of people. The staff all seemed to be of student age, smiling, casual, obliging; and if I was reminded of anything, it was of a university common room or a union office—an air of precarious organization. The word you were tempted to use—I thought of the hand-written posters and the single, small-screen televisions relaying information to potential crowds of hundreds—was 'amateur'. You had to remind yourself that a month ago the machinery of opposition and free information simply hadn't existed; and that, at a deeper level, all revolutions must appear to be started by amateurs.

Furthermore, if these were the amateurs, who were the professionals? No doubt, when the communist leaders were first compelled to negotiate with Civic Forum they must have stifled the thought (it was creepily instructive to have shared it) that the situation was preposterous—they were dealing with amateurs. But were they themselves professional in anything other than their official possession of power? Professional, in terms of expertise, responsibility, knowledge, capacity? The answer I got to this was to be repeatedly and vehemently 'No'. The constant cry—with a gush of relief now that at last it could be uttered openly—was that in a totalitarian regime stupidity floats to the top. At every level, control had passed for years into the hands of people with no qualification other than their Party allegiance. What Czechoslovakia desperately needs now is intelligence.

Jiří Wolf's name struck no immediate chords at Civic Forum. We asked after several of the names we had, some of them VONS people. Yes, one or two had been here, but they had gone. There was a little further conferring among the reception staff. Then someone disappeared and came back with a piece of paper. On it was written Wolf's name and a Prague telephone number. As simple as that.

It was well into the evening but we went to Alžběta's office and phoned the number. No answer. We tried several times. Meanwhile we talked and Alžběta studied the PEN dossier I had given her. It was clear that she had not fully appreciated how central to my visit was the search for Wolf, but she was becoming rapidly involved in it. We had a phone number, and it was perhaps now a straightforward matter. But there was a puzzlement which Alžběta shared. Why had she never heard of this man? And why had so many people, many of them on the circuits of information, at best only vague knowledge of him?

As we left the office and walked to get a meal, I began to feel that Wolf was having a distinct psychological effect on Alžběta— on top of all the emotion that the present crisis had brought. Here was a man whose painful history had been unknown to her only days before, and here was the prospect that soon many other such secrets must come to light. I did not imagine for one moment that Alžběta did not know of, better than I, the things that had been perpetrated in her country. But the individual case was acting, rightly or wrongly, as a catalyst to the assimilation of events.

As we walked, she spoke of things which do not often get mentioned in the West. How Charter 77 was in many ways, for all its courage and worthiness, an élitist and divisive body, exerting a tacit reproach against those who did not sign it, and throwing up within itself an inner circle of eminence at the expense of many an 'ordinary' signatory. It is generally true that in the West reference to Charter 77 evokes a handful of names. One forgets, firstly, that even by 1980 Charter 77 had more than a thousand signatories, and, secondly, that its total number of signatories was only ever a tiny proportion of the population. Alžběta was gently scoffing of those now flocking to sign the Charter. She also spoke of the pressurizing that had surrounded the signing of other petitions, such as that for the release of Havel; of a contagious attitude of 'if you are not for us, you are against us', which she pointed out was exactly the stance of the Communist Party.

What Alžběta was revealing was perhaps the inevitable nervousness and complexity that follow the simple, inspiring and hardly believable fact of revolutionary action. You could see the mechanisms of suspicion and trust, immunity and risk, rivalry and resentment beginning to turn themselves inside out: how good a non-communist were you? Old, familiar emotions were starting to flow stickily in a new direction.

I phoned the Wolf number that night. No answer. The next morning I tried again: same result. Alžběta had arranged a mid-morning meeting with Ludvík Vaculík; I was to go to her office first. I phoned Miloš to say we had Wolf's number and would keep trying it. Miloš was tied up for the day anyway. I then phoned a contact at the British Embassy Cultural Section to ask if someone could keep phoning the Wolf number through the morning. I then went to Alžběta's office on Národní Street.

Alžběta had had no luck with the Wolf number either. We tried again from her office without success, then walked to the Café Slavia at the far end of Národní Street to meet Vaculík.

Vaculík is a short, rather leonine-featured man in his sixties, with a thick, grey moustache and long, thick, grey hair. He is perhaps best known abroad for his novel *The Guinea Pigs*, written after the Soviet invasion, but his best work is considered to be *The Axe*, published before 1968. For a long time his work has been largely confined to essays, necessarily published in foreign and *emigré* journals. He is currently busy with volumes of diaries and correspondence. He remains one of Czechoslovakia's leading literary figures.

I had been warned that he was difficult, 'morose', that he might react contrarily to questions. In fact he was amiable, humorous, freely gave me his time and insisted on paying for the drinks. Vaculík rejected communism in the 1960s, but desribed himself as having had a 'lasting battle' with communism ever since he joined the Party. The Soviet invasion and subsequent crack-down meant the virtual loss of all previous freedoms. He spoke of his disbelief and despair at the time; a feeling—echoed by others I spoke to—that his life was lost, that the effects of the invasion would last and that he would not live (he gave a wry smile) to see them end.

He was forbidden to publish in Czechoslovakia and endured a

kind of house arrest. His decision to publish regularly abroad was effectively a decision to be regularly interrogated, and, like so many Czechoslovaks, he was obliged to keep monthly appointments with the police. His refusal to do menial work led to the threat of criminal proceedings for 'parasitism', though the charge was never brought. He had lost his pension rights, and he had no recourse to the assistance normally available for treatment following a gall-bladder operation. He was imprisoned once, for two days, for signing a petition to nominate Jaroslav Seifert for the Nobel Prize.

How did he view present developments?

He was a 'sceptical optimist'.

Was he bitter, did he regard the past as an evil joke?

No, it had to be viewed as a great, if terrible, lesson for world history and it should not be vulgarized.

How did he see the future?

There were two futures: one before and one after elections. Elections in the spring of 1990 seemed to him a reasonable possibility, with time enough to form parties and find personalities to stand.

Would he wish to stand himself?

No, it was his 'secret wish' to have nothing to do with politics.

In this last, frank admission Vaculík belied the stereotype of the Czechoslovak writer and perhaps expressed the inner feeling of many of his fellow authors. He exuded the dignified desire to protect his own independence. Our discussion moved on to the Czech Writers' Union, even then being denounced as a restrictive organ of the State. Vaculík, of course, was not a member, but nor did he wish to join the new free writers' association that was being formed. The scepticism in his optimism was apparent and even extended to some reservations about Civic Forum.

Did he think the perpetrators of repression should be punished?

An emphatic yes. But the punishment should be by law, not in the spirit of revenge, and those accused should include not only those responsible for the persecutions and imprisonments but those who had wreaked economic and environmental damage. One might need to accept that the punishment would not correspond to the guilt, since the degree of criminality might never be properly determined.

What of the punishment for those personally involved in his own suffering?

Here Vaculík's individuality reasserted itself. He would like, he said, with a slyly wistful expression, to invite a certain police officer to his home, just as that police officer had issued many invitations to him. No one else, no publicity. A simple invitation to coffee.

Finally I asked Vaculík if he knew about Wolf. Once again, there was the vague recognition of the name, but he could not help me further.

A fter lunch I called in at the Cultural Section of the British Embassy. Had they got an answer from the Wolf number? Yes.
Would Saturday morning be all right for a meeting?

Mr Wolf couldn't give a precise time as yet, but would call back. And he only spoke Czech.

I was amazed. My goal appeared to have been achieved in less than twenty-four hours. And, with all my readiness to pursue numerous Czech contacts, it was a section of the British Embassy that had made the connection. I was still baffled. How had he sounded on the phone? Was he genuinely ready to meet or perhaps a little cautious?

Oh, perfectly ready, perfectly positive about it all. And he sounded fine.

As it happened, I was able to hear for myself. They had forgotten to give the number he should ring at the Section, so a further call was made to him, in Czech of course. The voice I overheard issuing from the receiver was business-like and robust. One image I had of Jiří Wolf, as a man physically and mentally wrecked and beyond rehabilitation, faded.

Back at the hotel, I phoned Miloš to tell him the news. Would he be free to act as interpreter?

Only if the meeting was early. Could it be on Friday instead—he had the whole day free?

I said Wolf had to choose the time. I could probably find

someone else for Saturday. It looked as if I might never get to meet Miloš.

This was late afternoon on Thursday the seventh. There had been stories during the day that Adamec, the prime minister, was threatening to resign. A stalemate seemed to have been reached between Civic Forum and the government. Civic Forum wanted a reformed government (with a non-communist majority) by Sunday, otherwise the general strike would go ahead. Adamec's position was that he would reform the government but would not act under pressure and ultimatums. If they continued, he would resign. Since Adamec was, temporarily at least, a significant figure in negotiations for both sides, this was not a desirable outcome.

Alžběta had arranged a further meeting with another writer, Eda Kriseova, that evening between six and seven. Kriseova spoke English and would come to the hotel, but I was not to be surprised if she did not show up. I fully expected her not to appear, since she was closely involved with Civic Forum and was currently privy to discussions with the government. But she was also a writer, and perhaps sometimes it is true that writers like to meet writers. At six o'clock she phoned from the lobby, and, though we could have talked in the hotel, we hurried across the street to a café.

Obviously in a hurry and excited, but smiling and genial, she was the first person I met who seemed truly charged with the electricity of events. She was also the first person to convey a real shiver of fear. She had been on a tram just now and people were saying that Adamec had resigned. If this had happened, then everything was thrown into flux. There would be a 'constitutional crisis'. There might be a 'putsch'. She used this word several times, as if she had not chosen it thoughtlessly.

This was unsettling, to say the least. I shared the generally accepted view that the way ahead for Civic Forum was not easy but that the current of change was essentially irreversible. Correspondents in the Western press at least were ruling out intervention by the army. But Kriseova seemed convinced it was still possible. 'I don't see many uniforms about,' I said rather obtusely, remembering that a year ago it was hard to get away from them.

'Exactly,' she said. 'Where *are* they all?'

It was hard to get the measure of Kriseova. She seemed both to have acquired a special grip on events (given her closeness to the centre of things, you could not deny her privileged viewpoint) and to have lost some normal hold on them. She herself seemed to acknowledge this. Her language had a heightened, even ecstatic quality. She spoke of the 'existential' nature of recent experience, of being 'on a wave' and having no choice, of something working 'through her', of events moving so fast that you were 'racing after history'. She also admitted to an uncanny sense of being involved in the unreal, to having asked her old friend, Havel: 'Václav, are we dreaming this? Are we acting this?'

The question reverberates. Theatrical metaphors need to be applied with care to Czechoslovakia where the theatre has traditionally involved itself very concretely in politics. It is no bizarre accident that the opposition movement was inaugurated by an actor (famous for his romantic leads), threw up as its protagonist a playwright, Václav Havel, and had its first headquarters in a theatre, the fantastically named 'Laterna Magica'. Yet here was Kriseova testifying to the actual feeling, as the Civic Forum leaders met inside a theatre, that surely they were in a play. No doubt all remarkable events may seem at first unreal, especially when they have the weight of twenty years to deny their possibility. For me too these days in Prague had an unreal tinge. But surely people *make* history, they don't act it (otherwise everything is excused). Nor do they run after it. Or do they?

Rapt as she seemed capable of being, Kriseova was full of earthy warmth and vitality, and she plainly had a bent for the practical. She described herself as Havel's 'fairy godmother', making sure, amid everything, that he got his medicine for the lung problems he has had since contracting pneumonia in prison. She was also, one guessed, a courageous woman. She spoke of the demonstration on the night of the seventeenth, at which she, her daughter and some five thousand others had been caught in the trap formed by the police in Národní Street, preventing access to Wenceslas Square. All sorts of accounts were circulating about this night. Some said that the police had been specially drugged; that they had used nets to snare small clusters of people; that bodies were seen lying under covers (this apart from the publicized rumour, later proved false, that a student had been killed).

What seemed beyond dispute was the ferocity of the police attacks and that this was a premeditated plan, executed to prevent the escape of a mass of people from a confined space. A public investigation (that unprecedented thing) was currently being conducted into the brutality. A neurologist had testified that the cases of shock were similar to those he had seen in people who had experienced bombardment in the war. Others pointed out that from the sheer weight of numbers and from crushing and confinement alone, fatalities would have been likely.

Absolutely beyond doubt is that 17 November was a turning-point in events and a colossal mistake by the authorities. The world changed overnight.

Like Vaculík, Kriseova had found herself stripped of hope in 1969. Formerly a successful journalist, she suddenly had nothing, and had to wrench herself from despair. She took work in a mental hospital, which she says saved her from going mad herself. She saw that the inmates were 'free' in a way those outside were not. Her first stories arose from her mental hospital experience. In the seventies she came under scrutiny and threats from the security police and after refusing to 'retract' had established, like Vaculík, a regular 'relationship' with an investigator and was, of course, prevented from publishing.

How did she get involved in Civic Forum?

She had once presciently told Havel that if he ever got drawn into things so much that he needed help, he should call her. He called soon after.

Was she bitter about the 'lost' years and did she want retribution?

You had to remember, she said, that the worst time was in the fifties. The generation that had known that time was conditioned by its terrible memories, numbed into submission. Even now many of them were sceptical. The generations of the sixties and after had not lost their hope. And you had to get retribution into perspective: one woman who had been assaulted at night in the street was found screaming, 'They are killing us now! They are going to kill us!' Her assailant was a solitary molester but the woman was a Party member and genuinely feared an opposition massacre.

The Prague streets did indeed seem a little darker after speaking to Kriseova. In the café the talk had been confirmed: Adamec had stepped down. But even as she hurried to a possible constitutional crisis, Kriseova was making arrangements to meet me again, to give me some of her stories. I must read them, we must discuss them. Writers!

At the hotel there were no messages about Wolf. I phoned Alžběta to tell her that we seemed to have a meeting with Wolf on Saturday. Could she possibly be there to interpret? I also told her what Kriseova had said and discussed the evening's news. I could hear anxiety creeping into her voice. I could not tell if this arose from her own assessment of the situation or from my words, the garbled, intrusive words of a foreigner clumsily relaying inside information from one Czech to another. The palpable throb of rumour.

The next morning was bright and clear. There were no uniforms on the street and the trams were crossing the bridge over the Vltava as usual. I had to be at Alžběta's office at ten-thirty to meet Ivan Klíma. (Alžběta seemed to have abandoned normal work, but a revolution was a good excuse.) I phoned the Cultural Section to see if there was a definite time for Wolf.

We're glad you phoned, I was told. You see, the thing is, there's been a mistake. The man we spoke to phoned back and said that, after thinking it over, it seemed a little strange that you wanted to meet him. You see, the fact is, whoever he is, he's the wrong man. He's not Jiří Wolf.

I called Miloš. I let the enigma of the bogus Wolf go. It was Friday, Miloš's free day. We were back to where we started. He was at my service. He would do some scouting while I went to see Klíma. I also called a number of contacts I had neglected to follow up, believing we had found Wolf. These included a man called Hejda, a man called Freund and a man called Doruzka, a leading jazz figure (this a recommendation from Josef Škvorecký) who might put me on to a man called Srp [sic] who might know Wolf personally. Hejda didn't know about Wolf but suggested someone whom I had already tried without success. Freund was out but his wife said she would pass on a message. Doruzka, in stylishly idiomatic English, sounded the key-note of my search so far: 'No, I am afraid this man's name does not ring any bells with me.'

Now that Wolf was once again a mystery, I could not resist indulging in dubious theories. Could it be that Wolf, on his release, had simply wished to disappear? Could it be that there was something about his personality that had kept him removed from the main circles of activists? Had he always been, perhaps, a little mad? Some of the names and phone numbers I had were copied directly from a typed information sheet on a window in Národní Street, giving details about Pavel Wonka, who had died in prison the previous year. It seemed extraordinary that, if such matters were now public, Wolf should be so elusive.

I told myself that my hypotheses were indeed indulgent. It was wrong to construct riddles merely out of my lack of luck in finding a man. I went to Alžběta's office to see Klíma.

I had met Klíma on my previous visit. He is a tall, rather gangling man, with straggly dark hair, a sort of misshapen handsomeness and a crinkly smile. He has the air of a veteran from beatnik days and speaks good English. Popular at the time of the Prague Spring, mainly as a playwright, he now has a high reputation, both in and outside his country, as a novelist. Much of his work, though perhaps not the very best, has appeared in English. His untranslated *Soudce z Milosti* is considered, along with Vaculík's *The Axe*, to be one of the great Czechoslovak novels of recent times.

Comparatively speaking, Klíma has not been severely persecuted during the last twenty years, and I wondered whether for some this has slightly diminished his otherwise considerable standing. Despite the ban on his work at home, he has been able to survive on foreign royalties, to keep up a steady rate of production, and he emanated relative contentment. His life, on the other hand, has scarcely been easy. In 1969 he managed to visit an American university, leaving on the very day (31 August) before the borders were closed. His passport was confiscated on his return and he was not able to travel for eleven years, and then only within Eastern Europe. He ceased to write plays because of the impossibility of seeing them staged. He was harassed, his home searched, his telephone tampered with, but he was never arrested or imprisoned.

Klíma is neither complacent nor possessed of any false guilt at not being in the top league of the persecuted. He has a strong sense of his own individuality—I suspect that he shared Vaculík's 'secret wish' not to be involved in politics—and even a rather gleeful sense of irony about how his case goes against the grain of some received Western ideas. He pointed out that he did not sign Charter 77, but, as many of his friends were signatories and he moved in Charter circles, he was none the less subject to scrutiny. He also implied that not signing Charter 77 might have been a tactical advantage: you could be active without advertising the fact. He was not snubbed for not signing. His position was that as an author he wished to sign only his own texts.

Unlike Vaculík, Klíma did not disdain manual work. Rather, he took the view that doing other, temporary jobs could be valuable for a writer; and he told a story which was a perfect explosion of the Western 'myth'. A famous Czech author is seen cleaning the streets by a friend of his at the American Embassy. The American goes into a fit of outrage at how the authorities humiliate the country's best minds. But the writer (could it be Klíma?) is doing the job voluntarily: it is research for a book.

We discussed Havel, who conforms in paramount fashion to the Western myth and who at that moment was being tipped for president. There were two possible views of Havel in my mind. One, that he was a man moving willingly to meet his destiny as leader of the people; the other, that he was being sucked into events at some cost to himself, a writer uprooted from his true vocation.

But it seemed that Havel did not have the 'secret wish'. Klíma said that Havel was, of course, exhausted right now, but underneath he was happy. He called him a 'childish' man (I think he meant 'child-like'). He was happy to be the great citizen. He was a brave man, yes, but he had political ambitions—they were not thrust upon him. Klíma had always found Havel's essays and political writings more impressive than his plays.

We spoke of other Czech writers, the exiles Kundera and Škvorecký. Klíma thought Kundera was a great writer but self-interested. He played up to Western preconceptions in terms of both his own position and his portrayal of Czechoslovakia, which Klíma found often superficial and too eager for symbols. *The Unbearable Lightness of Being* was not entirely liked in Czechoslovakia. Škvorecký, on the other hand, retained a strong following, particularly among the younger generation, and was seen as the exile with the greater integrity.

We turned to Czechoslovak writing generally and to what the future held. Both Vaculík and Kriseova had spoken forcibly about the discrediting of the Czech Writers' Union, and Vaculík had wished to hold back even from the newly established free association of writers. Klíma seemed to be directly involved in the founding of this new association (*Obec*—'Community'), but some of the harshest language of a generally gently spoken man was reserved for the old Union. He called it an 'instrument of national treason' which for twenty years had accepted without protest that hundreds of Czech writers were suppressed and persecuted if not imprisoned. The Union, he said, was 'covered in shame.' However, there should be no 'craving for revenge.' Members of the old Union should be allowed, as individuals, to join the new Community. This was in accordance with the Community's overriding commitment to freedom of expression. But there was to be no 'fusion' between the two bodies.

What of the Union's money, its assets?

Klíma said, with some bitterness, that the Union had no assets, only tables and typewriters. Then he said there should be a calling to account for the 'abuse of literary funds'.

I half appreciated what he meant. I knew that all writers, Union members or not, were obliged to pay a percentage of income to a Literary Fund. In effect, writers who were banned were forced to pay for the privileges of the approved.

From my visit of the year before, I had a graphic illustration of what these privileges might entail. I vividly remember being taken from Bratislava on a snowy day to a 'castle' in the Slovak countryside, which was owned by, or rather allocated to, the Slovak Writers' Union. I have to say that those who took me did so in a spirit of hospitality but also with detectable unease.

The 'castle' was a grand country house, set in extensive grounds and approached along a magnificent avenue of poplars. I was told that for a very small payment writers could come here to work; though few of the many rooms seemed occupied. None the less, we were greeted by a permanent staff and ushered into a building that was as warmly heated as it was immaculately decorated and furnished. I was given a brief tour and shown one of the best bedrooms—one of the most sumptuous and elegant guest-rooms I have ever seen. Brezhnev, I was told, once slept here.

For their small payment, writers were also fed. There were only four of us, and the place really did seem empty, but a table (dwarfed by the proportions of the room around it) was laid for lunch, complete with fine cutlery and glassware. While snow fell outside on to noble trees, a waitress served us a meal worthy of any restaurant, in an atmosphere of Cinderella-like fantasy.

I asked Klíma what would become of such places and of the Literary Fund. He said the Literary Fund and all that it paid for—the 'castles', the Union buildings, offices, secretaries—all belonged to the Ministry of Culture. The Union owned nothing. He did not know what would happen now. He said that foreigners often overlooked the abuses in his country that were insidious and did not form neat or dramatic symbols. Of course individuals had been martyrs and suffered terribly and bravely, but the real damage was the gradual erosion of the self-respect of a whole people, the spread of corruption and the simultaneous ruination, by progressive mismanagement, of the economy and the environment.

It was perhaps the wrong moment, but I asked Klíma about Wolf.

No, Wolf's case was not familiar to him.

I lunched with Alžběta. I had told her about Wolf proving not to be Wolf. She seemed in a low mood. I was not sure if this was because she had entered the spirit of the search and felt thwarted or because she was anxious at the uncertainty still surrounding Adamec's resignation. Klíma had a theory that Adamec had resigned with the hidden purpose of popping up again as president. The ultimatum of the general strike stood. The streets were still calm. I went back to the hotel and waited for a call from Miloš.

Miloš duly rang, in positive mood. He had inquired again at

Civic Forum. No success. Then he had tracked down some VONS people and had been given an address for Wolf in Prague. No phone. He had gone to the address and found no one there. But he had left a note on the door, with a brief explanation, asking Wolf to call him or (if he spoke English) to call me at the hotel. So far, no replies. But we could only wait and see. I made a note of the address and we agreed to phone each other as soon as we heard anything.

I waited. The situation was a considerable improvement from the morning—at least I knew Wolf was in Prague. But, as time went by, I started to have doubts. Wolf did not have to be at the address at all. I also reflected on the wisdom of leaving notes on doors. Surely this was rash, even now. A forgotten fact came back to me: Wolf's sentence had included not only six years' imprisonment, now served, but also three years' subsequent 'protective surveillance'.

Late that evening there was a knock on my door. Surely not? No, it was Eda Kriseova, eyes bloodshot with fatigue, but smiling, dressed in a trench coat and chic black hat and clutching a folder of papers. The scene was straight out of a spy movie.

Would she like a drink?

No, she was too tired; she had been all day with Civic Forum; she had to go and rest. But here were the stories and extracts from a novel she had promised to bring me. We talked for a moment in the corridor. She told me that Civic Forum had reached provisional agreement for a reformed government and that President Husak would resign that weekend. I hardly registered the full import of these quietly spoken words. I took the folder and wished her good night.

Two things struck me. That despite what was clearly an exhausting and historic day, she was still writer enough to find time to bring me her manuscripts. Secondly, that this was one of Prague's 'international' hotels, much used by Western visitors, and three weeks ago one might legitimately have feared bugs and the ears of informers. But here was Kriseova announcing her momentous news in one of its corridors. Thus you learn of the fall of tyrants.

I began reading Kriseova's work immediately. The green light on my phone came on. Wolf? No. A message left by a Mr Freund, giving the same address for Wolf that Miloš had discovered.

It was snowing the next morning. I phoned Miloš, who had

heard nothing and would be busy until four o'clock. I had an arrangement to meet Igor from Bratislava at two in the hotel lobby. Miloš said he could find time to call me around one-thirty. The morning was free and, though I was beginning to lose hope, I resolved to go to Wolf's address myself on blind chance. Since this might have been fruitless anyway without someone who spoke Czech, I called Alžběta. If Kriseova was Havel's fairy godmother, Alžběta was surely the fairy godmother of my search for Wolf. It was Saturday, I could hear a child in the background, but she agreed to come.

By a stroke of luck, the address given for Wolf was not far from where Alžběta herself lived, south of the centre of Prague, some three stops on the metro from Wenceslas Square. Alžběta met me at the station and, following a street map, we walked through the snow. Wolf's street was a quiet cul-de-sac (though all the streets seemed quiet), with family houses on one side and a run-down apartment block, where Wolf lived, on the other. His door, with his name on it, was on the first floor. A cold, gloomy landing. We knocked. No answer.

Jammed in the door-frame was a pencil-written note on a scrap of paper, which, according to Alžběta, was to a woman and simply said, 'Wait for me here.' It seemed to have been written by Wolf himself and suggested he had been here recently. We knocked again, just in case, waited, considered; then knocked at a neighbour's along the landing. A burly man in a check shirt appeared, who did not seem unduly suspicious of us.

Yes, Wolf was around—he had seen him this morning. He had complained of not sleeping. Yes, he knew who Wolf was. Wolf was out and about a lot; he was still 'active', perhaps. Yes, my own son is with Charter 77.

Did Wolf look well?

He didn't look so bad.

We deliberated. Alžběta was for waiting; then for leaving a note. I was unsure. This would be the second note from a stranger on his door in twenty-four hours. I was beginning to think that the truth of the matter was that, whatever Wolf was doing now, he did not want intrusion; perhaps he should be left alone. And I was beginning to question my persistence in seeking him out—the whole absurd folly of a Western visitor trying to find an elusive Czech dissident. Was I not conducting a grotesque parody of the 'protective surveillance' that, for all I knew, Wolf was still subject to? I had got carried away with the detective-hunt element of things and had somehow pushed to the back of my mind the terrible facts that had provoked my interest in the first place. As though merely finding him mattered!

Alžběta left a note, this time giving her phone number as a further point of contact. We walked back to the metro in a subdued mood. I would probably not see Alžběta again before I left. She was sorry that with all our efforts we had not met with success. The search had led us only to mutual self-searching.

At the hotel there were no messages. Igor was due shortly. I looked forward to his arrival. I had called him from Prague at a point when I illusorily believed that my task would be accomplished by Saturday afternoon: the time would be free. I would have to explain what had happened, but I felt the situation was essentially unchanged: I had done all I could. Just before I met Igor, Miloš phoned, as promised. No further news. I explained that I had been to Wolf's address myself and that my feeling now was that Wolf was a man who wanted to keep to himself.

'No, no,' said Miloš, with some emphasis, 'my information about him is that he would not find this intrusive; he would be ready to meet.

I wrote a note for the reception desk, saying that if I had any callers or visitors, especially a Mr Wolf, I would be back at six. Then I waited in the lobby for Igor. He showed up, wearing the badge of Civic Forum's Slovak sister movement, People Against Violence, and we went off to a café on the Old Town Square. We intended to take a walk across the river to Hradčany, but the weather was bitter and, with much to talk about, we were still sitting there at five.

Igor's presence was a reminder of the elementary fact that Czechoslovakia is a federation of two states, the Czech and the Slovak. The negotiations to reform the government, going on even as we spoke, involved a good deal of juggling of Slovak against Czech as well as communist against non-communist representation. The Slovaks are proud of their Slovakness—in Igor's company you learn not to use the word 'Czech' to apply to the country as a whole. But Igor was generally sceptical of the notion that political changes might lead to an awkward upsurge of Slovak nationalism.

Events in Bratislava appeared to have run a parallel course to those in Prague, with the Bratislavs having the particular excitement of being suddenly allowed to travel freely across the Austrian border, less than five miles away. In practice, Czechs and Slovaks are still restrained from foreign travel by the lack of foreign money. But here was a chance to to-and-fro across a ghostly Iron Curtain just for the sake of it, East Berliner style, several return trips a day.

Were there any problems peculiar to Slovakia?

Yes, eastern Slovakia was a notoriously 'remote' part of the country and the spread of information from the capital had proved difficult, meeting with confusion and distrust. (Vaculík and Kriseova had made the same point about the rural areas generally). The authorities seemed to have colluded in the problem, since there was a remarkable incidence of power-cuts at the same time as opposition broadcasts. But not all Igor's stories raised laughter. There was the one about the Russian soldier (the Soviet army was still there of course, keeping a *very* low profile) found hanged near a railway station. Suicide? Or something else?

At five-thirty we walked back to the hotel. Igor was good company. My pensive mood of the morning had lifted and I was now sanguinely resigned to the fact that I would not meet Wolf. When we entered the lobby I could see there was a message for me next to my key. It said: 'I am tall with bushy hair and glasses. I am waiting in the lounge. When you read this Mr Wolf will probably be waiting too. Miloš.'

I am still confused as to how this small miracle occurred: whether Wolf and Miloš converged on the hotel by mutual arrangement or by some remarkable coincidence. Even after later hearing Miloš's account, I am not entirely sure of the exact sequence of events.

I walked, with Igor, round the corner into the lounge. There was Miloš, as described. There, introduced by him, was Wolf. And there was a third man, who spoke English and gave his name as Weiss. We moved to another part of the lounge which could accommodate us all, and the whole strange, short encounter began.

The first element of strangeness was the setting. To repeat, this was one of Prague's big hotels. It was a Saturday evening. The lounge was busy and hung with Christmas decorations. We might have gone to my room, or somewhere else, the choice was Wolf's; but we were sitting down to talk in a place that only recently would have been quite unsafe, and perhaps still was. I was conscious throughout that people *were* listening to us (who would not have eavesdropped?). I vividly recall the young waiter, with the face of a bespectacled sixth-former, who brought our drinks and stared boggle-eyed, transfixed by what Wolf was saying.

A second element of strangeness was the air of feverish, if business-like haste. From the moment he sat down, Wolf launched into a monologue, interrupted almost exclusively by Miloš's disciplined translations. There were no questions put to me about the nature of my interest and no opportunity for me to explain it voluntarily. Nor was there much opportunity for me to ask questions. The nearest thing to small talk came from Weiss, who was the third element of strangeness. I had not anticipated a mystery companion, though such a figure should not have been so unexpected. It became plain that Weiss was not just there for his English; he was looking after Wolf in some way. He said of Wolf at one point: 'He is part of my family now.' It emerged that Weiss had been a prisoner too, for several years, some of them in Valdice.

The contrast between Weiss and Wolf could scarcely have been more pronounced. Whereas Wolf was all contained nervous energy and concentration, Weiss was relaxed, smiled a lot and was ready, when he could, even to joke and digress. He apologized for his teeth, which had been damaged in prison, but the defect hardly marred a kindly, avuncular face. Weiss was dressed in a casual cardigan; Wolf in a suit and tie which, if it were not for a general dishevelment (the tie was quickly loosened), might have been called dapper. The clothes had been sent from America.

In the space of an hour, I learned a little about Weiss, the man:

that his passions were airplanes, that he had a library of eight thousand books. I learned very little about Wolf. When Wolf said that his wife had divorced him because she did not wish to be married to a criminal, there was no emotion and the remark was made almost incidentally. Weiss chipped in that his wife too had divorced him when he was a prisoner, but, on his release, they had met up again and married for the second time; and he was evidently delighted to repeat the story. It was as though Weiss was there to give the picture of a man who had been a prisoner yet was restored to a benign, rounded humanity.

Wolf was short, with the sort of slight frame that often suggests an intense mental life. Afterwards, when I asked myself the question, 'If you hadn't known who Wolf was, what would you have taken him for?' I answered: I would have taken him for some *distrait* chess-player, an obsessive academic, a mathematician. His face was distinctly Jewish, and I wondered how this may have affected the treatment he received from prison guards. He blinked a lot, with a twitch to his cheek, a definite tic. He sat on my right, with Miloš to my left. He spoke rapidly, a little breathlessly, mostly looking straight ahead or at Miloš, but now and then turning to me with a sort of uncertain smile, which I rightly or wrongly took as a seeking of reassurance. His hands were in contrast to the rest of him: thick, blunt fingers, with very little spare nail.

What did he say? In one sense he said what I had already heard, since the substance of his monologue, elaborated and extended, was similar to that of the dossier I had read on him and covered much the same ground. It was the third-person, case-history Wolf of the dossier, rather than the direct, first-person, intensely pitiable Wolf of the prison writings. There was, of course, something utterly new and strange in hearing facts already half-known issuing from the lips of the man himself. But I confess to more than once having the absurd urge to stop him and say, 'I think I know this. Tell me about *yourself.*'

There was also the sense that what he was uttering was prepared, rehearsed, had often been repeated. He had certain things to say, then he would finish. It did not take long to surmise that Wolf had probably been doing a lot of this recently. Telling a lot of different people or groups of people, if rarely stray visitors from

England, the facts. This was his work now, his task, the way in which, according to his neighbour, he was still 'active'. It was also, at some deeper level, the way he wanted, and was able, to deal with things. Weiss later confirmed the intuition. He said, 'We are very busy politically.' He spoke of fears that the prisons would be slow to change, that there would be a conspiracy to destroy prison and court records, a general hushing-up.

The repeated note from Wolf was forensic and legalistic: the attestation to accumulated injustice. He was not interested in his 'human story', nor in sensation, nor, save when he referred to Czechoslovakia's 'Gulag', in rhetoric. When he stated that he had received ten days of solitary confinement and a halving of rations for having a loose button, and I had to ask him, in amazement, to repeat what he had said, he did not dwell on the matter. When he remarked that a 'co-defendant' had been released after one year and was working 'to this day' for the state security, it was spoken without special stress or elaboration, like the reference to his divorce.

His release on 17 May had been at the full term of his prison sentence. He had been ill for a month and was treated by a neurologist. Necessary follow-up treatment proved unforthcoming, partly because doctors were afraid of his reputation with the secret police. When fit to do so, he was required to report to the police every day. There were problems with both employment and accommodation, and there was pressure on him to leave Prague.

He was held in custody twelve times after he was released that spring, with a flurry of detentions in August. Court proceedings were opened against him twice. The police entered his flat several times, sometimes at night. The last such visit was on 15 November, less than three weeks ago. In the same month, when he was working as a stoker in a boiler-room, he was visited by police who threatened to throw him into the furnace. On 17 November he was arrested at home and held till eleven that night to prevent his participation in the events of that day. Since 17 November he has refused to go to a police station, but since the seventeenth (the finality of that day!) persecution of him has ceased.

Wolf spoke of his years in prison with the intent but impersonal tone of a man in a witness box. There was little actual description. In ten years, prison rations were cut by half, but the work-loads of enforced labour were increased. Prisoners were required to *pay* for their maintenance in prison, but because of reductions in their wages for forced labour and because of other financial penalties, the 'bill' could never be met. Wolf is still technically in debt to the state for 4,200 crowns for the privilege of six years' brutal punishment.

Conditions for political prisoners were worse than for others, one aspect of their degradation being that they were thrown in with the worst criminals (Weiss's foreman at one time was a triple murderer). Political prisoners were selected for the worst work and were not allowed to associate with each other. They were subjected to close scrutiny of their behaviour and speech and to regular reports by warders, who were directed to destroy prisoners psychologically. All prison functionaries, medical staff as well as guards, colluded in the cover-up of breaches of law and human rights.

Wolf was manifestly a brave man, but his readiness to endure the worst showed a staggering single-mindedness. When his half-sister asked for remission for him, Wolf refused to sign the application, on the grounds that only those who were guilty could ask for remission: accepting remission amounted to retraction. When he received his six-year sentence he also refused to appeal, on the grounds that he did not accept the legality of the verdict. He annulled an appeal made on his behalf by a lawyer. Pressure was put on him to bring an appeal, to demonstrate the fairness of the courts, and he was promised one year off his sentence. Wolf did not comply. In the twenty-two months interval, between his two stretches of imprisonment, Wolf had been offered political asylum in France. He had refused on the grounds that, if he were granted asylum, all *other* political victims should be offered the same.

After making this last point, Wolf brought things to an abrupt close. I had been wondering how long he would continue, whether there would be a more flexible stage in which he would be open to question. But now he gave a quick expulsion of breath, said something which I was sure was the Czech equivalent to 'That's it', and made the knee-patting gesture of a man about to depart. I looked at Igor, who looked bemused, and at Miloš, who wore his interpreter's mask. There was a reaching for coats, some final hand-shaking, some pleasantries from Weiss, and then the two were gone, as if hastening to some other, similar appointment, leaving behind them a vacuum of bewilderment and the consciousness that all around us were eyes and ears.

Why should I have been so stunned? Given Wolf's history, I had been ready for anything, so why was the reality so confounding? And why, beneath it all, did I have a perverse feeling of disappointment? I had met him; he had spoken, on his own terms, which were the only proper terms; I had listened. Why should I feel sorry if I felt I was nowhere nearer to knowing the man? What right did I have to know him? If I could conceive at all of what ten years of his kind of imprisonment might take away from a man, how should I expect anything to be rendered to me in an hour?

I had never asked him about his writing. What happened to that earlier work? Confiscated, destroyed? Did he (absurd question somehow) still want to write? It was ironic that I had met three other writers who, each with their own personal nuance, had transcended the image of the 'suffering Czech', yet Wolf had given it back to me in hard, annunciatory fact, as if at a press conference, with scarcely a touch of the personal.

Miloš had to leave. I thanked him for all he had done. Igor and I had a strong desire to be out of the hotel. As we walked off, I, for one, could not resist looking over my shoulder. We began the process of analyzing what we had just experienced, but this slid into the anaesthetic urge to find a restaurant that served Slovak food, to drink several glasses of vodka, followed by several glasses of wine. A radio was switched on in the restaurant. It confirmed what Kriseova had told me in the hotel corridor: a new government would be sworn in tomorrow; the president would resign. It was the end of an era.

Walking late that night across the lower end of Wenceslas Square, I was stopped, not by a secret policeman, nor by a celebrating citizen, but by a street huckster with a small, puckered, toothless face. I thought my English would deter him, but he grabbed my hand, studied my palm and, with a confident American twang, assessed my life and character as follows: I had been a naughty boy, oh yes, a very naughty boy; and I would live to be seventy-four. This cost me ten crowns.

My last morning in Prague—Sunday the tenth, the day communist domination would cease—bloomed brilliant and clear. A huge rally was planned for the afternoon in Wenceslas Square when the new government would be announced. But I had to be at the airport at two, and in any case had the feeling I would be an intruder at someone else's party. On my last day I wanted to do what I had not yet done: to cross the river, to walk up the Hradčany, to the castle, and appreciate that Prague is beautiful. A year ago the beauty had seemed bogus, even sinister. What place did aesthetics have in politics? But now, perhaps, Prague could be truly, unashamedly beautiful again. And so it was, its valleys and crests of architecture rising out of the dazzle of the winter morning.

Igor came with me. We crossed the Charles Bridge, seagulls squawking around us. What place did aesthetics have in politics? Seifert, whose love of Prague was as fierce as it was gentle, and who did not live, like Vaculík, to see the end of repression, wrote, with his own terrible heed of aesthetics:

> When I shall die—and this will be quite soon—
> I shall still carry in my heart
> this city's destiny.

> And mercilessly, just as Marsyas,
> let anyone be flayed alive
> who lays hands on this city,
> no matter who he is,
> no matter how sweetly he plays
> on his flute.

The Czechoslovak people, the guide-books say, have always honoured their writers. The road up to the castle is named after a writer, the poet Jan Neruda, from whom Pablo Neruda borrowed his name. Hunched against the castle walls is the impossibly tiny, fairy-tale house where Kafka wrote part of *The Trial*. And all over Prague there were poems, of a kind, blossoming on walls and windows and statues. Someone will anthologize them, if they haven't already. Igor translated: 'Husak, you talked a lot, but you said nothing.' 'He has eyes but he does not see; he has ears but he does not hear: who is he?'

Writers, writers!

We walked through the courtyards of the Presidential Palace, where even at that hour, perhaps, Husak was enjoying or suffering his last lunch as president, and over which flew the presidential flag with its motto which, on this day, could not have been more ironic, more Delphically barbed: 'Truth Shall Win.'

Igor insisted on coming to the airport to see me off. With events just beginning on Wenceslas Square, this seemed a considerable sacrifice. Perhaps he shared the 'secret wish'. Did Wolf have— would he, could he, ever have that wish?

Later, on the phone, Igor told me he had gone back and caught the last of it: he 'couldn't resist.'

A television in the airport concourse showed pictures of the jubilant crowds. The plane left on time, minutes after the president's resignation. There were several Czechoslovaks on board and I wondered how they felt, to be flying out of their country on the day of its deliverance.

Neal Ascherson
Borderlands

You did not engrave yourself into popular memory, Byelorussia. You did not confiscate the liberty of others or plunder foreign lands or murder people who came from beyond your neighbour's furrow. You gave to strangers respect and the cake of hospitality; you gave to robbers your last cow and the last crumb of rye bread with the sign of the Cross... When I remember Byelorussian words, when the wind blows from the north-east, when I see a linen shirt with that sad embroidery, when I hear a cry of pain which does not blame... then I always feel the sudden chill of vague accusations of conscience, a sense of shared guilt and of shame. Byelorussia, Byelorussia, grey-green with a huge sky over your faded head, you are too good and gentle and generous for our times.

Tadeusz Konwicki, *The Calendar and the Hourglass*

Here is the forest. Not just a forest, but a *puszcza*: a Polish word that means a world of trees which have never been felled since the first bands of human beings arrived to hunt here. The *Puszcza* of Kniszyn, which begins north-east of the Polish city of Białystok, must be ten thousand years old.

To reach the village of Lipowy Most, I set off from the city Białystok along the road which leads to the Soviet frontier. I turned off the tarred highway at the spot where an oak tree grows upon a mound, a tree on which the Russians hanged Polish insurgents during the January Rising of 1863. That is to say: the vain Polish insurrection for independence which began in January but which lasted for fifteen months—for even longer, in the *puszcza*.

The road to the village is made of sand and dust. It ends in a wide clearing, large enough for fields of rye and a cluster of wooden houses. The history of this village began in 1918, when the three empires which had partitioned Poland between them for 123 years—Russia, Germany and Austria—collapsed almost simultaneously. Poland stood up among the ruins and reclaimed its independence, and the new government decided to honour a man, by then old, who had fought for the nation in 1863. It gave him this land for his six sons, and their descendants are still here. But the government also intended, by settling veteran patriots and their children on this land, to post more sentries along what the Poles consider to be the eastern frontier of Europe— the *przedmurze* (bastion) of the Catholic West.

Lipowy Most is still a Catholic village. But the peasants who inhabit other clearings in this forest are not Catholic: they are Russian Orthodox. They, the original inhabitants, are Slavs but neither Russian nor Polish. They are Byelorussians.

The forest edge is a few hundred yards away from the village, past two wooden crosses wreathed with herbs and rowan. Deer, lynx and boar live here, beavers and wolves and—further south—a few bison. I am sitting on a bench with my back against one of the houses, at the end of a summer day, doing nothing more than inhaling: sorting out the scents and tasting each, like a dog. The smells from the forest itself—pine-needles and resin, heather, sphagnum moss, the whiff of boletus mushrooms, moist earth—mix with wood-smoke, trodden rowan berries, long grass heated by the sun, cooking in one of the cottages, a dish of apples. It is entirely silent. Then a voice echoes against the forest wall and dies away.

How would a shot resound, a shot fired deep in the forest by a survivor from an invading army or a partisan band, by somebody who had stayed among the trees and never given in? Through the door of one of these huts, they carried young men wounded in the 1863 Insurrection. The Home Army resistance fought the Nazis here, and some of its detachments fought on against the Communist government long after the war. A few armed men remained in this forest, so the villagers say, until 1957. Kazimierz Brandys wrote a short story called 'The Bear' about a partisan man who wouldn't come out of the trees. In the end he lost his shape, became a tale to scare children, a shadow at dawn near the forest edge, the booming echoes of a rifle-shot heard between dreaming and starting awake.

The children of a Białystok doctor, here for the summer holidays, spend their days exploring in the forest. On the wall of the barn, they hang the helmets they find. Two German ones, rusted and pierced. Today the boy found a Red Army helmet, not much corroded, which he spotted lying half-buried in the bank of a stream. Patriots, bandits, fugitives and their pursuers, Scottish mercenaries, Swedish musketeers from the Great Northern War,

Russians and Germans, all have fallen here and disintegrated into the moss. I know a man who went mushrooming and found, in a distant clearing, the wreck of a French supply-wagon from the 1812 Retreat from Moscow, with Grande Armée buttons scattered around it. The *puszcza* has been swallowing the dead for many centuries.

There are also mass graves in the *puszcza*, where the skeletons lie face-down in rows, their hands bound behind them with barbed wire. North of here, they are digging into the sandy forest floor at Giby, where they know that anti-communist Poles and Home Army men were murdered in 1945. They have found corpses, but so far they are all German soldiers. The women of Giby have dreams; they give new directions to the diggers.

I have been reporting from Poland, on and off, for more than thirty years. But I had never before come to this north-eastern corner of Poland, wedged up against the borders of the Soviet republics of Lithuania and Byelorussia. Białystok was a town on the way to nowhere else, not specially historic, not a perch for brilliant minds. I knew that non-Polish minorities lived round here: Lithuanians and Byelorussians whose ancient territory had been transected by the frontier. But I also knew that they lived under such close surveillance by the Party authorities and the security police that it would be a long job getting them to talk.

Then, in the summer of 1989, Poland became the centre of the world, as it had been exactly fifty years before. World War Two began here; now the Cold War, perhaps even the Bolshevik Revolution itself, was ending here. The communist era of Polish history was over. In June, there were the first even semi-free elections to be held in the Soviet zone of Europe for forty years. Two years before, a few crazy optimists predicted that the Soviet Union might tolerate such an event early in the twenty-first century.

The end came suddenly. After the second wave of strikes in 1988, General Jaruzelski and his prime minister Mieczysław Rakowski surrendered. They summoned a round-table meeting of opposition and régime, of Solidarity leaders and those who had recently been their gaolers. Sessions began early in 1989. Decisions came rapidly. Solidarity was re-legalized, and 'free' elections were announced. Their freedom was qualified because the electoral law included a quota of reserved seats, designed to guarantee that the Communists—Polish United Workers' Party—had a majority in the Sejm, the lower house of parliament.

But the June elections produced a vote of universal, merciless hatred against the candidates of the United Workers' Party and the Communist-led 'coalition'. Almost every regime name that the voter could identify was crossed out. Nobody, not even Solidarity, had expected such a devastating result. The regime began to come apart, the satellite parties defected and sought alliance with Solidarity and the round-table deal (which had foreseen Solidarity only as a 'constructive opposition') swiftly unravelled. On 13 September, Tadeusz Mazowiecki formed the first essentially non-communist government in Warsaw since 1945.

These were extraordinary weeks to be in Poland, and yet weeks weirdly lacking passion. I thought at first that I had grown too cynical for joy, but then I found that Poles, too, seemed to feel that this couldn't really be happening. There was little exaltation, no visions: none of the intensity I remembered from the weeks in the Lenin Shipyard in 1980 or during the first visit of this Pope to his homeland in 1979. From the balcony of the Sejm, I looked down in serene disbelief at people I had known as fugitives, martyrs and revolutionaries, now sprawling on the benches or darting to the tribune as if they had been parliamentarians all their lives: Jacek Kuroń, Adam Michnik, Janek Lityński, Janusz Onyszkiewicz.

A year ago, these were still people who always ate when they sat down. They would hurry into the clandestine committee meeting, throw themselves into a chair and—in a single movement—pull from their brief-cases leaflets, typed reports, bread and sausage. They would eat mouthfuls between reading paragraphs about underground cells in the Ursus tractor plant. Then they would gulp a glassful of tea, grab a cigarette and be on their way. In the cool white corridor of the Sejm, one of them said to me: 'Now I'm the honourable member for S . . . But when we take our seats and Jacek starts speaking, I still feel my belly rumbling.'

I first went to Białystok in June 1989, to see the climax of the election campaign. In the park, there was a Solidarity mass rally with the candidates, pop groups, the cabaret star Jan Pietrzak. The whole town seemed to be spending its Sunday afternoon there. But then, on the way out with a Polish friend, we passed the new concert hall. On an impulse, my friend persuaded the janitor to let us slip in.

Darkness, devotion, opulent bass voices. Here, packed and entranced, sat another and quite different Białystok listening to a Russian choir singing Orthodox harmonies, a Białystok to whom Solidarity's supreme festival of Polish patriotism and liberty a few hundred yards away meant little. These were the Byelorussians, and their dream was not the same.

In the town, beside the Solidarity posters, there were a few small posters in Cyrillic script. I asked a Solidarity man who the faces on them were. 'Oh, that's Sokrat Janowicz. He's a fanatical Byelorussian nationalist—bilingual street-signs and all that.'

And this face?

'That's Gienek Mironowicz. Another Byelorussian activist, a schoolmaster.'

In Warsaw, Lech Wałęsa and the main Citizens' Committee (the name for Solidarity's campaign bureau) had pressed Solidarity in Białystok to put Mironowicz on their regional candidates' list for the Sejm. But the local Białystok Citizens' Committee had decided against him. 'We reckoned that nobody would have heard of him . . .'

After that conversation, I knew that I was going to have to come back to Białystok. Elsewhere, Poland can seem almost one-dimensional: anarchic in detail but uncannily uniform in outline. Practically everyone speaks Polish with the same accent; practically everyone is Catholic; practically everyone is anti-communist and anti-Russian and quotes the same verses from the same Romantic poets. But here, in the north-east, was a place where I could stand and see Poland in a new way. Here at last were the normal differences which most European countries contain—differences of language and religion and political outlook. Here, I thought, 'Polishness' would suddenly stand out in perspective, in light and shade, in three dimensions.

When I returned, it was 13 August. In the frowsy heat wave, Białystok looked less like a city than a cluster of worn-out villages. The pink stucco railway station, blocked with queues waiting for tickets or newspapers or a bottle of mineral water, seemed too small for a place with 166,000 inhabitants. The taxi to the Hotel Cristal bolted along empty streets, past patches of waste land, wooden shacks, a few rows of petty shops. Where was this city, anyway? I remembered that the writer Maria Dąbrowska called this place 'shockingly ugly.' And that was in the 1930s, before it was twice captured by the German armies and once by the Red Army. In the final 'liberation', the Russians contrived to set the whole town centre alight while trying to bomb the railway station, which they missed. Most of the quarter down by the Biała stream had already been levelled by the Germans, who had used it as a ghetto until the time came to drive the Jews of Białystok to the gas chambers. I thought that I would do a couple of interviews and then get back as soon as decently possible to Warsaw.

Nobody has ever loved Białystok, and it shows. This was a textile city of little brick mills and plank-built sweat-shops. Białystok grew suddenly large and rich in the last century, when the Russian occupiers set up a customs border between the heartlands of the empire and what had been the old Kingdom of Poland. The cotton mills of Łódź in central Poland found themselves beyond the line, but Białystok was on the Russian side and its exports into the empire's endless market stayed duty-free.

On my first afternoon, I walked down Lipowa Street. The queues were forming for meat, children's shoes, some rolls of cloth I couldn't see properly past the heads of shoppers. The kiosks had two notices glued up, written in ball-point. One said 'STRIKE ALERT'. The other said: 'BRAK . . .'—lack of: today, it was lack of cigarettes and matches.

Elderly men with noble faces cadged from one another without loss of dignity. Sir John Gielgud, wearing a brown suit and sandals, shuffled across the café to the Pope who—in a short-sleeved tartan shirt, sitting in front of a glass of beer—had just mashed out a Marlboro.

'Please, let the gentleman feel free to take two.'

311

'I thank the gentleman graciously; he is too kind.'

Politically, Poland was being reborn. Economically, it was dying day by day. A kilo of *polędwica* (sirloin) now cost one-sixth of the average monthly wage. A taxi cost seventy-five per cent more than it did five days before. A small cup of coffee in Warsaw's Holiday Inn cost more than a first-class rail ticket to Białystok. And there were no matches in Warsaw either.

But everywhere in Białystok the Solidarity election posters had been reverently left on the walls to bleach away. I recognized them from June: the Byelorussian ones, in contrast, had all been scraped off. Next to the Catholic church on Lipowa, somebody had chalked: 'Communism to the junk-heap of history!' Somebody else had been at work with a home-made stencil—a tank, a star and the words: 'Soviets Go Home.'

In New York, you can buy a pastry called a Bialy. It is softer and chewier than a bagel, and it doesn't have a hole. This is about the only tangible relic of one of the world's great Jewish cities; there were times in the last century when most of Białystok's inhabitants were Jews. Samuel Pisar, one of the very few of them to have survived World War Two, lists in his book *Of Blood and Hope* some of those who began life here: Ludwik Zamenhof, inventor of Esperanto; Maxim Litvinov, Soviet commissar for foreign affairs; General Yigal Yadin, Israeli chief of staff and the archaeologist of Masada; Dr Albert Sabin who invented the oral polio vaccine. The Jews, more than the Poles or the Byelorussians, were the real founders of this city, the creators of its wealth and its culture, the only people—perhaps—who did love it. To Samuel Pisar, Białystok was 'once known as the Town with the Golden Heart.' Nothing of that remains. A few buildings survive from the wartime ghetto quarter, with a bust of Zamenhof and a street named after Melmud, the hero who flung sulphuric acid at the SS during the final ghetto rising. The Germans razed everything else. Where the ghetto was, there is now an east-west bypass road, a strip of park, a weedy sports ground. When I went there, they were digging a new drain down by the Biała stream and, in the sand, lying exposed at my feet, was the archaeology of the ghetto: foundations, glazed tiles, fragments of china and glass. A rat, scrabbling to keep its balance, was clambering over a mass of rusted bed-frame.

Back in the middle of town, I asked an old man where the synagogue had been. He pointed at an apartment block across the street.

It was there until that fire. It had a magnificent cupola. He used to pass it every day going to work. That was the Great Synagogue, and all the houses round here had been Jewish.

In those times, did he have Jewish friends?

'No, no,' he said, surprised. But then he went on: 'Of course, we were all at school together. There were so many Jewish boys in our class, so many . . .' Suddenly his face twisted and furrowed; he began to sob loudly. He said: 'I saw it—we couldn't help them—they were beyond help.' He turned away, choking on his tears. I put my arm round his shoulders, and we stood awkwardly together for a moment until he shuffled away. At first I thought that he was a bit deranged. But then it occurred to me that he had spoken those last few sentences not in Polish, but in a sort of German. Just possibly, he was himself Jewish.

I didn't follow him but walked across the street. On a tablet in the wall, it was written in Polish and Hebrew, that in this place, on 24 June 1941, the Germans burned 3,000 Jews who had been driven into the Great Synagogue. Two days after Hitler's invasion of the Soviet Union; two days after the Germans had captured the city for the second time.

From there, a taxi took me to the remaining Jewish cemetery on Wschodnia Street, on the outskirts (the old central cemetery has been bulldozed away to make a park). There was an iron Star of David on the gates, which were rusted open. Beyond them, I pushed my way into a dense little wood of thorny trees in which hundreds of tombs were sinking into the undergrowth. Many were broken, many looted for their marble slabs. Physically, I told myself, this was no worse than the condition of many Victorian Christian cemeteries in London. And yet the oblivion is infinitely deeper. Nobody comes or reads the Hebrew on the graves; nobody will ever come; there is nobody left. This stony thicket on Wschodnia Street now seems to have only one purpose these days: it provides a path—a short cut—to the Catholic cemetery next door. There, candles glow and families move busily among the graves.

T hat particular afternoon, the cemetery was busy: the Polish Catholics of Białystok were celebrating a big anniversary. The fifteenth of August is *Maria Wniebowzięcie*, the Assumption of the Virgin. But it is also the day of the Miracle on the Vistula. In 1920, the Bolshevik armies invaded newly independent Poland and at Białystok they installed a committee of Polish communists assigned to convert the nation into a Soviet republic. The Red Cavalry rode victoriously forward until it was approaching the suburbs of Warsaw. Then Józef Piłsudski, Poland's liberator and commander, mounted a counter-offensive that tore right across the Bolshevik rear, cutting off whole armies and severing their lines of communication. The Bolsheviks, whose advance patrols had been about to cross the German frontier into East Prussia, now fell back in disorder and were chased eastwards across Poland into the distant borderlands.

The Catholic families laying their flowers on the graves at Wschodnia Street told me that the big commemoration was on the other side of town, in the St Roch cemetery. At St Roch cemetery there was a wooden church, where I found crowds honouring the Virgin and the victory at once; a portrait of Piłsudski beside the altar and ribbons of the 1920 volunteers draped about.

With helpful gestures, the priest explained how Mary really was lifted up by the angels into the sky, just like in the pictures by Wit Stwosz and Murillo. He went on to imitate the Polish soldiers in 1920, who (he said) shouted, 'Long Live Maria! Let's die for her!' as they charged against the Bolshevik hordes. Poland, continued the priest, is the eastern bastion of Christendom. And that is why, he explained, the Polish soldier does not drink or steal or lie or kill anyone except his enemy. That is why every drop of blood shed by a Polish soldier is taken up to Heaven. That is also why every Polish soldier's suffering and torment is noted down by God. In 1920, 1939, 1944 'and afterwards' (he meant the savage partisan war against the communist regime that lasted for several years in the forest) the army of Poland has shed its blood so that we might live.

At the end, everyone sang 'The First Brigade', the marching song of Piłsudski's legions.

On Sunday I went to a Russian Orthodox Mass. The church, on Lipowa Street, is in the town centre, a decorous Palladian building from the 1840s, where Czarist bureaucrats and Russian officers worshipped in the years when Białystok was a city of the empire. Now the worshippers are not the rulers but the underclass: the Byelorussian minority.

I was surprised to see so many young men in the congregation. The older generation tends to be squat and short-legged. But these were giants in T-shirts: they crossed themselves in the wide-sweeping, plucking Orthodox custom, and yet they looked out of place both among their parents and amid the conspicuous self-abasement of the ritual. Over and over again, the priest and the acolytes intoned the same solemn bass phrase; the worshippers drifted away into their own private raptures; the candles were raised and displayed and lowered again. Some men prostrated themselves. It was strange to attend, in Poland, a religious ceremony that seemed to have no nationalist emotion in it.

Or so I thought. Later I discovered that these same big, young men were the very representatives of nationalism: it was they who were the ones determined to graft Byelorussian politics into the Orthodox community. There may be shows of private rapture, but there was also public scheming. These young people were tired of their Church's passivity, exasperated that it clung to the Russian 'old Slav' language in the liturgy. They were pushing for the vernacular—Byelorussian, which is neither Polish nor Russian—to replace the Russian that was used in church. They were supported, I would also learn later, by the large emigrant Byelorussian communities in North America.

As things are, though, the Orthodox church in Poland feels like an outpost of Russian culture. This doesn't make it popular. And even before the war the Polish state encouraged Orthodoxy here for that very reason, calculating that its Russian flavour would alienate Byelorussian intellectuals, driving them gradually away from their own culture and towards integration into 'Polishness'. Since 1945, the new Communist regime in Poland has seemed at times to be protecting the Orthodox religion for the same devious reasons.

The last thing communist Poland or the Soviet Union wanted was an authentic Byelorussian revival. Phoney, controllable revivals, on the other hand, have frequently been useful. For many years the Byelorussians in Poland were restricted to a 'Social-Cultural Association' set up in the post-Stalin years under close supervision by the Ministry of the Interior. All attempts to set up genuine organizations for the Orthodox laity were squashed by the security police. The result was that a Byelorussian samizdat emerged alongside the enormous 'unofficial' literature of the Polish opposition, with periodicals like *Sustreci* and *Dakumenty*. This year, the Białystok authorities did finally agree that a lay Orthodox society called 'The Brotherhood' could be established. But their agreement amounts to too little, too late: 'The Brotherhood' is notably cautious and unpolitical and uses the Polish language, which isn't enough for the young militants of the Byelorussian cause. The attendance at Byelorussian cultural festivals and religious rallies this year was many times larger than it has ever been: a sign that the resistance of the Orthodox clergy and establishment to Byelorussian nationalism is going to break under pressure from below.

Across the frontier, the Byelorussian movement is moving more slowly. The Byelorussian grouping which calls itself 'Rebirth' is not as confident or militant as the National Fronts in the Baltic republics or as the 'Ryukh' movement in the Ukraine. Its programme so far is only to 'raise national consciousness' and to defend Byelorussian language and culture. But the authorities in Minsk, capital of Soviet Byelorussia and one of the last fortresses of unreconstructed Brezhnevism, refused for as long as they dared to let 'Rebirth' meet on their territory. Its founding congress had to be held at Vilnius, in Lithuania. Modest as it is, 'Rebirth' seems to have found the inevitable leader-icon which most nationalisms require: a young archaeologist Zenon Pozniak, described to me—without irony—by one Byelorussian as nothing less than the 'new Robespierre—an utterly true spirit.'

It wasn't until I was back in London that I read what Lech Wałęsa had written about all this, in the 'Letter to the Polish Electorate', published in April. He spoke of the national and religious minorities that still lived in Poland—calling them 'our rare and precious inheritance from the past'—and pointed out that 'they are concerned for the preservation, within the Polish environment, of their own religious and ethnic identity. They are concerned for their cultures, their schools, their churches. They want dignity, without having to 'change into Polish clothes.' Wałęsa insisted that the minorities should be involved in Solidarity's election campaign: that they should 'participate with the dignity to which they are entitled.'

There have been two competing ideologies in modern Polish nationalism. One is 'National Egoism', assuming an almost totalitarian priority for the interests of Poland at the expense of the interests of other nations. The doctrine implies that the true Poland is Catholic and Slav and that the other nationalities in the country—the Jews, above all, but also the Byelorussians, Ukrainians, Lithuanians and Germans—constitute a threat to Polish identity. The threat is both racial and political: these other peoples could not be expected to understand the absolute imperative of the Polish national struggle to regain the independence lost with the partitioning of the country in the eighteenth century. In the early years of this century, 'National Egoism' was the principle upheld by the politician Roman Dmowski, leader of the National Democrat movement (*Endecja* in Polish).

The other tradition is that of Józef Piłsudski, the man of the Miracle on the Vistula. The National Democrats and Roman Dmowski never managed to take power, but Piłsudski dominated independent Poland from 1918 to his death in 1935. Piłsudski, although authoritarian, believed in Poland as a multi-national federation. His dream was to revive the ancient Polish-Lithuanian Commonwealth, by recovering the eastern Borderlands which lay between Poland and Russia.

The Polish Commonwealth was an astonishing place. It matters now because of what is starting to happen in the territory between Poland and Russia. Before the Commonwealth was destroyed at the end of the eighteenth century, when Russia, Prussia and Austria partitioned the Polish state between them, it was, at its best, not only the biggest but the most tolerant state in northern Europe. It began from the medieval union of the Kingdom of Poland with the Grand Duchy of Lithuania. In the

Commonwealth, all subjects of the King and Grand Duke were 'Poles': Protestants and Jews as well as Catholics, Balts and Tartars, Scots and Byelorussians, as well as 'ethnic' Poles. It was a ramshackle structure whose tolerance at times broke down. It was, certainly, 'pre-modern'. But while it lasted the Commonwealth was one of Europe's nobler achievements.

Lech Wałęsa has made his own ideology clear. His nationalism, like that of the whole leading group in Solidarity, is Piłsudski's kind. But the nationalism of ordinary Poles, whether they are coal miners or peasants or petty officials, often has a lot of Roman Dmowski in its mix. Political anti-Semitism is common in its vulgar equation: Jew equals Red equals traitor to Polish independence. But the Slav minorities, the Byelorussians and Ukrainians who are mostly non-Catholic, are suspect too. These are the prejudices that arose from the Partitions and that continue today, reinforced by the practice of whatever regime is in power of divide-and-rule: bribing religious or national minorities in order to dissolve their alliance with the Polish-Catholic majority. As a result, the Ukrainians are accused by Poles of collaborating with Germans or Russians in order to further their own national cause, while the Byelorussians, almost all of them Orthodox in religion, have acquired a name for being ungrateful and untrustworthy.* After 1945 (this is what Poles in Białystok and the surrounding countryside constantly told me), the Byelorussians let themselves be used as the spoiled brats of the new communist regime. There were ushered into powerful jobs in the local Party and administration, while Orthodox applications to build churches got kinder treatment than those from Catholic parishes.

This isn't how the Byelorussians see it. Some 200,000 of them live in the Białystok region of Poland, a tiny overflow from the Soviet republic of Byelorussia with its nine million people. Their tradition has been to keep their heads down, a lesson learned from

---

* Since last summer, the opening of the Soviet frontier allowed Polish visitors to discover more about the genocidal massacres of the Polish minority committed by Ukrainians during the three years of Nazi occupation. In the region of Volhynia, for instance, whole villages were destroyed and all the inhabitants killed.

two centuries of intermittent Russian tyranny. But there was a time when Byelorussians were assertive and proud.

On my first night in Białystok, I went to see the Byelorussian intellectual Sokrat Janowicz in his small flat near the town centre. He told me that the Grand Duchy itself had once been Byelorussian in race and language. Lithuanian? In those days, Janowicz said, the word meant Byelorussian. The people who now call themselves Lithuanians, he assured me, were a backward Baltic race who in those days lived in the swamps of Zmudź. It was only after the fall of the Grand Duchy that the nature of the Byelorussians began to change, transforming them into the most humble and least assertive of all the peoples of the Borderlands. They became—and Janowicz quoted the passage cited at the beginning of this piece—the people whom Konwicki thought 'too good and gentle and generous' for this world.

Until last summer. Then, in the Poland of Solidarity's triumph, Byelorussians began to raise their heads. Byelorussian nationalists campaigned openly and dared to use their own language on public election platforms. But all the suspicions of recent history revived as well.

Today Solidarity and the new Byelorussian movement seem to agree on only one point: that the communist system has been a calamity. Beyond that, though, they don't know what to make of one another.

After the Orthodox Mass, I walked across the city to Bem Street. I had heard something about its open-air market; this was the place to see Soviet Byelorussians, who were pouring across the frontier in order to trade. Once the old town of Grodno on the river Niemen had been the natural capital of the whole region, but in 1945 it had vanished behind the new Soviet border. Now, Soviet Byelorussia was coming across into Poland, making Białystok its market-place.

If there's nothing to buy in Soviet shops, it must be because it's being sold on Bem Street. Hundreds of cars with Soviet plates were drawn up round the market field. Whole families had spread out their goods on folding tables, on car bonnets, on gaudy scarves laid across the mud, and they were selling things they had bought 'over

320

there', or inherited, or made, or simply stolen from their work-places. Polish buyers—from Warsaw or even further—come to Bem Street for bargains.

This trade, though done with money, was really an exchange of manufactured goods for food. It may seem incredible that anyone should travel to Poland in order to buy food. But conditions in the western Soviet Union are so bad that they make even Poland look abundant. For Polish zloties, the Soviet Byelorussians were selling car parts, rugs, cosmetics, Indian toothpaste, Aeroflot cigarettes, pencil sharpeners like miniature lathes, lavatory pans, caviar, Turkish sweaters, computer games in Cyrillic, packets of Georgian tea, knickers and bras made in the Ukraine, hairdryers, electric samovars . . . Soviet television sets, half the price of Polish ones, were now a banned export. Instead, there was an inrush of the ugliest toys in the world: purple Lunakhod moon-buggies, four different sorts of battery-driven tank with red star and working missiles, glumpish dolls, clockwork bears which shake their heads slowly from side to side and groan.

At one side of the field, among the sausage-stalls, women were selling gold, whispering in bad Polish to their customers. Men wandered through the crowd with notices hung round their necks: 'I buy dollars, marks, forints, crowns.' Some even bought roubles at the discounted Polish price. Eventually all the devalued zloties earned on Bem Street would be spent in the food shops or even at the back door of meat-processing plants. There was a nasty fight this June at the town of Ełk, when the regular black-market purchasers from Grodno turned up at the canned-meat plant with an articulated truck and found that a strike was going on. Everywhere in the region, somebody knows somebody who actually saw the back of a Soviet lorry burst open and release an avalanche of loaves and rolls over the highway.

Once, Białystok had an Orthodox church, a Catholic church and a Great Synagogue, all about the same size. But between the wars, after Poland had regained its independence, the Catholic Poles began to erect the St Roch Basilica, a monster of concrete fretwork and lattice blocking one end of Lipowa Street. After 1945 there was an Orthodox counter-offensive. It started with a crop of onion domes in the villages of the region and culminated in a cathedral that was completed this year in the Antoniuk suburb of Białystok. Then came Solidarity. Opposite the Orthodox cathedral in Antoniuk, a new Catholic church, the size of an airship hangar, was slowly crawling up its wooden scaffolding. Near the towers of the Sloneczny Stok housing scheme, the foundation for yet another church had appeared.

You could argue that, in a country with a shortage of building materials, where the waiting time for a flat can be thirty years, this was a queer way to use its resources. But nobody would listen to you. The rattle of Orthodox and Catholic collection-boxes was loud and urgent. Much of the Orthodox building programme was being paid for by the Byelorussian emigrants in Canada and the United States, which was why—in the end—the Byelorussian language would get into those churches whatever the misgivings of the priesthood. As for the Polish Catholics, the building of a church still amounted to the raising of one more tower on that 'bastion against the East'. Especially in Białystok.

The day before I left, I went out to a block of flats at Sloneczny Stok, on a windy slope south of the city. The tower-block was new, but already decayed. Here lived a man and his daughter who, I had been told, would give me a insight into the spirit of Solidarity in Białystok. The father was an old man He produced a photograph of his own father as the only Polish clerk in a Czarist Russian bank in Białystok. The old man himself had been in a Soviet prison, in the Home Army resistance against the Nazi occupation, in three concentration camps (Gross-Rosen, Nordhausen, Bergen-Belsen). He said to me: 'Poland is fulfilling its mission. In 1920 we saved Europe from Bolshevism. So now Poland has begun the destruction of communism all over the world, even in Russia. Only Solidarity made Gorbachev possible, and only Solidarity could show the way ahead to national movements everywhere . . .'

His daughter Zosia came in from Mass. She was a member of the regional executive of Solidarity: the trade union, that is, not the Citizens' Committee wing that had organized the election campaign. She worked underground with the union throughout the years of martial law after 1981, when it was banned, but she escaped arrest.

I had met Polish women of Zosia's kind before. She was beautiful, utterly sure of herself and of the righteousness of her cause, a severe moralist. Women who fought in the Warsaw Rising of 1944 are often like her, still measuring their own behaviour and that of others by the purity and devotion of those sixty-three days. To behave loosely or basely is to betray the sacrifice. Virtue is the true patriotism.

We talked about who was supposed to control the new Solidarity parliamentarians: the senators and deputies in the Sejm. I couldn't work out to whom they were democratically accountable: was it to Solidarity, or to their electors or to the Citizens' Committees which selected them as candidates in the first place?

Zosia simply didn't see a problem. It had to be Solidarity. Why should there be a separate political party in addition to the union? 'In the Citizens' Committee here, there is an ambitious group, but I say that, ethically and morally, the group is not entitled to be in the position to govern. We, in the union, on the other hand, we have passed the eight-year test of clandestinity; we were persecuted and lost our jobs. It is we who have the moral right to instruct the parliamentarians. And if they need an annual conference on policy, then they can attend the congress of Solidarność—the union's own congress—alongside the ordinary delegates from the factories. Solidarity is universal.'

I asked her about Byelorussian candidates in the June elections. Was it true that Lech Wałęsa had urged the Citizens' Committee here to run an Orthodox candidate for the Sejm and had suggested the schoolteacher Eugeniusz Mironowicz? Had there been a hope that, in such a case, the Orthodox bishop might instruct his flock to vote for Solidarity? And why did the Białystok Citizens' Committee decide against Mironowicz *and* against the idea of running Sokrat Janowicz, the Byelorussian writer, as a candidate for the Senate? Was the Citizens' Committee's membership exclusively Polish-Catholic?

Zosia replied that, when the next elections were fought, she would want to see a candidate from the ethnic minority on the

Solidarity list. She knew Mironowicz and his brother well; she had taught them both history. But she complained that the Byelorussians did not yet have a coherent or united attitude to Solidarity. 'Yes, we were asked if we would adopt Sokrat Janowicz for the Senate. But he wrote a poem attacking the Pope. It was impossible!'

Her father, listening closely, broke in. 'We had Orthodox boys as well as Catholics with us in the Home Army. And they fought and died for Poland at Monte Cassino too . . . '

Listening to father and daughter, I saw that there was no way to fit their view of what had happened to that of the Byelorussian politicians. I had already been to see both the men she had mentioned: Janowicz, on my first evening, and Mironowicz in his comfortable wooden house in the outskirts, where the streets become sand-tracks and run into the fields. Both insisted that they had never had any intention of joining the Solidarity platform, although both were invited to do so. And both of them swore to me that as Byelorussians they would have been committing political suicide by associating with Solidarity.

In the end, they had run as independent Byelorussian candidates for Senate and Sejm. They lost. But they scored impressively in some of the Orthodox villages, where Solidarity did very badly.

Mironowicz turned out to be precisely one of those tall young men I had seen in church, with a rich moustache. Sokrat Janowicz, an older man with many books to his name, is a dark, square-set man with a bad leg. Janowicz told me: 'The Byelorussian people are afraid of Solidarity. They think it represents the recidivist Catholic fanaticism of old Poland, and if the Byelorussians thought I was with Solidarity, I would be finished.' In fact, exactly that rumour had been put about. The Orthodox church, still nervous of the Byelorussian nationalist revival and frightened of Polish reprisals, spread the rumour that Janowicz was 'crypto-Solidarity' and backed its own candidate against him (who campaigned exclusively in the Polish language). The Communists, sly to the last, also warned the Orthodox community that Janowicz was a Solidarity man. Solidarity, in return, contrived to imply that Janowicz was actually a Communist puppet wearing Byelorussian folk-costume.

It was a mess. But next time, the two men say, it will be better. A Byelorussian Citizens' Committee is soon to be set up, the nucleus of a political party which will contest the local elections. At this stage, the aims will be modest: 'cultural autonomy', their own language in the schools, bilingual road signs, a say in regional planning to halt the drain of population from the villages.

But 4 June—election day—was none the less a turning-point for the Byelorussians in Poland. As soon as Sokrat Janowicz began to speak in Byelorussian from a platform, a dead hush fell. 'I felt my own rashness, breaching this moral complex, using a tongue until now spoken only at home or among friends, or maybe at functions with invited guests, but never at a public rally. I was warned by other Byelorussians not to dare, because there was sure to be some Polish chauvinist around who would start throwing stones.'

Are matters that bad? Sokrat Janowicz rages against 'Poles who are ill with an anti-Russian complex, and a Catholicism sick with colonialism. Poland and Russia have the same imperial complexes, the one about empire lost, the other about empire won . . .' But he admits that 'we have no problem with the younger Polish generation.'

I asked Janowicz who now had the effective power in Białystok.

He shrugged. The Communist authorities, he said, were still going to their offices. Local government remained for the moment in their hands, and the First Secretary of the Party in Białystok was still a personage. But now, as that dustbin of history opened for them, Janowicz reported that the Communists had changed tactic. After decades of playing the Orthodox community off against the Catholics without giving much to either, the Communists were spending their last months granting all the Byelorussian demands that they used to reject: access to local radio, teaching in Byelorussian, special grants to farmers in Orthodox districts.

Perhaps, as Janowicz thought, it was because they had lost their sense of power. Perhaps, though, this was only another hand in the divide-and-rule game, one more shuffle and deal of that greasy old minority card—this time, against Solidarity.

Neal Ascherson

History will label 1989 as the Third Springtime of Nations. There was 1848 and then 1918: the dream of escape from empires, and then the awakening as the empires collapsed. Now comes 1989, in which every nation between the Elbe and the Pacific is simmering: 'historic' nations like the Magyars, Serbs and Georgians, suppressed nations like the Lithuanians, Byelorussians and Meshketians, recently-invented nations like the Azeris or the Macedonians. But the reviving of nations is not the raising of a Lazarus from the dead. The problem is that under one Lazarus there generally lies another. Poland rises joyfully from the grave, disclosing buried national minorities which in turn wriggle to be resurrected.

The Annus Mirabilis is breeding national movements and revivals throughout the swathe of territory which separates Poland from the heartlands of Russia: in Lithuania and the other Baltic nations, in Soviet Byelorussia, in the Ukraine. At the same time, the present Soviet frontier which divides those people from their kin within Poland has suddenly turned porous.

In the age of the Commonwealth, it was Poland rather than Russia which was the imperial power in these borderlands. There are still many Polish patriots who assume that, once Russian power fails, the smaller nations in between will gladly return to Polish protection.

But this is wrong. None of these national movements, from Sajudis in Lithuania to Ryukh in the Ukraine, wants to exchange Moscow for Warsaw. The future depends, first, upon what happens to Mikhail Gorbachev. But after that, if there is to be any kind of distinct future for the borderlands, everything will depend on the form which Polish nationalism takes.

Tom Nairn, in *The Breakup of Britain*, made popular the idea of nationalism as a Janus: one face turned to the future, another backwards towards the past. The dualism in Solidarity is about the two Janus-faces of Polish nationalism, the most striking of all examples to support Nairn's argument. It is exactly the backward-looking face of Polish patriotism which bears the features we would now call 'progressive' or 'enlightened'. The Wałęsa leadership looks back to the Commonwealth (naturally through a golden haze) for holy notions like tolerance and the ideal of multi-racialism. The

326

nationalism of Roman Dmowski and the *Endecja*—in its way 'modern' if compared to the revivalism of a pre-modern past— taught the then-fashionable doctrines of state-worship, the mass party, national egoism and racial destiny. But those values, in contrast, have long since been discarded along with the rest of Europe's reactionary rubbish.

It comes hard to most Poles to accept that Poland could be perceived by weaker nations as an oppressor, aggressor or imperial power. That doesn't fit the image of Messianism: of Poland-as-immaculate-victim, of the curriculum which presents Poland as Europe's martyr and redeemer. In Białystok, Polish faces would change from bewilderment to outrage when I quoted Sokrat Janowicz's remarks about what Byelorussian voters thought of Solidarity. But that self-obsession, that lack of the capacity to think oneself into another's skin, has to break down if there is to be safety in Eastern Europe.

For the moment, Poland is in the right hands. Tadeusz Mazowiecki and his cabinet belong to the sort of Polish patriot who fought all over nineteenth-century Europe 'for your freedom and ours'. The new government in Warsaw represents that young element in Solidarity which cleans up Jewish graveyards and campaigns for the re-opening of Ukrainian churches. Yet Poland is once again on the way to becoming a power in east-central Europe. Nationalism is breaking loose in the old lands of the Grand Duchy, as Russian control slackens. Nobody yet knows what might replace the Soviet imperium in the borderlands—a new alliance, or supra-national trading bloc, a political federation?—but whatever grows up through the threadbare remains of the Warsaw Pact and Comecon, Poland will have the capacity to dominate it. The way Poland behaves in the next couple of years towards its own national minorities—difficult and elusive groups, who often don't clearly know what they want—will tell the rest of the world something about how the Poles will use that power.

ISABEL HILTON

THE GENERAL

I can see now where this story ended, although for a long time I was playing with other endings, reluctant to let go. It ended with that moment of cinema, crossing General Stroessner's spongy lawn and looking back to see him, framed in the doorway, waving. I waved, went through the gate and into the General's car, and the world rushed in around me, hotels, luggage and airports—everyday people, everyday lives.

I didn't go back—that was one possible ending, that I would return—I told myself there was no time and it was true. But the story wouldn't go away. The kitchen telephone would ring and it would be Gustavo Stroessner, the General's son, bellowing in that strange accent down a fuzzy line from Brazil, like an unruly fictional character nagging for a larger part in the plot.

'Hello, Colonel. How are you? How is the General?'

'Do you need any material?' He would answer. 'How is the work going?' None of the 'material' ever arrived, but it didn't matter. I knew what it would have been and was glad he hadn't sent it.

But where had the story begun? It had been there for years, but I always found something else, wars, elections; Latin America was never short of events clamouring for attention. Except in Paraguay. Paraguay was a situation, rather than an event. It was wrapped in a layer of clichés, and, when events poked through, they seemed only to reinforce the clichés. Josef Mengele was in Paraguay; fascist army officers from Argentina fled to Paraguay when their *coup* plots failed; Indians in the Paraguayan jungle were hunted by fundamentalist American missionaries with rifles. Stroessner had been there for ever and always would be.

Then, suddenly, in February 1989, he wasn't.

I wasn't there either. I was in Jamaica, watching a more orderly change of government. I called my newspaper from Kingston, cursing my bad luck—a journalist in the wrong place. It was too late. Stroessner had been hustled out of the country and had gone to ground in Brazil, where he sat in his beach-house, under siege from a press corps in bathing-suits. No interviews, no comment, no recriminations. Nothing.

He had never been a great one for interviews, but now he had a further excuse. He was in asylum and that imposed silence. After an interlude of disorderly scenes at the beach-house—photographers on step-ladders peeping over the wall, helicopters chartered by TV companies chattering overhead—he was moved. Some said to São Paulo; others said Brasília. At any rate, he had vanished behind another set of walls, another set of guards. He was rumoured to be ill and had a brief spell in hospital, then silence.

Six months later, I decided I would try to find him, to talk to him, and I had mixed feelings about the prospect. I knew nobody had and I didn't really see why I should be different, though I also knew that the unpredictability of Latin America could precipitate you as easily into a president's office as into a jail. I had set out on similar quests before and knew that they followed no timetable and that you just had to go where they led you until you either gave up or found yourself pushing an open door. I also knew that the last door always opened on to another, that it was hard to stop going through them and that there was never going to be enough time; I would end up, I feared, with one of those hollow-hearted stories which reconstructs the drama without the main character.

But even with that risk, it was a tempting drama. I knew that Stroessner's Paraguay had featured a kind of rampant official gangsterism, racketeers masquerading as high officials, contraband pretending to be business. There was a constitution, a state structure; there were laws, elections: but none of them was real. What was real was power, cronyism, corruption, the righteous men in jail and the criminals in government. At least, that's what I had been told. I didn't doubt it, exactly, but I hankered, foolishly, for evidence. I wanted to meet someone who had been cheated and robbed; I wanted to know exactly who had done it. I wanted to follow a thread to the Presidential Palace.

I set off for Asunción at the beginning of September 1989 with a suitcase of research I had only just begun to read and a list of names and numbers. Apart from one detailed academic political study and some slim volumes published by human rights organizations, there was remarkably little about Stroessner's Paraguay. It was, as someone was to say, in the et ceteras in the list of nations. It was like the silent planet, on a different radio frequency from the outside world. It fought savage wars with its neighbours, in which thousands died; created passionate myths and legends, but who cared? It changed presidents so often that when Alfredo Stroessner staged his coup, in May 1954, then sanctified his newly acquired throne with rigged elections, he must have seemed like just the latest man through the revolving door.

When he fell, thirty-five years later, he held a number of records. He was the longest-serving dictator in the western hemisphere and the second longest in the world: only Kim Il Sung outlasted him. The world had lived through thirty-five years of history, but three-quarters of the population of Paraguay had known no other leader, and there was not an institution or political party in the country that had not been shaped by his presence.

I had read that his image and name were everywhere. A neon sign flashed the message in the Plaza de los Heroes in Asunción: 'Stroessner . . . Peace . . . Work . . . Well-being'—on, off; on, off; on, off, twenty-four hours a day. Television began and ended with his heavy features and a march named after him. There was a Stroessner Polka, for more light-hearted occasions. The airport was named after him. The free-port on the Brazilian frontier was called Puerto Stroessner. There were Stroessner statues, avenues and roads, and official portraits of him hung in every office and school.

When I got to Paraguay, six months after he fell, he had been painted over. The portraits had gone, the airport was renamed, the march was no longer played and some of the statues, at least, had disappeared.

Democratic ideals were now the height of fashion. General Andres Rodriguez—who had led the February *coup* against Stroessner, his old friend, mentor and relative by marriage—had sanctified his position, like Stroessner, with electoral holy water: he got seventy-four per cent of the votes. Everybody knew there had been fraud, out of habit, if nothing else, but since Stroessner used to get over ninety per cent, Rodriguez looked like an honest man. Many people, I was to discover, liked to think that Rodriguez's less than perfect elections were free and fair. There had been something so grubby and humiliating in the last years, to be living in

Stroessner's Paraguay, that people fell upon the idea that this was now democracy and used it to wash away some of the slime. So large had the tyrant loomed that it only required his removal to encourage the hope that democracy was possible. From there it was a short step to pretending it had arrived.

Rodriguez was immensely popular. He was cheerful, where Stroessner had been bad-tempered; vigorous, where Stroessner had been in decline; available, where Stroessner had been withdrawn. Rodriguez never troubled to hide the fact that he had grown immensely rich in Stroessner's service but he had been forgiven his sins for this one act of deliverance. Only a few, with a natural bent towards scepticism, reflected that in May 1954 it had seemed like a new dawn too.

I was shown to a room in the Hotel Excelsior, proprietor Nicolas Bo, friend of General Stroessner. It was pitch-dark.

Was there another one? I asked.

Yes, but a room with daylight is extra.

I paid extra and got a view of a huge building site across the road. Every morning, at seven, I would be woken by the clink-clink of hammers on concrete. While I was there, the building rose a whole floor. I used to look out of my window, wondering who was out there in the city who could help me and what I had to do to find them.

It was Saturday when I arrived, the traveller's dread weekend. I looked through my list of names and numbers. The shops were shut, the town was quiet, the phones didn't answer. I began to read again, trying to absorb the country's tortured history.

Asunción—still sleepy, but sleepier then. When Stroessner came to power only one square kilometre of Asunción had running water. The rich lived in colonnaded houses along Avenida Mariscal Lopez, rattan chairs set out on deep verandas. Water and milk were sold off mule-carts, and the life of the town centred round the railway station where the peasants came in from the country to sell vegetables and chickens.

Outside the capital, red dirt roads turned to mud in the tropical rains. The wars that had kept the country backward had affected its society too. In Bolivia or Peru, there were enough of the Spanish-speaking élite to colonize, to relegate the Indian population to a despised under-class. In Paraguay, although tribal Indians were being steadily exterminated, their culture had always been accommodated in the past, even absorbed. The indigenous language, Guarani, is as important as Spanish, spoken by every populist politician. And, in spite of the strength of the Church, the need to repopulate the country after the worst of the nineteenth-century wars had left a legacy of *de facto* polygamy.

I would get to know Asunción a little, peeling back its layers of history: single-storey homes and grid-patterned streets running down the hill to the river; flashy high-rise buildings in the centre and, scattered through the outskirts, some giant institutional relics of a building boom in the late 1970s. Nobody had been very interested in roads or drains, it seemed. The streets were full of pot-holes, and had been scoured and carved up by the tropical floods that coursed down them. A few ostentatious hotels, décor somewhere between an ersatz gentleman's club and a high-class brothel. On the shores of the river, there were the shanty towns, squalid, but not as many as in Lima or Rio de Janeiro.

It was a quiet town, still. It woke up at six in the morning and went home at noon for lunch and a long siesta. At five business started again and by seven or eight it was all over: the rich went to their dinner parties and cocktails; the poor hung about under street lamps, where there were any; the modestly comfortable listened to lyrical Paraguayan music in bars. They sang in Guarani, because, they said, it was more expressive and passionate than Spanish. There was very little crime on the streets—less than the crime in the police or the government. Women sold their babies to foreigners who favoured Paraguay because the babies were less likely to be black than in Brazil; and they sold themselves in several well-known sites around town. On Sundays, everyone went to mass.

I bought all the newspapers. There seemed to be several free shows in town: political rallies at which factions of factions of parties attacked each other before thin crowds; the law courts where a succession of fallen grandees of the Stronato, Stroessner's system, bandits all, appeared in court protesting their innocence against charges of grand larceny. One general, who swore he never stole a centavo, nevertheless offered, as a gesture of solidarity to the new government, to donate—on a purely voluntary basis—one million dollars to the public purse. Many of the names in the newspapers were familiar from the books I had read: those who had jumped early enough and were still cruising town in their chauffeur-driven cars, still making deals; and those, the famous figures from the opposition, who had been jailed or exiled, and who were now in Congress, making politics.

The weekend wore on in the half-life of the hotel. On Sunday, a telephone number finally answered—some friends of friends, intellectuals. We had lunch and talked about Stroessner. They were not the sort who knew him or wanted to. They had tried to live their lives in spite of him, to create a cultural island in a bandit state. Did I realize, they said, that in thirty-five years Stroessner had never thought of building a national museum or a gallery? Sitting in their house, listening to music, I picked up the telephone book and looked up Stroessner, Alfredo. He was there, followed by 'Stroessner, Frederico' and 'Stroessner, Graciella', all with numbers and addresses. I imagined a citizen ringing the president to complain about the drains.

On Monday morning, I started in earnest down my list— politicians, journalists, other people's contacts. Talking to people who hated him would be easy, I thought. Talking to those who had been close was the challenge. Of those, Conrado Pappalardo's name stood out.

2

Conrado Pappalardo, a friend had told me, knew everything. He had been Stroessner's political intimate and presidential secretary for years. Pappalardo was also a survivor. He had switched sides at the eleventh hour; he remains presidential secretary, now to President Rodriguez.

The presidential palace lies down near the river, a low, grey building that could never quite make up its mind which architectural style it was imitating: Greek classical? Colonial? Was that square tower English? There were palm trees and dark-suited security men, immobile, their hands hanging by their sides or clasped behind their backs: whatever way I approached the presidential palace, I had to pass one of them.

It was very early in the morning, but there was already a gathering at the door: television and radio reporters, rural officials, the claque of the local press.

To get to Pappalardo, I had first to make a courtesy call on the press office where I found Oscar, the presidential press officer.

Oscar used to be on television, but this was much better. He was very proud to be serving democracy. No, he had no material about Stroessner, but as many copies as I liked of General Rodriguez's speeches.

I took a copy, and thanked him. A photograph of President Rodriguez hung behind his desk. I asked him what had happened to the thousands of portraits of President Stroessner.

He didn't know, he said.

Along the corridor from Oscar's office, near the main entrance and overlooking the river, was a vast salon where petitioners sat, waiting for an audience with the president. Whether that audience was granted depended on the decisions taken in the last room between them and the inner sanctum, Conrado Pappalardo's office, where power was discreetly, but enduringly, exercised.

Pappalardo was smooth, rich, and elegantly dressed; his manners were impeccable; he was the perfect servant. Someone told me that, as well as having once been Stroessner's secretary, Pappalardo was also Stroessner's godson. Stroessner, patriarch of the nation, had many godsons.

I made my speech of introduction and dropped a name, the son of a former Argentine ambassador who had known Pappalardo quite well. Pappalardo made careful note on a piece of presidential notepaper, under my name. He checked, several times, that he had spelled it correctly, then asked a few questions to determine how seriously he should treat the name-drop.

Pappalardo viewed Stroessner with affection and with sadness, the sadness of having watched his greatness decline into the foolishness of a sclerotic old age. He had been a great governor, Pappalardo told me, who had raised the people's living standards and insisted on raising educational levels to those of Italy. 'So obviously, once that happened,' Pappalardo said, 'the people wanted more liberty and Stroessner didn't want to give it. Until 1982, I was behind him. He was always polite, never angry, never irritated.' But in 1982, Pappalardo sighed, something went wrong. 'He seemed to grow bored, and the militants took over the government. His son, Gustavo, began to emerge. He spoke badly of his father, disloyally.

'Gustavo was always complaining,' Pappalardo added. 'He complained that there were women and children everywhere.' I had heard that that Gustavo, the heir apparent, and Pappalardo, the godson, didn't get on, that they were jealous of each other.

I had also heard that it was Pappalardo who managed the payroll for Stroessner's many mistresses, distributing the money on Fridays.

Was it true, I wondered? Stroessner acknowledged his children, didn't he?

Pappalardo frowned and sucked his teeth for an instant. 'No . . . He neither denied them nor acknowledged them.' Pappalardo started describing how Stroessner lived—'like a soldier, you know, a very spartan life, For years there was no hot water system in that house. He had one of those little showers that heated the water when you needed it.' We talked about Stroessner's house and Stroessner's marriage: he never paid much attention to his wife, Dona Eligia. 'He lives alone now,' said Pappalardo. 'Perhaps he's too proud to call his wife to ask her to join him.'

It was really only power, Pappalardo added, that interested Stroessner.

There was a red telephone on Pappalardo's desk, the presidential line. It rang and Pappalardo jumped. It was not a jump that implied any fear on his part, but rather a demonstration of his own importance and his gift for perfect service. When the president needed him, he must attend.

'Immediately,' he said into the telephone and left the room. People started entering his office, gossiping, waiting for a good moment to whisper a request to the fixer of fixers. Outside, in the public salon, more people gathered; I could hear the shuffling of their feet to mark the passing time. Pappalardo returned and continued his story, from time to time interrupted by his other duties, in and out of the President's office.

He himself had realized, Pappalardo said, that the old man had to go, and he told him so in 1982. 'Stroessner didn't reply, but he never really spoke to me after that. I offered him my resignation every year, but he never accepted it.'

What could the perfect servant do, but carry on?

But things had changed, he said. Stroessner became remote and lost his concentration. The government was run by low-grade advisors and scheming ministers. 'Stroessner spent only one hour here each day and he spent the rest of the time at home, reading. Nobody knew because everybody was so loyal to him that it was hushed up.'

Pappalardo mentioned other personal titbits. Stroessner, who was afraid of illness, cultivated the myth that he had perfect health. Once, said Pappalardo, he had an operation for skin cancer and refused an anaesthetic, preferring pain to the impotence of unconsciousness. Stroessner hated being touched, Pappalardo told me, and never embraced anybody. He never threatened or lost his temper, but then I doubted that Pappalardo had ever given him the chance.

Pappalardo was coming to the end of what he wanted to tell me. He gave me a copy of General Rodriguez's speeches. 'This will be of great interest to you,' he said.

I hid Oscar's copy under my handbag and said thank you.

I asked him if I could see Stroessner's house.

That, he said, would be difficult.

I asked him if I could see Stroessner.

He smiled. He had no contact and could not tell me who might have.

I asked if I could see those former ministers who were now in jail.

That, he said, would be up to the Ministry of Justice but he thought it would not be possible.

I knew I was becoming a nuisance and in danger of being dismissed. Then the door opened and a man came into the office. Pappalardo saw his opportunity. 'This is the man you should talk to,' he said. 'Ambassador to the Presidency, Miguel Angel Gonzalez Casabianca. This is the new Paraguay,' Pappalardo said, in the manner of a Harley Street gynaecologist modestly displaying the healthy outcome of a rather difficult breech presentation. 'Dr Casabianca was in exile for many years and now he is part of the government. You should get to know him. He could become president.'

The Ambassador to the Presidency made a face and sat down heavily at the table, pulling out a packet of cigarettes.

Dr Casabianca was a tall man with a large, heavy face, drooping eyes, the creased skin of a chain-smoker. He had a gloomy watchful air that I later decided resulted from having subordinated most other things in life to a political struggle that must have seemed, for most of that time, hopeless. I waited, not yet knowing where Casabianca fitted so not sure where to begin.

The door opened again, and a delegation of local party bosses shuffled into the office. They had come to invite the president to their folk festival. They were small, dark and weather-beaten, dressed in the dateless style of the South American cowboy. They would have figured as fittingly in a 1911 daguerreotype as in a street-corner band. Pappalardo stood up and received them graciously, paying elaborate tribute to the beauties of their town.

Pappalardo returned for a moment and I tried my luck with one more direct question: Were the stories of Stroessner's promiscuity true?

Pappalardo answered. There was more to it than showed in public, he conceded. 'Never in public and never orgies.' And then he deftly shifted the subject again. 'But he talked very little about his personal life . . . He was never concerned about his children. He was only interested in power,' he repeated. 'He wasn't,' added the man who had served Stroessner for more than thirty years, 'all bad. Whenever a Paraguayan drives on a paved road or comes into that airport, or switches on a light, they should be grateful to him. Yes there was contraband . . . But people here don't think of that as a crime. If you brought the Queen of England to Paraguay she would run contraband too. Up to 1982 he was a good president, but then he began to weaken.'

A bugle sounded outside his office, and there was a rush of footsteps. The president was leaving the palace. Pappalardo swept up his briefcase and glided definitively out of the room. The palace had emptied as if by magic. It was like a stage set after the show was over.

It rained most of the day, a chilly rain, and in the evening I met up again with Dr Casabianca at a German *bierkeller*. Casabianca drank whisky, chain-smoking Kents and talked about the years of hopeless exile politics, watching twenty-five years of life slip by and the dictatorship remain as firm as ever.

While Pappalardo had been oiling the wheels of the Stroessner machine—'He's a hard man for a government to do without,' Casabianca had said earlier, smiling one of those private, exile's smiles, 'so many years here, helping everybody'—Casabianca had been one of those whom the machine had all but crushed.

And how had that been machine made?

Before Stroessner came to power, there had been eleven presidents in nineteen years—Stroessner had conspired against five of them—and if there was a lesson in Paraguay's bloody history it was that weakness was the only political crime. Since the late nineteenth century, few Paraguayan presidents had had more than a few months in office, a year or two at most. Stroessner set out to be different.

There were two potential pillars of power in Paraguay—the army and the right-wing Colorado Party—and it was Stroessner's trick to use each to dominate and control the other. Stroessner became president as the Colorado Party's candidate—he was already commander-in-chief of the army and he then consolidated the army's obedience by making membership in the Colorado Party compulsory for all officers. But the party was the problem: the only reason he had been nominated was because the members of each one of several factions thought they could use Stroessner to destroy the others.

In the first few years, Stroessner set out to purge the party, helped by a young member of it, Edgar Ynsfran. Edgar Ynsfran later became first his chief of police and then his minister of the interior. Ynsfran, supported by a network of informers, turned out to be ruthless. The year after Stroessner was elected he created the legal instrument Ynsfran needed—the 'Law for the Defence of Democracy', under which opposition activity was labelled communist. Stroessner also continued the state of martial law, which suspended all constitutional guarantees and allowed Ynsfran's police to detain and torture whomsoever they chose. Martial law had been in force since 1929.

By the late fifties, however, Stroessner's greatest challenge came from yet another faction in the Colorado Party, whose members wanted an end to the police state and demanded political normalization. Casabianca was among them. He had been a student leader and then a congressional deputy and had supported demands for political reform—an amnesty, a new electoral law, press freedom. The leadership of the Colorado Party then backed the demands as well, and Stroessner appeared to agree.

Shortly afterwards there was a student demonstration, and Stroessner took advantage of it to throw everything into reverse The demonstration was violently repressed and turned into a pitched battle between students and police. When Congress complained, Stroessner dissolved Congress. A reign of terror began. The state of siege, which had been briefly lifted, was reimposed, and a vast round-up, master-minded by Ynsfran, began. Over 400 Colorado politicians who opposed Stroessner were jailed or fled into exile, where they founded the Popular Colorado Movement.

With the crack-down Casabianca went into hiding in the Uruguayan embassy in Asunción. Six months later he left the country. He had always been one of Stroessner's favourites, but thereafter Stroessner persecuted Casabianca wherever he went. 'Stroessner was always very indulgent but finally he would never forgive you if he thought you had betrayed him.' He had a long arm, Casabianca said, and a long memory. Casabianca scraped a living in Buenos Aires, working in the central market, eventually working his way up to be supervisor of supplies to the city's markets. But then, following the *coup* in Argentina in 1976, Casabianca was suddenly thrown out of his job again. 'After that, I did whatever I could, buying and selling, an estate agent for a while. Now here I am, working alongside the people responsible for all those years of persecution.'

Casabianca is a public figure now. He has a huge office in the presidential palace and is greeted with respect in restaurants. He drank several more whiskies and sent the coffee back, complaining it was cold. 'All the waiters here used to be police informers. Now some of them work with us. Now all my friends who weren't around all those years are reappearing. Still, you can't blame people for that. The consequences are too serious here.'

Driving home, the Special Ambassador to the Presidency fiddled unsuccessfully with the car heater. 'They just gave me this,' he said, 'I still don't know how it works.'

The next morning, I went back to my list of names and numbers. Pappalardo had started as my best hope. Seeing him had left me flat. I needed some allies, some strategic advice. I had the number of a lawyer, Felino Amarillo. I had been told that he would make me laugh and that he could introduce me to the Asunción underworld. I rationalized my need to laugh with the thought that perhaps, if the government wouldn't help, the gangsters might. I never met them; but I did meet Felino.

After a long telephone chase, he turned up at my hotel, lounging there in one of the pompous leather chairs, a slim young man with his black moustache, looking round a lobby that was overflowing at the time with society women rehearsing for a charity fashion show.

I introduced myself.

'Why do you stay in this brothel?' he said.

I rode down to Plaza Independencia on the back of Felino's newly acquired motor bike. He rode a motor bike, he told me later, because he couldn't afford a car. At least, he couldn't afford a legal car. Half the cars in Paraguay were not legal. They had been stolen in Brazil and driven over the border. They are called mau cars, because, like the Mau-mau, they came in the night. It was one of the army's sidelines.

Why didn't he buy one of those?

He gave me a pained look. 'In the first place, I wouldn't buy a mau car. And in the second place, as soon as someone like me did buy a mau car, the police would come and arrest him for having it. You can only drive a stolen car if you are in the police or if you're a friend of a policeman.'

We took the lift to the fifth floor. Someone had scratched the name Felino Amarillo in the paint-work. 'Young people,' Felino observed, 'no standards.'

'Hey, Gordo! [Fatso!]' he yelled, when we got into his office. There was a groan next door. 'Stop sleeping and come here!'

A man appeared, rubbing his face. 'I wasn't sleeping, I was reading.'

342

Felino bellowed with laughter. 'May I present Dr Rafael Saguier. Rafa, this distinguished English journalist wants to know about Stroessner.'

'*La puta madre*,' said Dr Rafael Saguier.

'Scottish journalist,' I said.

'Make yourself at home,' said Rafael. 'Stroessner. *La puta madre*. We must take her to the *escribano*.'

I never quite understood why I had to see the *escribano*, except that he was considered to be both wise and knowledgeable. For Rafael and Felino it was clearly imperative, in any case, that I did, so I found myself out in the street again, dodging along the narrow pavements, Rafael on one side and Felino on the other, both talking at me, shouting scurrilous Stroessner anecdotes over the roar of the traffic.

It was my turn to be self-conscious. I kept my eyes front, wondering who was watching, who could have seen from a passing car. It was a feeling that I was to have often. Asunción was a small town in which everybody knew everybody. Every time I talked to someone, I wondered who would find out about it, what they would hear. I felt no closer to finding Stroessner, but there was the sense that behind one of those windows there might be people who could, if they chose to, if I could convince them, open the door.

We got to the *escribano*'s office. He sat under a slowly revolving fan in a room shuttered against the sun. 'In Paraguay,' he said, 'the usual gap between the Third World and the developed world is even greater. So what is the aim of ideology? In the underdeveloped world ideology is a system of lies which stimulates people to survive. Truth and science are the monopoly of the developed world. Stroessner was thirty-five years of no truth and no science.'

3

Back in his office, Felino said, 'I'm going to lend you, lend you mind, a real treasure.'

He reappeared a few minutes later with a book. He was hugging himself with glee. He read out the title, *The Golden Book of the Second Reconstruction*, and fell back in his chair, bellowing with laughter. For the Stronato historians, Felino explained, the first 'reconstruction' was that of Bernardino Caballero, a nineteenth-century tyrant who fathered over ninety children and, at the end of his reign, left the country with sound finances, a trick rarely repeated in Paraguayan history. The second 'reconstruction' was Stroessner's. And it was this that *The Golden Book* described.

The prose of *The Golden Book* strains against the outer limits of adulation. When mere words are inadequate to describe the greatness of Stroessner, a common failing apparently, the very type is forced to unnatural extremes. Felino began to read:

> We have seen Alfredo Stroessner, THE LUMINOUS LIGHTHOUSE, in his various facets dissipating the shadows of PARAGUAYAN NIGHT. We have not been able to embrace the totality of his life because that would be a labour requiring more breath than we have . . . We will not enter into an analysis of whether he had or has defects. It is human to have them in the midst of the great virtues which he possesses. But, yes, we consign to you what he once said: 'One cannot be perfect because perfection belongs only to God, but we must try, as far as possible, to reach a degree of perfectibilty which will take us closer to God.'

'What's the book about?' said Felino. 'What's anything about in this country: money and corruption.' Felino showed me the back pages, which were advertisements, the paid and signed subscriptions to the cult of the dictator: '___ _____ would like to congratulate the author on his luminous work of history . . . '
'___ _____, patriot and outstanding citizen, salutes President Stroessner.'

'Outstanding citizen,' snorted Felino, 'he paid to have that advertisement put in. About himself!'

'Look at this one,' Felino said, flipping through the pages, pointing to another advertisement: '*Obra util.* Useful book: declared such by that minister means that every school then had to buy this useful book.'

I took *The Golden Book* back to my hotel and continued to

read it, wincing with pain. Every page revealed the writer's effort.
There was, for instance, the challenge of turning Stroessner's
unremarkable parentage and early life into the nation's destiny.
This is what I read of the first meeting between Stroessner's father
Hugo, an immigrant German brewer, and the local girl he was to
marry:

> A fifteen-year-old girl passed [Hugo] one day and
> powerfully attracted his attention. In romantic terms, he
> had been struck by an arrow. He united himself with
> her. It was an instantaneous decision. HERIBERTA
> MATTIAUDA, thus was the name of the young woman
> who moved [Hugo's] most intimate fibres. She was a
> descendant of a well-known family in the area, and in
> her were united the features of wit and beauty and the
> gallantry and the presence that belong to Paraguayan
> women . . . Heriberta had once read about Charlemagne
> in a novel, and her suitor was like a Blue Prince, since his
> eyes were blue.

I read on, by now enjoying the pain. Two sons and a daughter were
born, and briefly mentioned. Then came the birth of Alfredo,
whose cries 'already seemed to announce a new dawn for
Paraguay,' and who, in the eyes of his father, 'had some connection
with the product of his labours, seeing him as blond as the liquid
product of his noble sacrifices.' I read the sentence again, in
disbelief: Alfredo was as blond as a pint of German beer?

Sadly, the effort of this prose proved too great to sustain, and
most of *The Golden Book* is a tedious transcription of the official
diary. Not a ceremony missed, not a decoration unrecorded. There
were many ceremonies, an embarrassment of decorations: natural
tributes of a world rushing in to honour the greatness of Alfredo
Stroessner. For the outside world, Stroessner was not an
unwelcome figure. The United States pumped in military and
economic aid, and trained the officers of Stroessner's police and
armed forces. He was, after all, a staunch anti-communist. For the
Brazilians he was a loyal friend, stability on their southern flank.
For his fellow dictators in the 1970s he was a compadre. The
international approval rolled in—Order of Merit of Bernardo

O'Higgins, Chile; Order of the Condor of the Andes, Extraordinary Grand Cross, Bolivia; Collar of the Order of the Liberator, Venezuela; Order of Aeronautical Merit, Grand Cross, Venezuela; Grand Cross with Diamonds of the Order of the Sun, Peru; Golden Wings of Uruguay; Honorary Aviator, Chilean Military Medal; and from General Sam Shephard, US Army, the Medal of the Inter-American Junta of Defence. In a lull in the proceedings, he gave himself the Paraguayan Diploma and Brevet of the Naval Pilot.

There was more: the United Arab Republic, Holland and Japan. In 1961, Queen Elizabeth remembered the General and gave him the Order of Victoria (the Caballero Grande, as *The Golden Book* describes it). Prince Philip, Duke of Edinburgh, followed with the Grand Cross of the Knights of the Order of St Michael and St George in 1962, and General de Gaulle pinned the Legion d'Honneur on to what was, by then, one of the most crowded chests in South America.

I trudged on—past sinister photographs of the members of Stroessner's cabinets being sworn in with a straight right arm salute, of a multitude 'delirious with enthusiasm' acclaiming its leader at a rally—searching for some coded trace of reality, some acknowledgement that not everyone had applauded. There was none. There was no mention of the opposition, the dissenters—no name was allowed to challenge the omnipresence of Stroessner's. There were, instead, a number of familiar faces. There was, among them, Conrado Pappalardo in 1969, slimmer and wearing a moustache. 'State Director of Ceremonial,' read the caption, 'a man who, from the first moments was and is at President Stroessner's side.' And there was another name, one that ran like a counterpoint through the diary, heading a delegation here, presiding over a ceremony there, leading the applause at meetings, standing in for the absent president when he went abroad. Over and over again, the name of Juan Ramon Chaves.

Juan Ramon Chaves—his nickname, I learned, was Juancito the Liar—was on my list and I had been trying to find him. Juancito was the man who had run the Colorado Party for Stroessner, frightening off the opposition, delivering the renominations, managing the conventions that rewrote the constitution to prolong

Stroessner's rule. Juancito had been president of the party for twenty-five years, Stroessner's political right arm, until Juancito came out on the wrong side of a party split in August 1987. But when Stroessner was overthrown, Juancito, like Pappalardo, got his old job back. I was told that he was nearly ninety now and was running the party again.

The Colorado Party headquarters is a vast building in the centre of town. Like the Communist Party palaces of Eastern Europe, it is a testament to years of domination and robbery. You approach it up a steep flight of steps from the street and then enter a cavernous hall. Once Stroessner had subdued the internal opposition, the Colorado Party enjoyed huge revenues based on a compulsory subscription from the salaries of all public servants. Everybody had to join, from the humblest army cadet to the beauty queens. It was the patronage machine: local section bosses ruled like petty kings—they enjoyed *mbarete*, or 'clout', and, in return, delivered raised hands at convention time.

Juancito Chaves ran all this, Stroessner's system, one organized along fascist lines with branches in every village and with a network of paid informers. They reported chance remarks, unwise jokes and, of course, conspiratorial intentions. If the penalties for disloyalty were absolute, the rewards for service were great.

The security apparatus, the adjunct to the party network, consumed thirty per cent of state revenues and was sustained by military aid from the United States and from development aid, some of which also went to build the roads and bridges that Stroessner always pointed to as the emblems of his 'modernization' of Paraguay.

In his modernized Paraguay, there was, above all, peace, but it was a peace punctuated with episodes of savage violence directed against peasant organizations, trade unions, the Church or anyone who showed a capacity for organization outside the Colorado Party. The price of peace—a phrase that became part of official terminology—was the division of spoils: monopolies of contraband pacified the military and police—whisky, cigarettes, electronic goods, cars stolen in Brazil—and high officials took a percentage of every government transaction. The Party enjoyed the privileges of the one-party state. And holding it all together, at the centre of the web, the all-pervading image of Stroessner.

He held it all together through fear, but fear was not all. As I talked to people, I realized that Stroessner's domination was a subtle balancing act between co-option and terror, sometimes within the same individual. Those who served him feared him, but serving him was also the quickest way to get rich. And those who were closest to Stroessner were not serving him out of their fear of him, but because they wished to share a little of the power and a lot of the money. Fear was just what the opportunity cost.

He maintained a cynical show of formal legality. When he needed to reinforce the appearance of democracy, he tempted the opposition into co-operation with the promise of participation, then snatched it away. The constitution was amended twice to allow him a further term in office, in 1967, at a constitutional convention attended by almost all political parties—except, of course, the banned Popular Colorado Movement—and again in 1977, to perpetuate his rule for life. Both these conventions were run for him by Juancito the Liar.

Juancito's daily routine was a legend in Asunción. He left his house at dawn and got into his car. He appeared briefly at the party headquarters and then returned to his car. From then until evening, he roamed the town. If Juancito didn't want me to find him, Felino had said, I wouldn't. The only man in Asunción who knew how to find him was the man who brought him cheese from the market.

I made appointments, but he didn't keep them. In the end, I just sat, conspicuously, and waited with the others in the huge hall outside his office, under the eye of his door-keepers, watching his machine at work.

A woman began a litany of complaint. 'They don't let you see the president. They won't let you talk to him. They'll make you wait fifteen days, come back tomorrow, come in the morning, come in the afternoon.' Barefoot shoeshine boys polished the boots of party members. Others appeared, also barefoot, selling the party paper, *Patria*, for years the most unconditional supporter of Stroessner: under Stroessner, all public servants used to subscribe; the money was deducted automatically from their paypackets.

Then came the nod.

Juancito's office was vast. At the far end, crouching next to a bank of telephones behind an immense desk placed beneath an outsized portrait of President Rodriguez, was a shrunken old man. Little Juan the Liar.

'Well, Señora?' He rasped out his words. In the pauses, a little lizard tongue flicked across his lips. 'What do you want, Señora?'

'To talk about Alfredo Stroessner.'

'Who?'

I thought perhaps he was hard of hearing. 'Alfredo Stroessner,' I repeated, louder.

He waved his hand impatiently. 'Oh, I can't talk about that, that's all past. It's a local subject, a subject for us.'

'But you knew him well.'

'No. I didn't admire him. I didn't admire him. I opposed him.'

'But you were close to him for many years.'

'No, no, I opposed him. Let's talk about now, today, about the future.'

He launched into his set-text for foreign journalists—all about the excellent situation of Paraguay now that it had been liberated from the tyranny of Stroessner. Four lines about the economic programme, four lines about the political situation. I dutifully took notes.

'The situation is good, it's democratic, without authoritarianism.'

He slowed down, watching my pen move across the paper, making sure that I kept up, that I got it down precisely.

I had expected a defence, a justification of those long years at Stroessner's side, self-serving but reasoned. An explanation of how, at the end, Stroessner had crossed some final line of tyranny. I was not prepared for his flat denial of involvement.

'Did you know the coup was coming?' I asked him.

He waved his hand in a gesture of dismissal. 'I can't talk about that. It would take too long. But he didn't fall by himself, did he? He fell because something happened. But I can't talk about the past. There is complete freedom of the press here.' He glared at me myopically. 'Nobody bothers you, do they? You can come here in absolute freedom, can't you? Well then.'

The lizard tongue again. The old man's fidgeting. 'Stroessner!' He spat the word out. 'We didn't support Stroessner, we struggled against him for years.' He looked at me, perhaps wondering what I knew. 'At the beginning, he was a man of much hope. But then he made mistakes and made a bad government.'

'Which year was that?' I asked. I knew that Juancito had never defected. He had just been elbowed aside, at the next to the last moment, by the new crowd, the *militantes*.

'I don't remember exactly which year it was. We opposed him for many years. The militants had the power. We had none.'

Juancito had been thrown out of the party presidency on 1 August 1987, at a famous party convention. His faction, the traditionalists, had tried to fight off a takeover by the militants, the young turks who saw their chance to use the last powers of the ageing president to secure the party and the government. They were friends of Stroessner's son Gustavo, and he, it was said, was their candidate for the throne. The traditionalists lost.

'But before that you had power,' I insisted. 'You were a key man through most of the Stroessner years.'

He spluttered with rage. 'No, no. It was Stroessner who had power, who had all the judicial and executive power. We didn't have power. I wasn't a key man in the Stroessner years. I was a key man in the opposition.'

'Did you approve of nothing he did then?' I asked, wondering how far this fantasy would go.

'A few things perhaps,' he said. Stroessner had, he acknowledged, built a little. 'But material things are not the only thing that matter,' said Juancito. 'What matters are the spiritual values of democracy, liberty and justice.' I looked at his huge desk, his bank of phones, trying to find a way through this monstrous lie, some small admission that Juancito might once, perhaps long ago, have supported Stroessner. In the face of this flat contradiction, I would have felt it a victory. But Juancito was a hard man to induce to reflection. His look was growing more venomous. He had begun to chew the air, an old man's habit. The flunkey was entering the middle distance, headed in my direction. Time was running out.

'But your photograph is in *The Golden Book*,' I said.

'*Golden Book*? What *Golden Book*? No such thing. Never

existed.' And then a thought clearly struck him. 'You've seen it? Which one have you seen . . . all three?'

'Yes,' I lied. Three *Golden Books*? I hoped I didn't have to read the other two.

'You've seen all three?' he said. Now he was thinking, talking fast, wondering whether to make an admission. He didn't wonder for long. 'I'm in it, you say? Really? I have never seen it. I didn't know anything about it. Is my signature there? Do you have it with you?' I didn't, and he embarked on his bamboozle-the-jury performance again. 'Someone must have forged my statement. My photograph? I don't know anything about photographs. Talk about the future. That's what matters, not the past.'

He turned the outsized leather swivel-chair towards a phone and picked it up. The grim flunkey gestured me to the door.

'Well, what did he tell you?' asked Felino later. 'He said he was a key man in the opposition,' I said. I thought Felino would never stop laughing.

In the end, there wasn't a politician in Paraguay who had not been formed by Stroessner. For those who played the game, there was a seat in Congress and a share of the spoils. For those who didn't, there was ruin, torture, imprisonment, exile or death. And there were very few who didn't play the game, at least at first. Talking to people in Paraguay is like peeling an onion. The outer skin is anti-Stroessner. Perhaps the next two layers are layers of persecution. But get to the centre and you will come across a layer of co-operation. Juancito the Liar and Pappalardo are collaborationist onions covered over with the thinnest skin of repudiation. But so many of Paraguay's famous opposition figures, heroes of the later years of struggle, have, buried inside, that core of collaboration.

Looking through *The Golden Book* I had found an entry that surprised me: in 1962, it said, President Stroessner inaugurated Radio Nanduti.

I was taken aback. There were two media in Paraguay whose closure had caused an international scandal, and one of them was Radio Nanduti. I remembered running the story at the time, as a short item in the newspaper. It had been a violent affair, in 1986.

CENTRAL SOUTH AMERICA

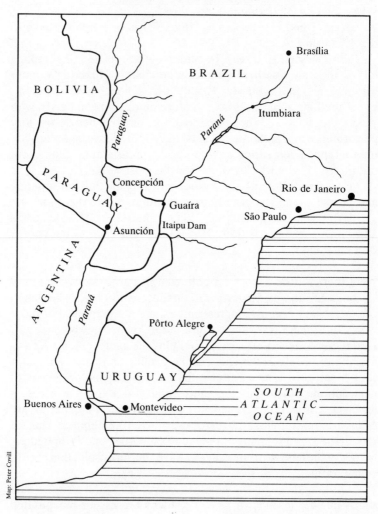

The military arrived in trucks, shouting, 'Death to the communist Jew,' and sacked the radio station. The sacking was broadcast as it occurred, until the plug was finally pulled.

The 'communist Jew' in question was Humberto Rubin, one of the names that everybody had given me. He was the radio station's proprietor, chief broadcaster and known as an intelligent and implacable opponent of Stroessner's. I had planned to see him anyway, but now I wanted to ask him how was it that Stroessner had opened his radio station: just who was Humberto Rubin in 1962?

I was shown into a small shambolic studio where a bearded man with a rumpled face was talking into the microphone. Humberto Rubin seemed to live in the studio, in constant dialogue with his huge audience. The only way to interview him was to be interviewed by him, on air, and squeeze questions into the commercial breaks.

Yes, Rubin said, he had invited Stroessner to open the radio station, not just because he was *El Presidente*, but because Rubin had believed in him. He had believed in Stroessner first because he was grateful and then because he hoped Stroessner would bring democracy.

'Look,' he said, 'from 1947 until Stroessner came to power it was chaos here, parents against children, brother against brother. When someone arrived saying we were now going to live in peace all of us hoped there would be at least some security. Democracy didn't even matter that much. All that mattered was that there were no tanks in the street. Until Stroessner came we never knew who had the power.'

Rubin had thought that things would be hard, but that they would get better. 'The Stroessner chapter was unfortunate,' Rubin said, 'but he didn't create it alone. We all helped.'

Stroessner's other famous closure was that of *ABC Color*, the biggest newspaper in Paraguay before it was shut down in 1984. It has an equally famous proprietor and editor, Aldo Zuccolillo. Zuccolillo comes from one of the richest families in the country. His enemies make a point of insisting that Zuccolillo's family fortune comes from trading in contraband sugar with Paraguay's old enemy, Bolivia. Zuccolillo's brother was appointed by Stroessner as ambassador in London—appointed in fact shortly before *ABC Color* was closed down.

Stroessner closed the paper because it had annoyed him. It had annoyed him because it was publishing about Itaipu.

Itaipu was the most grandiose of many grandiose projects. Its beauty was that it combined several of Stroessner's fetishes—the friendship with Brazil, a project of Pharaonic proportions, electrification and almost unlimited opportunities for corruption.

It was sold as a triumph. The Guaira Falls on the Parana River had been a source of tension between Paraguay, who claimed possession, and Brazil, who occupied them in 1964. In 1966, Stroessner signed the Act of Iguazu with Brazil, agreeing to joint exploitation of the enormous hydro-electric potential of the falls and thus implicitly relinquishing Paraguay's claim to sole possession. In 1973, with the Treaty of Itaipu, construction of the dam was agreed. It was to be financed by loans raised by Brazil, and Paraguay was to pay off its share by selling back to Brazil, at preferential rates, most of the electricity produced.

Many Paraguayans believed the treaty made Paraguay into a virtual colony of Brazil. Paraguay had little control over the cost of the dam, which rose from the original estimate of 1.8 billion dollars to seventeen billion. And in return, Paraguay received only about fifteen per cent of the contracts.

But the impact of that fifteen per cent on the tiny economy of Paraguay was staggering. The money had never rolled so freely. 'Before Itaipu, the Paraguayan upper classes' idea of a good time was to go on a trip to Buenos Aires,' said Felino. 'Then they suddenly had so much money they didn't know what to do with it.' Asunción became a sybaritic society. Petty officials who had lived in miserable little houses suddenly had two cars and domestic servants and Asuncion had more Mercedes than any other capital in Latin America. 'We were all corrupted,' said a friend. 'We all got used to drinking French wine and eating Dutch cheese, to having dishwashers and videos.' Mass opposition was tranquillized by the flood of money. 'If Stroessner had retired in 1980,' said Paul Lewis, author of a study on Stroessner, 'he would probably have gone down as a great president.'

Paradoxically, for Zuccolillo, Itaipu was a catalyst that forced him into taking up with the opposition and that led to the closure of his newspaper. He told me his story, one that I was finding increasingly familiar: how at first he had supported Stroessner; how, in the late 1960s, that support had become a qualified one, followed by disillusionment and then opposition and finally repression. Even so, *ABC Color*'s record is one of courage. In the seventeen years the paper published, Zuccolillo's journalists were jailed on thirty-two occasions. It became the practice for everyone to keep an overnight bag in the office, in case of arrest, and Zuccolillo himself was in jail twice. The end came in March 1984, also a familiar story: fifty police with machine-guns, a man with a piece of paper on which was written the charge—promoting hatred amongst Paraguayans.

Between the closure of *ABC Color* and the coup, every paper in the country that wasn't owned by a Stroessner friend or relative was either closed or its staff harassed. The opposition weeklies *El Enano*, *El Radical*, *Dialogo*, *La Republica* and *El Pueblo* all went. The staff of *Nuestro Tiempo*, a church-backed monthly, was persecuted. Radio Caritas, also backed by the Church, tried to fill in some of the space left by Radio Nanduti and was told to stick to prayer.

After the February coup, *ABC* came back and Zuccolillo had fun exposing the crimes of his fallen adversaries. He published a series of articles on the fabulous mansions built by Stroessner functionaries, and his guided tour—'the tour of Asunción's corruption,' as he calls it—is on the itinerary of every visiting journalist. The tour includes the market, where the contraband ranges from cases of Scotch to plastic buckets from Brazil; the Central Bank building, which contains an Olympic-sized swimming-pool and a theatre, true cost unknown; the mansions of the Stroessner clan, family and mistresses, former ministers and army officers. Zuccolillo's own home is also a mansion; in fact it is a mansion as large as most of those on his tour, as his wife was the first to point out to me.

The tour also includes General Rodriguez's French château, though that was left out of the newspaper series.

I asked him why.

'Because of what he did in February,' he said. 'I have forgiven all his sins.'

4

I was still looking for Stroessner.

Juancito Chaves hadn't helped, even with his memories; in their way, both Rubin and Zuccolillo had, but they didn't know Stroessner's whereabouts. I had searched through the official histories for clues to the man behind the deadly prose. I had walked around his city, trying to imagine how it was when his presence filled it. Nobody would admit to being in touch with him. Those who wanted me to talk to him couldn't help. Those who might have helped didn't want to.

But I was beginning to understand why he fell. After the easy money that followed the Treaty of Itaipu, his own system had begun to rot. By the time the dollars stopped flowing in, his two pillars, the army and the party, were crumbling. But there was also something else. There was social protest.

There were peasants demanding land, citizens demanding human rights and the Church, steadily, quietly, preaching solidarity and justice. In the land of no-science and no-truth, there were now groups burrowing away in the structure of the big lie, collecting information, writing news-letters, worrying the system. The Data Bank was one of them.

The Data Bank's members always knew that information was subversive, but they never knew what information exactly would bring the police down on them. When Stroessner's police finally raided, they didn't just take away the people; they stripped the place bare. Typewriters, photocopiers, even the electric wiring out of the walls—all of it went (and when they raided a home, they took everything down to the last pair of socks). Even afterwards, no one could be sure what it was that they had done, this time. José Carlos Rodriguez, a sociologist at the Data Bank, one day found himself on the run with an order out to shoot him on sight. He escaped by hiding in the belly of the beast, taking a military flight to the Brazilian border, then hitching a ride with a police chief. 'Nobody checks the papers of anybody who's with a police chief,' he said. Back home, the police followed his child for six months, waiting for the father to make contact.

Rodriguez at least knew he was guilty, even if he wasn't sure of what. But there were many who were genuinely innocent: when the Data Bank was raided, a passer-by, who had gone inside to use the lavatory, was arrested with all the others. Who could know when he would be released? A famous case is Nelson Ortigoza's. What he did, if anything, is now so lost in myth and counter-myth that it has ceased to be the point of the story. Nelson Ortigoza was in solitary confinement for twenty-five years. For the last two, his cell was bricked up. He was eventually released into house arrest, but escaped, helped in fact by my two friends Felino and Rafael. They say that when Stroessner heard the news he had a coughing fit that lasted four hours.

The resistance was growing, nevertheless, and, as more and more people were prepared to protest, more lawyers were emerging prepared to defend them. One of them was Pablo Vargas. Vargas had been in prison sixteen times, beginning in 1956 when he was thirteen. He was tortured four times, the first time when he was sixteen. In one session in 1969 he lost a kidney.

Vargas worked for the Church Committee, an inter-denominational body that had been set up in response to a particularly brutal repression of a peasant organization in 1976.

I asked him if his work had been dangerous, and he gave me a weary look. We were sitting in a cool, whitewashed room, shafts of sunlight filtering through the shutters. I waited for him to answer, half-listening to the murmur of the street below. My question, I realized, must have sounded banal.

'I saw many people die under torture,' he said finally. 'People used to ask me why didn't I write about it, but I never wanted to because torture is something that nobody can describe. At one time I went to see all the films in which there was torture to see if it could be portrayed, but I found it was romanticized, idealized. What I saw on the screen seemed to me like a game for children.'

A person who is tortured, he said, becomes an animal. 'It's the most miserable thing there is. They tell you, "Rest. We will come for you at three o'clock." And you watch the time pass. If they don't come you pray that they have forgotten or that they have gone for somebody else.'

Inside those jails, the routine of torture had its own ritual, one that the prisoners got used to. When they heard loud music, they knew that, for somebody, the dance had begun. 'I remember the *pileta*,' he said. The *pileta* is popular in Latin America. It is simple, cheap and effective. It consists of holding a prisoner's head down in bath water until he is nearly drowned. Then you haul him out. Then you put him back. Sometimes the water is clean, sometimes it's sewage. 'It was just a metal bath,' said Vargas. 'It had feet like lion's claws. How often did I lie on the ground, looking at those feet?'

He was hunched over in his chair, looking at his hands. He stopped suddenly and looked round. The room was silent.

'Why am I talking about this? I have never talked about this.' He shrugged, his chair creaked. 'When they begin,' he continued, 'you are naked. Your hands and feet are tied. The bath had one tap, and I would lie there, listening to that tap running, to the sound of the water changing as the bath filled, trying to guess how deep it was.'

He looked up. 'The *picana* [electric prod] and the *pileta* don't hurt, you know. People think they do, that the torture is pain. It's not pain. It's worse than pain. It's like a small death each time: you long for pain in the end. It's better to feel pain than that absolute despair. When they use the *picana*, you think you are going to explode.'

'You talk to your torturer,' he continued, 'about anything. About fishing or food, trying to postpone the moment. The torturers tell you that they don't like doing it and ask you to help stop it, to tell them something. But there's nothing you can tell them. I have seen people tortured for twenty-nine days on end.

'I could guess from the way they walked which one was coming for me. They were all different. Normally an interrogator would torture a man for half an hour at a time; then there would be another one, and then it would be back to the first. Sometimes they would torture two at a time, all the while comparing observations. And sometimes there were sessions that lasted four to five hours at a time, and during them they would talk about your performance. They killed a man once within the first half-hour, and they were very contemptuous of him. They'd had a girl of eighteen who had survived hours of it. "What kind of a man would die after half an hour?" they said. A good torturer doesn't kill. You knew, if they broke somebody's bones, it was because they were going to kill him.'

Torture had left him with bad dreams, he said, but he wasn't unusual. 'In Paraguay, fear was like a second skin, something we all wore on top of our normal skin.'

Today, Vargas is a senator. He is forty-six. Of the seventeen people who were in the leadership of his party when he was twenty-two, five are still alive. 'You feel like an old man, at forty-six,' he said. 'Stroessner stole thirty-five years of my life. Thirty-five years of systematic human rights violations while the rest of the world was completely silent. One of my friends was arrested at nineteen and got out at forty. There were people who were in jail for twenty-two years without trial. There were cases of mistaken identity in which the accused were released after six months, but there were others in which they were forgotten for ten years.'

Like the man in the lavatory of The Data Bank, I thought, wondering how long it would be before he was set free.

I walked back towards the centre of town, to get some air, and found myself in the square, looking at the neo-classical Congress building. In front of it was a little Bolivian tank, a trophy from the Chaco War, painted the same municipal green as the benches and the little bronze statues that had been imported from France. The heat was suffocating except for a light breeze.

I sat on an empty bench and looked at the statue of Mariscal Francisco Solano Lopez, president of Paraguay from 1865 until his death in the disastrous War of the Triple Alliance in 1870. Lopez had nearly wrecked Paraguay, having been lured into a war against Argentina, Brazil and Uruguay; and, by the end, half of Paraguay's population was dead. The last battles were fought by children from the cadet school, with painted-on moustaches.

Someone told me that his rearing horse had started out on ground level—it now rests on an oversized plinth—but the children used to daub him with paint. I liked the idea of the children's revenge.

Behind me was the police headquarters. It takes up an entire block. The torture chambers were 300 yards from where I was sitting. Could the street noises be heard in the cells? What would it be like, to listen to the footsteps, people coming and going, indifferent? Almost everybody I met seemed to have been in jail. It was almost a commonplace, but few paraded their suffering.

Sometimes there would be a look: it was like the look you imagine crossing a soldier's face when a kid asks, 'What's war like?' Sometimes you could tell that there were questions that were being thought but not asked: Where were you when it was happening? Were yours among the indifferent pairs of feet I listened to from my cell? Why do you come now, wanting to know, when it's all over? Where were you with your questions when my son was kidnapped outside my front door, when my brother was exiled, when I was in the *pileta*?

I went to have a coffee with Felino.
   'You want to know where they tortured people?' he asked.
'Everywhere.'
   I wanted a list.
   We went out on to the balcony and looked down on the city. It was late afternoon, and the roofs were bathed in a rich, golden light. Felino began to point out the buildings which had cells and torture chambers. After five, I stopped taking notes.
   Rafael had been in most of them, said Felino. The windows of Rafael's office, next door, had much the same view. I wondered: what did he think when he looked out?
   'Jail wasn't so bad,' said Rafael. 'All the nicest people were there. One time I met a kid whose only crime was that he was a brilliant basketball player. His team was coming up against a general's team, so the general had him arrested.'

I was getting depressed, wondering what I was going to say about Stroessner's Paraguay that didn't make it sound like a bad novel with an exotic backdrop: the comic opera dictator with the oversized hat, covered in gold braid. And where was the man, at the heart of it all? Nobody could tell me. They all had their own, oversized image. I was beginning to hear the same stories.
   What made him laugh? I asked.
   People stared back.

I phoned home, upbraiding them for the pain of my own absence, for the frustration of the story. My daughter had had an accident, in the playground, a cut over her eye. She was fine, I was told. I put the phone down and began to cry with the shame of not being there.

I turned over my notes, wondering if I had enough to stop.

I could see how it had all begun to fall apart, around the ageing dictator. He grew tired and no longer put in the hours. He began to ramble on old themes, to go off and play cards and chess with his cronies, to visit his mistress. His health began to give him trouble, and he didn't like it.

What I didn't know was how he felt about it. Whether he knew that he was losing his grip. What did he think about when he took off the gold braid and climbed into bed? Did he worry about his paunch? Did he notice his legs were growing thin? Did the decay of his body disturb him as he took those young women to bed?

I felt I hadn't made sense of the women and it annoyed me. I wanted to know what it was like to be debauched by Stroessner. Did his subjects admire him for his appetite for teenage girls or detest him for his insistence on his rights as the national stud?

And why so many? Had he mixed up his appetite with his sense of national destiny? It wasn't an entirely idle question. There had never been enough settlers in Paraguay. There had been too many wars, too many exiles. Everybody had a story of a grandmother, an aunt or even a mother abducted when a schoolgirl by a predatory male.

Stroessner's neglected wife, Dona Eligia, was more pitied than resented. Behind the official first family pomp, people said, was a *campesina* who chewed tobacco, a concubine from his days as a junior officer whom he kept on as a wife, a prisoner of his insistence on the myth of official respectability. She could be got into evening dress for state occasions, but mostly she kept in the background, bringing up their three children, Gustavo, Freddie and Graciella in the official residence on Avenida Mariscal Lopez. Stroessner had separate quarters at the back.

Stroessner did not build lavish mansions on every corner. The public myth is of a man who lived ascetically, though, as someone pointed out, why bother, when the whole country is yours? But his

361

way of affirming the reality of his possession, his absolute right, was through the women. The younger, it seemed, the better. His annual pilgrimage round the high schools presenting diplomas was mentioned in *The Golden Book*. The President, it said, took a keen interest in education. From the school platforms he would inspect the rows of schoolgirls and, when he spotted one he liked, she would be delivered to him.

In the early years, a Colonel Perreira acted as procurer for Stroessner. There was little point in resisting, and, in any event, the girls and their families were well rewarded. 'You had hit the jackpot if your daughter came to the notice of a *capo*,' said Rafael, 'and if it was Stroessner, well, your dreams were made of gold.' Nobody knows exactly how many girls there were, or how many children he had by them. When he tired of the girls, Stroessner had them married off to army officers who swallowed their pride and acknowledged his children as their own. But one or two lasted long enough to become public figures in their own right. I had tried to find some of these women. I talked to one on the phone, but she wouldn't meet me. I talked to people who knew them, slightly, but it was gossip, funny stories of other boy-friends hiding on the roof when the General called unexpectedly. Nobody seemed to know or care what they really felt.

Then I met a woman who did, a friend of Maria Estela Legal, known as Nata, Stroessner's most famous mistress. 'I'll tell you about her,' she said. 'But don't use my name. I was just her friend, nothing political. Just her friend.'

Nata's story, she told me, was a very Paraguayan one. She was the natural child of parents who each married somebody else. Stroessner picked her out of a school procession, when Nata was fifteen, and her mother gladly sold her.

Since she was too young to be given a house of her own, Nata was sent to live with one of Stroessner's generals and his wife. The girl spent the first few months weeping with misery, but gradually resigned herself to her situation. In any event, there was no choice.

Stroessner talked to her regularly, took her on fishing trips. 'He probably showed her the first real kindness she had known,' said her friend. Nata became pregnant, and after her first daughter was born she was given her own house, where Stroessner would visit, every afternoon. She had a second daughter two years later.

Nata could have anything she wanted—cars, money, jobs for the relations who came flocking round. Her friend insists she didn't abuse her power. She was nearly arrested once, by a zealous and ill-informed policeman who pointed out that the car, a present from the president, had no number-plates. She didn't make a fuss, said her friend, and would have gone to the police station, but a street-wise kid selling chewing-gum alerted the policeman to the fact that he was on the brink of an important career error.

But it was a lonely life. In official circles, the done thing was to support the myth of the first family. At Nata's parties it was always the same crowd, a couple of generals, a senator, her doctor, a plastic surgeon and two or three friends. Nevertheless Stroessner was devoted to both her and the daughters.

He went shopping at the supermarket himself and then went round to cook them meals. He helped the girls with their homework and was always there for birthday parties, answering the door himself. 'He loved them, in his way,' said her friend, 'but I couldn't have stood it. He was so authoritarian. They were never allowed to wear trousers because he said it was unfeminine. And he was fantastically jealous. Whenever Nata went out, he had her followed. I have seen him following her himself, all alone in a black car.'

Nata, as she grew older, tried to escape several times. Once, after a row about one of Stroessner's many other amours, she left. She went to Switzerland and married an Italian antique dealer. Stroessner was desperate. He did everything to get her back. He hung on to the daughters, then aged eleven and thirteen. Nata was away for six months and then returned to visit her children, intending to stay for two weeks. She stayed three months. The Italian husband became jealous.

It was an impossible situation and eventually she came back. She had been married about four years. 'It was so sad,' said her friend. 'She had been such a different person in Switzerland. She was able to go out, have a coffee, talk and laugh, just like anyone else.'

She was back but she was still lonely. Eventually she persuaded

Stroessner that she needed to marry. A husband was found, an architect. The wedding was held in a house she had shared with Stroessner by the lake in San Bernardino, fifty kilometres from Asunción. The guests, on entering, walked under a large portrait of the president hanging in the entrance. None of Stroessner's friends went.

After the marriage, it was business as usual, except for the husband, whose presence clearly irritated the General. Stroessner continued visiting the house that he had built for Nata on the airport road, always after the regular Thursday meetings of the army chiefs that he chaired as commander-in-chief, but on several other days too. At first the husband waited on the veranda but finally he was told to remove himself further and he took to playing bingo in a hall near the house. As it happened, the bingo hall belonged to Gustavo Stroessner. Stroessner was visiting Nata when the *coup* started.

5

People had begun to feel that change was coming. Dr Casabianca felt it. He had returned to Paraguay in 1983 after the newly elected President Alfonsin in Argentina had interceded on behalf of the exiled members of the Popular Colorado Movement. (Stroessner said that of course there was no problem, the members of the Movement had always been free to return, and that they should have asked sooner.) Dr Casabianca returned the next week and then spent the next five years being followed, harassed and arrested. When he was in prison in December 1988—one of the last political prisoners of the Stronato—he said he felt then there was a change coming. 'The police were polite to me. It was as though they knew it couldn't last.'

The issue, finally, was the succession.

In most ways, Andres Rodriguez was the natural successor to Stroessner. For years he had been part of the corrupt inner circle. He had grown rich in the drugs traffic and had invested in land, breweries and a currency-exchange empire. By the 1980s he had shown signs of becoming nearly as respectable a businessman as Paraguay permits. He was commander of the cavalry, a key army corps, and he had a dynastic connection through the marriage of his daughter to Stroessner's son, Freddie. For all these reasons, he was seen by the militants as the principal threat to Gustavo's succession.

Gustavo had acquired a reputation for brutishness and greed, which might not have done him any harm, but also for homosexuality, which certainly did. If the father lived austerely, the children squandered lavishly. Local journalists estimate Gustavo's winnings—culled from gambling, the drug trade and a string of 'business' interests—at 100 million dollars. His rise in the armed forces was viewed with resentment, and it ate away the foundations of Stroessner's second pillar of power.

The militants—new money and friends of Gustavo—had won control of the party at the disastrous and violent convention in 1987. Juancito the Liar and his friends were ignominiously thrown out, and Sabino Montanaro was elected the new party president. He was also minister of the interior, had part of the stolen car concession, sold passports and dabbled in narcotics. He had been excommunicated at one point, for torturing priests.

The plan, people now say, was to call another constitutional convention and make Gustavo vice-president, ready to shove him upwards when the vacancy appeared. Gustavo's friends and several die-hard militants deny this; some thoughtful bystanders wonder if Gustavo wasn't so unpromising that even the militants had their doubts. Whatever the plan, it was true that this was the last, truly decadent stage of the Stronato, a combination of grand larceny and radical violence in the face of decay and no control.

The displaced Colorados plotted their revenge and the times were with them. Things were moving on the streets, strikes and demonstrations, backed by a Church led by the wise and courageous Archbishop Abimael Rolon. In January 1989, Gustavo was promoted to colonel and 150 officers above him were retired. Many of them were Rodriguez's cronies, and Rodriguez began to smell a rat. The junior officers, for their own reasons, were bordering on a revolt. Rodriguez realized he was about to be caught between his junior officers—he would be engulfed in their revolt—and the new militant faction. And then Rodriguez was warned—people say that it was Pappalardo—that Stroessner planned to retire him. That was why, the story goes, Rodriguez pretended to have broken his leg and did not attend the usual Thursday general staff meeting, the week of the *coup*.

They moved the next day.

Ammunition and radios for the *coup* had been supplied by some wealthy industrialists, as, even in his decline, Stroessner was too canny to hand out too many bullets to his own army. In the afternoon, Nata's house was attacked: Stroessner was there having his customary siesta. His bodyguard gave the old man enough cover to allow him to escape, and he went off with his own élite unit, the presidential guard, although even here, few fought with any conviction. His generals had so long neglected military affairs that they could scarcely remember how to give orders, and the tanks in the élite unit couldn't move because the man with the keys was out of town. Only around the police headquarters was there serious fighting. By the next morning, Stroessner and his family were packed off on a flight to Brazil, and there was dancing in the streets.

Felino told me how he went out looking for a statue to topple. 'They were surprisingly hard to find. After thirty-five years we finally noticed he didn't put up statues.'

Felino found one in the end and knocked it over.

Some peasants occupied the cathedral hoping now that the dictator had gone they might get some land. The chief of police accused them of being communists and produced as evidence a tin of Russian prawns that he claimed they had been eating.

Nata put to rights the house and grounds that had been ravaged by the assault and sat down to await developments, consoling her daughters, who were, perhaps, the only people in Paraguay who genuinely mourned the exile of their father. The younger one stood out in the wrecked garden, it was reported, watching Stroessner's plane fly off, tears pouring down her face.

6

I had a pile of notebooks; I had a new circle of friends; I was even beginning to fall into the routine of life in Asunción. But I hadn't found Stroessner. I felt frustrated: I wasn't really any closer to finding him than I when I arrived. I had one last hope—the militants who had kept the faith. The important ones were in jail, and I wasn't allowed to see them. But there were one or two others, lesser figures, who had not been arrested. One was Benitez Rickman.

Benitez Rickman is a notary public, but in the last fifteen months of the regime he had been the minister of public relations. I couldn't say, from the evidence, that he had done a brilliant job, but it had become a hard item to sell. I had seen him once before in his office, a room filled with German military regalia, mementoes of his grandfather, and Stroessner souvenirs: photographs of Rickman and the General, newspaper cuttings about the great man. Rickman had advanced the theory that Stroessner had been punished by both the Russians and the Americans. I was sure he had stayed in touch.

I had listened sympathetically and was rewarded with an invitation to his house, to look through his library. I went, thinking that perhaps I could pass some test and be given Stroessner's telephone number in Brazil. My appearance at the gate of his mansion sent his Alsatian dogs into a tedious frenzy. I began to feel that I should have known better.

There was another guest sitting in the study, an Argentine man in his sixties from the provincial town of Salta. His hair was dyed an implausible chestnut. He wore an extravagantly double-breasted brown suit; a shirt with red, white and blue stripes; and a paisley cravat. He talked incessantly, between long pulls of beer, in a voice like a band-saw, fidgeting from chair to chair. He was introduced as an old friend of the family.

The maid brought some red caviare. 'What's this?' the family friend croaked. 'Red caviare. Shouldn't caviare be black? Is it Chinese?'

I made a joke about Russian prawns, but nobody laughed.

The Argentine talked on and on, about the purity of the Argentine 'race' and his own European ancestry. Then he got on to Jews.

Benitez Rickman's Stroessner library was the largest collection I had seen of official eulogy: *The Golden Books* (all three), *Panorama* magazine, glossy brochures for the public works, treatises on Latin American genealogy that were beached on the further shores of social Darwinism.

Could Rickman really be serious?

The evidence suggested that even my host, who must be among Stroessner's most ardent admirers, had not managed to get very far through his own collection: *Alfredo Stroessner, Politics and Strategy of Development*; *Stroessner, Defender of the Democratic Institutions*. There were Stroessner's acceptance speeches on his many nominations. There were the rally speeches: Stroessner on democracy and communism; Stroessner on communism and democracy. There was a commemorative volume published in 1987, the centenary of the founding of the Colorado Party, with chapter headings like 'The Unity of the Colorado Party is the Basis of Public Peace.' 'Never again,' ran the text, 'must it be admitted that a Colorado is the enemy of another Colorado. The best friend of a Colorado is another Colorado.' *Stroessner, Imbatible*—this title was heavily underlined, especially at the beginning. I pictured Benitez Rickman, in an evening of especial piety, sitting down to study and learn, even to memorize passages. But the underlining stopped abruptly after the first twenty pages. I felt touched. It had defeated him, too.

There were souvenirs as well. Benitez Rickman showed me a bottle of champagne, presented to Stroessner. 'That champagne costs 400 dollars a bottle,' he said, laying the bottle carefully back in its presentation case.

Meanwhile, the Argentine was becoming embarrassing.

Our host fidgeted. 'My friend is a bit of a Nazi,' he said with a laugh. Then he lapsed into silence, visibly dejected by the impossibility of shutting up his guest without breaching the rules of hospitality. He shrank into his leather armchair and stared at the wreckage of the red caviare. The Argentine poured another glass of beer which foamed over on to the tray. I picked up yet another book, *Stroessner City, the Construction of the Century*.

'Can you put me in touch with President Stroessner?' I asked Benitez Rickman.

'Why?' he said, as had so many others. I always thought it was an odd question. 'What do you want to talk to him about?'

'His thirty-five years in power,' I said.

'He isn't seeing anyone. He can't talk about politics in his situation.'

I had asked so many people the same question. I had asked a friend of Gustavo's, a businessman who had told me about the exemplary family life the Stroessners led.

Was he in touch? Would he send a letter for me? A copy of *Granta*? The editor had thought it would help.

The businessman promised he would, but his expression of studied innocence told me that it probably wouldn't get further than the waste-paper basket. I had begun to give up hope of getting at Stroessner through Paraguay. I had begun to give up hope of getting at Stroessner.

It was the next morning when the phone rang in my room. It was a call from Brazil, where I had some lines trailing in the water. I had become so discouraged in Paraguay that I had almost forgotten them. Suddenly it seemed as though there was a way of delivering a letter, if I was still interested.

I had a letter. I had carried it around, trying to find a way of sending it. It was letter from the editor of *Granta*, to Stroessner. At the time it had seemed like a good idea. I took it out and read it through, wondering whether I really wanted to send it. Tactically, I had to admire it, but it still made me squirm.

I visited Felino.

'Does Stroessner read English?' I asked.

Felino spluttered into his *mate*. 'No! He's underdeveloped. Like me.'

Well, you'll have to help me translate this, I told him.

But then I had to give up on Felino. Even as a joke, he couldn't bring himself to get the tone right. We called in Rafael's wife Solange.

She read the letter and gave me an ironic look. 'You want to talk about his achievements? Is this for real?'

I fidgeted. Well, I said, I want his point of view.

'You'll get it, I'm sure,' she said tartly. 'Except that he won't see you.' Solange added some touches of her own.

Do you have a doctorate? she asked.

No, I said, I never completed my thesis.

What was it about? she asked.

Metaphysical Chinese poetry in 1920s Shanghai, I said. That, I added, was why I never finished it.

'I think you deserve a doctorate,' she said, inserting '*Doctora*' in the text.

I took the letter back to the hotel to fax it to Brazil. The receptionist stared at me but decided against comment.

That night I went out to dinner with Rafael and Solange, to the Yacht Club, a grandiose development where the rich and their children idle at the weekends. 'You could drop a bomb on this place,' said Rafael, 'and not damage humanity one bit.' At dinner Rafael and Solange told stories about their adventures in the opposition: how Rafael went into the cathedral on the day of the March for Life, one of the last, great demonstrations, disguised as a woman. His wife began to laugh and soon none of us could stop.

'You should have seen him,' said Solange, tears rolling down her face, 'in my fish-net tights and a skirt he borrowed from his mother, tittupping along in high heels. He was just like Benny Hill. Everyone who saw him said, "Look, there's Dr Rafael Saguier dressed as a woman." '

'There were supposed to be more of us,' said Rafael, trying to rescue his dignity. 'A group of seminarists was supposed to come but the bastards pulled out. So there I was, all by myself, in the darkest corner of the cathedral, carefully taking off my fish-net tights, when this priest finds me and threatens to call the police if I don't leave immediately. Call the police! They were ten-deep outside. You can imagine what it would have done to my reputation to be arrested disguised as a woman.'

'But why, Rafa?' I gasped, helpless with laughter myself, 'why did you go to the cathedral disguised as a woman?'

'To occupy it, of course.'

'*Gordo*,' said his wife, wiping her eyes and putting her arm round him. 'You were a lovely woman . . . '

The story was almost over and I missed my children. I had been told for two weeks that Stroessner was unseeable, and I was resigned to a few days of boredom in Brasília for form's sake. I said goodbye to my friends.

'Come back soon,' said Rafael, 'and we'll write a book

about Napoleon Ortigoza and his twenty-five years in solitary confinement.'

I promised I would.

7

Stroessner had begun his exile, appropriately enough, in Itumbiara, as the guest of Brazil's electricity company, but the locals complained and the governor was hostile. There had been too much contraband, he said, too many murders. Stroessner moved to his own beach house in Guaratuba, but that didn't last either: it turned into one of the most popular stake-outs in the history of journalism, a long beach party. They moved on again, while Gustavo looked round Brasília for a house. Stroessner's wife and family went to Miami. Perhaps Dona Eligia, like Nata, saw her chance of freedom. Gustavo, for whom there was an implausible extradition request, stuck close to his father, counting on the Brazilians to look after him. Stroessner was reported to want to go to the United States, but it was made clear that he would be turned down.

I had forgotten what a vision of hell Brasília was: the illegitimate offspring of an intellectual love affair between an architect and a dictator. Everyone must have cheated on the contracts, because what had once been intimidatingly new was now shabby and peeling. I was in Metropolis, locked in the past's vision of the future. I felt nostalgic for Asunción's haphazard charm. I chain-smoked and looked out of the window of my hotel, watching the traffic accidents five floors below. It was a landscape of modernist blocks marching across bleak open spaces. In the afternoon, the sky blackened and a deluge hosed all the people off the landscape.

I looked down the list of people I might call, at least to avoid eating alone for three days. But first, I rang my contact.

'It's all fixed,' he said.

'What do you mean, fixed?'

'The gentleman you want to see has said yes. Let me give you his telephone number.'

'He said yes?' I repeated foolishly.

I began to feel as though I was in a bad film. I rang the number and got Gustavo. He was extremely affable. There had been some awful casting error. It was the wrong movie.

'We were expecting your call. When do you want to come? Are you alone? I think I should come and meet you at your hotel to discuss how to proceed.'

The catch, I thought. He'll come. He'll smell a rat.

But he kept on phoning after that. He dropped the idea of coming and rang instead with questions that, asked by someone else, would have been endearing. 'Would it be all right if we don't wear suits?' he asked.

Quite all right, I said.

'You won't take pictures, will you, if we're not in suits?'

Wouldn't dream of it.

They would send a car, he said, to my hotel. He rang back again, to reconfirm the time.

I was alone in Brasília. There was nobody I could tell. I turned on the air-conditioning unit, and it fell out of the wall. I phoned Cambridge. I phoned London. I phoned Florida to talk to Paul Lewis. What would he ask Stroessner? I asked him. I found myself worried. I imagined myself forgetting to ask the most obvious question, paralysed by the absurdity of the situation.

I went out to buy a camera and got soaked, somewhere in no man's land. That night I went through my notebooks. I couldn't think of a single thing I could ask him that he would possibly want to tell me.

I waited in the lobby for the car. It was a long wait of a kind I had had before, a woman hanging around a hotel lobby, trying simultaneously to look out for one particular stranger yet avoid eye contact with all the others. A blue Chevrolet Commodore pulled up outside and a burly Brazilian got out. He struggled with my name at reception. We pulled out into the traffic and took the road to the South Lake Residential Zone, over the bridge and into Sector Nine, medium to senior bureaucrat-grade villas with small swimming-pools and hibiscus hedges. We pulled up, the car's nose pointing at a high metal gate. The driver hooted his horn. The gate opened, and we drove straight into a garage.

Gustavo was there, waiting in the garage. He opened the door of the car, and we greeted each other warmly. He was effusively welcoming.

'Are you sure,' he asked, 'that you don't mind the sneakers?'

He apologized his way up a path of stepping stones that had been set into a spongy tropical lawn. 'You must excuse the conditions in which we have to receive you. We still haven't got all our things yet. It was all rather hurried, leaving. We are rather camping here, birds of passage, you might say.' The front door opened on to a living-room, furnished with brocade chairs. It was tasteful, I thought, and realized I was childishly disappointed. Opposite the door, French windows stood open on a garden, and I glimpsed a swimming-pool. It was very quiet, except for the crickets.

I turned round from the garden at the moment the General made his entrance. It was as though the photographs had come alive. That heavy face, the pouchy blue eyes, the full underlip beneath the moustache and the slightly receding chin that folded into a flabby neck. His blue-silk suit was carefully buttoned over a paunch. The General was clearly not given to sneakers.

'Welcome,' he said, 'a great pleasure to receive you.' We shook hands, and he gestured me to one of a group of chairs arranged around a glass coffee-table. He sat, quite still, on an upright chair while Gustavo lounged and fidgeted in an armchair opposite me.

Stroessner cleared his throat and began to make a speech. 'In Paraguay,' he said, 'there was democracy. A fully democratic system, with absolute independence of the judges and the parliament. Then there was great progress. Great progress. Development.' He stopped.

I fished the tape recorder out of my bag and put it on the table. Gustavo was still fussing.

'This isn't going to be published here, is it?' he asked. 'We . . .'

The General interrupted. 'We can't make any statements here. We can't talk about the internal politics of Paraguay.' My heart sank. 'A lot of people have asked for interviews, but we have said no. This is a special case. But we are in political asylum. We have to be careful.'

I wondered why they had made an exception. Occasionally, walking down a street in Asunción, there had flashed into my mind the preposterous thought that my package had reached them and that the two of them were sitting poring over *Granta*. It had made me laugh out loud. I recalled once sitting in the Moneda Palace in Santiago, Chile, in deep conversation with one of Pinochet's close political advisors, certain that at any moment someone would burst through the door and bundle me out of the room, shouting that it was a case of mistaken identity. Now, I kept expecting the telephone to ring, and some security man to tip them off, or perhaps a loyalist in Asunción who had seen me laughing in a café with the wrong people. I wondered if he knew anything about me, about the people I had been seeing. At any moment, I felt, the director would shout, 'Cut!' But he didn't.

Stroessner showed no signs of resuming his speech. Perhaps that was it. His statement had been made.

'Where shall we begin?' I said. 'Perhaps you could tell me something about your early life, your childhood.'

Stroessner cleared his throat and returned to his formal manner. 'I have visited many countries in Latin America . . .'

'Your childhood,' Gustavo interrupted, 'she wants to know about your childhood.'

The old man closed his eyes in exasperation. 'No, no, this is up to me now.'

He started again. 'I have visited many countries. Here in Latin America. I am not going to quote them all because I have visited almost all of them, including . . .' He tailed off, paused and started on a different tack. 'I have received many visits from the great personalities of the world, heads of state who include General de Gaulle. Also that . . .' He stumbled, searching for the name. I felt my stomach tensing. 'General Péron,' he said. I relaxed again. 'On two occasions as head of state. Also Chile, General Pinochet, and Ibanez del Campo, and I have been in all the countries like Ecuador, Venezuela. And I have been in Brazil I don't know how many times, on many occasions.'

He was clearly a man for lists. The recitation seemed to have tripped him back into his speech 'Paraguay and how I built It.' 'Now,' he went on, 'with support and co-operation, Paraguay developed considerably. And had peace, peace and respect for the constitution and laws.'

'You know this is being recorded,' said Gustavo.

'I know, I know. I am not going to—I am going to be careful.' He resumed in a firm tone. 'Now I am going to tell you. Paraguay was always a patriotic country. And it had a lot of internal and external problems. From 1904 to 1940 it had twenty-one presidents, an average of one each year and a half. For each government. This was all they had. From 1940 to 1948, I was the eighth president. So when I became president, I took'—he corrected himself—'we took measures to do what the country needed.' He was both stumbling and unstoppable. I wondered how much they had talked about what they were going to say.

'Asunción had no running water,' he was saying, 'and we made the road to Paraná, to the Friendship Bridge. With the co-operation of Brazil we built the Friendship Bridge, and we also built the hydroelectric plant Icarai, and the bridge was finished by Brazil. We also used the Brazilian road to reach the Atlantic, for exports and imports to Paraguay. We fostered the production of soya, cotton and all the agricultural products. And we built a lot of roads, a lot of roads, that . . .' He tailed off again, and Gustavo jumped in.

'In Paraguay,' he said.

'Yes, yes,' said Stroessner, 'I'm talking about Paraguay.'

I smiled encouragingly.

'Five thousand kilometres of roads,' said Gustavo.

'Asphalted,' said Stroessner.

'No,' said Gustavo, 'No. Asphalted, 700 kilometres. And 6,000 kilometres of dirt roads.'

'No, no. More, Gustavo.'

'Well, 10,000 kilometres of dirt roads then.'

'No. Asphalted.' He began to list them. 'The TransChaco road, how long was that? The road to Encarnación, how long was that?'

'Well, let's say 1,500 asphalted. Let's say that,' said Gustavo.

The old man ignored him and continued to recite his rosary of roads.

'Well, let's say 1,500 kilometres,' Gustavo said, louder, with the air of a man forced to pay more for a car than it was worth, but bored with the bargaining.

'And the road to . . .' The General had forgotten where the road was to. He paused and moved on to the next item on his mental agenda. It was the economy.

'And we managed to balance the budget. Balance it. We did that. It was possible. And we managed not to have too much external debt. It was under control. So it's not a pressing problem for the country today.'

'And the electricity. And the water,' said Gustavo, hurrying on to his own shopping list.

'I have already said that,' snapped his father. I felt a certain sympathy for the General creeping up on me.

'Now,' he continued, 'we built bridges with the co-operation of Brazil on the Paraná. The co-operation of Brazil on the Paraná, the Friendship Bridge . . . And the bridge over the Paraná is under construction with Argentina.' I began to wonder if it was me or him. It was hot, and the effort of remaining affable and interested was telling. Was there anything in there? I wondered, and how was I to get to it? 'And then the one over the Paraguay River. I should also mention the co-operation of Spain. And then the bridge at Concepción towards the Chaco.'

I began to wonder if I had enough tape.

Stroessner was still going. 'Now as to energy. The country didn't have any. The truth is when we built Icarai with the . . . also Itaipu'—he paused, realizing that he had left off an item on an earlier list—'Yes, Itaipu, which is now, which will be, the biggest dam in the world. Also Yacyreta, with Argentina. And we were doing studies about another dam. And this is thanks to the co-operation of world financial institutions like the World Bank and Inter American Development Bank.'

I asked him how he achieved his economic stability.

Gustavo answered. 'Twenty-two years,' he said.

I asked the question again. He had nothing to say, I realized later, to questions like how?

'There is no doubt,' said Stroessner—it was one of his verbal mannerisms, like 'Now I'm going to tell you . . .'—'that the exporters asked for a larger quantities of the local currency in exchange for the export dollar.' They certainly did. Fiddling the export dollar was one of the many means of growing extremely rich in Paraguay. Even the Central Bank was on the fiddle. I found myself wondering if it was a game, after all. If he was ticking off a list of possible accusations and offering his pre-emptive defence, closing off the issue to further exploration.

He went on about the stable exchange rate, told me how he had never needed to knock off zeros. That was true, too. I recalled the restaurant in Buenos Aires that was wallpapered with worthless currency, a citizen's satire on incompetent government. But not in Paraguay.

He had jumped again, without pausing, to another subject—the next accusation on his imaginary prosecutor's list. 'If I was there for several terms of office,' he said, 'it wasn't because I wanted to be. It was because the people insisted. The country was developing, and it was necessary that President Stroessner continue.' He had slipped into the third person.

He got back on track again, listing endorsements this time, tailoring some of them, it seemed, to please me. 'Now what comes to my mind is that I had many friendships. Good friendships.

'I received a book from General Alexander, who was Montgomery's commander, and I read it. There was a book about Cunningham. I always read a lot. We had many delightful visits. I was also in Europe, in various countries—in Spain, in France. In France,' he repeated, losing it slightly, 'it was Pompidou who was president then. I was in Italy as well. I was also in Bavaria, in Germany, to see my relatives, my father's family. He was from Hof. He was born on 17 May 1867. He came to Paraguay as a tourist, to see Iguazú, the waterfall. Then he went to Encarnación and he saw that circumstances were very good and he stayed and built a brewery at the beginning of the century. I was also in Asia, in Japan and in Nationalist China, Taiwan, South Africa, always with the idea of developing the country.' It had come neatly back to his central mission.

'Morocco,' said Gustavo. We both looked at him. 'Morocco,' he repeated. 'You were in Morocco.'

'Yes, I was in Morocco,' Stroessner admitted, irritably. 'But just to see it. Just a visit.'

I was still trying to provoke some opinion, something beyond this. I asked him who had impressed him, of the leaders he had met.

He began another list. 'I also met President Nixon . . . and Eisenhower.'

'Ford,' yawned Gustavo, from deep in the chair.

'Ford. And that one, what was his name—who replaced Kennedy?'

Gustavo was silent.

Johnson, I volunteered.

'President Johnstone. I was invited to the US specially by him. Now there is no doubt, that of all the heads of state who impressed me . . . '

'Franco,' said Gustavo, firmly, but perhaps unwisely.

'Him too,' said the old man. Now I knew he was second guessing me.

'Franco,' insisted Gustavo, oblivious of his *faux pas*. 'And Pompidou, you said . . . '

'I have already mentioned him.' Stroessner was trying to cut him off. I pictured a little boy at his father's knee, being told about the great General Franco. But Pompidou?

'But she asked who most impressed you,' Gustavo insisted.

The old man became stubborn. 'Well, they all did; they were all impressive. Now General de Gaulle, in Asunción, he had a very good impression of the country because he saw the youth, the army, the people. He said things about Paraguay.' He straightened himself in his chair, as though he was going to recite a poem. 'He said the following: he said very short things. He said, "A great people, a great government and . . . and . . ."'

'A great race?' said Gustavo.

The old man ignored him, rummaging in his memory, trying to put it in order, to make it come out right. 'He said.' He began again. 'What was it he said? He said three things. "A great race, a great government . . . a great . . ."' He couldn't remember, but then he cheered up. 'But he said other things about other countries that I am not going to repeat,' he concluded.

'I knew the president of Panama,' he added, as an afterthought.

He started to tell me about the great English personalities who had visited Paraguay, then veered off again. 'Why don't they serve coffee, Gustavo?' We dropped the English personalities and turned to his military career.

378

'Now there is no doubt,' he resumed, 'that I entered the Military College in 1929.' Well that's a relief, my inner voice whispered, childishly. It was beginning to mock me, that voice. I struggled on.

Why had he chosen a military career? I asked.

His were patriotic motives, he said. Then he jumped to the civil war, the rebellion, as he called it.

There was a long pause, but, as I drew breath for a question, he came to life again. 'Well, I became president,' he suddenly said. 'There was half a political party in the government. Then we made the electoral law. And there were more parties in the government. Because the government is the high political body that runs the country. One definition. That's all I can say.' He veered straight off again, on to the great increase in Paraguay's exports under his rule.

I tried his childhood again.

'I liked the primary and secondary schools,' he said. 'I read a lot. I read everything, everything I could when I was a child.' And that was the end of that.

'Now I always cared about the country,' he continued, 'I always believed that the laws should be respected. I always tried to instil in school-children and university students . . . I was always in contact with the people. And I always held audiences for the public. Not just for officials but the general public.'

'So people would come to the Palace,' I said. I realized I was humouring him. I wondered if he had noticed, but it didn't seem likely.

'Oh, yes. And they would wait, and if there was time . . . A lot of people came. Problems of every kind. Education problems. They came. And I would talk to the education ministry. Land problems or personal requests. Yes.' He spoke in bursts, then would sink into what was almost a reverie. He pulled himself up again. 'So I,' he began. 'There is a phrase that we used: "He uselessly strives who tries to please everybody." ' He smiled, the patriarch, happy with this piece of political wisdom, wiser than his brood, children who thought you only had to ask and it could be given.

'So I satisfied as many people as I could, of those who came with their requests. And when they invited me to the interior, I said, "If I come I want a school to be painted or finished." Because we

379

built a lot of schools . . . ' I thought of the generals, building him little projects so that he could go there and untie the ribbons—such a small price to pay for what they got in return.

'Secondary schools,' said Gustavo, rolling the words slowly round his mouth. 'Universities.'

I shifted in my seat, trying to shake off my drowsiness. Gustavo was suddenly attentive. 'Would you like to change your chair? Are you comfortable?'

The whole room started to take on the qualities of a dream. The light seemed to come and go. I could feel my own will to find a way through to this man slipping away into the warm air.

'Going back to that difficult time,' My voice sounded suddenly loud, 'before you became president—'

'That was the politicians,' said Stroessner, 'creating problems. Ambition for power, to dominate. Beating the people, quarrelling among themselves. It's a very long story. Books have been written about it, all the intrigues of that time.' I recalled Juancito the Liar snapping the same phrase at me, trying to dismiss me when I had asked him about the *coup*. 'None of them lasted. They were there only a short time. The movements, the intrigues, the barracks revolts.'

How had he put a stop to all that? I asked.

By development, he said, building things. I looked at him, puzzling over the connection. 'Insisting on peace,' he added, 'insisting on what the country needed, not the senseless political movements. Political movements—' He was searching for a phrase again. 'Avoiding negative political movements.'

A uniformed maid appeared with a tray of coffee and orange juice. In the break, Stroessner allowed himself a comment. 'She seems familiar,' he said to Gustavo, looking at me, 'as though I knew her from somewhere.'

Gustavo had come back to life. 'We are going to write history together,' he boomed. 'History!'

There were the sounds of voices in one of the other rooms.

His mother and sister, Gustavo explained. A family reunion. I wondered if they were tempted to listen at the door. The house didn't seem that big. Were they sitting in the kitchen, waiting for me to leave?

'I hear you have been in Asunción?' Gustavo said.

Stroessner suddenly focused. 'In Asunción? When were you in Asunción?'

I told him I had just come from there. 'But I wasn't there very long,' I added, limply, dreading the questions that would follow.

'And do people remember the General?' asked Gustavo, eagerly. I felt like a drowning man.

'Oh, yes,' I said.

'And what do the people in the street say?'

I searched my mind for an acceptable quote. I couldn't find one. My smile was becoming rigid. 'Some remember you with great affection,' I said, thinking of Benitez Rickman. 'Although the politicians are different.' I heard the tone in my voice, appeasing, and hated it.

Gustavo joined in. 'The politicians speak badly of him. They say the works were Pharaonic projects, that people stole.' He recited the case for the prosecution.

Yes, things like that, I said.

'It's not true,' said Gustavo.

'They say those things to inflame,' said Stroessner.

'Some of the people who say those things were at his side for a very long time,' I ventured, prodding for a reaction.

Gustavo pulled the shutters down. 'That's all right,' he said, 'they were good people.'

But Stroessner was interested. 'She said people who were at his side.'

'Yes,' said Gustavo. Then to me: 'But they didn't betray him. Very few betrayed him. They were all good people. They were called to co-operate and they did. They were not traitors. We don't consider those who are co-operating traitors.' Gustavo didn't want any trouble.

'There might be some,' said the General. 'There might have been some.' The General and I looked at each other, and I began to wish Gustavo would go to the lavatory.

'That is what we have said, in general.' Gustavo was trying to steer back towards the harbour.

'A few are against us,' said Stroessner, giving in. 'The rest are with us.'

381

'What do the humble people say?' asked Gustavo. He genuinely seemed to think this was safer ground. 'Twenty-two years without inflation?' he prompted me. 'All those things?'

'The universities,' said Stroessner, 'the Catholic University . . .'

He began the list again, without waiting for the humble people's view. The airports. Asphalted. Energy. Electric light.

We talked about his great obsessions, stability and the communist menace. When he first came to power, he said, his main concern was just to keep power, day by day, worrying about whether he would make it to the end of his term of office.

'To get through the first year,' interjected Gustavo, 'the first month . . .'

'The first month then the first three months. Then the first year,' resumed the old man. They mused on, in their querulous duet.

I asked him about communism, and the threat posed to the continent by the Cuban revolution, a subject to which he had devoted the bulk of his speeches for thirty-five years, drawing heavily on the Cuban threat in order to milk defence dollars from the United States. I braced myself for a harangue. I had read it, but I wanted to hear him say it.

He seemed surprised to be asked about the effect of the Cuban revolution in Paraguay. 'In Paraguay, we always talked about democracy. I don't know if they had democracy there.'

Cuba? I thought. Democracy? Had he heard me correctly?

'Cuba was a very long way from Paraguay,' said Gustavo helpfully. 'So it didn't have a lot of influence.' His father agreed.

'Did it have no repercussions for you?' I asked. I felt suddenly off-balance. I pictured Benitez Rickman's library of Stroessner's speeches on the communist threat; all those State Department reports of Stroessner's complaints that his strategic country's fight against Cuban infiltration was underfunded.

'No,' said Stroessner, 'in Paraguay there was a stable regime. Stable.'

'But there was so much talk,' I insisted, 'of the danger of communism in the continent.' This was a subject on which I had come prepared to be bored, to be lectured, to be treated to banalities. This was the man who had hosted conferences of the

World Anti-Communist League, attended by the real hard core. The White Hand from Guatemala, d'Aubuisson, the killer from El Salvador. The Argentine dirty warriors, the South Koreans, the Taiwanese, the South Africans. This was the man who had teased the world over Mengele. I couldn't believe this was happening.

'Yes. That's what Vice-President of the United States said,' the General said. 'That Vice-President. What's his name?'

'Nixon,' I said, still in my own thoughts, in my memories of Stroessner, the well-paid subaltern on the western front of the Cold War.

'Quayle,' said Gustavo.

'Quayle?' I said. What did Quayle have to do with it?

'He said there were three problems,' said Stroessner. He remembered all three this time. 'Drugs, communism and the debt. Yes.'

And what do you think? I asked, clutching at this implausible straw.

'Listen,' said Stroessner, clearly bored with my insistence on communism. 'I am a democrat and I have always demonstrated it.' My head began to swim.

But the attempted revolutions in Paraguay? The guerrillas? I couldn't let it go. I was sounding like him. He was sounding like me.

'A few,' said the old man. 'But they were very small in number. They were of no importance.'

I thought of those peasant massacres, armed assaults on people seeking land-reform, tortured oppositionists, all condemned as communists. Of Archbishop Rolon, Humberto Rubin. Of the language of the Cold War, preserved in the rare air of Asunción. And he didn't believe it? Never had?

'There was no reason for a revolution in Paraguay,' Stroessner added, by way of explanation.

I tried a few other ways of asking the question and gave up. Stroessner simply refused to worry about communism.

I tried another line of questions, on the problems of authority. Did he feel, always, that he was being told the truth by those who served him?

'Yes, always,' he said. Another dead end, I thought. 'Though,' he added, after a pause, 'one can always be wrong, given what happened.'

I looked up at him. He was smiling at the floor. I hadn't expected irony.

He seemed to be thinking about it, talking from inside at last. 'I was always confident that I knew. I never expected this . . . this'—he searched for the word—'this *cuartelazo*.' For reasons that are not hard to find, there is, in Spanish, more than one word for a *coup d'etat*. The most derogatory is '*cuartelazo*', a barracks revolt, a rabble got out of hand.

'But the people,' he said, 'the people had no part in this. The people were always at the margin of these events.'

Gustavo had wandered off, at last. He had answered the telephone, then loped into a room at the back of the house. The General's tone had changed, his voice had dropped, had become more personal without his shambling minder to steer him back from forbidden ground.

How did he feel about it, I asked him, wondering how long I had.

'Look, what can you do in these circumstances . . . "*A lo hecho, pecho*"—take it on the chin. It happened. Taking into account all the other things that happened in the past, what happened to me is not extraordinary.'

He returned to his consolatory recital. 'Paraguay had a long period of progress, tranquillity and peace. It took giant steps.'

Gustavo came back and the morning drifted on. I could smell their lunch. I had my own plans and I wanted to get out. I left, arranging to return later, when the day was cooler.

'It's too hot to wear a suit in the afternoon,' said the General. I looked at Gustavo's sneakers. I wondered how long his father had nagged him about them and why Gustavo had held out.

8

Outside, I felt normal again, but needed someone to talk to. I had an arrangement to meet a Brazilian diplomat. He was the perfect companion, full of charm and cynicism. He also knew something about Stroessner: he had been the one sent from the foreign ministry to meet Stroessner on his arrival in Brazil.

We met for lunch. After the Stroessner's household, Brasília
was suddenly bustling, nearly human. According to my companion,
the restaurant was the best one in town, not for the food but for the
politicians. 'They come here to plot. So all the journalists come here
to watch them. So all the politicians come here to be seen by the
journalists.'

He told me about going to meet Stroessner. It had been the
beginning of carnival, he pointed out, a fact that I, in my Anglo-
Saxon way, had overlooked: not the best moment for a diplomatic
crisis. The capital had emptied, and he himself was about to leave
for Rio when the minister called. A plane was waiting, the minister
said, to take him to Itumbiara. He had no idea where it was; when
he got there he still didn't. After having to fight his way past all the
journalists, he finally found Stroessner, poring over a map.

He then sat there on behalf of the Brazilian government,
listening to the radio with Stroessner and his family, occasionally
going out to answer some questions for the press corps. There were
solidarity visits from some right-wing politicians who wanted to get
their pictures in the papers. Considering all things, he said,
Stroessner was holding up well. 'Imagine,' he said, 'it's not as
though he'd had time to pack or go to the bank.' Stroessner read the
papers and watched the television news, but couldn't lose the habits
of control: afterwards he would come in, upset and angry, saying:
'Do you see this? They're calling me a tyrant. A tyrant!' Then he
would walk up and down, muttering to himself, 'This has got to be
stopped. This has got to be stopped.'

The car was late for my second appointment. I began to
wonder. Had he changed his mind? Had I said something
that afterwards struck him as unfriendly? Perhaps I had been
indiscreet on the telephone.

I was about to call when the car appeared, forty-five minutes
late, pulling up in in front of the hotel.

The route was the same. You turned left off the main drive
from the lake, went over the speed bump and then stopped by the
corrugated steel fence. I opened my own door; it wasn't armour-
plated. In his own exile, did Stroessner recall the fate of Tacho
Somoza, blown to pieces on a street in Asunción under the noses of

the security services?

Gustavo was waiting again, and we walked through the door from the garage, across the small garden and up the stone path. The General was dressed in the same dark blue silk suit.He was wearing a red tie. 'Be careful of this rug,' he said, taking my elbow. 'It can sometimes trip you up.'

'No it doesn't,' said Gustavo.

I heard voices and sounds of another meal in preparation, occasional laughter. At one point Gustavo called in his wife to be introduced: a small, fair-haired, fine-boned woman, very good looking with blue eyes, dressed in shorts. Gustavo made her tell me about the time she attended a horse show at Olympia and another time at some other place that we decided must have been Windsor. She excused herself as soon as she could. 'I shall leave you to work.'

And then we sat down—Stroessner in the same upright chair again, with the same disciplined stillness.

Occasionally he grew impatient and made as if to rise or dismiss me, but it seemed to me that it was only the old dictator's habit of rationing his audiences. When I misjudged one of his pauses, left the silence unfilled too long, he would put his hands palms down on his knees and say, 'Well, we have talked a great deal,' or, 'I think we have covered everything,' and I would have to rouse myself to a new line of questioning.

It must have been odd, to have this stranger sitting there, hour after hour.

This was his last display. The General had dusted off the president, put on a suit and performed for history as well as his rambling old age would allow. Gustavo, with his fears, his bad conscience, was playing the minder, fearful that reality might break through the recitation of roads, airports and electric lights, and that the General might say something which would annoy Asunción, stimulate someone there to reach out for Gustavo and mean it this time. At odd moments, when Gustavo was answering the telephone or had simply fidgeted his way out of the room, the General would almost seem to want to talk, to drop the show, to gossip. He couldn't disguise his interest in what had been said of him by his former collaborators—Pappalardo, Juancito the Liar, Ynsfran.

'He said that?' he spluttered, when I told him of my interview with Juancito. 'Chavez said that? He was always the first and loudest in his praise, the most obsequious. Well,' he said dismissively, 'it's best not even to think about that one any more.'

But these were exceptional moments. I had come for my second interview wanting to get some sense of how the General felt about the *coup*—what led to it? why he thought it had happened? did he think that things could have turned out differently?—but I was not to have much success.

There were so many things Stroessner clung to: that the army had not been unhappy; that he had never insisted that officers join the Colorado party (I had seen a photocopy of the regulations, but what was the point of insisting?); that those who ousted Stroessner were members of a small clique who did it for no other reason than that of squalid personal ambition.

Under Stroessner, life in Paraguay had always been marked by peace, order and an absence of serious social conflict. The problems with the Church were a matter of a few individual priests. The problems with the United States were some minor difficulties (with one ambassador). The problems with the 'exiled' opposition were exaggerated ('There is no doubt that you can't satisfy everybody, but the truth is that they [of the Popular Colorado Movement] came back, were in the country, had all their liberties and guarantees'). The problems with the press were only because some members of it had been advocating violence. Paraguay, under Stroessner, was a fully democratic society.

I reminded him that he had closed down newspapers.

He disagreed. 'Only *ABC*, and only because it was advocating violence.'

'Disorder,' boomed Gustavo, from deep within his armchair, and Stroessner agreed, this time, with the interruption.

'Yes, disorder. They would say things like: "Tomorrow the chief of police will be replaced," when the chief of police wasn't going to be replaced. Things like that, things that were completely untrue. Free expression has its limits and reaches only to where the freedom of another begins.' A decision was taken, he said, by the

Supreme Court, a legal decision, because subversion cannot be allowed in a democracy. 'But there were all the other newspapers. Paraguay never had so many newspapers as now. And they said what they liked about my government. I read them every day. There was no censor.'

I t was true that there had been no censor. A censor is a hard thing to explain away in a fully democratic state. Besides, a censor implies someone to argue with. One of the beauties of Stroessner's state of terror was the very uncertainty about what was permitted.

I was starting to see that, at the heart of it all, there were just too many things that could not be reconciled: a clear white space between the Paraguay of Stroessner's vision and the Paraguay I had got to know. There were also two Stroessners: one, the beloved father of the people, progressive and popular; the second, the man who, for thirty-five years, ran a state of terror in the name of national security and the fight against communism. Now, in exile, he chose to forget the second Stroessner; or, at least in my company, he had chosen to forget him, and there seemed to be little that I could do about it.

I asked about the conflict with the Church, but that hadn't existed either. His government had looked after the Church; it had funded the parochial schools. How could there be a conflict with the Church? Only a few, a very few, individuals, misused the pulpit for purposes that were not religious.

'A few, who disagreed with the government,' explained Gustavo.

'There was some resistance,' admitted Stroessner. 'Some . . .' he groped for the word, 'politics.'

'They wanted an accelerated agrarian reform,' said Gustavo.

'And you have to impose order,' Stroessner said. It wasn't a word he shouted, but it was one whose sound he liked. There seemed to be something reassuring about the way he said it. '*Orden*,' he would say in the Spanish. '*Orden*,' rounding out the first syllable, rolling the 'r' slightly.

We talked about the Pope's visit to Paraguay, and Gustavo explained liberation theology to me. Priests in Paraguay, he said, agitated among the poor, suggesting that they were entitled to other

388

people's land. 'The peasants believed them. The Church should have talked to the rich first and convinced them that they had to donate part of their wealth to the poor, not just teach the poor to shout at the rich.'

'Yes,' he repeated, pleased with his idea. 'Rather that the rich give to the poor in good grace . . .'

I asked about Archbishop Rolon.

Stroessner started to say that the Archbishop had always acted correctly, but Gustavo chipped in. 'No,' he said, 'Rolon hadn't acted correctly for a long time.'

Stroessner started to argue.

'There were confrontations,' said Gustavo, sticking to his guns.

'Not confrontations,' said Stroessner.

'She has already interviewed Rolon,' said Gustavo.

'Is that true?' said Stroessner.

'Yes,' said Gustavo, 'she's said so.'

'*That* Rolon?' asked Stroessner, as though the idea that he could be sitting with someone who had interviewed the archbishop was too bizarre to grasp.

'Yes,' said Gustavo.

Stroessner changed his tack. '*That* Rolon has some family members who are in politics, and he couldn't keep his nose out of it. But we didn't have any conflicts. It might be that he thought in a certain way, but this happens sometimes.'

'There was no personal problem,' said Gustavo, perhaps recalling the unfortunate excommunication of Sabino Montanaro, the one who tortured priests.

'Oh, no. Nothing.' said Stroessner. 'We always had . . . I always went to mass. To the military chaplain.'

Gustavo began to explain that the Church itself was divided, and that part of it supported the government, and part of it was against it.

Stroessner, however, was already trying to claw back the argument. The Church was not divided, he said. 'There were just a few priests who . . . It was a personal thing.'

A short silence fell.

Gustavo broke it. 'Did Monseignor Rolon say there was any conflict?'

Yes, I said.

Archbishop Rolon, who was entitled to a seat in the State Council, had refused to take it up because he did not want the Church to be associated with the government. I had seen Rolon in Asunción, and he had explained all this to me. He also recounted explaining all this to an emissary that Stroessner had sent to see him, and in the end the emissary had pointed to the crucifix on Rolon's chest and said, 'You should wear a hammer and sickle, not a cross.'

Gustavo tried to make the best of it. 'It's not that Rolon went to the State Council the first time and then refused to go after that,' he said. 'From the very first day Rolon didn't go. Never.'

'But what I'm saying,' said Stroessner, his voice growing harder, 'was that Rolon was sworn in, as a member of the State Council.'

'But he never, never went,' insisted Gustavo.

'I've already told her that,' snapped the General.

'And that's what I'm saying!' Gustavo turned to me: 'You see we never had a disagreement with Rolon,' he said, trying to help, 'because we never saw him at the Council.'

'And that was what was unconstitutional,' said Stroessner, making a bid for the last word. 'You have to obey the constitution and the laws as a citizen, really.'

There was an uncomfortable pause.

Then Gustavo said: 'My nephews are in an English school, an Anglican one.'

I thought he was changing the subject.

'The headmaster is a Mr Venables.' Mr Venables and the Anglican school were famous in Asunción for managing to impose some discipline on Stroessner's grandsons. Zuccolillo's wife and daughters had lots of stories about it. I remembered the one about one of Stroessner's grandsons throwing all the toilet rolls into the lavatory and being made to pick them out again.

'I am very keen on religion,' Gustavo was saying, still trying to mend relations with the Church. 'I am a friend of lots of priests.' He laughed. 'But we never talked politics.'

'Well, that's enough of that,' said Stroessner.

I rather agreed.

I gave up on the Church and turned to the army—surely here the old soldier would recognize that things had gone wrong?—but he held firm to the vision of himself as the beloved patriarch. It was a mystery, really, how the *coup* could have come about.

He started to tell an anecdote that got nowhere, about a British general in Africa, waiting for information and smoking. 'Just smoking and smoking,' he said, 'waiting for information that never arrived.' I pictured a general, in his khaki shorts, waiting for information. 'A *coup d'état*,' Stroessner said, 'is something that one doesn't expect. It's about a lack of information.' This was related to the British general in Africa but I was not entirely sure how, except that the British general, like Stroessner, did not expect what happened next.

I tried another approach.

How had he interpreted the demonstrations in the last months of his regime?

'Oh, they were,' said Stroessner, 'an entirely normal thing in a democracy. Entirely normal.'

'Did you not object to them?' I asked, recalling descriptions I had heard of how savagely the police had responded to the exercise of these democratic rights.

'No, never.' he said.

I tried again. 'On reflection,' I asked, 'was there something now, knowing what you do, that you would have done differently?'

It was still no. He had been firm, had never weakened and had always acted against corruption.

He decided to explain the *coup* to me. 'What happened was this,' he said. 'I'll tell you. When the Convention came, the Colorado Party had three factions [*listas*]. And one of the factions won. And the others lost. And those who lost began to conspire—that's what it was. It wasn't anything else. The losers conspired.'

Had he known at the time that the losers were conspiring?

He had not. He had noticed that they had been complaining—even expressing their complaints in the press—but it was, as they say, a free country. Those were the reasons for the *coup*.

'The *cuartelazo*,' Gustavo corrected him.

'The *cuartelazo*,' he agreed.

Gustavo went out of the room and returned. He had been

looking for a book but he couldn't find it. It was written by a man called Levin. He didn't remember the title, but it was about Paraguay and had been, he said, very successful both there and in Argentina.

Might that be Lewis, I suggested, Paul Lewis?

'What was it called?' asked Gustavo.

I told him.

He claimed to have read it. He said that he had liked it.

The General said, no, he hadn't read it. Neither seemed to recall that they had banned it for years.

9

That night, in the hotel, I listened to my tapes. The next day would be my last. I had a ticket to return to London, and Stroessner had agreed to see me again in the morning before I left. I had little to lose, I thought, in confronting him with some realities. That's what I decided I would do: I would make Stroessner confront Stroessner.

I would talk to him about torture.

I began by citing Amnesty International. A simple statement: that Amnesty International had consistently reported that in Paraguay there was torture.

'Rupture?' said Stroessner. 'No there was no rupture. We always answered the questions.'

There was never a rupture or there was never torture? I asked, deflated by this attack of deafness.

'No,' he said, 'never a rupture. We answered all the questions quite normally.'

But what about the allegations themselves? I said. The physical mistreatment in the prisons?

'No. Absolutely not,' he said. 'I don't remember any such allegations. Or any such information coming to me through such organizations.'

'So the behaviour of the Paraguayan police was—'

'—Correct,' he interrupted.

'Correct?' I said.

'Correct,' he repeated.

What about the state of siege? I asked, determined to poke my finger through the ideal democracy of Paraguay. 'Did not the state of siege act as an impediment to justice?'

I had made him irritated.

'Look,' he said. 'The state of siege was necessary. There was subversion in Latin America. It was more of a preventive measure. It wasn't used much.' He, he said, would have preferred to have lifted it. It was not what he wanted.

But I had crossed the line.

'These are things that have already been judged. Things in the past,' he said. 'I have to think of my status as a resident in this country. But I do insist that in Paraguay there was order [*orden*]: the judiciary had the power of complete independence; justice was fully exercised.'

I asked him if he regretted the way things had turned out.

'Oh, yes,' he said. 'I went in by the front door and had always wanted to leave by the front door. But circumstances didn't allow it. But I don't want to make any accusations. Everything that happened, happened, and, if I had known—well, we are all wise after the event . . .'

'Well,' he said abruptly, 'I think we have talked quite a lot. I was at the head of the government—by popular choice—and Paraguay progressed. That's all I can say, Isabel Hilton,' he said, his pronunciation of my name laboured. 'The chain of hotels. Is it written the same way?'

Gustavo came to life suddenly and gave me a short lecture on the Latin antecedents of Conrad Hilton. It did not interest the General.

'I think I have given you all the time necessary,' he said. 'We are fine here in Brazil, but it is transitory. I am not used to Brazil. The climate is good, but I miss Paraguay, the ambience. You get used to your friends. It's easier there. But I have a lot of company here.'

'More or less,' muttered Gustavo, 'more or less.'

I wondered how deposed dictators go about building a social circle.

'We have nothing to complain about,' said his father sharply.

'Do you still play chess?' I asked.

'No,' he said, 'I have nobody to play chess with.'

W e chatted about the weather and fishing. I thought of my Paraguayan friends and made one last try. I asked him about Jimmy Carter.

'Carter,' he said, 'had asked me what I had seen at the NASA space museum. A lot of interesting things. I was given some moon-dust, you know.'

And what had he thought of Carter's human rights policy?

'I thought it was very good,' said Stroessner. 'I have always thought that human rights are very important for the whole world.'

Had he read what human rights reports said about Paraguay?

He couldn't remember the details, he said. 'But we were always concerned about human rights on a permanent basis.'

It was over.

The General had said his last word. He showed me to the door, pointing out again the dangerous rug. He clasped my hand and thanked me. Gustavo walked me across the lawn, and I took advantage of the moment to ask him whether there had been a plan to make him president.

Absolutely not, he insisted. Never.

As we were talking I glanced back at the house and realized that the General was still standing there, waving, as though seeing off a visiting head of state, patiently waiting through this unexpected hitch in protocol.

Embarrassed, I waved again and we retreated out of sight.

It was absurd to feel sorry for him in his loneliness, I told myself. He had always been lonely, despising those close to him, taking refuge in his relationship with Nata and a series of court-jesters, human familiars whom he adopted.

Meanwhile, Gustavo was chattering on, tumbling over himself in his strangely ingratiating manner. How had I become their last hope of vindication? Because I had invited them to think that, I supposed. I didn't like it.

Gustavo followed the car out into the road, shouting 'Goodbye! Have a good journey!' I set off back to the hotel behind the taciturn Brazilian driver. I thought of the people I had met in Paraguay, the overwhelming kindness of strangers. I thought of all those people who had suffered at Stroessner's hands. I wondered what they would have done, if they had sat down for three days with him. I thought of all the people who had clung to him when he was in power, who had grown rich for the sacrifice of a few scruples and a little pride. 'Stroessner didn't do it on his own,' Rubin had said. 'We were all in it.'

His greatest gift had been his power to corrupt. His great good fortune that so many were willing to be corrupted. He had distorted meaning so far that finally there was none. How long would he last, I wondered, in this little domestic prison, adding up the mileage of asphalted roads?

What did he say? people asked me. What was he like? I found it impossible to describe. 'I saw Stroessner,' I said to one friend, a man who knows as much about Latin American dictators as anybody.

'Did he say much?' he asked.

'No,' I replied.

'I'm not surprised,' he said. 'They never do.'

CHRISTOPHER HITCHENS
ON THE ROAD TO TIMIŞOARA

On Christmas night, stuck in freezing fog at the Austro-Hungarian border, I had telephoned my best Budapest friend and spoken across an insufferable line, fed with near-worthless *forint* coins cadged from a friendly guard. 'Have you heard?' said Ferenc, 'Ceauşescu has been *assassinated*.' The choice of word seemed odd. 'Murdered' wouldn't do, of course, in the circumstances. 'Killed' would have been banal. 'Executed'—too correct. And Ferenc always chooses his terms with meticulous care. No, a baroque dictator who was already a prisoner, and an ex-tyrant, had somehow been 'assassinated'. I took the first of many resolutions not to resort to Transylvanian imagery. Yes, there had been King Vlad, known as the Impaler, reputed to drink blood as well as spill it. Every writer and sub-editor in the trade was going to be dusting him off. Still, I found myself wondering just how Ceauşescu had been 'assassinated' after his capture. A stake through the heart? I had read that the chief of Ceauşescu's ghastly Securitate was named General Julian Vlad, but I was determined to make absolutely nothing of it.

A sorry-looking shop-front, which was in one of the radial streets off Calvin Square in Budapest, housed the Alliance of Free Democrats (SDS), Hungary's main opposition party. It resembled the headquarters of every 'movement' I'd ever visited. The stickers and posters in haphazard pattern gave promise of an interior of clanking duplicators, overworked telephones and bearded young men in pullovers. One of the stickers was fresh and blazing with colours—the national colours in fact. It read: TIMIŞOARA=TEMESVAR. To any Hungarian, it summoned an immediate, arresting image. On the plains of Transylvania, near the town the world now knows as Timişoara, the Hungarian patriots of 1848 were scattered and cut down by the Czar's Cossack levies, lent as a favour to the Austrian emperor. Near Temesvar, as the Hungarians call it, the national poet Sandor Petofi lost his life. At nearby Arad, the thirteen generals who had sided with the 1848 revolution were put to death. Now, under its Romanian name, this lost city so well-watered with patriotic Hungarian gore was again an emblem.

Today, the first day of the post-Ceauşescu era, the office was crowded to the doors with people of every class and category, standing around wearing intense expressions. Most wore buttons reading simply: TEMESVAR. Others displayed the more reflective symbol of two ribbons, one in the Hungarian colours and one in the Romanian, arranged over a black mourning stripe. Nationalists and internationalists, they were all waiting for the Romanian border to be declared open so that they could get to the stricken field of Transylvania and the wounded city of Timişoara. A volunteer convoy was in formation, with taxi drivers, workers, housewives and students offering to donate, or to transport, food and medicine. As so often in the course of the astounding Eastern European revolution of 1989, people seemed to know what to do. And they seemed to know, what's more, without being told. My companion and I, who continually needed and sought advice and instruction, felt this keenly.

The Romanian Embassy in Budapest, scene of numerous protests (some of them cynically encouraged by the nearly defunct Hungarian Communist Party), had offered exactly the wrong kinds of reassurance. 'No problem,' said the greasy officials who had just run up a hand-stitched 'National Salvation' banner on the balcony. Had the border, sealed by Ceauşescu, been reopened by his death? 'No problem.' (I find these the two least relaxing words in the lingua franca.) Visas were said to be obtainable at the border. Or at the embassy, of course, with a wait on the cold pavement. And there would be a fee. In dollars. In cash. For some reason, we couldn't give hard currency to these soft, shifty figures, who were still dealing with the public through an insulting grille.

As the ten cars, one truck and one taxi that together comprised the Hungarian dissident convoy prepared to set off, I got an idea of how excited and intimidated they were by the whole idea of Transylvania. We got a short and cautionary talk from Tibor Vidos, an SDS organizer, who specialized in taking the romance out of things. 'There's to be no driving at night once we cross the border . . . We pick up the blood supplies before we meet at the check-point . . . No car is to pick up hitch-hikers, however innocent-looking they are. Secu men have been taking lifts and getting out while leaving plastic bombs behind . . .' Carrying blood to Transylvania? No, too glib an image and indecent in the context. Dismissing Dracula once more, I went for a swift meal with

Miklos Haraszti, author of *The Velvet Prison*, a book which relates the trials of writers and intellectuals in the 'goulash archipelago'. He had been to Timişoara/Temesvar years before, to see the now-famous Father Laszlo Tokes, and had been detained and tortured by the *Secu*. Haraszti comes from Leninist stock; his Jewish watchmaker parents left Hungary for Palestine in order to escape fascism, but quit Palestine in 1948—the year of the proclamation of Israel—in order to come back to a people's republic. His own disillusionment had taken him through Maoism before fetching him up with the majority of Budapest's 'urbanist' intellectuals into the ranks of the liberal SDS.

Haraszti told us of something that had just happened to the convoy in front of ours. 'One of the volunteers was pulled from his car, not by the *Secu* but by the Romanian crowd. They said he looked like an Arab, and that Arab terrorists had been helping Ceauşescu's gangs.' This was an instance of the *grande peur* that infected Romania in those days, and that was to poison the inaugural moments of the revolution. Not a single Arab corpse was found, nor a single prisoner taken. Yet the presence of Libyans, Syrians, Palestinians in the degraded ranks of the *Secu* was something that 'everybody knew'. The cream of the jest, as Haraszti went on to say, was that the 'Arab-looking' volunteer seemed exotic in appearance because he was a Budapest Jew. 'One of the few New Leftists we still have. He probably does sympathize with the PLO.' Nobody knew what had become of this hapless comrade, because the convoy had been too scared to stop. As we concluded our meal, the waiter brought us the last of several predictions about the time at which Hungarian TV would transmit video pictures of the Ceauşescus' execution. At that stage, excited rumour was calling for an actual sequence of the bullets hitting the couple. Neither he nor his customers could wait for the event. I vaguely recalled seeing television pictures of the dead General Kessem after a coup in Iraq in the colonial fifties, but couldn't otherwise think of a precedent for a prime-time 'assassination' of a fallen leader. 'The genius of the Carpathians', as Ceauşescu characterized himself, hogged the stage until the very last.

I describe this hesitation on the border of Transylvania because it shows, even in small details, the way that Hungarians felt

Romania to be *in partibus infidelium*. Romania is much larger than Hungary, by virtue of having absorbed so much of it, and Ceauşescu was the perfect ogre neighbour from the point of view of the regime. Not only did he run a terrifying, hermetic police state, the weight of which was felt disproportionately by the Hungarian-speaking minority, but he flaunted a mad, grandiose, population-growth policy which overtopped the megalomania of a Mussolini. And, as he raved from his balcony, it seemed to ordinary Hungarians that the Bucharest crowd supported him, at least passively and at least in his 'Greater Romania' fantasy. I asked Haraszti if this had made him feel nationalist in turn. 'The fact that the Romanian revolution was started by Hungarians,' he said firmly, 'is a miracle.' Almost at a blow, the mutual xenophobia had been dispelled. Neither regime could ever again easily mobilize or distract its people by fear of the other. This is no small issue for Hungarian democrats, who remember that their country took the Axis side in the stupid, vainglorious hope of 'redeeming' lost Magyar territory, and instead lost most of its Jews and decades of its history as well as its national honour.

As the convoy got on the move, and as people were allocating and being allocated their tasks and their cars, I was brought the news that Queen Elizabeth II had rescinded her award of the Order of the Bath to Nicolae Ceauşescu. There were polite Hungarians who felt that I might wish to know this, and who added that the decision was taken not a minute too soon. Bloody hell, I think, it's like Chesterton's definition of journalism—telling the public that Lord X is dead when the public didn't know that Lord X had ever been alive. I'm sure most people didn't know that Ceauşescu was sporting a Windsor honour. And, by the way, for what was the Order bestowed? The brute got 'most favoured nation' status from the United States, the Order of Lenin from Moscow, the moist thanks of international bankers for exporting all his people's food, pay-offs from Israel and the Arab League and solidarity from Beijing. He was the perfect postmodern despot—a market Stalinist.

Departure was announced for two in the morning, so that all night-time driving could be done on Hungarian territory, and everyone was ready to move out on time, and did move out, without being told. Our car was the property of a man who normally drove a beer-truck, and looked like it, and drove like it (the image of the SDS as an intellectual and élitist party is misleading). The freezing fog had thickened. At first light, after frequent stops and regroupings, and a detour for the blood pick-up at the border town of Gyula, all the cars met again at the border-point. Here people started to get nervous. It would have been a good thing to have had a leader or a commander. We knew that the previous convoy had been shot up and had lost one of its Bohemian-looking members to the liberated populace.

The Romanian border guards were in the very act of revisionism when we turned up. A large blank space on the wall spoke eloquently of yesterday's *Conducator*, as Ceauşescu got himself called, and various party and state emblems were being hurriedly junked. Still, the place wore the dismal, dingy aspect of a little machine for the imposition of petty authority. Everything from the lavatories to the waiting-room was designed for insult, delay and humiliation, and there was no one-day, quick-change cosmetic to disguise the fact. The unctuous, ingratiating faces of the guards who were 'making nice' for the first time in their lives, only reinforced the impression they were trying to dispel. Eager to please, they overdid their hatred of the *Secu* to whom they had deferred the day before. They even suggested that we not proceed. 'They are firing from cars. There is no law, no authority.' Without orders, they had no idea what to do. When I said, quite absurdly and untruthfully, that I was given 'clear instructions' from the capital that visas were free of charge today, they gladly waived the fee. There was a pathetic relief in the gesture of acquiescence.

Quitting the stranded, irrelevant guardhouse, and holding perhaps the last stamps that read 'Socialist Republic of Romania', we fell back a few decades. The Hungarian town of Gyula had amenities, as Americans say. Shops and telephones, restaurants, street lamps. Across the border there were herds of pigs and geese, horse-drawn wagons and wayside hovels. The first cars to be seen were waiting in an abject queue, not because of the upheaval but because today was the day when the exiguous petrol ration was issued. The people at the side of the road looked like caricatures of

Eastern European misery, in their shapeless bundles of coats and scarves. But there was a palpable lift in the atmosphere even so, because every person raised a hand in a V-salute at the sight of the Hungarian flag (or was it our reassuring Red Cross?). These villages had been the targets for 'systematization', perhaps the nastiest political neologism since 'normalization' in Czechoslovakia, and were saved from bulldozers and unheated tower-blocks where the water-pressure sometimes got as far as the first floor, and where the official cultural activity was praise for the *Conducator* and the denunciation of fellow sufferers.

At the city of Arad, our first major stop, we found what we were to find everywhere, which was that the centre of activity had shifted to the gates of the hospital. The *Conducator*'s cops had been vicious and thorough in their last stand, whether from panic or from sheer professional pride it is hard to say.

In the street an army lorry screamed to a halt and I heard the sound of boots hitting tarmac. This forbidding noise heralded a squad of uncertain young soldiers, steel casques reassuringly askew, who held up traffic with large gestures before entering the crowd and fraternizing. In the Romanian attitude to the army there was something of the Stockholm syndrome. The soldiery had changed sides at the last minute, and some of the brass (including the excellent-sounding General Militarescu) had been in touch with Party dissidents when it was dangerous to do so. Thus there was a popular willingness to smile, to repress unease, to cry, 'Army and People.' It became an article of faith that the soldiers who had fired on crowds on Christmas Eve were not really soldiers at all, but *Secu* devils in disguise. To have armed men on your side at long last, for whatever reason, seemed worth the sacrifice of pride. So the classic photograph became that of old women handing scarce food and drink to tank crews. Which indeed happened, showing in the oddest way that Brecht was right when he said that every tank had a mechanical weakness—its driver.

The beer-truck chauffeur, who seemed a stranger to exhaustion, had had the idea of stuffing his back seat with bales of Hungarian newspapers, including the daily organ of the Communist Party he despised. To stand in the streets of Arad and hand out free copies of yesterday's Budapest editions, was to court instant popularity. Every hand reached for a copy, probably because a good deal of Hungarian is spoken in these parts and probably because there hadn't been any newspapers for days, but also and undoubtedly because the front page bore the death-masks of Ceauşescu and his wife Elena. Watching people rivet themselves to this photo-exclusive, I again fought down the impulse to Transylvanian cliché. They had to see the dead monster, had to know he was dead. The Ceauşescus' 'trial' had been a shabby, panicky business with unpleasantly Freudian overtones (Elena: 'I was a mother to you all.' *BANG!*), conducted by a tribunal which feebly refused to show its members' faces; but their execution had a galvanic effect on the morale of Transylvania and a correspondingly lowering effect on the fighting spirit of the *Secu.*

All had been festivity on the way to Arad, and as we left we met bystanders who were happy and eager to point the way to Timişoara. Wayside saluting and waving seemed inexhaustible. It was like being in Orwell's Barcelona, or in Portugal in 1974, or even like being on the skirts of a liberating army. But everything changed as we approached Timişoara. There were fewer people on the roads, and they seemed less keen and animated. As we found the outlying bits of the town, we noticed that our salutes were not returned. All the window-glass in the city seemed to have gone. Except for some flags with the now famous hole cut in the centre (a borrowing from Budapest in 1956), there were no signs of anything except shell-shocked, sullen wretchedness. I felt almost cheated. Here was the town of the resistance, of the revolutionary epicentre; the town that had lived up to 1848—and won this time. Where were the garlands, the proud slogans, the maidens in national dress, the gnarled old men with fierce tears in their eyes?

How could I have been so romantic and vulgar? Timişoara was the scene not of a triumph but of an atrocity—a sort of distillate of twentieth-century horrors. The inhabitants had been strafed from the air like the people of Guernica. They had been shot down in heaps like the victims of Babi Yar, and buried like refuse in mass graves in the forest on the pattern of Katyn. Many had been raped and mutilated like the villagers of My Lai. Before he left on a state visit to, of all places, Iran, Ceauşescu had given explicit orders that the city be punished. This was his Lidice; his Ouradour. At least the people who had been through such a digest and synopsis of horror could tell themselves that they were the last carnage of the last European dictator. But this obviously was not much of a consolation on the day after.

Again, it was at the hospital that everybody gathered. Timişoara is a superficially uninteresting town with a dull, routine Stalinist design. The box-like buildings even have generic names stencilled on the outside: 'Hotel', 'Restaurant', 'Cultural Centre'. It was a surprise to learn that the fateful, desperate demonstration in support of Father Tokes had taken place in Opera Square, because Timişoara doesn't look as if it rates an Opera House. Opera Square, on the other hand, doesn't disappoint your imagination of what a Transylvanian provincial city might boast after twenty-five years of philistine despotism. What a terrible place to die, I thought grotesquely, especially if you feared you might be doing it for nothing. On the other hand, a perfect place for concluding that you had little or nothing to lose.

We entered the hospital, and were led through a morgue which perfectly misrepresented the proportions of casualties. It contained one third civilians, one third soldiers and one third *Secu* men. I had come this far to see my first dead secret policeman—a great twentieth-century experience and only partly an anti-climax. He lay in his scruffy black livery, balding but thickly furred like some once vigorous animal, and looked alarmingly intact, with no outward mark of whatever violence had taken him. One of his companions, however, had been got at by the crowd and given a thorough kicking—the more thorough, by the look of it, out of frustration at that fact that he was dead. There was a pure hatred in the way that people spoke of the fallen regime and its servants. 'Our first happy Christmas,' said Dr Istvan Balos, without affectation, when I asked him for a reaction to the shooting of the Ceauşescus. Caligula once said that he wished the Roman mob had only one head so that he might decapitate them all at one stroke. The Romanian crowd wished only that the Ceauşescus had had a million lives so that everyone could have a turn at killing them.

Just before I left New York for Eastern Europe, I had been talking and drinking with Zdeněk Urbánek, original signatory of Charter 77, friend of Václav Havel and Czech translator of Shakespeare. Most of our conversation concerned the problem of vengeance, and the argument over amnesty and prosecution in newly emancipated Prague. Urbánek took the view that there should be no retribution, and his analogy was from Rome also. Remember, he said, that *Julius Caesar* is called *Julius Caesar* even though the eponymous character disappears after a few scenes and about fifteen minutes. 'But after he is murdered his influence remains over everything, pervading everything. That is the result of blood and the effect of revenge.'

The elevated sentiments of Prague and Bratislava were alarmingly remote from the Timişoara morgue. On a slab neighbouring that of the brutish-looking *Secu* man lay a dead young soldier, his eyes wide open and very blue, and on adjacent tables were two older civilians—man and wife, we were told—who had worked at the hospital. Their corpses were being processed in some ghastly way that involved the stench of formaldehyde. If it hadn't been for this stench, in fact, I might have been spared the moment I had in the corridor outside. My nostrils only started to wrinkle just as I felt my soles getting sticky, and the smell of drying blood hit me precisely as I realized what was gumming up my feet. A blood-bath has taken place here, I thought. A fucking *blood-bath*. All these people, killed like rats after leading such miserable, chivvied existences. Life-blood on my shoes.

'We have given the *Secu* another twenty-four hours to give up,' said Dr Balos, 'after which they are subject to a popular tribunal and a summary verdict.' As he was announcing this he dropped his voice. 'Do you see that man there?'—he indicated a tall and rather handsome man in a hospital housecoat who was talking easily with colleagues—'He's *one of them*. We can do nothing now, because there is no law. But soon. . . ' He spoke as if he was still living under occupation or dictatorship.

There appeared to be a delayed reaction in the Romanian psyche. It took the form of believing, not every rumour, but every rumour that had the morbid odour of pessimism or foreboding. This was where Caesar had his posthumous revenge. There were no apparitions exactly, but an unusual number of people said that they thought the trial video was a fake, the corpses phoney, the 'live' Ceauşescu a double. In his madness, it seems Ceauşescu had commissioned a few doubles for purposes of security (or perhaps of perverted vanity or repressed self-hatred). This is only a step away from having food-tasters and granting audiences while perched on the can, but it wasn't hard to believe about the *Conducator*. I began to soften in my anti-Dracula resolve when I learned from Transylvanian historians that Ceauşescu had forbidden all mention of the Bram Stoker book or the legend. The idea that he still walked seemed implicit in his entire cult of death and in the haunting effect of his undead minions.

In Budapest, Miklos Haraszti had spoken with approval of the decision to kill the Ceauşescus and with enthusiasm of the proposal to ban the Communist Party. 'It proves that it's a real revolution,' he said decisively, adding after a pause, 'in the dirty sense as well.' As Ryszard Kapuściński once remarked, 'Hunger revolutions are the worst.' The people of Romania and especially of Transylvania were starved in every sense of the term. Kept on short rations, kept in the dark, in the cold, kept from anything that could be called culture, screaming with boredom and groaning with humiliation; forced to applaud a mad gargoyle for whom they felt puke-making hatred. In Timişoara one could see all the bitterness and futility as well as all the grandeur of a hunger revolution. One could also get premonitions of the disagreeable things that lay ahead for the country—the crowd-pleasing decision to restore capital punishment, the hasty ban on the Communist Party (the only such ban in the 1989 European revolution), the evasive answers on the make-up and origin of the Council of National Salvation, the awkward hysteria about the body count, the ambivalence about the place of the army in politics. People were— are—hopelessly rattled and furious and confused.

I had had the vague idea of finding out the true body count of the Timişoara massacre, because cynical reporters were already saying that there 'hadn't really been all that many' casualties. Nettled at this, many citizens of the town were staunchly reiterating unbelievable death-tolls. I sickened of the task, not just because of the stench of blood around the morgue but because it seemed vile to be disputing the statistics of something evidently awful and sacrificial. It gave one the same rather creepy feeling that is engendered by an argument with Holocaust revisionists about Dresden or Auschwitz. I cleaned the soles of my shoes, remembered the packets of Hungarian coffee sugar I had pocketed on leaving Budapest, distributed them to some ecstatic and unbelieving children and made ready to leave the hospital. In the reception area, patients were sitting dully watching the television. All that could be seen on it was a test card. But they sat passive and fascinated, gazing at the flickering, improvised logo that read: *Romania Libera*.